THE HANDBOOK OF DEVELOPMENTALLY APPROPRIATE TOYS

THE HANDBOOK OF DEVELOPMENTALLY APPROPRIATE TOYS

Edited by Doris Bergen

ROWMAN & LITTLEFIELD
Lanham • Boulder • New York • London

Published by Rowman & Littlefield
An imprint of The Rowman & Littlefield Publishing Group, Inc.
4501 Forbes Boulevard, Suite 200, Lanham, Maryland 20706
www.rowman.com

6 Tinworth Street, London SE11 5AL, United Kingdom

British Library Cataloguing in Publication Information Available

Library of Congress Cataloging-in-Publication Data

Names: Bergen, Doris, editor.
Title: The handbook of developmentally appropriate toys / edited by Doris Bergen.
Description: Lanham : Rowman & Littlefield, [2021] | Includes bibliographical references. | Summary: "The handbook is expected to serve both as a reference for educators, parents, toy designers, and other interested readers, and as a catalyst for further research and ongoing toy development"—Provided by publisher.
Identifiers: LCCN 2020040144 (print) | LCCN 2020040145 (ebook) | ISBN 9781475849196 (cloth) | ISBN 9781475849202 (paperback) | ISBN 9781475849219 (ebook)
Subjects: LCSH: Educational toys—Handbooks, manuals, etc. | Child development—Handbooks, manuals, etc.
Classification: LCC LB1029.T6 H36 2021 (print) | LCC LB1029.T6 (ebook) | DDC 371.33/7—dc23
LC record available at https://lccn.loc.gov/2020040144
LC ebook record available at https://lccn.loc.gov/2020040145

♾ ™ The paper used in this publication meets the minimum requirements of American National Standard for Information Sciences Permanence of Paper for Printed Library Materials, ANSI/NISO Z39.48-1992.

CONTENTS

FOREWORD

Reading this book is a concierge tour of toys. The contributing authors shift the reader from the brokered experience of current digital technologies to personally real social, physical, and direct aesthetic experiences. Three-dimensional toys serve many developmental achievements. Physical manipulation affords opportunities for comparisons, connection making, and predictions. They are the foundation for three-dimensional, spatial imagery relevant to the development of STEM (science-technology-engineering-mathematics) and concepts of geography. The reader is invited to savor the impressive variety of toys that can replicate the three-dimensional world, engage imagination, pretense, embellishment, and assure personal power.

The opportunities for *pretense* with ambiguous materials and toys is so essential that children in impoverished or dangerous situations create their own imaginary toys with found materials in their environments. Pretense begins with the third dimension and serves as a continuous pathway toward three-and two-dimensional representations in the arts, invented writing, writing-into-reading, and reading. There is *empowerment* in the multiple ways that three-dimensional and imaginative toys have acceptable, creative uses. It is possible to make the case that a personal sense of empowerment could reduce bullying and antisocial behavior. Children at play demonstrate the ways in which they regulate their own behavior and can persevere within their self-motivated engagement. Imaginative social play with others—sociodramatic play—builds social competence, language development, connection making, and language expansion. The author-experts in this distinctive and authoritative book provide a wonderful panorama of memorable, multidimensional, and authentic experiences that empower players and remind the reader that it is worth making time to play.

Doris Fromberg, Professor Emeritus, Hofstra University

PREFACE

Since earliest time children have played with objects specifically designed for their use and enjoyment (e.g., toys), but although some of these toys have contributed greatly to children's social, emotional, intellectual, and physical development, there have not been many attempts to discuss thoroughly why toys have been so important and engaging to children (and to some adults!) over the centuries. This handbook was developed in order to bring together the body of knowledge that has accumulated for many years about a wide variety of toys, and to discuss their importance for the development and cultural awareness of children.

The handbook is expected to serve both as a reference for educators, parents, toy designers, and other interested readers, and as a catalyst for further research and ongoing toy development. Its purpose includes helping readers to gain knowledge that enables them to more fully appreciate the value of children's toy play, find out more about the favorite toys they had in childhood and relive those satisfying play experiences, and learn how to foster the learning, physical development, and social-emotional growth that comes from such toy play. As both a long-time play researcher and as a life-long toy player, my hope is that the reader will gain both a greater appreciation for the important role toys, and in particular, specific types of toys, have performed and continue to perform in children's (and many adult's) lives. In addition, by learning more about toys and their major influence on children's lives, the reader should gain a stronger commitment to advocacy for supporting the continued importance of child-directed toy play in this increasingly automated entertainment world.

INTRODUCTION

This handbook is organized purposefully in order to facilitate readers' access to the information on toys that is of most interest to them. An initial section discussing the historical and cultural significance of toys, their developmental impact, enduring popular characteristics, and changes over time is presented.

The majority of the handbook is composed of chapters by authors who discuss the important features of particular types of toys, provide information related to the developmental importance of this type of toy, discuss social and cultural issues engendered by play with such toys, and review the available research on the characteristics and potential impact on children's developmental progress of toys of that type. Both traditional toys and technological toys are discussed.

The handbook concludes with a section focused on the process by which new toys are developed and speculates on the potential role of toys (both traditional and contemporary) on children's development in the future.

THE ROLE OF TOYS IN PROMOTING CHILDREN'S DEVELOPMENT

Doris Bergen

This handbook celebrates the universal and historical uses, the many meanings and purposes, and the developmental value of toys. A toy is "an object for a child to play with, typically a model or miniature replica of something" (Toy, 2020). While almost any object (real or imagined) can be played with, toys have always had a special place in children's lives because, in contrast to most of the objects in the child's world, they are objects specifically designed for children. Thus, they are especially valued because they have the power to enrich the variety and quality of children's play.

According to Kudrowitz (2014), any object can become a toy if it is used in playful ways. However, a "toy product" is "an item that is intentionally designed for the primary purpose of play" (p. 237). Thus, most of the toys discussed in this handbook are really "toy products" because the specific purpose of their design has been to stimulate, enhance, and expand children's play experiences. While many of the toys discussed in the handbook have been designed by toy manufacturers, many other toys have been designed, built, sewed, or otherwise made or invented by family members or by children themselves. "Homemade toys" were especially common in past eras because manufactured toy products were not as available.

Presently, there are many manufacturers who market a plethora of toys and many children from families with some financial means have a good supply of such toys. With the advent of new technological enhancements in toy production, the marketing of toys with such computer-driven enhancements has become extensive and these toys are becoming the predominant type in many children's lives. Also, because the manufacture of toys has become a lucrative business, "homemade" or "craftsman" types of toys are much less in evidence.

THE PERVASIVENESS OF TOYS

During the many years of toy product development, a range of materials have been used to make toys, including wood, clay, paper, cloth, grass, string, and, more recently, plastic, metal, and other human-engineered materials. Often child-designed or parent-designed toys have been made spontaneously, with whatever materials were at hand and since early times toys have been made by adults expressly for the purpose of being playthings for children. Such toys are often replicas of the "real world" objects that adults were using.

From early human existence, it seems that adults have realized that children's play with replica objects from the real world is important for enabling the children's developmental progress, introduction to the culture, and future life success. Other toys, however, have represented fanciful objects not found in the real world and these also have contributed to children's creative and imaginative development. Some of these "toy products" have existed since prehistoric times, and they have been found at many archaeological sites.

Toys found in excavations from other early civilizations (1010–1400 BC) include small carts, bird whistles, and toy monkeys on strings. Toys also have been prevalent in many diverse cultures, as a painting of two children playing with paddle balls by a Song Dynasty artist, Su Hanchen (1130–1160) suggests. Archeologists have found that Egyptian children played with wigged dolls with movable limbs, and children from Greece and Rome had wax or terracotta dolls, bows and arrows, and yo-yos. Different types of puzzles also have been found at excavation sites in various parts of the world. The origin of the word "toy" is not known, although that word seems to have been in common use by the fourteenth century.

By the eighteenth century, in the Enlightenment era, when childhood began to be considered a special time period, specifically designed toys became more evident and began to focus on promoting children's learning and intellectual skills. For example, in the seventeenth century, putting numbers on blocks to teach literacy was suggested by the theorist, John Locke (Williams, 1990). In the 1800s, Friedrick Froebel designed balls and a variety of blocks as learning "gifts" for young children (Hill, 1908). Thus, adults have been aware of the importance of toys and toy play as influential for children's experiences and, presumably their development, for many years.

In later eras, as children's developmental progress became a focus of study, the importance of toys as stimulators of children's social, emotional, physical, and cognitive development has increased, and today, children from middle-income and high-income families in most societies typically have a plethora of toys. However, manufactured toy products may often be a luxury for children from low-income families and those in many parts of the world. Toys are much less in evidence for children who live in subsistence environments. Such children may have little time for play, and they may possess few manufactured toys. When they do have time for play, however, children from these cultures continue to devise toys with materials from their environment.

With more recent centuries of technological progress, toy products have become increasingly diverse and complex. However, there are many modern toys that are similar versions of the types of toys found in archeological sites. These classic toys continue to be part of the toy product world and they are still enjoyed by today's children. The authors in this handbook discuss the wide range of existing toys, including many newer types of toys, that have gained popularity over the years, and they give information on historical trends and cultural changes in such toys.

Because of both advancements in technological designs and intense business marketing practices, the variety and complexity of toys have greatly expanded, and there is a plethora of toys now in existence. Many of these newer toys have expanded children's play world. Some adults (e.g., developmental psychologists, educators, physicians, parents) have raised concerns, however, related to what effects play with some of these newer, primarily technology-enhanced toys will be on traditional types of toy play.

Such play has influenced children's cognitive, physical, language, moral, social, gender role and other areas of development in past centuries. These "enhanced" toy products also may be expanding children's abilities and making them more competent for functioning in present and future time periods. A brief overview of the major findings related to how play with toys are related to children's development and learning provides a context for the following chapters.

TOY PLAY, CHILD DEVELOPMENT, AND LEARNING

Because, over many centuries, adults have encouraged children's play with toys, it seems evident that they have believed that toy play would increase the child players' cognitive, language, physical, social, moral, and/or gender role development. In more recent years, many theorist and researchers have studied and discussed the role of toy play of various types in influencing other areas of children's development. Presently, child play with many traditional toys is decreasing in favor of technology-augmented play materials, and thus, the question has been raised as to whether toy play with "typical" toys is essential for various developmental achievements. A sample of research on the toy/development relationship is provided.

Cognitive Influences

Researchers who studied how toy play may foster cognitive development have presented evidence of toy play-developmental connections. For example, Uzgiris and Hunt (1974) reported that infants used similar actions (e.g., mouthing, shaking) of toys initially but by 9–12 months they use differentiated actions, shaking rattles, banging blocks, and holding a soft doll close. These examples of early types of toy play are related to the development of "enactive" cognition (See Bruner, 1964).

Research on toddlers has described how their toy play, clay manipulation, and structure building enable them to learn what the affordances of the objects enable them to do (Gopnik, Meltzer, & Kuhl, 2001). Preschool play also involves the use of toys in pretense and early games, fostering theory of mind development (Bergen, 2002). Kami (2015) has demonstrated that various types of mathematical knowledge, such as numeracy and classification, are fostered by children's playful interaction with mathematical materials and games.

Wolfgang and colleagues (2001), in a longitudinal study of preschoolers who engaged in complex block play, reported that these children showed long term gains in mathematical cognition. Ramani and Siegler (2008) also have reported that when low income children play number board games their numerical knowledge is increased. Also, Roskos and Christie (2001) have described young children's growth in literacy skills during play with literacy toys and materials.

Language Influences

Newland and colleagues (2001) have reported that maternal responses to infant toy initiations, as well as manipulation and labeling of toys at 11 months were related to the infant's language at 14 months. In a study of the influence of books and toys on the development of young Latino children, Tomopoulos and colleagues (2006) found that the presence of toys in the home at 6 months and 18 months predicted 21-month-old children's receptive language level, while book reading predicted both cognition and receptive language.

Bergen and Mauer (2002) reported that preschoolers with high levels of play with literacy toys were more likely to be spontaneous readers of signs and have greater pretend language in a "town-building activity" at age 5. Also, toy play has been found to improve the communication skills of 4- to 6-year-old children identified as autistic (Toth, Munson, Meltzoff, & Dawson, 2006).

Physical/Motor Influences

In a study of lower-income families, Saccani and colleagues (2013) reported that when there was a variety of toys in the home environment and parents encouraged infants to interact with them, the children's motor development was optimized. However, they noted that in such families, access to toys is often not a priority. Valadi, and Gabbard (2018) also found that the availability of fine-motor toys was a significant predictor of fine-motor skill and Miquelote, Santos, Cacola, et al. (2012) found that there was a positive relationship between play materials in the home and infant global motor performance, fine-motor performance, and later cognitive behaviors.

Social Influences

Research on father-toddler social toy play in Early Head Start showed that father-toddler social toy play was more complex among fathers in this program and predicted better cognitive and social developmental outcomes for their young children (Roggman, Boyce, Cook, Christiansen, & Jones, 2007). In a study comparing the results of child use of "social" and "isolate" toys in an integrated preschool setting that included children with special needs, Martin, Brady, and Williams (1991) found that the social toys encouraged more social interaction among these groups. Although some educators have been concerned about the social effects of child play with "war toys," other researchers (e.g., Hart & Tannock, 2013; Pellis & Pellis, 2007) have indicated that engaging in sociodramatic play involving play fighting and war toys may be beneficial for social development.

Moral Influences

Although there are fewer studies of toy play focused on moral influences, Tulviste and Koor (2005) reported that in four- and five-year-old preschool dyads, boys were significantly more likely to bring up justice and rights issues. Girls mentioned conventional rather than moral rules more often, but both genders applied moral rules more in play conflict situations. Relationships to justice issues (e.g., fairness in toy sharing) were the moral rules most often engendering conflicts. In a study of how children use dolls to address moral dilemmas, Woolgar and colleagues (2001) reported that children's use of non-physical discipline for the dolls was related to their awareness of moral issues such as honesty.

Gender Role Influences

The question of toy choices of boys and by girls has been studied extensively, especially in relation to the gender-related marketing of toys, which is prevalent at the present time. Such marketing in toys seems to be stronger now than in the past because, before 1975, only about 2 percent of toys were labeled by gender, whereas today on the Disney store's website, almost all toys are labeled by gender (Auster & Mansbach, 2012; Miller, 1987). Apparently, the message that some toys are more appropriate for males and others for females is taught early and the lesson is long lasting. Even at 18 months of age, children begin to show stereotypical toy choices (Powlishta, et al, 2001).

Auster and Mansbach (2012) reported that on internet marketing sites bold-colored toys of action figures, buildings, weapons, and vehicles were targeted for boys while pastel-colored toys of dolls, cosmetic, jewelry, or "domestic-oriented" types focused on girls. Also, toys marketed as "gender-neutral" had a color palette that more closely resembled toys marketed primarily to boys.

Cherney and London (2006) reported that elementary-age children continue to show gender-linked differences in their preferences for toys, television shows, computer games, and outdoor activities and Blakemore and Centers (2005) have noted that college-age students who rated four sets of toys associated girl's toys with nurturance, domestic skill, and attractiveness while boy's toys were rated as violent, competitive, exciting, and dangerous. Educational and artistic toys were rated as neutral or moderately masculine.

An emphasis on "gender-appropriate" toys seems to be worldwide, as a study of 8- to 12-year-old children in Italy showed that technology, warfare, locomotion, and construction toys were attributed to boys and the number of toys for girls was less extensive (De Caroli & Sagone, 2007). Although these studies of gender choices and gender marketing of toy selection and play continue to show gender differences, however, there is little research on whether and what might be the long-term results of such gender-influenced play.

EFFECTS OF TECHNOLOGY-AUGMENTED TOY PLAY

Presently, there is great interest in whether children's development will be enhanced or affected negatively by their play with technology-augmented toys. Some developmental psychologists have raised questions about potential negative effect on children's development. For example, David Elkind (2005, p. 11) has written, "Too many toys, given too often, made of synthetic material, and run by computer chips have denied children many of the benefits they once took from interacting with less high-tech playthings." Research on effects of such toys is only beginning but there is some evidence that children's play patterns, and thus possibly their development, may be changed both positively and negatively by such toys.

Kahn, Friedman, Perez-Granados, and Freier (2006) compared play with a robotic toy with a typical toy and found few differences in what children said about the two toys, but they concluded that the children's interactions with the robotic toy resulted in "impoverished" relationships. Other research on effects of technology-enhanced play on social interactions found that young children observed each other, commented on the actions, shared and helped with software-related problems, and also had conflicts over taking turns (Heft & Swaminathan, 2002).

In studies comparing children's play with augmented (i.e., "talking") action figures and nonaugmented figures, Bergen (2004, 2006) found that children had greater initial exploration of the augmented toys but after an exploratory period, the play actions of the two groups were similar. The ability of children to override the technological message to play in a certain way was sometimes accomplished. For example, one group of children avoided the "life-saving" messages of the toy and instead had the toy figures go to a "family dinner." As more research on the developmental implications of technology-augmented toys is collected, the effects of children's play will become clearer.

SUMMARY

For most of human history, there have been universal, relatively unchanging types of toys, but in the present era, some of these toys are undergoing technological enhancements. The authors in this handbook are providing an in-depth description of toys as they have been and of toys as they are changing and expanding. They are also suggesting the ways children's play with these many varieties of toys have played a role in children's development and how they will play a role in children's future as well.

REFERENCES

Auster, C. J., & Mansbach, C. S. (2012). The gender marketing of toys: An analysis of color and type of toy on the Disney store website. *Sex Roles*, 67(7–8), 375–88.

Bergen, D. (2002). The role of pretend play in children's cognitive development. *Early Childhood Research and Practice*; 4(1): 2–1. http//ecrp.uiuc.edu/v4n2/Bergen.html.

Bergen, D. (2004). Preschool children's play with "talking" and "non-talking" Rescue Heroes: Effects of technology-enhanced figures on the types and themes of play. In J. Goldstein, D. Buckingham, & G. Brougere (Eds.) *Toys, games, and media* (pp. 195–206). Erlbaum: Mahwah, NJ.

Bergen, D. (2006). Play and the brain. In C. Ferguson & E. Dettore (Eds.). *Play: An endangered species*. Olney, MD: Association for Childhood Education International.

Bergen D., & Mauer, D. (2002). Symbolic play, phonological awareness, and literacy skills at three age levels. In: Christie, J, Roskos, K. *Literacy and play in the early years: Cognitive, ecological, and sociocultural perspectives*. New York: Erlbaum: 193–204.

Blakemore, J. E. O., & Centers, R. E. (2005). Characteristics of boys' and girls' toys. *Sex Roles*, 53(9–10), 619–633.

Bruner, J. S. (1964). The course of cognitive growth. *American Psychologist*, 19(1), 1.

Cherney, I. D., & London, K. (2006). Gender-linked differences in the toys, television shows, computer games, and outdoor activities of 5- to 13-year-old children. *Sex Roles*, 54(9—10), 717.

De Caroli, M. E., & Sagone, E. (2007). Toys, sociocognitive traits, and occupations: Italian children's endorsement of gender stereotypes. *Psychological Reports*, 100(3 suppl), 1298–1311.

Elkind, D. (2005). The changing world of toys and toy play. *Exchange-Exchange Press*, 166, 11.

Gopnik, A. M., Meltzoff, A. N., & Kuhl, P. K. (2001). *The scientist in the crib: How children learn and what they teach us about the mind.* New York: Harper Collins.

Hart, J. L., & Tannock, M. T. (2013). Young children's playfighting and use of war toys. *Encyclopedia on Early Childhood Development*, 1–6.

Heft, T. M., & Swaminathan, S. (2002). The effects of computers on the social behavior of preschoolers. *Journal of Research in Childhood Education*, 16(2), 162–74.

Hill, P. S. (1908). The value and limitations of Froebel's gifts as educative materials (Part I, II). *The Elementary School Teacher*, 9(3), 129–37.

Kahn, P. H., Friedman, B., Perez-Granados, D. R., & Freier, N. G. (2006). Robotic pets in the lives of preschool children. *Interaction Studies*, 7(3), 405–36.

Kamii, C. (2015). Play and mathematics in kindergarten. In Fromberg, D. F. & Bergen, D. (eds). *Play from birth to twelve: Contexts, perspectives, and meanings, 3rd ed.* New York: Routledge. 2015: 197–206.

Kudrowitz, B. (2014). Emerging technology and toy design. In Foller, J. (Ed.), *Designing for emerging technologies.* Massachusetts: O'Reilly Media, 237-253.

Martin, S. S., Brady, M. P., & Williams, R. E. (1991). Effects of toys on the social behavior of preschool children in integrated and nonintegrated groups: Investigation of a setting event. *Journal of Early Intervention*, 15(2), 153–61.

Miller, C. L. (1987). Qualitative differences among gender stereotyped toys: Implications for cognitive and social development in girls and boys. *Sex Roles*, 16, 473–87.

Miquelote, A. F., Santos, D. C., Caçola, P. M., Montebelo, M. I. D. L., & Gabbard, C. (2012). Effect of the home environment on motor and cognitive behavior of infants. *Infant Behavior and Development*, 35(3), 329–34.

Newland, L. A., Roggman, L. A., & Boyce, L. K. (2001). The development of social toy play and language in infancy. *Infant Behavior and Development*, 24(1), 1–25.

Pellis S. M., & Pellis, V. C. (2007) Rough-and-tumble play and the development of the social brain. *Current Directions in Psychological Science, 16*, 95–98. doi:10.1111/j.1467-8721.2007.00483.x

Powlishta, K. K., Sen, M. G., Serbin, L. A., Poulin-Dubois, D., & Eichstedt, J. A. (2001). From infancy through middle childhood: The role of cognitive and social factors in becoming gendered. *Handbook of the Psychology of Women and Gender*, 116–132.

Ramani, G. B., & Siegler, R. S. (2008). Promoting broad and stable improvements in low-income children's numerical knowledge through playing number board games. *Child Development*, 79(2), 375–94.

Roggman, L. A., Boyce, L., Cook, G. A., Christiansen, K., & Jones, D. (2007). Playing with daddy: Social toy play, early head start, and developmental outcomes. *Fathering: A Journal of Theory, Research, and Practice about Men as Fathers*, 2(1), 83.

Roskos, K. & Christie, J. (2001). Examining the play-literacy interface: A critical review and future directions. *Journal of Early Childhood Literacy*, 1: 59–89.

Saccani, R., Valentini, N. C., Pereira, K. R., Müller, A. B., & Gabbard, C. (2013). Associations of biological factors and affordances in the home with infant motor development. *Pediatrics International*, 55(2), 197–203.

Tomopoulos, S., Dreyer, B. P., Tamis-LeMonda, C., Flynn, V., Rovira, I., Tineo, W., & Mendelsohn, A. L. (2006). Books, toys, parent-child interaction, and development in young Latino children. *Ambulatory Pediatrics*, 6(2), 72–78.

Toth, K., Munson, J., Meltzoff, A. N., & Dawson, G. (2006). Early predictors of communication development in young children with autism spectrum disorder: Joint attention, imitation, and toy play. *Journal of Autism and Developmental Disorders*, 36(8), 993–1005.

Toy. (2020). In Oxford Online Dictionary . Retrieved from https://en.oxforddictionaries.com/definition/toy

Tulviste, T., & Koor, M. (2005). "Hands off the car, it's mine!" and "The teacher will be angry if we don't play nicely": Gender-related preferences in the use of moral rules and social conventions in preschoolers' dyadic play. *Sex Roles*, 53(1–2): 57–66.

Uzgiris, I. C., & Hunt, J. M. (1974) *Assessment in infancy*. Chicago: University of Illinois Press.

Valadi, S., & Gabbard, C. (2018). The effect of affordances in the home environment on children's fine-and gross motor skills. *Early Child Development and Care*, 1–8.

Williams, A. D. (1990). *Jigsaw puzzles: An illustrated history and price guide*. Radnor, PA: Wallace-Homestead Book Co.

Wolfgang, C. H. Stannard, L. L., & Jones, I. (2001). Block play performance among preschoolers as a predictor of later school achievement in mathematics. *Journal of Research in Childhood Education*, 15: 173–80.

Woolgar, M., Steele, H., Steele, M., Yabsley, S., & Fonagy, P. (2001). Children's play narrative responses to hypothetical dilemmas and their awareness of moral emotions. *British Journal of Developmental Psychology*, *19*(1), 115–28.

2

DEVELOPMENTAL INSIGHTS FROM THE NATIONAL TOY HALL OF FAME

Christopher Bensch

The Strong National Museum of Play is home to the National Toy Hall of Fame, as befits its status as the museum with the largest, most diverse collection of toys, dolls, games, and video games in the world. The museum opened to the public in 1982 and focused its mission on play beginning in 2003. Since then, The Strong has dedicated itself to exploring play and the ways in which play encourages learning, creativity, and discovery and illuminates cultural history.

The Strong collects and preserves, interprets and educates, and provides outreach programs that serve a diverse audience of adults, families, children, students, teachers, scholars, collectors, and others. Through all these activities and more, The Strong seeks to ensure that present and future generations understand the critical role of play in human physical, social, and intellectual development and the ways in which play reflects cultural history. As part of those endeavors, The Strong began housing the National Toy Hall of Fame in 2003.

ORIGINATION OF THE NATIONAL TOY HALL OF FAME

The National Toy Hall of Fame began in 1998 at what was then called A. C. Gilbert's Discovery Village in Salem, Oregon. With an intent to recognize and celebrate classic playthings, that first year the National Toy Hall of Fame inducted 11 timeless toys: marbles, Crayola crayons, Play-Doh, Monopoly, Etch A Sketch, Frisbee, Barbie, Teddy Bear, Erector Set, LEGO, and Tinkertoy. In succeeding years, the groups of inductees decreased in size as critical mass had been established—inducting six toys in 1999, five in 2000, and two each in 2001 and 2002.

Leading up to the 2002 induction, A. C. Gilbert's Discovery Village found itself the subject of an intensive lobbying campaign by the fans of Raggedy Ann. Determined to get their favorite rag doll into the hall, the Raggedy Ann advocates deluged the museum with letters and petitions, tied up the telephone switchboard with calls, and even posted a picketer dressed as Raggedy Ann out front. Whether that lobbying paid off or whether it was purely on her own merits, Raggedy Ann was indeed inducted in 2002 along with the jigsaw puzzle, but the process had exhausted the A. C. Gilbert's Discovery Village staff and revealed that the hall of fame was the tail wagging their institutional dog.

THE STRONG'S NATIONAL TOY HALL OF FAME

For years, the senior staff of The Strong in Rochester, New York, had considered establishing a toy hall of fame to leverage the museum's status as the holder of the largest, most comprehensive collection of toys, dolls, and games in the world, but abandoned that idea once they were scooped by the museum in Oregon. However, later in 2002, fate brought The Strong's president, Rollie Adams, into contact with the president of A. C. Gilbert's Discovery Village at a museum conference.

Adams conveyed the message that The Strong had always envied A. C. Gilbert's hall of fame and was both surprised and pleased when the effective response was "for the right price, it could be yours." The result was that in 2003, the National Toy Hall of Fame's collection and brand moved to The Strong. Since then, The National Toy Hall of Fame has gone on to become one of the museum's most prominent elements and a driver for global visibility with more than 1.5 billion media impressions each year, largely concentrated around the induction time in early November.

CRITERIA AND PROCESS FOR SELECTING TOYS
FOR THE HALL OF FAME

The National Toy Hall of Fame induction process solicits nominations from the public throughout the year, typically generating thousands of nominations for more than 400 or 500 different playthings. An internal team at The Strong considers those nominations and distills them to a dozen finalists based on four criteria:

- Icon status: The toy is widely recognized, respected, and remembered.
- Longevity: The toy is more than a passing fad and has enjoyed popularity over multiple generations.
- Discovery: The toy fosters learning, creativity, or discovery through play. (Note that a toy may be inducted on the basis of this criterion without necessarily having met all of the first three.)

Assembling the list of the 12 finalists each year also involves balancing toys and games that fit different developmental stages (toddler versus tween, for example), represent different types of play (large motor outdoor play, open-ended imaginative play, or social play, among others), and reflect both gendered and universal playthings and play patterns. The group is likewise mindful of the need to include a blend of both branded and generic toys in order to tap most viscerally into popular consciousness and to encourage maximum media attention.

The 12 finalists are then sent to the National Toy Hall of Fame Selection Advisory Committee, a group of approximately 24 external individuals with expertise in fields such as history, child development, toy collecting, creative endeavors, and the toy industry. The committee members each rank their top three choices for induction and the results of that ranking are compiled to guide the selection of the two or three toys that are inducted each year.

In their deliberations the National Toy Hall of Fame Selection Advisory Committee are guided by their historical analysis of the toys' cultural significance, persistence across time, and overall play value. The results meet the criteria that the two or three toys that are inducted each year represent the best qualities of play—offering children and adults rich imaginative, creative, physical, and social experiences—and demonstrate the playthings that have had the most significant impact on American popular culture broadly and on individual lives.

TOYS IN THE NATIONAL TOY HALL OF FAME

As of the induction ceremony in November 2020, the National Toy Hall of Fame had recognized 74 classic toys:

1998

Marbles Round stones and polished nuts sufficed for ancient games, but today's children play with spheres of colorful glass or steel, first mass-produced in the nineteenth century. Marble games demand both strategy and dexterity.

Crayola crayons The word *crayon* first appeared in 1644. But Crayola's multicolored, paper-wrapped, nontoxic wax drawing-sticks—named for the French words for "chalk" and "oily"—debuted in America in 1903. Children use billions every year.

Play-Doh This squishy, colorful modeling compound started out as a grade school art project using off-white wallpaper cleaner. It is easier to work than clay, and since 1956 children have sculpted hundreds of millions of pounds of it.

Monopoly This Great Depression–era board game that celebrated squashing competitors and driving up profits soared to popularity in 1934. Over the next 80 years, 275 million copies sold to players in 111 countries.

Etch A Sketch This nifty drawing tool became the Christmas toy sensation of 1960; Ohio Art has sold 100 million since. Knobs guide internal rods that move a stylus that tantalizingly traces lines or loops across a powder-coated screen.

Frisbee New England college students tossing pie tins and pretzel can lids inspired this plastic flying disk that debuted in 1954. Over the next 50 years, Wham-O and Mattel sold 200 million.

Barbie This biggest-selling-ever fashion doll appeared in 1959. Tall and curvy, she became the career girl of the 1960s, driving a pink Corvette. Afterward, as a dentist, firefighter, or pilot, she mirrored gender-role changes.

Teddy Bear The most popular plush toy ever began as a cartoon of a cute cub that President Teddy Roosevelt spared on a hunt in 1902. Boosted by mass production and print advertising, "Teddy" bears soon became standard for cribs.

Erector Set This construction toy from 1913 let boys and their fathers play together at building. Over the years, they teamed up to build superstructures for mini-buildings, bridges, cranes, machines, and ships.

LEGO These phenomenally popular building bricks originated in Denmark in 1949 and still let children explore spatial relationships. Just six blocks can be connected 102,981,500 ways. *Leg godt* ("LEGO") means "play well" in Danish.

Tinkertoy Launched in 1914 and still popular, this toy provided kids with loose parts to endlessly reconfigure. Advertising spotlighted the educational value of play, and parents appreciated the training in spatial intelligence.

1999

Duncan Yo-Yo This popular, age-old Philippine toy came to America in 1929. A top-turned-sideways, it spools away with a wrist-flick, and then returns, winding up its string. Learning to make it sleep or spin in place enables tricks.

View-Master Introduced at the 1939 World's Fair, this rotary viewer produced three-dimensional effects for photos of natural wonders, exotic cultures, and foreign royalty at first, but later—and profitably—Disney characters, too.

Roller Skates Invented in the eighteenth century and perfected in the twentieth, roller skates depend upon and train balance. Learning to glide on four wheels courts calamity but bestows grace. Toe-stops and heel-brakes now make the ride safer.

Radio Flyer Wagon This little red wagon, popular since 1930, remains a hybrid—part racer that merrily careens down driveways, part hauler that in the past helped paperboys deliver the morning news. The sturdy cart lasts for many years.

Lincoln Logs Introduced in 1916, and later promoted on 1950s TV shows *Pioneer Playhouse* and *Davy Crockett*, these notched "linkin" logs helped kids develop spatial understanding as they built millions of sturdy cabins.

Hula Hoop In 1957, the hoop—a traditional wooden toy for rolling and spinning—became the hollow plastic tube named for the swivel-hipped Hawaiian dance. Millions sold almost overnight and the fad never faded.

2000

Jacks Children from every culture have sat cross-legged to play a version of this, one of the world's oldest playground games. Once played with stones and bones, it continues as a red rubber ball and spiky metal jacks.

Jump Rope Popular as a boys' competitive game among seventeenth-century Dutch settlers, rope jumping in sociable groups—accompanied by songs and chants—gained popularity among girls in the nineteenth century and now belongs mostly to them.

Mr. Potato Head This comical toy sprouted as a cereal box prize. But in 1952, it sold four million units on its own as a package of assorted plastic eyes, noses, mouths, ears, hats, and a pipe designed with prongs for poking into a spud.

Bicycle Part child's toy, part adult athletic gear, and part basic transportation for all, bikes became popular in the 1890s. Since then, they have given riders thrills, pleasure, exercise, and freedom to move.

Slinky In 1943, a nautical engineer looking for ways to keep delicate instruments steady at sea noticed how a loose spring slinked off a sill. This toy began flying off store shelves in 1945 and still does.

2001

Silly Putty World War II chemists seeking a rubber-substitute made a bouncy colloid useless for tires but fun for parties. Sales soared after marketers packaged the goo in plastic eggs and kids used it to lift newsprint images.

Tonka Trucks Tonka started in 1947 with a single steam shovel and now sells more than 30 sturdy, lifelike work vehicles. Mighty dump trucks, bulldozers, and road graders drive children's pretend play in backyard sandboxes across America.

2002

Jigsaw Puzzle In the 1700s, English mapmakers played at reassembling pieces of maps they had dissected and pasted on wood. In 1930s America, mass production of cheap cardboard puzzles helped spark a lasting problem-solving pastime.

Raggedy Ann and Raggedy Andy (2007 addition) These cuddly rag dolls, perennial favorites for pretend play, began as plucky fictional siblings who first appeared in the popular *Raggedy Ann Stories* (1920–1938). They spring to life when humans aren't looking.

2003

Checkers Since at least the 1600s, players have used colored stones, painted wood chips, corn cob slices, or plastic pieces to play checkers on boards scratched in the dirt, sawn from wood, or printed on cardboard.

Alphabet Blocks For more than 300 years, these colorful cubes embossed with letters have taught basic literacy lessons disguised as fun. When stacked the blocks make words; when linked they build sentences.

2004

Scrabble A hit in 1948, this board game sustains its appeal by asking players to search their minds and trust their luck as they spell out words with tiles of assigned value. Electronic versions now appear on the web.

Rocking Horse Since woodworkers joined curved boards to carved horses' heads 500 years ago, children have imagined galloping steeds while rocking back-and-forth to create the illusion of speed.

GI Joe In 1964, this fighting man action figure with moving parts helped boys create stories of power and control. In 1970, Hasbro gave Joe peaceable adventures to sustain sales that totaled 400 million in 40 years.

2005

Jack-in-the-Box Since the 1500s, this music box has triggered anticipation and surprise; two powerful reasons to play. Crank a verse of "Pop Goes the Weasel" and the lid springs open and Jack leaps out. Then children ask for more.

Candy Land When created in the 1940s, this game aimed to keep young bedridden polio victims busy and happy. The Peppermint Stick Forest, the Gumdrop Mountain, and the Ice Cream Floats soon drew other fans by the millions.

Cardboard Box This toy is not manufactured; it is rescued for pretend play. Children use scissors and crayons to turn empty boxes into pirate ships, princess's castles, and other imaginative creations.

2006

Easy-Bake Oven Roving pretzel-vendors on New York's streets inspired this toy in 1963. Heated initially by 100-watt light bulbs, these ovens turned millions of cake mixes into cupcakes and millions of children into bakers.

Lionel Trains Customers clamored for electric trains after they saw Joshua Lionel Cowen's store window model layout in 1900. Sales soared as pretending to run a railroad made boys feel like men and men feel like boys.

2007

Atari 2600 Game System In 1975, Atari's *Pong* brought electronic table tennis home. Two years later, the company's 2600 game system offered a library of affordable game cartridges and made Atari a synonym for video games in that era.

Kite Tethered silk kites flew in China 3,000 years ago. The familiar bowed diamond still decorates the sky, but breezes also float triangles, boxes, birds, and dragons. All lift the flyers' spirits and imaginations.

2008

Baby Doll After the mid-1800s, doll makers sought to provide truer-to-life pretend play experiences. Little girls dressed, fed, carried, scolded, and cuddled a long line of increasingly realistic baby dolls.

Skateboard Late 1950s California surfer kids nailed roller skates to boards and created a new sport that soon attracted millions. In the 1970s, plastic wheels enabled acrobatic tricks that demanded strength, balance, and creativity.

Stick Possibly the world's oldest toy, and surely the cheapest, sticks prompt pretending. Children at play imagine sticks as bats, batons, bows, swords, spears, light sabers, magic wands, flying broomsticks, and fishing poles.

2009

Ball Soft or hard, round or oval, solid or air-filled, when thrown and caught, bounced, batted, or kicked and chased, this simple, low-cost, ancient plaything makes possible more games than any other object.

Big Wheel Old-style, top-heavy steel tricycles tipped easily. In 1969, Louis Marx & Co. introduced this low-slung, fast, stable, and exciting alternative made of red, yellow, and blue plastic. More than 40 million have sold since.

Nintendo Game Boy Appearing in 1989, this videogame platform came preloaded with absorbing games—*Tennis*, *Baseball*, *Super Mario Land*, and the popular puzzle *Tetris*. Hand-held and battery-powered, it changed how children play.

2010

Playing Cards Originating in China 1,200 years ago and popular ever since, palm-sized decks allowed matching (Rummy), fishing (Go Fish), and accumulating games (Slapjack). Card players always hope for a good hand and a fair deal.

The Game of Life In 1866, The Checkered Game of Life, the first popular parlor game, valued virtue by sternly punishing vice. A century later, Milton Bradley produced a new, gentler version. Recent editions feature cheerful endings.

2011

Blanket When children pretend, this toy becomes a crime-fighter's cape, a genie's magic carpet, an explorer's tent, or a princess's flowing gown. Such inventive play helps children develop mentally, socially, and emotionally.

Dollhouse In the late 1500s, wealthy Europeans displayed miniature rugs, tables, chairs, and beds in fine cabinets called baby houses. During the 1800s, mass-production made dollhouses and pretending accessible to the masses.

Hot Wheels Mattel introduced these tiny tricked-out American muscle cars in 1968. Springs gave them realistic wheel-bounce. By 2014, the company had designed more than 800 models and sold more than 4 billion.

2012

Dominoes This 700-year-old tile game from China still teaches math skills through games such as matador, chicken foot, five up, and Mexican train. Other players simply enjoy toppling long rows.

***Star Wars* Action Figures** Since 1977, the Star Wars franchise has spawned hundreds of character-based toys that empower children to act out stories of mystical heroes vanquishing demonic villains. Adults join the fun as collectors.

2013

Chess With roots in seventh-century India, chess migrated to Europe and by 1475 evolved into the game people recognize today. Players exercise strategic decision making as they move six pieces endowed with a range of powers.

Rubber Duck This buoyant toy has been turning bath time into play time since the 1940s. After Ernie, the Sesame Street Muppet, sang his hit tune "Rubber Duck-ie," in 1970, the toy became a cultural icon.

2014

Bubbles Blown from a wand or blooped from a gun, these perfect soap-film spheres shimmer in the light and float on the breeze. They pop instantly but endure as playthings. Shops sell 200 million bottles of soap bubbles a year.

Little Green Army Men Legions of two-inch-tall unpainted plastic toy soldiers that appeared after World War II still join backyard sandbox battles. These little warriors, cheaper than old tin or lead versions, now sell by the bag or bucket.

Rubik's Cube In this puzzle, players move 27 boxes hinged cleverly on a rounded core, spinning rows to match colors. A few champs now solve Rubik's Cube in seconds; since 1977, more than a billion fans have labored over it.

2015

Puppet Since ancient times, people the world over have used puppets to present tales of fantasy and make-believe. Puppets also help kids develop imagination, creativity, and dexterity.

Twister Using people as playing pieces made Twister unique among boxed games in 1966. First thought to be too suggestive, Twister has become a standard for playrooms and parties, producing laughter and fun for all ages.

Super Soaker In the twentieth century, kids waged water wars with tiny squirt guns. Dr. Lonnie Johnson's 1990 Super Soaker, with its large water tank and pressurized delivery system, changed outdoor play forever.

2016

Swing Ancient drawings and sculptures document humans on swings. A pastime of French royalty in the 1700s, the swing became a playground favorite for children in America in the 1900s. Today many youngsters enjoy swings in their own backyards.

Fisher-Price Little People First offered in the 1959 Safety School Bus, Fisher-Price Little People have helped generations of small children imagine big adventures in play sets representing farms, schools, airports, and other fascinating places in their worlds.

Dungeons & Dragons In the 1970s, two serious gamers added the concept of role play to strategy games. Their innovation brought fantasy and imagination into games for adults and paved the way for the computer games of the twenty-first century.

2017

Clue Inspired by English mystery parties in the 1920s, the board game Clue challenges players to solve an imaginary murder. The fun and suspense of a mystery come to life as players deduce not only who, but also how and what, dispatched the victim.

Paper Airplane Although science and technology have brought vast improvements in flight over the years, the simplicity of a plain paper airplane made it a fixture of play through the twentieth century and into the present.

Wiffle Ball For more than 60 years, children have started their baseball careers swinging at a Wiffle Ball, a perforated plastic orb designed for pick-up games among a few friends.

2018

Magic 8 Ball Magic 8 Ball has entertained millions by letting them flirt harmlessly with fortune telling. Expectations for the future lie between idle longing and fervent wishing. This novelty provides answers that swim randomly out of its inky depths.

Uno Uno's simple rules and bright graphics offer a variation on the classic card game crazy eights. Children and adults alike can compete to be the player to announce they have just "Uno" card left and then discard it to win.

Pinball With their roots tracing back to an eighteenth-century French parlor game, pinball machines saturate players' senses, challenging them to use flippers to aim, control, and fire steel balls across a miniature playground of ramps, bumpers, and obstacles.

2019

Coloring Book Children express their creativity with coloring books, popular since the early twentieth century. Whether the subject is today's favorite superhero, beloved pet, or cartoon character, the books invite children and adults to add their favorite colors.

Magic: The Gathering Inventor Richard Garfield's Magic: The Gathering collectible card game was the first game in which individual cards can change rules and affect the outcome. Designed by artists, each card carries unique powers in an expanding mythical universe.

Matchbox Cars A formula for high quality and low prices set Matchbox cars apart from their competitors when they debuted in 1952 and fueled such an enduring success that, even today, some people call a miniature car, no matter the maker, a "Matchbox."

2020

Sidewalk Chalk Chalk has few limits to what people can do with it. Every sidewalk square, patio, and driveway holds the potential for chalk to turn it into a work of art, a winning game of strategy and cleverness, or a demonstration of physical agility, poise, and balance.

Baby Nancy In 1968, Shindana Toys' Baby Nancy, a baby doll with a dark complexion and Black features, exposed a long-standing demand for ethnically correct Black dolls that the mainstream market had failed to deliver.

Jenga Based on Leslie Scott's childhood play with wood blocks in East Africa, the game Jenga received worldwide admiration. Simple to understand and play, it appeals to multiple generations, promoting patience, balance, and manual dexterity.

INFLUENCE OF THE TOY HALL OF FAME SELECTIONS

In building its collection of National Toy Hall of Fame inductees, The Strong has pursued the creation of deep and comprehensive holdings that both represent continuity over the years and illustrate the ways that playthings have changed within their genres and brands to remain appealing and relevant to new generations. The Strong has assembled large and outstanding collections of the individual toys and games—more than 7,200 jigsaw puzzles, 2,600 Barbies (including her friends and paraphernalia), 150 Monopoly variants from the United States and around the world, 2,500 Star Wars action figures, 475 rubber ducks, 650 Hot Wheels vehicles, and 1,800 yo-yos, among many other Toy Hall of Fame holdings.

Examining and analyzing these large groups of timeless playthings reveals ways that popular culture has shaped play and playthings, particularly in the Baby Boom years and beyond. Increasingly enduring toy brands seek to amplify their contemporary appeal by applying licensed characters and media properties to their products. The results—*Simpsons* Magic 8 Ball, *Star Wars* Clue, *Toy Story* little green army men, and Thomas the Tank Engine Uno, to name just a few—offer a glimpse of marketing strategies intended to keep evergreen play products pertinent to consumers and to stand out online or on store shelves as not just a standard toy, something your parents played with when they were kids.

Whether these media licenses do anything to enhance the play value of the toys is less clear and, in fact, superimposing characters and back stories on the playthings may constrict rather than augment the types of engagement that the toys and games suggest. Often the induction of alternative or highly generic toys has generated the highest public and media response for the National Toy Hall of Fame, reinforcing the appeal of less commercialized playthings and the ways that they resonate with people. That dynamic first emerged in 2005 when the National Toy Hall of Fame inducted the cardboard box.

The outpouring of responses from the public, waxing rhapsodic over the joys of refrigerator boxes (Spaceship? Castle? Little House on the Prairie?) and inspiring people to share stories and photos of children delightedly playing with boxes—sometimes completely ignoring the manufactured toy that had come in the box. Even when The Strong exhibited the cardboard box at Toy Fair, the annual trade show of the toy industry each February, the reaction of attendees was not resentment of this noncommercial alternative to their carefully designed, manufactured, and marketed playthings, as might have been anticipated. Instead, the commentary universally celebrated the creative spark that "discovered" toys can tap into and inspire. Later years' inductions have gone on to include the stick, the blanket, the ball, and the swing, each possessing incredible potential for open-ended play.

ENDURING VALUE OF TOYS

From another vantage, the inductees to the National Toy Hall of Fame can be categorized by their suitability for five primary types of play activities: building, competing, creating, imagining, and moving. Building toys clearly include LEGO, Erector, and Lincoln Log sets, but also encompass such toys as Lionel trains and jigsaw puzzles, since the pleasure of play with those items largely resides in assembly. Still, it is worth noting that the types of play are not mutually exclusive.

The games in the Hall of Fame, such as Uno, chess, Monopoly, and Scrabble, easily fit into the competing category, but so too can movement playthings like skateboards and Frisbees as participants compete with one another or individually set themselves challenges to accomplish. Similarly, Crayola Crayons, Play-Doh, and cardboard boxes all fit on a spectrum between creativity and imaginative play, depending on how the individual player chooses to use them.

Over its years of inductions, the National Toy Hall of Fame has accumulated a representative sample of timeless toys that suit different phases of children's development and that bridge dividing lines between different ages and generations. For the youngest children, toys such as rubber ducks, teddy bears, and alphabet blocks may find use in play that emphasizes their tactile qualities and encourages large motor skills. But those same toys, as children age, might be incorporated into imaginative play—teddy bears having tea parties with baby dolls or Raggedy Ann and Andy—or construction play—alphabet block towers adjacent to LEGO buildings or serving to create a corral for a Fisher-Price Little People farm set.

Those malleable qualities and generous affordances are among the characteristics that have kept these playthings pertinent across time and through individual lives. In turn, that adaptability has reinforced the evergreen qualities that have kept these toys in production for decades. Adults often feel a particular fondness for the play they recall with these toys and games, inspiring them to make sure that the children or grandchildren they care most about have access to those same items in their own childhoods. And thus the cycle begins again, cultivating new generations' attachment to these classic toys and ensuring that the toys and games in the National Toy Hall of Fame remain valued and vibrant elements of childhoods for decades to come.

REFERENCES

The Strong National Museum of Play, 1 Manhattan Square Drive, Rochester, New York 14607
www.museumofplay.org
National Toy Hall of Fame, www.toyhalloffame.org

3

CULTURAL HISTORY OF DEVELOPMENTALLY APPROPRIATE TOYS

Dorothy Sluss

When did children begin to play with toys? Did it occur when stone-age children played with sticks, leaves, and dirt? Was it when children skipped rocks across the top of water? Or perhaps when the first doll was made? Although it is not known specifically when children began to play with toys, children have played with toys since records were first kept. Historical documents show that children in Greece played with yo-yos in 500 BCE, children in China played with kites in 1000 BCE, and children in India played with animal toys with and without wheels in 2500 BCE (McMahon, 2020).

These records show that the toys were culturally specific. That is, the makers of toys produced items that represented things considered important in their culture such as animals, wheels, and flying objects. Were these toys aligned with and/or reflective of their age and stage of development? That is, were these toys developmentally appropriate and if so, what is the cultural history of developmentally appropriate toys? That is the question that guides our exploration.

The term *developmentally appropriate practice* (DAP) was popularized in the1980s with the publication of a book by the children's advocacy group, the National Association for the Education of Young Children (NAEYC) (Bredekamp, 1984). Developmentally appropriate practice references educational practices that are age appropriate, individually appropriate, and culturally appropriate. Those who value developmental practice select developmentally appropriate toys that are aligned with the child in terms of age, capacity, interests, and cultural milieu.

Because of the use of DAP since the 1980s, many people, especially educators, are familiar with this term and strive to select toys and learning materials that meet the standards of developmental practice (Copple & Bredekamp, 2009). In response stores, toy manufacturers, and online sites often suggest appropriate toys for specific ages and stages of development. However, there is less attention to which aspects of culture are being represented. In recent years, advocates of developmental practice have urged manufacturers to provide toys and materials that reflect the wide-ranging diversity of physical attributes, social practices, and skills valued in various cultural situations.

EARLY AGES

Most information from the early ages comes from the birthplace of Western civilization, Greece and Rome. In early Greece, boys were included in the preparation for the Olympic games so their play may have reflected the perspective that it would prepare them for both adult work and games. Their toys would have included materials found in the games such as a rope, a smaller spear, or a lighter discus. Accounts about their play are found in the literature that has been handed down, but there are no supporting artifacts (Huizinga, 1950). In the same way, girls from around the world and in many different cultures have engaged in activities to prepare them for women's roles as defined in their culture. For example, miniaturized pots have been found in Egyptian tombs and archaeological sites in Crete (Cleverley & Phillips, 1986).

According to Barnes, "No doubt girls planned imaginary meals featuring olives, dates, bread, and honey more than thirty centuries ago" (1998, p. 6). Unfortunately, the interface of children and toys from countries with limited written historical documentation is more limited so we study tribes and groups of people who still exhibit some of these traditions such as the !Kung in Africa (Lancey, 2007). Although we may not know the specifics of how children played with toys at the beginning of our civilization, we can surmise that all children played when they had opportunities to play and much of their play reflected their culture.

MIDDLE AGES

Written records and images from the middle ages provide a glance into how children were viewed and the toys that were prescribed to them by society. At one time, there was a view that children in the Middle Ages were not accorded a childhood and instead were viewed as adults (Cleverley & Phillips, 1986). Indeed, that may have been the case for many, but the current view suggests that adults in that era ensured that some children had time to play and encouraged their play. Orme (2003, p. 101) notes that "Archaeologists have discovered everything from toy knights and horses, to tiny cooking pots and pans. . . . Children played ball games, stick games, and sports, as well as what we'd now call board games like backgammon and chess. In the cloisters of Canterbury and Salisbury cathedrals, nine men's Morris boards carved into the benches by medieval children are still visible today."

Other toys, such as the roly-poly toy, were developed in China and Russia. According to Kyburz (1994), a roly-poly toy is usually a round-bottomed doll with a bottom that is roughly a hemisphere, so that when it is pushed over, it can right itself. It is considered as one of the oldest toys in history. Although there are many version (e.g., animals, clowns, people), they symbolize the ability to have success, overcome adversity, and recover from misfortune (Kyburz, 1994).

The most famous image from the Middle Ages period that reflects the play of young children is the 1560 painting, *Children's Games*, by Pieter Bruegel the Elder. Perhaps no other image captures their play as well as this painting. The variety of play and toys evident in the painting reflect a society that valued play for both boys and girls. In this image, boys are observed playing with sticks, hoops, flying objects, and barrels with other boys, and girls can be seen playing games on the ground with objects from a basket with small round parts. Boys and girls are observed playing apart and with each other. Although the picture shows gender specific games and toy play, it also shows opportunities for all children. Although this was not meant to be a depiction of children but rather a satire of adults, it still indicates that these materials were available and that toys were a valuable part of their daily life.

MODERN AGES

In Europe and the colonies, children from all but the wealthiest homes were involved in work that sustained the family. When they played, their play was functional in that it served the purposes of the adults. At that time period in Europe and America, children were viewed as miniature adults. American toys included materials for hunting and fishing for boys and dolls for girls (Chudacoff, 2007, 2011).

Girls' play with dolls and miniature household items was intended to prepare them for skills that would need as a woman, while boys hunted, raced, and roamed together in their male-only world (Chudacoff, 2011). Because tea had been imported into Europe in the 1700s, tea sets for young girls became a highly desirable toy (King, 1979), and some tea sets probably found their way to the colonies. Also, after the American Revolution, coffee pots were included in many of the dish sets as young girls poured coffee instead of tea, thus reflecting the cultural change.

THE GOLDEN AGE OF TOYS

If there has ever been a Golden Age of toys, it has occurred since the beginning of the nineteenth century, again reflecting changes in society's view of children. In the 1800s, for example, children began to be viewed differently by scholars in Europe and America. Rousseau's view of the child as innately good and John Locke's focus on the child as a *tabula rasa* were examples of this change, and, as the view of children changed, so also did their toys. For example, John Locke created the first alphabet blocks by pasting letters on the side of a six-sided die. He thought by observing the die, children would learn their letters. This was perhaps, the first toy designed specifically to educate children.

In 1843, the grandfather of kindergarten, Friedrich Froebel (1782–1852) created a set of gifts/toys that he used with children. Though these materials may not be viewed these as toys now, they are credited with giving rise to technical toys. A museum display in Germany reflects the history of this movement. According to Yagou (2016, p. 1), "The Deutsches Museum toy collection covers the period from 1880 until today. It has been exhibited since 1984 in four sections based on material (wood, ceramic, metal and plastic) and has been unchanged. It is based on the premise that play is a way to acquire skills, understand technologies and develop the imagination. Additionally, toys reflect the state of technological advancement and the public perception of technology."

The industrial revolution in the mid 1800s enabled the design of wheeled toys, board games, dolls and doll furniture, which were mass produced on an assembly line. However, construction toys were considered strictly for boys and homemaker toys were for girls (Mergen, 1982). The "availability of mass-produced toys, games, dolls, and books increased dramatically after the Civil War, transforming commercialized playthings from instruments of instruction to items of joy" (Chudacoff, 2011, p. 105).

The dawn of the 1900s saw a child-study movement in which childhood was recognized as a distinct period of development and children were no longer viewed as miniature adults. Caroline Pratt (1867–1954) was influenced by Froebel, but she thought that children should have toys that they could freely manipulate so she invented unit blocks. John Dewey also supported Pratt's unit block creation, and for this reason, toy manufacturers invited early childhood educators to help develop educational materials that would stimulate children's imagination and self-expression experiences with concrete, self-expressive materials such as blocks, clay, paint, and wood. Additionally, they encouraged children under the age of six to play with language and rhythms and to invent their own games instead of playing games with rules (Sluss, 2005).

In spite of the influence of the child study movement, consumerism and gender stereotyping of toys were rampant throughout the 1960s. The mainstream holiday, Christmas, (not others such as Hanukah) was the main time when toys were advertised by manufacturers and mail order catalogs were the conduit for toy purchases. In 1955, the first toys tied to a television show (the "Mickey Mouse" show") began, and the Mattel Toy Company targeted advertising for toys on a daily basis with such shows. According to Rancese (1985, p. 121), that is when there began a trend "for children to get more decision-making authority and exercise that authority at younger and younger ages." This targeted marketing suddenly created a large market for toys and rapidly eclipsed the freedom inherent in many of the "classic" toys.

In the 1970s, parents started trying to diminish gender stereotyping. Although Federal laws initially prevented toy manufacturers from marketing toys from movies and television to children, in the 1980s, television was deregulated so that commercials during children's prime time could show toys in a way that encouraged gender stereotyping and depiction of acts of aggression. For example, toys suggested that boys were expected to be violent and girls were sexually precocious. In response, a movement gained momentum to remove gender specific toys and labels.

The technical design of toys initiated by Froebel gained momentum in the 1980s. A technological revolution occurred as children played with media-related figures that replicated what children viewed on the television set in their home. These highly structured toys often limited the imaginative possibilities of children's creative play and increased the level of violence found in play (Carlsson-Paige & Levin, 1987). On the other hand, electronic figures that communicate feelings were also popularized. Many toys now have a digital component such as the digital dolls replicating traditional dolls on computers. However, with the prominence of adult-controlled environments where children could be observed, there was a focus on more indoor toys, rather than toys used in outdoor play.

In contrast to earlier views of toys that were valued for supporting cultural transmission, this period witnessed a greater focus on the use of toys to facilitate children's development. Toys have a "logic of action" that suggest how the toy is to be used. For example, some toys suggest activities that lead to fine and gross motor development, such as fine motor toys like pegboards, pattern boards, and puzzles. Sensorimotor toys such bouncing balls, shaking rattles, spinning tops, and rocking horses give rise to repetition and to the joy of making things happen with objects.

Miniature animals, vehicles, houses, utensils, furniture, and dolls facilitate enactment of actions observed in particular cultures. Constructive toys that can be manipulated and used to create something new, such as Bristle blocks, wooden blocks, LEGOs, and Kapla or Keva blocks offer opportunities to develop creative thinking with understanding of the mathematical relationships of shapes, sizes, and contours. Locomotion toys, including tricycles, bicycles, scooters, and wagons, facilitate gross motor development, understanding of one's body, and have the added benefit of offering the joy of movement. Although development might be the intended goal of these toys, children have and continue to use the toys according to their own agenda.

CURRENT FOCUS ON TOYS (2000–2020)

In the past thirty years, the United States and other industrialized Western nations have focused attention on children's toys and activities that are not gender-restrictive (Barnes, 1998). Often at the urging of feminists, child-development specialists, and early childhood educators, boys have been encouraged to play in miniaturized kitchens, learning to wash dishes, set tables or serve food, push replicas of vacuum cleaners and small brooms and mops, and play at shopping for household foodstuffs in child-sized supermarkets. Similarly, girls have been more encouraged to play with blocks, computers, and running games.

Research supports the value of play with different kinds of toys in terms of cognitive, emotional, and social benefits. When children play with different type of toys, they develop a variety of skills that help them understand the acceptable behaviors in their culture. In this way, gender-typed play both reflects and codifies gender stereotypes as it develops children's later social roles (Weisgram & Dinella, 2018). For this reason, understanding how best to ensure opportunities for girls and boys will continue to be a major focus of study in the future.

CULTURALLY APPROPRIATE TOYS THROUGH THE AGES

Toys that reflect the culture move from one generation to the next in ways that adults approve. For many years, culture and gender have had the most impact on selected toys and their use, mass produced toys fostered stereotypical roles for girls and boys, reflected the culture of the majority of society, and dominated the market. Today, there is a growing market for toys that foster gender equity, reflect the values of society and especially parents, and enhance development in a way that is enjoyable and beneficial for all children.

Basic Characteristics of Toys from Many Cultures

An inspection of toys from any part of the world will find some type of ball or projectile for throwing. Children have even used animal intestines that can be blown up to make a ball. Because these reflect the shape of the sun and moon, it might seem logical that toys are inspired by natural surroundings. In some way, they do reflect the natural and human made materials that are available to them. A common characteristic is that toys reflect the natural and manmade environment that surrounds them.

Additionally, toys are useful for transitioning children into successful adult society. This occurs through either imitation or instruction (McMahon, 2020). As children imitate their parents, they act out activities of their parents that reflect basic activities for survival such as hunting or gathering food, protecting the family, and caring for or feeding the family members. In the same way, instructional toys such as alphabet blocks, games, and a host of technological toys encourage appropriate cultural development.

Toys that invite children to imitate adults at work, rest, or dancing are found in all cultures. These include dolls, balls, guns, stick horses, and ropes. Toys that foster affection and care for the family range from dolls, doll houses, Russian dolls sets that tell a story, and dishes that allow children to imitate cooking and eating. Indigenous toys are more reflective of adult activities related to daily survival, such as rocks that can crush corn for dinner. In the same way, toys in more developed societies reflect a current technological approach. Both, however, reflect the activities of the adults in their culture and are developmentally appropriate for the children playing with the toys.

Toys that inspire children to jump, run, and throw are found throughout the world. These toys may have wheels, ropes, or a combination of different mechanisms. From the first wheeled elephant to the current four-wheeler, from the first horse on a stand with springs to a trampoline, children delight in using toys that encourage movement.

The child's environment, along with imitation, instruction, and movement, is reflected in all toys. They manifest in ways that adults approve and provide common playthings when children from different groups intersect. Though the rules might differ, the game of marbles can be played by children from different cultural groups. They only need to negotiate the rules that will be used. The marble, itself, is the same.

FEATURES OF TOYS THAT INITIATE CHILDREN INTO THE CULTURE OF THEIR TIMES

Gender

Because children imitate adults, gender is a feature that has influenced toys throughout the ages. From the tombs of Egypt to the toys found in any mall, small pots and plates reflect a specific role for young girls who play with these materials. In the same way, boys used bow and arrows or toy soldiers in the middle ages. Today, many toy stores have several aisles of action toys and toy guns. In fact, many toys are viewed as either pink or blue, with pink for girls and blue for boys. Van Hoon Monighan-Nourot, Scales, and Alward (2015, p. 315) noted that "once a toy has been classified as gender specific, the reasoning continues that 'If I am a girl, I play with this and if I am a boy, I play with this.'"

Gender differentiation has resulted in targeted marketing for boys and girls. Observations of families in toy stores have shown that some parents tend to encourage their children to move to either the pink or blue toys and that some parents actually move boys away from the stuffed animals and toward the action figures (Sluss, 2002, 2005). In this way, toys that support traditional gender identity are encouraged by some parents as they prepare children for the roles that they want them to assume in society.

At the same time, there are also toys, such as jump ropes, bicycles, and skates, that can equalize the play of children, which in turn will lead to more equal roles and opportunities for adults. For this reason, toys that promote STEM (science, technology, engineering, math) have been created in pastel or pink colors, potentially to appeal to girls. A recent study found that boys are more likely to play with toys deemed masculine, but girls are more flexible in playing with toys viewed as masculine or gender neutral (Wohlwend, 2018). For both boys and girls, advocates for gender equality prefer to enlarge children's options by expanding the range of toys offered to them in childhood (Greenberg, 1978).

Race and Ethnicity Issues

Race and ethnicity are factors that are reflected in varying degrees in toys that initiate children into the culture (Barton & Somerville, 2016). In the middle ages and modern years, when an adult made a doll or toy for a young child, the doll or toy generally reflected the culture of the person who made it. With mass production, however, white dolls were the norm during most of the twentieth century and few dolls of color were created. Commercials and catalogs featuring advertisements for toys during the 1920s to 1960s showed pictures of white, well-dressed children at play. This sent a message that this toy was designed for white children. Since the 1960s, however, there has been a push for more dolls and other toys that represent different races and ethnic groups.

It is important to note that indigenous groups around the world create toys that are reflective of their unique culture. As they interact with more developed groups, they acquire these toys and become more acculturated to the larger group, thus losing some of their own culture. One example of this occurred along the border of the United States and Mexico. During the day, both groups of children were in their own schools and used their own language and play with toys from their own culture. In the afternoon, they played together with toys from each group. The end result was that the toys from each group were transformed into a new creation

Toys for Children with Special Needs

The capacity of the child to use a toy determines how the toy will be used. With mass production, there is a focus on creating toys that everyone can use, but some children still cannot use these toys and need adaptations. Today, there is recognition that toys for children with special needs must be accessible, adaptable, and lead to cooperative interaction. Specifically, a ball may be fine for some children who can toss it and catch it easily. However, this is a virtual impossibility for a child who is visually impaired.

Instead, a ball with marbles or other material inside it (so that they can located it in space) will let them play with the ball. In the same way, children may not be able to complete the fine motor actions that some toys such as puzzles require and need special pegs on top so that they can move the puzzle pieces. Today, a large market offers toys specifically designed to encourage play among children of widely varying abilities and needs.

Affordability and Commercialization

Socioeconomic status affects selected toys and how they are used. Children in the United States have a great deal of access to toys. By the age of one, most children have at least 25 toys (Sluss, 2019). However, there is also a great deal of poverty. The Children's Defense League (2020) reports that one in six, or over 11.9 million children live in poverty. Many of these children live in single-parent homes or with a grandparent or other family member. This affects the choice of toys as they may not be able to afford developmentally appropriate toys and may be given free toys by charitable organizations.

Middle class and affluent parents have more options available for selecting toys that are aligned with their child's age, stage, needs, and desire. Many of these parents are concerned with the commercialization of childhood and the overt push for children to become consumers at an early age. When companies create a movie and sell toys that depict the individuals in the movie, children want to play with these toys. If parents are unable to purchase these toys or believe that the toys are not appropriate for the child, tension occurs between the child and parent. This affects their relationship and how they are acculturated into society.

Violent Toys

Perhaps no other issue is impacting children more than violence. Violence is a feature that is marketed in some toys and this has created tension in the early childhood community. Guns, bows, and arrows are toys found in many societies, and boys have long been encouraged to play with such toys to prepare to hunt with the adults or to engage in military operations. However, some nations such as Sweden now ban the sale of all war-related toys They are concerned that children are being readied for war through play with these toys. In the United States, however, many toys and war-related toys are produced and marketed every year. This is a controversial subject, as many people want to ban war toys while others want to encourage war toy play. Both groups believe that they are reflecting a perspective that is developmentally appropriate.

SUMMARY

Throughout the ages, children have played with toys that reflect cultural and social expectations of the community. Today, there is a great deal of knowledge about the impact of toys on both the growth and development of children as well as on the eventual roles they believe they can and should assume in society. Gender, race, capacity, affordability, and violence are factors that create the most controversy and also have the most influence on the selection and use of developmentally appropriate toys. The intersection of these factors reflect current culture and will affect future culture and societal norms.

REFERENCES

Barnes, D. (1998). Play in historical contexts. In D. Bergen (Ed.) *Play from birth to twelve and beyond: Contexts, perspectives, and meanings* (pp. 5–13). New York: Garland Publishing.

Barton, C. P., & Somerville, K. (2016). *Historical racialized toys in the United States*, pp. 61–75. Taylor and Francis. E-copy.

Bredekamp, S. (1984). *Developmentally appropriate practice in early childhood programs*. Washington, DC: National Association for the Education of Young Children.

Carlson-Paige, N., & Levin, D. (1987). *The war play dilemma: Balancing needs and values in the early childhood classroom*. New York, NY: Teachers College Press.

Children's Defense League. (2020). Child poverty in America 2020. Retrieved from https://www.childrensdefense.org/policy/policy-priorities/child-poverty/.

Chudacoff, H. (2007). *Children at play: An American history*. New York: New York University Press.

Chudacoff, H. (2011). The history of play in the United States. In A. Pellegrini (Ed.) *The Oxford handbook of the development of play* (pp. 101–109). New York, NY: Oxford University Press.

Cleverley, J., & Phillips, D. (1986). *Visions of Childhood: Influential models from Locke to Spock*. New York, NY: Teachers College Press.

Copple, C., & Bredekamp, S. (2009). *Developmentally appropriate practice in early childhood programs, 3rd Ed*. Washington, DC: National Association for the Education of Young Children.

Greenberg, S. (1978). *Right from the start: A nonsexist guide to child-rearing*. Boston, MA: Beacon.

Huizinga, J. (1950). *Homo ludens: A study of the play element in culture*. Boston, MA: Beacon.

King, C. E. (1979) *Antique toys and dolls*. New York, NY: Rizzoli.

Kyburz, J. A. (1994). "Omocha": Things to play (or not to play) with. *Asian Folklore Studies*, 53(1), 1–28.

Lancey, D. (2007). Accounting for variability in mother-child play. *American Anthropologists*, 109, 273–284.

McMahon, F. (2020). Toy. Encyclopeadia Britannica, Retrieved on January 10, 2010 at https://www.britannica.com/technology/toy.

Mergen, B. (1982). *Play and playthings: A reference guide*. Westport, CT: Greenwood.

Orme, N. (2003). *Medieval children*. China: World Press, Ltd.

Rancese, P. (1985). *American demographic: Trends and opportunities in the children's market*. Ithaca, NY: Cornell University Press.

Sluss, D. (2002). Block play complexity among same-sex dyads of preschool children. In S. Reifel (Series Ed.) & J. Roopnarine (Vol. Ed.), *Play and culture series: Vol. 4. Conceptual, social-cognitive, and contextual issues in the fields,* (pp. 77–92). Stamford, CT: Greenwood.

Sluss, D. (2005). *Supporting play: Birth to age eight*. New York, NY: Cengage.

Sluss, D. (2019). *Supporting play: Curriculum, environments, and assessment*. New York, NY: Cengage.

Sutton-Smith, B. (1986). *Toys as culture*. New York: Gardner Press.

Van Hoorn, J., Monighan-Nourot, P., Scales, B., & Alward, K. (2015). *Play at the center of the curriculum, 6th Ed*. New York: Pearson.

Weisgram, E., & Dinella, L. (Eds.). (2018). *Gender typing of children's toys: How early play experiences impact development*. Washington, DC, US: American Psychological Association. http://dx.doi.org/10.1037/0000077-000

Wohlwend, K. (2018). Child's play: Reading and remaking gendered action texts with toys. In B. Guzzetti, T. Bean, & J. Dunkerly-Bean (Eds.) *Literacies, sexualities, and gender: Understanding identities from preschool to adulthood* (27–39). New York, NY: Routledge.

Yagou, A. (2016). The collection of technical toys in the Deutsches Museum, Munich, Germany. *Massachusetts Institute of Technology Design Issue*, 32(1), 87–92.

4

LARGE BLOCKS/UNIT BLOCKS AS BUILDING MATERIALS

Lynn Cohen

Daniel Kirk's (2005) illustrations in the children's book, *Block City*, inspired by Robert Louis Stevenson's poem in a *Child's Garden of Verses* (1885) begins with a question, "What can you build with blocks? A little boy plays indoors and builds castles and palaces, temples and docks. As the block city grows, the boy imagines that his city is real and he is the emperor of his imaginary world" (p. 53). Kirk's (2005) book reminds us that one of our longest-serving toys, unit blocks, encourages children's free play and imagination.

TYPES OF LARGE BLOCKS

Today, blocks come in a variety of shapes and sizes for infants to school age children. Blocks as a material and block play have been accepted as developmentally appropriate and as a method of learning by early childhood educators (Bredekamp & Copple, 2009; Hirsch, 1996; Provenzo & Brett, 1983; Wellhousen & Kieff, 2001). Varieties of materials fall under the general description of "block." Below is a description of unit blocks, hollow blocks, plastic blocks, and cardboard blocks.

Unit Blocks

The most widely known blocks used in early childhood programs are unit blocks. Caroline Pratt (Winsor, 1996) has been associated with the development of the basic wooden unit blocks based on proportions of 1:2:4 (half as high as they are wide; twice as long as they are wide). Common block shapes include squares, triangles, rectangles, cylinders, curves, and arches. The cylinders conform in height to the unit. The curves are of similar width and thickness (Johnson, 1996).

Unit blocks have been central to early childhood education since the late-seventeenth century when John Locke in his influential book *Some Thoughts Concerning Education and of the Conduct of the Understanding* (Grant & Tarcov, 1996) wrote of a father who replaced educating his children by repetition with a game played with four wooden blocks. The letters of the alphabet were pasted on the blocks, one block for vowels and the other three for consonants. Today's toy aisles reflect the pedagogical ideas of John Locke and educators such as Johann Heinrich Pestalozzi and Frederick Froebel who believed that children needed to touch and observe for themselves in order to learn. For over 200 years, letters and numbers have been painted and stamped on blocks, yet children continue to build towers and castles similar to Kirk's *Block City* (2005), "ignoring the attempt of elders to inject a dose of literacy" (Hewitt, 2001, p. 7).

A number of educators had a profound influence on the ubiquity of unit blocks as a toy and learning material in early childhood centers and children's homes. To Frederick Froebel (1782–1852) the block was where to begin an education. Author of *The Education of Man* (1826) and considered the founder of the kindergarten, he began a movement towards a systematic use of blocks for children to learn through play. Froebel's contribution was the development of a series of twenty educational toys and materials called "Gifts" and "Occupations" (Provenzo & Brett, 1983). The "Gifts" have influenced block play in early childhood classrooms. The "Gifts" were used to symbolically represent a larger world through Forms.

Froebel named these Forms of Life, Knowledge, and Beauty to correspond with nature (the physical world), abstract knowledge (math/science), and art (design/pattern) (Bultman, 2014). In Forms of Life, the cube could represent a house or a table. The sphere placed on top of the cylinder could be a person. More recently, Scott Bultman, author and toymaker (Bultman, 2014) continues to promote the Froebel kindergarten method to early childhood educators. Friedrich Froebel began a revolution that emphasized the importance of construction materials for young children. Other block systems were invented after Froebel's "Gifts."

In 1905, Patti Smith Hill, a faculty member of Teachers' College, Columbia University, recognized children's need to play, and developed a set of floor blocks consisting of large blocks, pillars, wheels, and rods to give children the means to symbolically represent their environment and build houses, stores, and boats (Provenzo & Brett, 1983). The Hill Blocks were manufactured until 1950 (Hewitt, 2001).

Caroline Pratt was inspired by Patty Smith Hill. Pratt began her training in 1892 at Teacher's College, Columbia University in kindergarten education where she observed children playing with the blocks designed by Patty Smith Hill (Winsor, 1996). During her training, she recognized the importance of blocks as a toy to appropriate meaning for children. A simple geometric shape could become any number of things to a child such as a barn, skyscraper, or entire community.

In 1913, Pratt (1990) made her earliest set of building blocks and applied them to children's play while teaching New York City children in settlement houses. She found that children used mental powers, reasoned out relationships, formed conclusions, and learned to think through the use of unit blocks. In 1914, Pratt started her own Play School in New York City, now called the City and Country School.

Hollow Blocks

Caroline Pratt also developed large hollow blocks for children to "build structures they can climb into and over, developing their strength, coordination, balance and self-esteem" (Cartwright, 2006, p. 133). Hollow wooden building blocks are the ultimate pretend play building blocks for young children. They are made of birch and maple wood, smooth, durable, with a washable finish. A typical large hollow building block set includes six half unit hollow blocks, five full unit hollow blocks, four double unit hollow blocks, four ramps, four short boards, and four long boards. Children can build houses, stores, farms, bridges, and boats. When children use hollow blocks they engage in rich dramatic play and take on roles of mothers, fathers, storekeepers, and restaurant owners. This toy provides complex imaginative play both indoors and outdoors. Cartwright (2006) describes indoor building as less on building and more on dramatic play as compared to outdoors where elaborate building takes place.

Large Plastic Blocks

Plastic blocks come in two different sizes and primary colors. They are similar to LEGOs because they are interlocking. Infants, toddlers, and preschool children can build, stack and design structures while using gross and fine motor skills.

Cardboard Blocks

These large blocks are inexpensive and light for infants and toddlers to carry and stack. Children can use their imaginations as they build towers and castles. A child as young as nine-months-old can actively learn to stack and balance structures when playing with these lightweight building toys.

VALUE OF UNIT BLOCKS

In the 1900s, researchers (Johnson, 1996; Guanella, 1934; Bailey, 1933) began to document the uses of blocks by children. These play scholars focused on the importance of block play for children's development, as well as symbolic functioning. These early scholars discussed the value unit blocks play in promoting interrelated aspects of child learning. Children at different ages will need different types of blocks and will use the materials differently. As they work through the learning of one stage they are ready to move on to the next stage. The stages are developmental, each one building on the last, but children advance at their own rate regardless of age.

AGE LEVEL DIFFERENCES IN BLOCK PLAY

Infants and Toddlers

Infants and toddlers use foam blocks, cardboard blocks and medium size wooden blocks. They usually stack blocks in straight lines then knock them down. They may push blocks around a small area and eventually carry them. Our youngest block experimenters repeat the same steps over and over before moving on to new experiments. They are experimenting with space, the nature of materials, and object permanence.

Preschool Children

Preschool children use a basic set of unit blocks that include cylinders, arches, and ramps for their buildings. A set of hollow blocks supports preschoolers' imagination, creativity, and dramatic play. They make stacks, roads, enclosures, and lines of blocks placed end to end. Also, three-year-olds also carry, push, and pile blocks. Children's learning and play develops at individual rates and it is important to watch and listen while observing, rather than judge. Preschool children can classify, sort, and match shapes and sizes. They begin to experiment with balance, symmetry, patterning, and problem solving. Language flourishes as they socially interact with other children.

Elementary Children

School age children are concrete operational thinkers who learn through active engagement with materials. They need a large set of unit blocks to give physical form to tackle complex problems, manipulate ideas, and integrate concepts throughout the curriculum. A complete set of hollow blocks is also important for dramatic play. Providing new materials such as loose parts (e.g., cardboard tubes, film canisters, craft sticks) often enhances the structure. Materials might represent ideas in direct, concrete physical ways. Representations are of real-life items and places (e.g., schools, restaurants, houses). This age group creates block structures for dramatic play scenarios that relate to their experiences.

DEVELOPMENTAL VALUE OF UNIT BLOCKS

The learning opportunities available when children play with blocks are many and varied. With blocks, a child acquires basic knowledge of the world in ways that are similar to many adult situations. As children use blocks to construct and represent their experiences in daily living, they grow across all developmental domains. Unit blocks enhance the physical, social and emotional, cognitive, and language and literacy development in children.

Physical Skills

Unit block building from a simple pile of blocks to a large structure requires children to use small and large muscles as they carry, lift, and stack the blocks on top of another. Children increase eye-hand coordination as they reach for a block and carefully place it on top of another block. They need to learn to achieve balance, control and spatial awareness as they place one block on top of another.

Social Emotional Skills

An important aspect of block building is social development as children work in groups to create structures and build together. When children are building with unit blocks they have to work in close proximity to one another and to share a communal toy. They are learning the core of social living and the value of making friends, sharing, and taking the perspective of other children while using blocks. According to Cuffaro (1995), "Negotiation, compromise, cooperation, caring and consideration, and the balance of individual and group rights are not abstract concepts but concrete, lived experiences as children work to resolve the dilemmas that arise when space and materials are finite and must be shared" (p. 38). They learn to express their feelings and ideas in a form that is observed, examined, and shared thus, building children's self-esteem.

Cognitive Skills

Symbolism

Blocks helps children strengthen symbolism and representational skills that are the basis for using and understanding the symbol systems of reading and math (Provenzo &

Brett, 1983; Wellhousen & Kieff, 2001). A child engages in symbolic play when a block represents a toy spoon to feed a baby, acts as a telephone, or very fast police car. Reifel (1981) examined symbolic representation in block play, as well as the spatial development of the representations between two age groups. The researchers read children a fairy tale and asked them to represent the story with building blocks. The children labeled and described each constructed representation. In a follow up investigation (Reifel and Greenfield, 1982) block play complexity was indexed by both spatial relationships and symbolism. Reifel and Greenfield (1982) devised a scale for evaluating symbolism and the spatial complexity of block play. They concluded that construction becomes more structurally complex with increasing age and suggested that cognitive structures also become more complex with age. The younger child simply designates parts of the house verbally, while the older child depicts them structurally (Reifel & Greenfield, 1982).

STEM Skills

Block play furthers children's conceptual understanding and understanding of relationships. It involves quantitative knowledge of shape, size, part-whole relationships, fractions, and measurement. As children use blocks they begin to recognize sizes and shapes as they choose and use long, short, triangular, square, or rectangular blocks. Concepts such as proportion and quantity become real as children use blocks. Hanline, Milton, and Phelps (2001, 2010) found a predictive relation between complexity of block play and later reading ability and self-regulation. Similarly, Wolfgang, Stannard, and Jones (2001) found that block play complexity in preschool was related to math achievement in middle and high school.

Blocks increase the opportunity for children to problem solve. Children can experiment with blocks and draw conclusions about which blocks work best for building a castle or a racetrack.

They also can experiment with physical properties of objects. Unit blocks are hard and smooth; they have weight and mass.

As children use and build with blocks, they learn the science concepts of balance and gravity.

Unit blocks are currently linked to important science, technology, engineering, and mathematics (STEM) learning (Lindeman, Jabot, & Berkley, 2013; Moomaw, 2012). Lindeman et al. (2013) illustrated a preschool boy using trial and error, as well as basic science and math principles, as he builds three different towers (p. 106). Moomaw (2012) described a block center where children can construct towers, houses, and other structures. Child-designs are described where children manipulate multiple ramps that connect to a vertical board in order to design creative ways for a ball (e.g., a table tennis ball) to move from the top to the bottom of the board, rolling down ramps and hopping from one ramp to another.

Researchers have also linked block play with spatial skills (Caldera et al., 1999; Ness & Farenga, 2007). Caldera et al. (1999) examined 51 preschoolers' play preferences, skills at assembling block structures, and spatial abilities. Play with art materials and reproduction of complex block structures were interrelated to tests of spatial visualization. Ness and Farenga (2007) found differences between four-year-old and five-year-old unit block structures. They analyzed videotapes of children's block play to observe and record cognitive abilities of the relationship between space and architectural thinking based on *The Assessment for Measuring Spatial, Geometric, and Architectural Thinking of Young Children*. Similar to Reifel's (1981) study on block complexity, Ness and Farenga (2007) found buildings for five-year-old children included more symmetry and patterns. This finding suggests that spatial relations within children's block building structures become more complex with age. Not only does block play support spatial reasoning thinking, which is crucial for STEM skills, blocks also increase children's use of spatial language, vocabulary, communication and literacy skills.

Language and Literacy Skills

Language flourishes as children interact with peers to discuss plans for building, negotiate with one another for needed blocks, and see the world from the perspective of another in conversation. Children are able to learn vocabulary for ideas they have created by building. Certain ideas are expressed by their words as to the structure they are creating, its size, where they will build it, and its purpose. Cohen and Emmons (2017) examined the use of spatial words with children aged three-to-nine-years that refer to spatial features and properties of blocks (e.g., big, little, tall, fat) or the shapes of blocks (e.g., circle, rectangle, octagon, triangle), and the spatial properties of blocks (e.g., bent, curvy, flat, edge, pointy). On average younger and older children produced 376 spatial words during play sessions with blocks.

Stroud (1995) found interactions while building promoted oral language development in three important ways. First, children communicated with one another by explaining and discussing their buildings. Second, children expanded their vocabulary during block play. As buildings are erected children learned new words from one another, books, or adults. Third, children incorporated pretend play into their structures, which provides opportunities for rich, varied language.

Cohen and Uhry (2007) observed individuals, dyads, and small groups of children in the block area and found children were able to acquire new words to define their ideas and learn new words from each other. Having children talk about what they built and asking questions enables children to share ideas that the child may have experienced or thought about. The dyads and small groups talked more than children building by themselves did. The dyads and small groups learned to work with their ideas and blocks by sharing and taking turns. They learned the valuable lesson of working together as a team and respecting the ideas of others. Communication between the children helps to develop self-expression. In addition, the process of putting the blocks away at cleanup time is an important part of the block experience. "If an adult gets involved by asking questions such as *How many blocks can you carry?* or *Where do these blocks belong?* language and thinking will be stimulated on the part of the child" (Provenzo & Brett, 1983, p. 90).

Blocks also promote an environment conducive to fostering important reading and writing skills (Wellhousen & Giles, 2005). Children can look at fiction books and informational books about architects and architecture that represent different cultures and countries (e.g., India, China, Mexico) (Cohen, 2009). After looking at the books, children can plan and draw an architectural design for building a structure. They further develop writing skills as they create signs for their building (Lee, Collins, & Winkelman, 2015).

Blocks as a toy offers a good balance of play behaviors across physical, social and emotional, cognitive, and language and literacy development. A complete set of hardwood blocks are simple classic open-ended toys that children can use and learn in multiple ways.

AN EQUAL CHANCE: UNIT BLOCKS FOR ALL CHILDREN

An aim of offering wooden blocks in classrooms and homes is to provide equality for children with and without disabilities and encourage cross-sex play. Given the known value of complex block play benefiting all developmental domains Hanline et al. (2001) recommends that teachers as well as parents provide guidance and instruction for children with disabilities when using unit blocks. Children with disabilities may need explicit modeling and prompting to increase block complexity (Lifter, Mason, & Barton; 2011). Studies with individual children and adults with children with disabilities have used contingent imitation (Barton, 2015) and play expansions (Frey & Kaiser, 2011) to facilitate new play learning for children with disabilities.

Barton, Ledford, Zimmerman, and Pokorski (2018) examined the use of imitation and play expansion to four pairs of children on the engagement and complexity of block play. Each pair included a target child with or at-risk for a disability and a peer without an identified disability. Results indicated that the target children increased levels of engagement when both imitation and play expansions were used but block play complexity increased only when adults offered visual and verbal prompts. These studies indicate that children with disabilities may need additional time and adult support when using and building with blocks.

Children are socialized into what is considered gender appropriate for both girls and boys. There are societal assumptions about the perceived roles and abilities of boys and girls. Anecdotal reports from classroom teachers and researchers report the differences between boys and girls in terms of their interest and engagement in block building. There is conflicting research related to blocks and cross-sex play. Goodfader (1982) and Sluss (2002) found a male advantage in the complexity of structures with boys building more complex structures than girls. Other studies in university child-care settings (Caldera et al., 1999), community-based childcare (Hanline et al., 2001), and age differences (Reifel and Greenfield, 1982) have not revealed gender differences in block play. Hanline et al. (2001) conducted a three-year study of developmental changes in block building. The amount of time in the block area was controlled so over the three-year period, boys and girls had equal time to play with blocks. They did not find any gender differences in block building complexity and the amount of involvement in block building over time was associated with the levels of complexity of the block structure for both girls and boys.

It is important to be aware of children's individual needs and differences. Parents and educators should strive to encourage children to seek solutions to their play as they use unit blocks to build castles, palaces, temples and docks. Time for all children to play with unit blocks is important so they can be emperors of imaginary worlds as Kirk (2005) so nicely illustrated in *Block City*.

SUMMARY

Large blocks have been in the field of early childhood education for a long time. Block building involves the whole child in meaningful growth to benefit the mind and body of the child. Blocks have been promoted as a valuable and complex play material with many contributions for early childhood curriculum.

REFERENCES

Bailey, M. (1933). A scale of block constructions for young children. *Child Development, 4*, 121–39.

Barton, E. E. (2015). Teaching generalized pretend play and related behaviors to young children with disabilities. *Exceptional Children, 81*, 489–506.

Barton, E. E., Ledford, J. R., Zimmerman, K. N., & Pokorski, E. A. (2018). Increasing the engagement and complexity of block play in young children, *Education and Treatment of Children, 41*(2), 169–196.

Bredekamp, S., & Copple, C. (Eds.). (2009). *Developmentally appropriate practice in early childhood programs*. Washington, DC: NAEYC.

Bultman, S. (2014). *The Froebel gifts. The building gifts 2–6.* Grand Rapids, MI: Froebel

Caldera, Y. M., Culp, A. M., O'Brien, M., Truglio, R. T., Alvarez, M., & Huston, A. (1999). Children's play preferences, construction play with blocks and visual spatial skills: Are they related? *International Journal of Behavioral Development, 23*, 855–72.

Cartwright, S. (2006). Learning with large blocks. In E.S. Hirsch (Ed.) *The block book*. (pp. 133–41. Washington, D.C.: National Association for the Education of Young Children.

Cohen, L. E. (2009). Exploring cultural heritage in a kindergarten classroom. *Young Children, 64*(3).

Cohen, L., & Uhry, J. (2007). Young children's discourse strategies during block play: A Bakhtinian approach. *Journal of Research in Childhood Education, 21*, 302–15.

Cohen, L., & Emmons, J. (2017). Block play: Spatial language with preschool and school-aged Children, *Early Child Development and Care, 187* (5–6), 967–77

http://dx.doi.org/10.1080/03004430.2016.1223064.

Cuffaro, H. K. (1995). Block building opportunities for learning. *Child Care Information Exchange, 103*, 35–38.

Frey, J. R., & Kaiser, A. P. (2011). The use of play expansions to increase the diversity and complexity of object play in children with disabilities. *Topics in Early Childhood Special Education, 31*, 178–92

Froebel, F. (1826, 2005). *The education of man*. (W.N. Hailmann, Trans.). New York, London: D. Appleton and Company. Froebel USA.

Kirk, D. (2005). (Illustrator). *Block City*. New York, NY: Simon & Schuster Books for Young Readers.

Goodfader, R.A. (1982). Gender differences in the play constructions of preschool children. *Smith College Studies in Social Work, 52*, 129–44.

Grant, R. W., & Tarcov, N. (1996) (Eds.). *The Works of John Locke. Some Thoughts Concerning Education and of the Conduct of the Understanding*. Indianapolis: Hackett Publishing Co.

Guanella, F. M. (1934). Block building activities of young children. *Archives of Psychology, 174*, 5–91.

Hanline, M. F., Milton, S., & Phelps, P. (2001). Young children's block construction activities: Findings from 3 years of observations. *Journal of Early Intervention, 24*, 224–37.

Hanline, M. F., Milton, S., & Phelps, P. (2010). The relationship between preschool block play and reading and maths abilities in early elementary school: A longitudinal study of children with and without disabilities. *Early Childhood Development and Care, 180* (8), 1005–17.

Hewitt, K. (2001). Blocks as a tool for learning: Historical and contemporary perspectives. *Young Children, 56* (1), 6–12.

Hirsch, E. S. (Ed.). (1996). *The block book*. (3rd Ed.). Washington, D.C.: National Association for the Education of Young Children.

Johnson, H. (1996) The art of block building. In E.S. Hirsch (Ed.) *The block book* (pp. 9–25). Washington, D.C.: National Association for the Education of Young Children.

Lee, J., Collins, D.A., & Winkelman, L. (2015). Connecting 2-D and 3-D: Drafting and blueprints, building, and playing with blocks. *YC Young Children, 70*(1), 32–34.

Lifter, K., Mason, E. J., & Barton, E. E. (2011). Children's play: Where we have been and where we could go. *Journal of Early Intervention, 33*, 281–245.

Lindeman, K. W., Jabot, M., & Berkley, M. T. (2013). The role of STEM (or STEAM) in the Early Childhood Settings, In L. E. Cohen, & S. Waite Stupiansky (Eds.), *Learning Across the Early Childhood Curriculum. Advances in Early Education and Day Care Series*. (pp. 95–114). UK: Emerald Group.

Moomaw, S. (2012). STEM begins in the Early Years. *School Science and Mathematics, 112*(2), 57–58.

Ness, D. & Farenga, S. J. (2007). *Knowledge under construction: The importance of play in developing children's spatial and geometric thinking*. Lanham, MD: Rowman & Littlefield.

Pratt, C. (1990). *I Learn from Children*. New York, NY: Harper & Row.

Provenzo, E. F. & Brett, A. (1983). *The complete block book*. Syracuse, NY: Syracuse University Press.

Reifel, S. (1981). An exploration of block play as symbolic representation. *Dissertation Abstracts International, 19*(10), (UMI no. 5901295).

Reifel, S. & Greenfield, P.M. (1982). Structural development in a symbolic medium: The representational use of block constructions. In G. Forman (Ed.), *Action and thought: From sensorimotor schemes to symbolic operations* (pp. 203–232). New York, NY: Academic Press.

Stevenson, R. L. (1885). *A Children's Garden of Verses*. Retrieved from Project Gutenberg, http://www.gutenberg.org.

Stroud, J. E. (1995). Block play: Building a foundation for literacy. *Early Childhood Education Journal, 23*(1), 9–13.

Sluss, D. J. (2002). Block play complexity in same-gender dyads of preschool children. In J. L. Roopnarine (Ed.), *Play and Culture studies: Vol. 4. Conceptual, social-cognitive, and contextual issues in the fields of play* (pp. 77–91). Westport, CT: Ablex.

Wellhousen, K., & Giles, R. M. (2005). Building Literacy Opportunities into Children's Block Play: What Every Teacher Should Know. *Childhood Education, 82*(2), 74–78.

Wellhousen, K., & Kieff, J. (2001). *A Constructivist Approach to Block Play in Early Childhood.* Albany, NY: Delmar Publishing.

Winsor, C. (1996). Blocks as a material for learning through play. In E. Hirsch (Ed). *The block book* (3rd ed.). (pp. 2–7). Washington, DC: National Association for the Education of Young Children.

Wolfgang, C. H., Stannard, L. L., & Jones, I. (2001). Block play performance among Preschoolers as a predictor of later school achievement in mathematics. *Journal of Research in Childhood Education, 15,* 173–80.

5

SMALL BLOCKS AND BUILDING MATERIALS

Eleni Loizou

Constructive play is a general term for block play, since, other than blocks, there is a variety of building materials that can provide children with multiple and open-ended opportunities to construct creatively, develop specific skills, and learn particular concepts. The elements that affect constructive play experiences involve the child herself, the materials, and the adult. These elements are in constant interaction and when the adult develops a constructive play program in a classroom, taking into consideration the four important elements: time, space, exploration, and interaction with others (Hobenshield, Moss, & Stephenson, 2015). Then children will present mature forms of constructive play.

Children in the context of constructive play can also use different materials realistically or symbolically to enrich their play. This chapter will provide information about children's constructive play actions, the relationship to learning and development, the diverse options of building materials, children's individualities in participating in this type of play, and the role(s) early childhood teachers can have during constructive play.

STAGES OF BLOCK PLAY

This section explains the stages of block play, unfolding the actions and behavior children are expected to present during each one. It is important to highlight that, depending on children's experiences and development, these stages may coincide or be blurred. Even though they are called stages of block play, there is not a direct sequence of these stages due to the diverse experiences and skills that children have.

Exploration

Children use all of their senses to explore and experiment the world around them. Thus, they try out construction materials by holding and placing them in their mouth or knocking them on the floor or banging them together. These behaviors show that children use exploration as their first action when interacting with constructive play materials such as blocks.

Transferring

Children begin to advance in their motor skills, walking and moving within space, thus becoming interested in transferring constructive play materials. They move them from one spot to another without necessarily showing interest in building something.

Simple Building (Rows, Columns, and Patterns)

Children begin to be able to co-ordinate their hands and eyes and begin to successfully place blocks one on top of the other while also try to build rows or columns. Depending on the materials they create patterns with colored blocks or with shape blocks. So, they try to combine and connect rows of blocks in different ways.

Building Enclosures (Bridges and Passageways)

Due to the development of fine motor skills, children can handle building materials better and, thus, build enclosures. They can place blocks sideways as a means to create an enclosure, using as many blocks as there are available. In addition, due to their language development, they name their constructions and also add different figures and other accessories to enrich their play.

Complex Constructions and Sociodramatic Play

Children build more complex structures using many more blocks, even small size blocks, since their fine motor skills are quite advanced. They build separate sections to their structure, taking into consideration scale details and the functionality of space. Different figures and accessories are central to their play. They name everything they construct as well as their figures. They take on a role, and a scenario is developed based on their construction. There is interaction between the children and they all participate in a scenario taking on roles, using materials in a symbolic way, with their construction being one of these.

TYPES OF BUILDING MATERIALS

There is a variety of materials provided in the market which can be used for children to participate in constructive play. The type of building materials leads children to specific constructions and supports specific skills. A variety of constructive play materials are presented and then discussed regarding their potential play use and impact on children's skills.

Blocks

Blocks of different types of materials, sizes and colors are the first toys one can place within the category of constructive play and building materials. Wooden blocks have been a traditional constructive play material, these being large or small ones. Wooden blocks are made of wood, originally in the color of wood, brown. But they have developed in different forms, shapes and colors, as well as material, and can be produced with foam or other light material. Blocks are considered as a very common building material which can normally be found in every house and classroom.

LEGO

Another traditional constructive play material are the LEGOs. LEGOs have been in the market and used for children's play since 1958. They come in different colors, sizes and shapes, which can be used to construct either specific/diverse figures and places. Also, currently there is a new line of blocks, being piloted, especially designed for children with visual impairments (LEGO Braille Bricks), which will help children recognize the various pieces they are using to build.

Clicks

This building material is made of plastic, has specific edges, either round ones or flat ones, which enable each one to fit in the other. They are also produced in different colors and other materials accompany them, such as sticks and wheels allowing for the construction of specific structures (e.g., a car or cargon).

Magnetic Blocks

These blocks are made of plastic and magnets, thus are used to make connections much simpler. All of their sides can be connected due to the magnets and they are made of different shapes and colors, providing opportunities to explore shape, color, and magnetic properties, all at once. This adds to the potential constructions children might develop.

Bristle Blocks

These blocks are colorful, have different shapes and stick together at any angle and side. They are soft and easy to stick together. There are additional pieces which enhance the creation, such as wheels creating motion to the construction. There is a large number of these blocks that make it functional to create different structures.

Connecting Cogs

These are plastic interlocking and stacking cogs. They are made of hard material in different colors and can be connected to create complex structures.

K' nex

This is a set of plastic colorful pieces that include wheels and cars and imaginary figures. The producers of the specific material support its usefulness towards STEM experiences.

Pipebuilders

These are plastic colorful pipes which can be combined creating unique constructions. The inside part of each pipe is empty thus they can be combined with other materials such as water and sand. There are different sizes and shapes allowing the child to create angles.

It is important to note that the above building materials are only a small part of what one can find in the market but they provide a wide range of possibilities for children's constructive play. One can find other similar material such us octons, pipebuilders, playstix, and gears.

LEARNING AND DEVELOPMENT SKILLS DEVELOPED DURING CONSTRUCTIVE PLAY

In considering children's overall development, there are specific skills children can develop when exploring constructive play materials. It is evident that small motor skills are essential in constructive play. Specifically, when children are involved in constructing with the above mentioned materials they learn to control their small motor muscles to perform simple tasks, develop hand-eye coordination and, thus, perform fine motor tasks, and strengthen their small muscles developing strength, flexibility and agility in their hand use. Their interaction with any type of construction materials has children using their hands, thus, the above- mentioned skills are important in every process.

Another area of development that is closely connected with children's experience with construction material is certainly cognitive development. It is evident that due to its functionality and potential constructive play can enhance children's conceptual understanding, constructing representations, problem solving, creative thinking, pretense, critical thinking, and metacognition. Children test and explore the different ways they can construct, put blocks together, connect, and disconnect to build what they plan in their minds. Often during the process, they change their mind and either add a section they did not think of before or remove one they cannot build the way they had planned it. When building, children can note, observe, and group the materials based on their similarities and differences, and use these to solve potential construction problems. The older they get, the more precise they become in constructing what they had originally planned (Bodrova, & Leong, 2012). After the construction of a structure, and thus the creation of a context (e.g., a castle) children use language to plan, pretend to take on different roles symbolically (e.g., queen and king) and improvise developing a scenario (e.g., there is an attack to their castle).

Social and emotional development is closely related to all play experiences, and consequently, to constructive play experiences. Children develop self-perception and begin to understand what they can do, and recognize their skills and abilities while involved in constructing with their peers. Moreover, they develop learning attitudes and show interest in new experiences, challenges, and knowledge, especially if there is a set block play program in their classroom (Hobenshield, Moss, & Stephenson, 2015). Children develop social skills, interacting and collaborating with other children in having a common goal and building together. Of course, during these processes, children learn to express their feelings, to recognize other children's feelings, coexist with others, and negotiate their needs. Table 5.1 provides the description of a constructive play episode where the skills of the child are analyzed and pointed out in order to bring light to the connection between constructive play and development.

CHILDREN'S INDIVIDUALITIES IN REFERENCE TO CONSTRUCTIVE PLAY

Research studies on constructive play pose different research questions which refer to gender play differences, how block play enhances or assesses children's math or literacy

Table 5.1.   Analyzing a constructive play episode to highlight children's skills

Description of constructive play episode	Constructive play actions	Learning and development skills
Alice (5.5 years) takes a box of wooden and colorful small blocks. She does not empty the box on the floor rather she picks some blocks from the box to begin to create her structure. She chooses same color and shape blocks and places them one on top of the other, creating two columns, one next to the other, allowing some space between them. She then takes two rectangular blocks and attempts to place them on top of the columns trying to connect them. She realizes that they cannot be connected so places them on the floor. She moves the columns closer to each other and looks for another block. She purposefully takes a block in the shape of an arc and places it on top of the two columns connecting them with a bridge. She then says that her structure can be different things such as a house or the bridge of a castle. Afterward, she takes more blocks places them sideways next to both columns trying to extend the structure and in the front of them creating an enclosure. She says that what she made is the bridge of a castle and at the same time removes two blocks opening up the enclosure and adding more blocks to make it larger. She states that she will create a palace, and because she cannot make a king and a queen with the blocks, she will bring her figure dolls to use them in her play.	Building enclosures	Movement skills: Eye-hand coordination Small hand muscle use (handling of small items) **Personal and social awareness:** Recognizes her skills and abilities **Cognitive empowerment:** Exploration and experimentation Observation Comparison Problem solving Language use: Expression of thought processes, and argumentation of choices

skills, or how children with disabilities respond to block play experiences. The chapter discusses children's individualities in this section.

There is a dilemma in reference to boys' and girls' involvement in constructive play and how they respond to it. Previous research studies considered constructive play as one that was mostly preferred by boys, but current research suggests differently. It seems that there are no specific gender preferences in constructive play (Ferrara, Hirsh-Pasek, Newcombe, Golinkoff, & Lam, 2011). Boys and girls, as well as children of all ages, show interest in this specific type of play. Ramani, Zippert, Schweitzer, and Pan (2014) have explored preschool children's block play during a guided activity, and their results suggest that there were no differences in building complexity, even though girls in their constructions included more symbolic features.

These specific researchers suggest that when boys and girls have equal experiences and guided ones, then block play can reduce potential gender differences. Moreover, the work of Casey, Andrews, Schindler, Kersh, Samper, and Copley (2008) on the development of spatial skills though block building activities showed lack of gender differences in block building or block design measures. And they suggest that guided experiences can support children to develop spatial skills.

Casey and Young (2008) suggest that boys show more interest in constructive play by building higher and more complicated buildings than girls, while girls construct flat buildings that they use during their sociodramatic play. In reviewing children's block play and its relation to spatial skills and other mathematical skills, there are different points of reference. Sluss (2002) suggests that boys' constructions look more like castles while girls' constructions more like enclosures. Moreover, Andrews (2015) suggests that boys shared their ideas more easily. They negotiated and discussed their choices. Children's personality traits, those who enjoy challenges, experimenting, and exploring, are more possible to display when children participate in constructive play. Also the choice of materials, type of structures built, and the role of the adult during constructive play can affect the way boys and girls respond to a building experience.

As in the case of all types of play, so is constructive play important for children's development and learning. For a child with or without disabilities, constructive play provides opportunities to practice specific skills that were not developed fully due to the different types, materials, size, weight, and shape of the constructive play materials. Hanline, Milton, and Phelps (2010) explored the relationship between block play and reading and mathematics abilities in children with and without disabilities. The study reveals that children who have higher levels of representation in their block constructions have higher reading abilities. And in reference to children with disabilities, they show that these children had lower predicted reading and math scores, as expected. It is significant to emphasize the need for modification of the different elements of a block play program (e.g., space, materials, time) in order to make it accessible to all children and provide equal quality play opportunities for all children.

TEACHER'S ROLE(S) DURING CONSTRUCTIVE PLAY

Teacher's involvement in play is a debatable issue in the literature. There is a dilemma whether teachers should or not intervene in children's play. However, teacher involvement is advocated by many authors and specific forms of involvement and participation are suggested in different studies (e.g., Trawick-Smith & Dziurgot, 2011; Hakkarainen, Brėdikytė, Jakkula, & Munter, 2013; Loizou, 2017; Loizou, Michaelides, & Georgiou, 2019). The main goal of a teacher participating in children's play is to enhance their play skills in order to support them reach mature forms of play. The roles teachers can take in play include observing, organizing, planning, intervening to support play, or to put limits or end it.

An agreed-upon role of the teacher is organizing the classroom environment; that is, the classroom space, materials, accessibility and time provided. For the development of a construction play center, the teacher needs to consider arranging the physical environment in order to ensure appropriate access for all children. For example, the teacher can consider to place the specific center close to the entrance of the classroom and can decide to use tables as work space rather than the floor to make it easily accessible for children on wheel chairs. The materials to be used also need to be wisely chosen to consider all children's needs and potential.

The use of big blocks is more appropriate for younger children, and the use of magnetic blocks is preferable for children with fine motor problems or visual problems. Moreover, the quantity of the materials needs to be such that will provide children the opportunities to expand on their structures and of course, to collaborate with each other. Finally, since exploration is vital for constructive play, in reference to materials and/or ideas, children need to have enough time to explore multiple ideas before they begin to build.

It is crucial for teachers to consider the above elements with the children and agree upon specific rules so that there is a common understanding how they could work independently.

The following example from practice elaborates on how constructive play can be integrated into the curriculum as a meaningful experience for the children. In implementing a transition program in a preschool classroom, the teacher arranged for the children to visit the neighboring elementary school. The children noticed that there were no big toys in the yard of the school and decided to write a letter to the school's principal to suggest some big playground toys. When returning to their classroom, the teacher invited them to consider what to write to the principal and draw on paper the toy they wanted the elementary school yard to have. The next day the children discussed between themselves about their toy suggestions, and the teacher proposed to use any of their building materials to build it.

During this process, and because of the continued interest of the children, there was a change in the morning schedule since children were provided with as much time as they needed to choose their materials, remove them from the shelves, and use them to construct. Also, constructive play was not limited to a specific area but all over the classroom. Teachers' actions aim at supporting children to explore, experiment, create, have fun, learn, take on roles, and improvise during constructive play. It is widely agreed that before any interaction in children's play, adults are expected to observe in order to note play needs and children's skills to make their involvement focused and effective. Teachers' involvement can be defined as direct or indirect depending on the above-mentioned points.

Teacher's Indirect Involvement in Children's Constructive Play

Indirect involvement refers to the adult observing children's play and providing suggestions, actions, and support to extend it. The adult, in an indirect way, either by taking on a role, providing a suggestion, or commenting on an existing situation, creates space for alternative ideas which children can choose to use or not. Depending on the children's needs, the adult can indirectly participate in their play to answer queries they might have, to give information necessary to enhance their construction or scenario.

For example, "Woao, how many animals do you have? You think there is enough space in your zoo? Let's ask the manager of the zoo to see if she thinks there is enough space." The teacher can also provide children with challenges or dilemmas within their play scenario and construction idea when she realizes that there is a need for flexibility and play advancement. For example, the teacher can say, "We have three new neighbors. But each family has three cars and we only have one available parking space. What can we do?" If after observation the teacher realizes that children are not using the materials appropriately, then the teacher can remind the rules by saying, "Remember to look at the signs we have for our play rules."

Constructive play is closely related to specific content areas such as mathematics, science, and/or language. The adult through specific questions and/or actions can support children's mathematical skills and enhance specific mathematical concepts, such as patterns, geometry, counting, addition-subtraction, and quantities. More specifically, if the adult is interested in supporting children's counting and observation skills, the teacher can state the following questions within the play context: "If the two buildings are made up with the same number of blocks, what makes this building higher? How can you tell whose building has the most blocks? How can we tell whose building is taller/the same as Melina's?" Or in considering the concept of balance the teacher can ask the following: "Why is it that your tower keeps falling down? How can we use these blocks to support your tower? Or how can we build something really tall or a bridge over our building?"

In reference to further supporting children's play and helping them construct a more complex structure, the teacher can ask questions such as, "How can we ensure that the animals will not escape from the farm" or "What will happen to your building if it starts raining? Can you do something different about that?" The adult can be a role model in using the materials during play (while in a role or not), especially if the teacher notices a need that has to do with the realistic or symbolic use of materials and better role development ("I think I will use the magnetic blocks to make the train tracks because it is easier to make curved lines").

Also, the adult can ask questions to find play needs when these are not so obvious through observation. For example, questions can be asked such as, "What you are making looks very interesting? What is this part?" Finally, part of the indirect involvement is for the teacher to play with the children, participate in their play, and converse with them about their construction. The teacher can say, "You have made a large two-story house. What can you build around this house?" as a response to the need of enriching and developing their scenario with language development and collaboration.

The children might decide to consider her question or decide to do something different.

Teacher's Direct Involvement in Children's Constructive Play

Direct involvement includes the teacher observing children's play and then participating by directly guiding them, providing them with information as to how they can play, or what to say, and by telling them what to do in order to support and develop their play. The teacher can ask questions or give specific information through direct involvement. For example, during constructive play, the teacher can say, "Let's make our fence taller so that the dog does not run away again! We need to put more blocks." With this comment, the teacher is being precise in order to support children develop their structure.

Moreover, through direct involvement the adult can share the roles children might take and give them specific tasks in order to organize their play. For example, "You can be the architect and tell the constructors about how they should build the new level on this building." The adult can also provide specific feedback in reference to the children's constructions, especially when problems arise. For example, "You have to place more blocks for the lower part of your construction if you don't want your castle to fall apart."

In addition, the adult who observes children having difficulties in collaborating as a team or who have a low self-esteem in reference to the specific type of play can give them specific information for what to do and how to participate, thus supporting them to become part of an existing team and construction process. "Costas, tell them what they should use to build a bathtub in pattern for your house" or "Nick can be the farmer who will ask for an extension to his farm." The teacher can also use positive commentary to encourage children and at the same time guide them to enrich their structure. "Your building is very impressive, but you could make it taller so that it becomes a skyscraper!" Also the teacher can remind children of the rules they have in reference to play and, thus, support the continuation of their play. For example, "When we knock down the blocks you might hurt each other. Remember our play rules."

Finally, during direct involvement the teacher can participate in children's play and state specific questions related to different content areas, which aim in advancing children's learning and play. For example, the teacher could ask, "How many cars can be parked in your parking lot? Let's count them." With this question, the teacher uses mathematical language and has the children count which might force them to consider extending their structure. Direct involvement is a way teachers can participate in children's play in order to guide it by being specific and precise in their input. The main aim is to extend children's play experiences based on their play needs. This type of involvement can be effective especially for children with disabilities as it provides the type of scaffolding that embraces and responds better to their needs.

RESEARCHING CONSTRUCTIVE PLAY

Constructive play needs to be further explored in order to unfold the impact it can have on children's learning and development. There are several factors that need to be considered in studying constructive play (e.g., materials used, teacher involvement, connections with content areas), thus it is crucial for the early childhood education field to consider a variety of research questions. Examples of such questions might include these: How can teachers' support mature forms of constructive play? What mathematical language and mathematical concepts do children use during their constructions? How does the construction material change children's play maturity? Obviously, learning outcomes can be related to constructive play, but it is important to highlight that play in general and constructive play in particular needs to be a process-oriented experience for children and not a product-oriented experience.

REFERENCES

Andrews, N. (2015). Building curriculum during block play. *Dimensions of Early Childhood, 43*(1), 11–15.

Bagiati, A., & Evangelou, D. (2015). Engineering curriculum in the preschool classroom: the teacher's experience. *European Early Childhood Education Research Journal, 23*(1), 112–128.

Bagiati, A., & Evangelou, D. (2016). Practicing engineering while building with blocks: identifying engineering thinking. *European Early Childhood Education Research Journal, 24*(1), 67–85.

Bodrova, E., & Leong, D. J. (2012). Assessing and scaffolding: Make-believe play. *Young Children, 67*(1), 28–34.

Casey, B., Andrews, N., Schindler, H., Kersh, J., Samper, A., & Copley, J. (2008). The development of spatial skills through interventions involving block building activities. *Cognition and Instruction, 26*(3), 269–309.

Ferrara, K., Hirsh-Pasek, K., Newcombe, N., Golinkoff, R. and Lam, W. (2011). Block talk: Spatial language during block play. *Mind, Brain, and Education, 5*(3), 143–151.

Hakkarainen, P., M. Brėdikytė, K. Jakkula, and H. Munter. 2013. "Adult play guidance and children's play development in a narrative play-world." *European Early Childhood Education Research Journal, 21*(2): 213–225.

Hanline, M., Milton, S., & Phelps, P. (2010). The relationship between preschool block play and reading and maths abilities in early elementary school: A longitudinal study of children with and without disabilities. *Early Child Development and Care, 180*(8), 1005–1017.

Hobenshield Tepylo, D., Moss, J., & Stephenson, C. (2015). Blocks: Great learning tools from infancy through the primary grades: A developmental look at a rigorous block play program. *Young Children, 70*(1), 18–25.

Kamii, C., Miyakawa, Y., & Kato, Y. (2004). The development of logico-mathematical knowledge in a block-building activity at ages 1–4. *Journal of Research in Childhood Education, 19*(1), 44–57.

Loizou, E. (2017). Towards play pedagogy: Supporting teacher play practices with a teacher guide about socio-dramatic and imaginative play. *European Early Childhood Education Research Journal, 25*(5), 784–95

Loizou, E., Michaelides, A., & Georgiou, A. (2019). Early childhood teacher involvement in children's socio-dramatic play: creative drama as a scaffolding tool. *Early Child Development and Care, 189*(4), 600–12

Nicole, A. (2015). Building curriculum during block play. *Dimensions of Early Childhood, 43*(1), 11–15.

Park, J. (2019). The qualities criteria of constructive play and the teacher's role. *The Turkish Online Journal of Educational Technology, 18*(1), 26–132.

Phelps, P., & Hanline, M. (1999). Let's play blocks!. *TEACHING Exceptional Children, 32*(2), 62–67.

Ramani, G., Zippert, E., Schweitzer, S., & Pan, S. (2014). Preschool children's joint block building during a guided play activity. *Journal of Applied Developmental Psychology, 35*(4), 326–336.

Schmitt, S., Korucu, I., Napoli, A., Bryant, L., & Purpura, D. (2018). Using block play to enhance preschool children's mathematics and executive functioning: A randomized controlled trial. *Early Childhood Research Quarterly, 44*, 181–91.

The benefits of toy blocks: The science of construction play. [online] Available at: https://www.parentingscience.com/toy-blocks.html [Accessed 20 March 2019].

Trawick-Smith, J., & T. Dziurgot. 2011. "'Good-fit' teacher–child play interactions and the subsequent autonomous play of preschool children." *Early Childhood Research Quarterly, 26*(1): 110–23.

Trawick-Smith, J., Swaminathan, S., Baton, B., Danieluk, C., Marsh, S., & Szarwacki, M. (2016). Block play and mathematics learning in preschool: The effects of building complexity, peer and teacher interactions in the block area, and replica play materials. *Journal of Early Childhood Research, 15*(4), 433–48.

Wolfgang, C., Stannard, L., & Jones, I. (2003). Advanced constructional play with LEGOs among preschoolers as a predictor of later school achievement in mathematics. *Early Child Development and Care, 173*(5), 467–75.

6

BICYCLES AND OTHER RIDING TOYS

Valerie A. Ubbes

Children use toys for play and interaction. Toys are important for children's overall development, self-regulation, and executive functioning. Toys can benefit children for their value in symbolic and pretend play, language development, fine motor skills, and gross motor physical development. The focus of this chapter is on the use of bicycles and other riding toys as key affordances in children's physical, cognitive, and social development. This chapter also discusses the features of bicycles and other riding toys, including gender, age, and special needs differences among children.

TYPICAL TYPES OF BICYCLES AND OTHER RIDING TOYS

Young children like to play with wagons and tricycles when they are three to four years of age. Children's fascination with wheels usually begins when adults in their environment model the use of wheeled tools like lawn mowers, shopping carts, and vacuum cleaners, which prompts their parents to purchase look-alike push toys for playtime. By age five, children like to ride scooters and bicycles with training wheels (Clements, 2004). Bicycles and other riding toys (e.g., wagons, scooters, tricycles) provide children with "an opportunity to explore and develop the knowledge of his own body parts and how they move" (Zimmerman & Calovini, 1971, p. 642).

Wagons

Wagons are low-riding toys that have four wheels for carrying a load. Wagons are usually pulled by children who have toys or objects to carry from place to place. Sometimes, children are placed into wagons for a ride if the wagon is of sufficient size and durability. A long handle is extended from the base of the wagon for pulling the load and for steering the direction of the vehicle.

Scooters

Scooters are riding toys that require the use of the hands or the feet to push and drive the vehicle forward. Scooters can be operated without handlebars or with handlebars depending on the body position of the children using the toy. If completely seated on a scooter base, children use their hands or feet against the ground to propel the scooter forward. If in an upright standing posture, children use their feet to propel them forward while holding onto handlebars for steering the scooter in a particular direction. Sometimes scooters can be arranged for children to sit upon a mid-height seat with one wheel in the front and two wheels in the back. Scooters designed in this fashion would not have pedals so children will need to use their legs and feet to move the riding toy in a forward or backward direction.

Tricycles

Tricycles are seated riding toys that are designed to move by two wheels in the back and one wheel in the front to form a triangle platform with pedals. Tricycles are moved by alternating the bent legs and feet against a right pedal and a left pedal. The speed at which children turn and rotate the pedals in an alternating pedaling action determines the speed of the tricycle. The vehicle is steered with hands holding onto a right and left handlebar. The gripping action of the hands keeps children from falling to the right, left, or back side of the seat. The dynamic coordination of the hand grip, seated posture, and foot pedal action enable children to balance in a triad like a three-legged moving stool. Children's tricycles are generally manufactured from steel, aluminum, or plastic parts. A children's tricycle seat may be comprised of rubber, foam, phone, leather, and plastic (Johansen & Mathiesen, 2012).

Bicycles

Bicycles are two-wheeled vehicles with one wheel in front and behind the other. Bicycles have a seat, handlebars for steering, and two-foot pedals to turn the wheels and propel the toy forward. Bicycle are fitted to the size of the rider and often have an adjustable seat and handlebars that move up and down. The tires of the bicycle have spokes that extend in a circular pattern around a sturdy rim that holds the tire in place. Tires must be inflated with air pressure for the bicycle to move forward. Bicycles have chains that connect the two wheels together near the pedals.

More advanced bicycles have gears and gear cables to regulate how easy or hard that children must pedal to move the bicycle forward. Although bicycles are meant to be ridden in a seated position, children can stand up to move the pedals in an alternating pattern while maintaining hand contact with the handlebars. The vehicle is stopped by applying a backward action against the pedals to activate brakes which will stop the wheels from moving forward.

LEARNING FEATURES OF BICYCLES AND OTHER RIDING TOYS

Bicycles and other riding toys are developmentally appropriate vehicles that afford children learning opportunities for gaining dynamic and static balance, muscular endurance, eye-hand coordination, and eye-foot coordination. The moving nature of bicycles and other riding toys require children to learn either a seated or standing posture with appropriate head lift, body lean, and eye scans. Bidirectional eye tracking is a fine motor skill that helps to establish equilibrium of the body during movement. Equilibrium or balance is a function of the cerebellum and the vestibular apparatus in the inner ear. When balance is developed in tandem with vision and auditory function, sensory integration results.

Wagons are often pulled toys that require an upright seated posture of children whose parents will pull them for a ride. Adults will pad wagon beds with comfortable blankets and upright walls to contain pretoddlers when being pulled in wagons. When toddlers have command of their own walking gait and directionality, they often show pleasure in pulling objects and toys in their small wagons while holding and pulling the wagon handle behind them. Children enjoy putting things into and out of wagons when playing with this type of riding toy.

Scooters are the next developmental riding toy that help to develop dynamic and static balance, muscular endurance, eye-hand coordination, and eye-foot coordination. Some scooters require a seated position on top of a wooded or plastic plank on four wheels. Because of its low position to the floor, children can cross sit their legs over the square seat then lean forward and scoot their body along the floor at various speeds with the propulsion of their hands pushing against the floor.

Other scooters that are higher off the floor require bent knees, seated position with hands holding onto the handlebars of the scooter and feet resting against the floor. Children initiate the movement of the scooter by lifting their knees slightly on each side of the scooter then pushing their feet against the floor to extend their bodies in the forward direction. The swinging pendulum of the hip and knee lift, in sequence with the foot placement against the ground, enables the toy to advance forward. When the scooter catches up with the location of the planted feet against the ground, the bent knee posture of the child allows for a slowing seated position until there is a dynamic action against the ground by the feet to propel the toy forward again. With some practice, children can reverse the action to push or thrust both legs against the ground to move the riding toy backward, or they can coordinate an alternating foot placement one at a time against the ground to simulate a pedaling motion either forward or backward.

More advanced scooters require an upright standing posture on straight legs with both hands on the handlebars. To initiate the movement, children place one foot stationary on the scooter base with the second free-moving leg swinging forward and backward in the air close to the ground. The free-swinging leg advances the scooter in a forward direction by also pushing against the floor to generate power and forward momentum. When enough speed is generated by the pushing foot, children can coast along and ride the scooter with both feet aligned on the narrow platform until more action is required.

Benefits of Riding Toys for Children

A toy is a learning material or object that stimulates children to discover relationships with themselves and things in their environment (Rambusch, 1968). Play behavior is defined as interaction with peers and objects (Loovis, 1985) and is considered a social determinant of child development. Wheeled toys help children to develop their upper and lower body coordination, gross motor skills, postural balance, and social cooperative play. Social peer interactions can occur around tricycles and bicycles because of the negotiations they need when asking to use the toy in educational and play contexts and when following rules associated with such play.

Toys should be challenging to use because they give children a chance to progress to their next developmental level. Toys that challenge children can help to motivate them to move to a higher level of physical and cognitive functioning (Zimmerman & Calovini, 1971). For example, wheeled toys often require children to develop and use a play language around positional and directional travel. Children also establish the concepts of spatial organization when learning to maneuver corners and negotiating forward, backward, and sideward movements with their toys.

GENDER DIFFERENCES IN USE

When children receive their first bicycle, it is seen as a milestone and a rite of passage (Judson, 2019). An Australian study (Bell, Timperio, Veitch, & Carver, 2019) found that boys cycled more frequently and for longer duration than girls. In their thorough investigation of individual, social, and neighborhood perceptions among children living in socioeconomically disadvantaged and mostly rural neighborhoods, Bell and colleagues (2019) found that enjoyment of cycling was the most significant predictor of cycling frequency and duration. Researchers also indicated that increasing parents' willingness to allow their children to cycle independently may increase cycling for the development of physical activity.

Supporting both girls and boys to participate in cycling is an important contributor to physical activity across all geographical and socioeconomic areas. In a systematic review of 39 studies from seven countries (United States, Scotland, Finland, Australia, Chile, Estonia, Belgium) found that two to six-year-old children lack in moderate to vigorous physical activity for at least 60 minutes per day (Tucker, 2008). Cycling is considered to be a viable public health intervention for children because "it is a low-cost lifelong physical activity" (Centers for Disease Control, 1997).

According to the National Association for Sport and Physical Education (NASPE, 2002), preschoolers should engage in daily structured physical activity and daily unstructured physical activity with wheeled vehicles and playground equipment for at least 60 minutes (or 120 minutes for both forms of physical activity). Activity-friendly play equipment added to an outdoor preschool playground has been found to increase the physical activity intensities of three to five-year-old boys and girls (Hannon & Brown, 2008).

The 2018 Achieving a State of Healthy Weight (ASHW) report was released by the National Resource Center for Health and Safety in Child Care and Early Education. The annual report, funded by the U.S. Centers for Disease Control and Prevention, assesses the extent to which Early Care and Education (ECE) licensing regulations follow the nationally recommended obesity prevention standards. Analyses of the 2018 data showed significant improvements by US states to strengthen childcare licensing regulations for the prevention of childhood overweight and obesity programs in early childcare education.

Five states (i.e., Alabama, Kentucky, Nevada, North Carolina, and Tennessee) adopted childcare licensing regulations that focused on the use of obesity prevention standards for physical activity, screen time, nutrition, and infant feeding. The report highlighted that 83 percent of the changes increased support for national obesity prevention standards, and 17 percent of the changes decreased support for national obesity prevention standards.

Caesar (2001) highlighted that wheeled toys aid in the progression of walking skills to running skills by developing arm and leg coordination. For example, use of a wheeled wagon encourages children to develop gross motor skills such as walking and reaching in order to move the wagon during play time. All wheeled toys help children to develop pushing and pulling actions (Hartley, 2012) of their arms and legs while activating their core muscles in their torso.

ADAPTATIONS FOR CHILDREN WITH SPECIAL NEEDS

Play helps all children to acquire a sense of control over their environments. Children with special needs might present with some unique problems in the mobility and manipulation of toys because their cognitive and/or physical abilities may not be congruent with their design (Loovis, 1985). Children with cerebral palsy often have muscle weakness and poor muscle control so adaptive tricycles can assist with mobility, especially those with recumbent pedaling (Judson, 2019). Research suggests that some children with orthopedic challenges will need to be taught how to play with riding toys supported by adults who will need to cue and reinforce them for longer periods of toy play (Loovis, 1985).

Harrington, Klein, and McHugh (2005, p. 56) report that "even for children with disabilities, the time required to master bicycle riding is relatively short, often a matter of a few hours or a few days." In a camp (or clinical environment) with a bicycle program for children who have a wide array of disabilities and needs, the presence of peer role models helps to build the key ingredient of "belief" or self-efficacy. To that end, 70 to 80 percent of the children attending the program were taught to ride two-wheeled bicycles (Harrington, Klein, and McHugh, 2005).

RESEARCH ON PLAY EXPERIENCES WITH WHEELED TOYS

Thompson (1993) outlines more than 70 developmentally appropriate activities for parents and teachers while emphasizing the close relationship between motor skills and cognitive development in the first two years of life with infants and toddlers. Thompson (1993, p. 3) states, "Gross motor movements dominate activity. Toddlers repeat actions over and over as if practicing to be able to do them perfectly. They gradually become more agile and coordinated. While the toddler spends a great deal of time working on his or her gross motor skills, fine motor skills are not neglected." Repetition has been noted as a key feature of children at play (Piaget, 1962).

Zimmerman and Calovini (1971) outline the characteristics of learning activities and their developmental purposes for one- to two-year-old children, two- to three-year-old children, three- to four-year-old children, and four- to five-year-old children. Samples of learning activities with wheeled toys such as doll buggies, wagons, tricycles, and scooters begin to be used by children between ages three to four years and continue being used by four- to five-year-old children. Early spatial awareness and balance are developed through the pushing, pulling, carrying, rolling, riding, walking, and jumping on and off actions of wheeled-based activities; these activities also foster dexterity through body handling of the toys and energy released through active large limbed muscles of children.

Outdoor play affords children a chance to improve their large muscle activity when using wagons, scooters, tricycles, and bicycles along with opportunities to explore different natural environments. Studies show that Canadian children spend less than 10 hours per week in outdoor play but 20 to 30 hours per week in indoor play (Dietze & Crossley, 2000). Similarly, 40 percent of Japanese children prefer playing indoors but like to chat with their friends, play ball, and riding bicycles when outdoors (Benese Corporation, 1999).

American children spend less time playing outdoors than previous generations, owing to children's increased use of televisions and computers despite the fact that their mothers recognize the important benefits of outdoor active play (Clements, 2004). Slutsky and DeShetler (2017) examined play in three to five-year-old children and found that they engaged in considerably more technology play (e.g., TV, tablet) and nontechnology play (e.g., toys, puzzles, reading) than outdoor play (e.g., playground, bike)

In a study by Egan and Pope (2018), outdoor play was assessed in Irish five-year-olds. There was almost universal access (99 percent) to outdoor play equipment such as a bicycle or roller skates. Results showed that most children rode a bike, tricycle, or scooter multiple times per week. Researchers found that to have agency in their play, children needed to take advantage of affordances found in their neighborhoods by using or modifying what was available in their immediate environments.

Tricycles were shown to be very important to children who were three to four years of age during a summer experimental preschool program for culturally deprived children (Gray & Klaus, 1987). In the first summer, children could only obtain a tricycle by asking for it as a way of delaying immediate gratification and to encourage the use of verbalizations. In the second summer, tricycles were used in a miniature traffic situation where children responded to traffic signs and hand signals to develop a meaning of symbols and gestures.

The type and frequency of human interactions were observed between children and staff in an outside playtime period in the UK where tricycles were available (Bilton, 2012). Types of interactions and utterances ranged from child extended, child domestic, adult extended, and adult domestic, with the latter dominating the outdoor play time. In the ten scenarios for child-initiated interactions at the school, asking for a bike by a child was considered a child domestic utterance that occurred second to talking about something the child had done, created, or made.

In some settings, bicycles and tricycles are considered an affordance (Gibson, 1979), meaning the quality of an object or environment that allows children to perform an action. Bilton (2012) suggested that future research might suspend the offering of bicycles since asking for a bike and using a bike tended to involve disputes over lack of affordances whereas the latter type of child domestic utterance involved extended conversations for developing their ideas and concepts.

RECOMMENDATIONS

Recommendations for safety when using wheeled toys is of paramount concern. Riding toys are the leading cause of toy-related injury (Stephenson, 2005). Parents and caregivers need to be sure that children use their wheeled toys away from stairs, traffic, and swimming pools (Stephenson, 2005).

Use of wagons, scooters, tricycles, and bicycles are an active form of transport that require children to demonstrate a developmental ability to "constantly make decisions to enable them to remain safe" (Lenton & Finlay, 2018, p. 2). Younger children may struggle when pulling wagons across different surface areas like stones, grass, and sidewalks until they have gained adequate experiences. When younger children learn to ride toy vehicles on hard surfaces and pavements, increased risks occur with body scrapes, bruises, and skin abrasions. Children need practice in identifying hazards in the form of objects, equipment, people, or environmental conditions that have the potential to cause harm during play (Lenton & Finlay, 2018).

Although the age of five can be a milestone for children learning to ride a bicycle, mastery is very dependent on a minimum of 100 hours of practice in steering, pedaling, and braking without falling (Anderson, 1982). Children often do not understand that people in other moving toys and vehicles cannot see them. Children also lack understanding about stopping distances, road signs, and traffic and weather conditions.

Children need to gain confidence in being able to steer their riding toy while performing hand signals and learning to brake with their feet. Other coordinated movements are learning to ride alone and with others, starting and stopping abruptly, and being able to negotiate straight, curved, and zigzag patterns with their wheeled toy.

The National SAFE KIDS Campaign (2019) recommends that parents buy helmets, horns or bells, elbow pads, and kneepads for children playing with scooters, tricycles, and bicycles. Bicycle injuries persist throughout all child development and is the sixth leading cause of injury from ages 1 to 18 years, but the leading cause of pediatric injury for ages 10 and 11, and third leading cause of injury for ages 12, 13, 14, and 15 (Schwebel & Brezausek, 2014).

The US Consumer Product Safety Commission reported 220,500 toy-related injuries treated in the United States hospital emergency department in 2006. Riding toys (including nonmotorized scooters) are associated with the most treated injuries for any other category of toys, and tricycles were associated with two fatalities when two children fell into in-ground swimming pools while riding their tricycles. Coffman (1991) highlighted safety tips for drowning prevention by keeping tricycles away from pools.

Although the London Handicapped Adventure Play Association (HAPA) recommended that physically impaired children have the "means for independent mobility" through the use of bicycles and hand-propelled tricycles, HAPA also outlines some concerns with such vehicles: (1) ramped surfaces and hard surface paths cost money and could be unsafe without adult assistance, (2) lack of playground space can cause congested areas and disrupt the play patterns of other children not using toy vehicles, and (3) replacement parts of the vehicles can be costly and require expertise in assembly, repair, and maintenance.

SUMMARY

The focus of this chapter was on the use of wagons, scooters, tricycles, and bicycles as key affordances in children's physical, cognitive, and social development. Features of riding toys were described, including gender, age, and special needs adaptations among children. Recommendations regarding safety and risk were highlighted. Children who play with riding toys require a growing capacity of safety decisions through practical experiences. Because learning to ride a bicycle, scooter, tricycle, and bicycle is an acquired competency, adult supervision and injury prevention strategies should occur in tandem when young children engage in these developmental play experiences.

REFERENCES

Anderson, J. R. (1982). Acquisition of cognitive skill. *Psychological Review*, 89, 369–406.

Bell, L., Timperio, A., Veitch, J., & Carver, A. (2019). Individual, social, and neighbourhood correlates of cycling among children living in disadvantaged neighbourhoods. *Journal of Science and Medicine in Sport*, https://doi.org/10.1016/j.jsams.2019.08.010

Benese Corporation. (1999). Kodomo tachi no asobi monogurafu shogakusei nau [*Children's play in elementary grade schools*], 19(1). Tokyo: Benesse Educational Research Center.

Bilton, H. (2012). The type and frequency of interactions that occur between staff and children outside in Early Years Foundation Stage settings during a fixed playtime period when there are tricycles available. *European Early Childhood Education Research Journal*, 20(3), 403–21.

Caesar, B. (2001). Give children a place to explore. *Child Care Information Exchange, 3*, 76–79.

Centers for Disease Control and Prevention. (1997). Guidelines for school and community programs to promote lifelong physical activity among young people. *Journal of School Health*, 67(6): 202–219.

Chowdhury, R.T. (2007). *Executive summary: Toy-related deaths and injuries. Calendar Year 2006*. Washington, DC: US Consumer Product Safety Commission.

Clements, R. (2004). An investigation of the status of outdoor play. *Contemporary Issues in Early Childhood*, 5(1), 68–80.

Coffman, S. P. (1991). Parent education for drowning prevention. *Journal of Pediatric Health Care, 5*, 141–46.

Dietz, W., & Gortmaker, S. L. (1985). Do we fatten our children at the television set? Obesity and television viewing in children and adolescents, *Pediatrics*, 75, 807–12.

Dietze, B., & Crossley, B. (2000). Young children and outdoor play. Belleville, Ontario: Loyalist College.

Egan, S., & Pope, J. (2018). On your bike: Outdoor play in Irish 5 year olds. *Children's Research Digest Children: Young People's Play*, 91–98.

Gibson, J. J. (1979). *The ecological approaches to visual perception*. Boston, MA: Houghton Mifflin.

Gray, S. W., & Klaus, R. A. (1987). An experimental preschool program for culturally deprived children. *Peabody Journal of Education, 65*(1), 15–28.

Hannon, J. C., & Brown, B. B. (2008). Increasing preschoolers' physical activity intensities: An activity-friendly preschool playground intervention. *Preventive Medicine, 46*, 532–36.

Hartley, R. E. (2012). Toys, play materials, and equipment. *Childhood Education, 45*(3) in Periodicals Archive Online, p. 122.

Johansen, J. B., & Mathiesen, L. (2012). Children's tricycle with adaptable seat. US Patent Number 8,276,987B1.

Judson, D., (2019) Adaptive tricycles: Their role as a mobility device in addressing domains of the international classification of functioning, disability and health. *Canadian Seating & Mobility Conference*, 77–81.

Klein, R. E., McHugh, E., Harrington, S. L., Davis, T., & Lieberman, L. J. (2005). Adapted bicycles for teaching riding skills. *Teaching Exceptional Children*, 37(6), 50–56

Lenton, S., & Finlay, F. O. (2018). Public health approaches to safer cycling for children based on developmental and physiological readiness: Implications for practice. *BMJ Paediatrics Open, 2*, e000123. doi:10.1136/bmjpo-2017-000123.

Loovis, E. M. (1985). Evaluation of toy preference and associated movement behaviors of preschool orthopedically handicapped children. *Adapted Physical Activity Quarterly, 2*, 117–26.

National Association for Sport and Physical Education. (2002). Active start: A statement of physical activity guidelines for children birth to five years. American Alliance for Health, Physical Education, Recreation and Dance, Reston, VA.

National Resource Center for Health and Safety in Child Care and Early Education. 2019. *Achieving a state of healthy weight 2018 report*. Aurora, CO: University of Colorado Anschutz Medical Campus. [https://nrckids.org/HealthyWeight]

National Safe Kids Campaign (2019). Report to the nation: Trends in unintentional childhood injury mortality and parental views. Retrieved June 25, 2019 from http://www.safekids.organd https://www.safekids.org/sites/default/files/documents/ResearchReports/Report%20to%20the%20Nation%20Trends%20in%20Unintentional%20Childhood%20Injury%20Mortality%20and%20Parental%20Views%20on%20Child%20Safety%20-%20April%202008.pdf

Piaget, J. (1962). *Play, dreams, and imitation*. New York, NY: Norton.

Raumbusch, N.M. (1968). *The learning child*. Englewood Cliffs, NJ: Respiratory Environmental Corporation.

Schwebel, D. C., & Brezausek, C. M. (2014). Child development and pediatric sport and recreational injuries by age. *Journal of Athletic Training, 49*(6), 780–85.

Slutsky, R., & DeShetler, L. M. (2017). How technology is transforming the ways in which children play. *Early Child Development and Care, 187*(7), 1138–1146.

Stephenson, M. (2005). Danger in the toy box. *Journal of Pediatric Health Care, 19*, 187–89.

Thompson, D. S. (1993). The promotion of gross and fine motor development for infants and toddlers: Developmentally appropriate activities for parents and teachers. ERIC ED361104.

Tucker, P. (2008). The physical activity levels of preschool-aged children: A systematic review. *Early Childhood Research Quarterly, 23*, 547–58.

Zimmerman, L. D. & Calovini, G. (1971). Toys as learning materials for preschool children. *Exceptional Children, 5*, 642–54.

7

THE DOLL IDENTITY

Race, Ethnicity, Gender

John A. Sutterby

Although dolls have long been one of the chief toys of children and are now nearly universal among both savage and civilized peoples, it is singular that few serious attempts have been made to study them (Ellis & Hall, 1897, p. 3). Doll play seems to have been around since there were cave drawings and other awareness of ourselves as humans. Why humans are attracted to dolls is an item for discussion, but that they are attracted to dolls there is no doubt. Most dolls prior to the nineteenth century were homemade dolls, often from scrap materials, like straw or corn husks. During the industrial revolution, mechanical processes allowed for commercially designed dolls. For the purposes of this chapter, commercially created dolls will be the focus as they represent a juxtaposition between what adults want children to play with and what children decide to do. The connection between dolls and the identities of children who engage in play with them is an important one to explore. Researchers today examine dolls from many different traditions, from anthropological to feminist to child development. They often approach questions about dolls from different perspectives. How much do children identify with the dolls they are playing with? How much impact do dolls have on children's behaviors?

First a definition: a doll is a play object that is meant to be a physical representation of a person. The author's first memories of playing with dolls involved Fisher Price Little People. Although they did not have the articulations of dolls like Barbie or G. I. Joe, they did allow playing out family dramas between the characters of fantasy. The author's children played with dolls, with Barbie and doll house play from a daughter and Power Ranger doll play from a son.

TYPES OF DOLLS, DOLL PLAY, AND AGE-LEVEL DIFFERENCES

Dolls generally come in three types with somewhat different purposes: baby dolls, child age dolls, and adult dolls. Baby dolls, like Betsy Wetsy dolls, are expected to encourage the child to engage in caregiving behaviors like feeding, bathing and dressing. Child-age dolls, like American Girl dolls, are expected to encourage companionship and sharing behaviors. These are meant to encourage cooperative play between two friends. Adult aged dolls generally are expected to encourage play reenactments of adult scenarios like dating, dressing, or shopping. This adult portrayal of dolls was for the most part initiated with Mattel's Barbie in 1959 (Walsh, 2005).

Doll Play Types

When parents think about dolls, they often like to envision their children in innocent doll play of family scenarios and caring for innocent children. On the other hand, children's play often does not live up to the innocent ideals of parents. An early study found that doll play was often not very sanitized. The categories of doll play recorded in the surveys of G. Stanley Hall (1907) include doll food and feeding, sleep, sickness, death, funeral and burial of dolls, dolls names, discipline, hygiene, toilet, and schools, parties, and weddings. Discipline included ripping off paper doll legs, deprivations, spankings, whippings, scolding, and in one case, a doll was "hanged with due ceremony" (p. 178).

Dolls and commercial doll play have been controversial for decades. Barbie dolls are often at the center of doll controversy. When they were first sold in 1959, parents were scandalized about how the dolls were dressed and the fact that they represented an adult woman; dolls that when stripped of their clothes were essentially naked, although without nipples, genitalia, and belly buttons. The possibility of exploring adult bodies by children was part of the concern with Barbie dolls (Stone, 2010). Dolls are at times critiqued for the messages they send. Are they too sexual? Do they represent materialistic culture? Are they too realistic? Do they portray girls as weak or bad at math? All of these are concerns for parents and educators. This chapter examines some aspects of commercial doll play along the lines of age level, gender, sexuality, race/ethnicity, and disability.

Age Level Differences

As children develop, their doll play changes. Infants may engage in looking at dolls' faces as something they are attracted to while toddlers begin their first acts of symbolic play when they engage with a doll and pretend that it is a living thing to be cared for.

Preschoolers engage in very deep engagement with dolls in creating scenarios for their play, based on their lived experiences. Elementary doll play is often media driven as the dolls they select to play with are tied to television and video media. Although the market for doll play has changed dramatically over the last few years, the original market for Barbie was what would now be called tweens (age 10–12) who would engage in fashion play with the dolls.

Dolls and Gender and Sexuality

Often doll play is associated with gentle play associated with caregiving for girls. This quiet doll play, however, was not necessarily popular with young girls who often preferred more active outdoor play. In addition, girl play with dolls often is not so sweet as their play frequently involves dismembering dolls, smashing dolls against walls, cutting up dolls, and even "killing" dolls in order to have mock funerals (Formanek-Brunell, 1992). For boys, dolls (action figures) are assumed to be violent and their play, therefore, can more freely express urges to more aggressive play. For girls, this type of aggressive play is seen as unseemly and forbidden. Hall (1907) unsurprisingly found that some parents and teachers frowned on activities that children did with dolls.

Gender and identity are complex. There is an intersection between what societal beliefs about how gender should be expressed and the internal emotional state about how one identifies self in terms of gender. Societal beliefs about gender and gender norms are constantly changing. Societal beliefs about gender may be congruent with how one feels about oneself or they may be incongruent (Killerman, 2017). For the sake of simplicity, the terms *girl* and *boy* will be used unless otherwise specified in the literature.

There has been a long and consistent debate about whether there is a biological versus an environmental difference in preference for doll play (Weisgram & Bruun, 2018). Both boy and girl infants prefer dolls over trucks, but by one year, boys begin to show a preference for trucks over dolls. Parental influence may be a driving factor by the cues they give children about what are appropriate toys, by toys they suggest, and by how many dolls or trucks are in the home. Parents support more gender conformity for boys than they do for girls. These research findings are fairly consistent over time (Boe & Woods, 2018).

Much of the recent research on dolls and identity has focused on the dolls that represent adult characters and how this may impact children's images of themselves. Dolls have been introduced that often push the limits of the play interests of children. When dolls push into controversial territory, they begin to face critiques, especially from popular media. Researchers and critical theorists also have critiqued dolls, most notably, Barbie dolls, for the messages that they send to children (Steinberg, 1997).

The American Psychological Association has investigated the sexualization of girls play and focused on some dolls such as Bratz dolls and a proposed line of dolls based on the musical group, Pussycat Dolls, that were to be released by Hasbro. The Pussycat Doll line of dolls was cancelled due to protests from consumer groups and advocacy groups (Meyers, 2006). Efforts to show the possible child cognitive/social emotional differences when playing with masculine versus feminine toys has been inconclusive (Fulcher & Hayes, 2017).

Social cognitive theory is one explanation for how dolls might influence children. Social cognitive theory of Bandura suggests that modeling, experiences, and reinforcements shape how gender is enacted in children. Parents, teachers, peers and the media act as important influencers of children's enactment of their identity. Dolls can be a part of this process in that they are portrayed by media, selected and purchased by adults and reinforced by other significant individuals like teachers and peers. Parents can either reinforce gender role stereotyping through how they reinforce dolls, they can reject it, or they can be neutral toward stereotyping (Kollmayer, Schultes, Schober, Hodosi, & Spiel, 2018). In their research study, Kollmayer and colleagues (2018) found that parents overall had more positive attitudes toward toys that reinforced gender roles or were neutral over toys that encouraged cross-gender roles.

The Barbie persona itself may have an impact on girls' attitudes about themselves. Sherman and Zurbriggen (2014) found that playing with a Fashion Barbie versus playing with a Mrs. Potato Head doll led girls to see themselves as having fewer career options in comparison to boys. Even when Fashion Barbie was dressed as a doctor, girls did not see this as a possible career for themselves in comparison to boys. The nonsexualized doll, Mrs. Potato Head, apparently did not lead to girls feeling the same limitations on possible careers as the Fashion Barbies did. So the attractiveness of the doll itself, despite the marketing of Barbie as encouraging girl empowerment, has not lead girls to believe Barbie is empowering.

Campaign for a Commercial Free Childhood is an advocacy group that tries to raise media awareness about how products are marketed to children. Their goal is to limit how corporations influence children's identities. One of the ways corporations influence children's identities is through doll and toy marketing. The controversial Bratz Dolls are the focus of how young children are being marketed sexualized images. Levin and Kilbourne (2008) document the media emphasis on the sexualization of girls and the violence marketed to boys. The integration of toys with media, video games, and advertising immerse children into a world where they are constantly bombarded with messages. Messages of sexuality and violence are often unmediated by adults. Young girls are sent messages that sexuality makes them attractive and boys are sent messages that violence solves problems.

Although those messages may result in children taking on whatever toy companies are marketing, children who actually play with the dolls create their own meaning making and storytelling. Often the marketing is subverted by the player. The Ken doll might be in a relationship with another man for example. Adults take control by subverting the messages of Mattel and making the dolls into images that embody stories that they can identify with (Rand, 1995; Stern, 1998).

One consideration of the concern over the sexualization of childhood is that it is a form of "moral panic." Moral panic occurs when some outside influence is seen as corrupting children so adults must act to protect children, often at great lengths, from that threat is. In many cases, dolls, especially dolls that represent adults like Barbie or teens like Bratz, are seen as sexualized threats to children, especially to girls. Adults may be overly concerned about the loss of childhood innocence rather than the children themselves. Blaise (2013) brought Bratz dolls into an early childhood classroom to examine children's attitudes toward the dolls. She found that young preschool age children did have curiosity about sexuality that was elicited from the dolls. Their interest in sexuality was often silenced by parents who wanted to silence any discussion on the topic.

Recently, Mattel has released a set of Barbie Dolls called the Fashionistas that have a range of body types from tall to petite to curvy. These new doll body shapes have drawn media attention as well as being described in a recent Hulu documentary, *Tiny Shoulders, Rethinking Barbie* (Crocker Riley & Blaugrund Nevins, 2018). The documentary focuses on the history of the dolls as well as their development and testing. In addition to the new body types, the Fashionista line also has dolls that represent different ethnicities, hair color, and style as well as disabilities. The purpose of the dolls is for children to more easily find a doll that resembles themselves or people they might encounter. There is a corresponding male line of dolls to go along with the female dolls. This new line of dolls has been a commercial success, especially attributable to the focus on race and Barbie (Peck, 2017).

Nesbitt, Sabiston, de Jonge, Slomon-Krakus, and Welsh (2019) explored the issue of body image using images of the new Barbie Fashionistas. The girls in this study made subconscious or unconscious self-other comparisons between themselves and the images of these dolls. This is important, in that media images as well as dolls can unconsciously lead to body image comparisons between the child and the image. Another interesting study result was that girls self-reported that the curvy doll was the most pleasant but least desirable. The original version and the tall doll were not seen as pleasant but were seen as desirable. The petite Barbie was rated the highest of all the doll shapes.

Action Figures

"You. Are. A. Toyyyyy! You are not the real thing. You're an action figure. You are a child's plaything!" (Arnold, Guggenheim, & Lassiter, 1995). Boy and girl toy marketing is mostly separate. Girls toys are marked with pink boxes in separate isles. Dolls marketed for boys are often called action figures and marketed with brown, black, or blue colors. The capabilities of male and female dolls are different. Male dolls have grasping hands and stand alone. Female dolls cannot stand alone and cannot grip things like weapons. The ways that boys and girls often play with dolls is different. Action figure play allows boys to play as if the doll is an extension of their body. They face the doll out from them for action. Girl doll play involves the girls interacting with their dolls. The girls face the dolls toward themselves. As the girl dolls do not have the capacity to hold things, this requires the girl players to hold and do actions for the dolls. Girl play was more based on narrative rather than action (see Nelson, 2011).

Doll play for boys has often been questioned socially in literature and in society. *William's Doll* (Zolotow, 1972) is a story about a boy who wants to play with a doll despite the concerns of his family members. Educators have encouraged this type of literature as allowing boys to break out of traditional gender roles. Perhaps allowing or encouraging boys to play with dolls may make them more positive caregivers to their own children and families (Malcom & Sheahan, 2018).

Like dolls marketed for girls, action figures are often criticized for encouraging negative characteristics in boys. Levin and Kilbourn (2008) suggest that violent cartoons and doll play create boys who are unable to relate to caring behaviors toward others. Ellis and Hall (1897), more than a century ago, suggested that moderate doll play for boys might encourage more prosocial behavior in adults. "Of course, boy life is naturally rougher and demands a wider range of activities. The danger, too, of making boy milliners is of course obvious, but we are convinced that on the whole more play with girl dolls by boys would tend to make them more sympathetic with girls as children, if not more tender with their wives and with women later" (49).

G. I. Joe, like Barbie, is based on a toy line of accessories, and like Barbie, G. I. Joe was articulated so that he could be posed. Jeeps, weapons, and uniforms were all designed to go along with the articulated body of the toy. The designers avoided using the term doll as it was marketed to boys thus initiating the use of the term action figure for dolls targeted to boys (Bainbridge, 2010). Transformers are another type of doll designed primarily to appeal to boys. All of these dolls have male voices in the cartoon that celebrates this toy. The toy is also active in that it can be changed from doll to truck, appealing to parents concerned about boys playing with dolls (Toffoletti, 2007).

DOLL IDENTITY, RACE, AND ETHNICITY

Many of the first manufactured Black dolls were not a fair representation of Black people as a whole . . . these dolls were inadequate representations with overly exaggerated features and outrageously dark complexions. Modern black dolls allow black children to see themselves in a positive light. They promote self-esteem, self-pride and self-acceptance (Garrett, 2003, p. 6).

Ellis and Hall (1897) found that fair hair and blue eyes were the favorites of most of their respondents in their doll study. However, some children did prefer Black dolls, and the prevalence of Black women caregivers then may have led to children preferring these dolls (Furmanek-Brunell, 1992). Clark & Clark pioneered doll preference in the 1940's. In the Clarks' research the participating children were more likely to select the White doll as having positive characteristics while the Black doll was more likely to be attributed to have negative characteristics. This research was used in part to overturn Southern segregation laws (Gibson, Robbins & Rochat, 2015).

A discussion of the Clark and Clark studies and some of the problems of the studies included that children were given a forced choice and could not select both dolls. In addition, the study children were not able to play with the dolls, not making it a very playful situation. Attempts to recreate the doll selection process using a doll house setting found that White children showed White preference while Black children chose randomly when selecting doll racial preferences. In addition, Black children were more likely to create mixed race doll stories (Jarrett, 2016).

White girls gave preference to White girl dolls over Black girl dolls and Male dolls in a recent study. Black girls on the other hand gave preference to White girl dolls over Black girl dolls. According to the authors, the difference may be explained by noting Black girls have more interactions in White environments than White girls have in Black environments. In addition, White parents may not discuss race with their children as much as Black parents (Kurtz-Costes, DeFrietas, Halle, Kinlaw, 2011).

Major toy manufacturers have included non-White dolls as part of their toy collections. Mattel released 'colored' Francie in 1965. Interestingly Francie was marketed as Barbie's cousin. The face and body for Francie was the same as Barbie, but darker. Although this doll was not commercially successful, many companies have released Black versions of their dolls to tap into this market (Garrett, 2010, February 18). Baby Nancy was released by the Shindana Doll Company in 1969. Baby Nancy was a black baby doll that had black facial features, and a short afro hair style. The Shindana Doll Company was a black-owned business that was sponsored by startup money from Mattel. Shindana has produced many more dolls that targeted the African American doll market (Goldberg, 2019; Stone, 2010; Garrett, 2012). Barbie also traveled to international locations in the 1960s, including Asian, Mexican, and European vacations. On these trips she often wore clothing that was supposed to represent touring these countries (Goldman, 2007).

Later Mattel offerings were more sensitive to the range of physical characteristics of the African American community. The Shani doll line released in 1991 had personas with different skin tones, facial features, body types, and hair styles. These were some of the first manufactured dolls lines to have such great detail. This line was more successful and was heavily promoted by Mattel (Garrett, 2017; Stern, 1998).

Dolls that were meant to represent Hispanic heritage usually carried the same body shape as the original Barbie with only a darker skin color and longer dark hair. The similarity in clothing and appearance for Latina Barbies from different countries suggests that Mattel has a limited idea of how to present Latina identity. "Latinidad is reduced to one easily consumable, stereotypical identity-in-a-box" (Goldman, 2007, p. 269). The styling of Latina Barbie as a darker skinned version of the Caucasian Barbie leaves out the indigenous and African heritage of most Latinas. The lighter-skinned and blonde Barbie sells better in South America as the middle-class elites typically are lighter skinned from a European Heritage (Goldman, 2007).

Manufactured dolls can also be used to subvert traditional cultural rituals. A quinceañera is a religious celebration of a girl's fifteenth birthday, common through Latino culture, especially in Mexico. The quinceañera is a coming of age ceremony where a girl becomes a woman. In the tradition the girl receives her last doll. For Mexican Americans, the alteration of tradition by American popular culture is found in religious traditions such as the quinceañera. Mattel has released a quinceañera Barbie to integrate itself into this Latino tradition blurring the line between the religious tradition and social event (Deiter, 2010).

Some manufactured dolls are designed to resist the Western tradition of Ken and Barbie. Dolls such as Fulla and Razanne are marketed with modest clothing, hijabs, and abayas to appeal to a Muslim audience. Jamila is another doll focused on the Muslim market. Jamila is married to Jamil and has two children, something Barbie would never have (Limbé Dolls, 2013, July 27). These dolls are sold in Muslim countries and are popular with Muslims living in the Western world. According to Fulla.com, "Fulla is sixteen years old. She's Arab, body and soul. She loves life and learning. She honors her parents and loves her family and friends. She's a good listener and takes care of brother and sister." Barbie is banned in Saudi Arabia for her skimpy clothing and her threat to morality. The Fulla and Razanne dolls are designed to be role models for girls and are marketed as educational toys. Both dolls come with fashionable clothing that is meant to be worn inside the home, with the jilbab and hijab to be worn in public (Yaqin, 2007).

American Girl Dolls were originally designed to fill a need that was different from Barbie and other adult fashion dolls. American Girl Dolls are girls supposedly be more like companion dolls. American Girl Dolls were created based on historical time periods and were marketed with period clothing and a book series, thus emphasizing their educational aspects. Like Barbie and Mattel, American Girl Dolls saw the importance of being inclusive as they released an African American doll (Addy) and a Mexican American doll (Josefina) in their second doll production (Acosta-Alzuru & Roushanzamir, 2003).

American Girl Dolls also recognizes the importance of a doll that resembles children. The line was originally called American Girl of Today (Acosta-Alzuru & Roushanzamir, 2003). Currently the line is called "Truly Me." They have a "create your own doll" choice, with options for facial features, skin tones, eye color, and shape and hair style. Designers can also create a boy doll with all of these features (Americangirl.com, 2019). The cost of these dolls means they are out of reach for most children and appeal more to adults' sense of wholesomeness and education (Acosta-Alzuru & Roushanzamir, 2003).

A feminist critique of American Girl Dolls notes that the dolls are designed not to be adults nor caregiving dolls. The girls can be styled as all sorts of races and ethnicities. It is also not a representation of sex or adult relationships. A major feminist critique of the doll is that they are very expensive and thus represent a play opportunity for a select group of children. The dolls are manufactured in low-wage countries and marketed at high costs. In addition, the marketing of the dolls involves skin and hair care as positive attributes of girl dolls and girl doll players (Davion, 2016).

DOLL PLAY FOR CHILDREN WITH SPECIAL NEEDS

Doll play for children with special needs tends to focus on three areas: dolls that resembled children with special needs, on play activities children engage in with dolls depending on their disability, and on interventions based on engaging in doll play. Wheelchair Barbie, when first released in 1997, was not considered a success. However, more recently the Barbie Fashionista line has introduced a number of Barbie's that have different physical disabilities, which have been much more widely accepted (Spinal Cord Team, 2019). Dolls that have physical characteristics that resemble a child with Down Syndrome also are available (Coady, 2019).

Doll play for children with disabilities is a complex topic to approach in that the type of doll play engaged in is dependent on the type of disability. Interventions are often focused on how to make the play behaviors of children with disabilities more resemble the play of typically developing children. For example, differences between typically developing children and children with autism were compared in a task of dressing paper dolls (Bancroft, Thompson, PetersDozier, & Harper, 2016).

CONCLUSION

Of any toy available, surely dolls draw the most interest. They represent people. They represent attitudes, beliefs and values about what people should look like and how they should act. Entire websites are devoted to all aspects of dolls. Dolls are featured in their own museums and are the focus of many toy museums. As long as there are dolls, there will be discussion and criticism of what they represent in a changing culture.

REFERENCES

Acosta-Alzuru, C., Roushanzamir, E. (2003). "Everything we do is a celebration of you!": Pleasant Company constructs American girlhood. *The communication review, 6.* 45–69. doi:10.1080/10714420390184150

AmericanGirl (2019). Truly Me. Retrieved from https://www.americangirl.com/

Arnold, B., Guggenheim, R., & Lassiter, J. (1995). *Toy Story.* United States: Pixar Animation Studios.

Bainbridge, J. (2010). Fully articulated: The rise of the action figure and the changing face of "children's" entertainment. *Continuum: Journal of media and cultural studies 24* (6), 829–42.

Bancroft, S., Thompson, R., Peters, L., Dozier, C., & Harper, A. (2016). Behavior variability in the play of children with autism and their typically developing peers. *Behavioral Interventions, 31* (2), 107–19. doi:10.1002/bin.1438

Blaise, M. (2013). Charting new territories: Re-assembling childhood sexuality in the early years classroom. *Gender and Education, 25*(7), 801–17. http://dx.doi.org/10.1080/09540253.2013.797070

Boe, J., & Woods, R. (2018). Parents' influence on infants' gender-typed toy preferences. *Sex roles, 79* (5–6), 358–73.

Bush, E. (2010). [Review of the book *The Good, the Bad, and the Barbie: A Doll's History and Her Impact on Us*]. *Bulletin of the Center for Children's Books 64*(3), 151–152. New York: Viking Books.

Coady, S. (November 26, 2019). Texas woman creates hyper realistic Down Syndrome baby dolls. *Metro,* Online at https://metro.co.uk/2019/11/16/texas-woman-creates-hyper-realistic-down-syndrome-baby-dolls-11167540/

Crocker-Reilly, C., & Blaugrund Nevins, A. (2018). *Tiny shoulders, Rethinking Barbie.* United States: Rare Bird Films.

Davion, V. (2016). The American girl: Playing with the wrong dollie. *Metaphilosophy, 47*(4–5), 571–84.

Deiter, K. (2010). From church blessing to quinceañera Barbie: America as "spiritual benefactor in la quinceañera. In I. Stavans (Ed.) *Quinceañera,* pp. 47–63. Santa Barbara, CA: ABC-CLIO.

Ellis, C., & Hall, G. (1897). *A study of dolls.* New York: E. L. Kellogg & Company.

Formanak-Brunell, M. (1992). Sugar and spice: The politics of doll play in nineteenth century America. In E. West & P. Petrik (Eds.), *Small worlds: Children and adolescents in America 1850–1950,* pp. 107–124. Lawrence, KA: University of Kansas Press.

Fulcher, M., & Hayes, A. (2017). Building a pink dinosaur: The effects of gendered construction toys on girls' and boys' play. *Sex Roles, 79* (5/6), 273–84.

Fulla.com (2019). Fulla. Retrieved July 30, 2019 from Fulla.com.

Garrett, D. (2003). *The definitive guide to collecting Black dolls.* Grantsville, MD: Hobby Horse Press.

Garrett, D. (2010, February 18). MIDBH: Early Black fashion dolls [Blog post]. Retrieved from https://blackdollcollecting.blogspot.com/2010/02/mibdh-early-black-fashion-dolls.html

Garrett, D. (2012, August 8). Baby Nancy, Shindana's first doll [Blog post]. Retrieved from https://blackdollcollecting.blogspot.com/2012/08/baby-nancy-shindanas-first-doll.html

Garrett, D. (2017, September 4). The marvelous world of Shani and her friends [Blog post]. Retrieved from https://blackdollcollecting.blogspot.com/2017/09/the-marvelous-world-of-shani-and-her.html

Goldberg, R. (2019, March 12). Baby Nancy, the first "black" doll, woke the toy industry. *Los Angelas Times.* Retrieved from https://www.latimes.com/opinion/op-ed/la-oe-goldberg-baby-nancy-black-doll-shindana-20190312-story.html

Goldman, K. (2007). La princesa Plástica: Hegemonic and oppositional representation of Latinidad in Hispanic Barbie. In M. Mendible (Ed.) *From bananas to buttocks: The Latino Body in popular film and culture*, pp. 263–78. Austin, TX: University of Texas Press.

Hall, G. (1907). *A study of dolls*. T. Smith (Ed.) Aspects of child life and education (pp. 157–204. Boston, MA: Ginn & Company Publishers.

Jarrett, O. (2016). Doll studies as racial assessments: A historical look at racial attitudes and school desegregation. In M. Patte & J. Sutterby (Eds.) *Celebrating 40 years of play research: Connecting our past, present, and future. Play and culture studies, 13,* pp. 19–38. Lanham, MD: Hamilton Books.

Killerman, S. (2017). *A guide to gender: The social justice advocates handbook, 2nd edition*. Austin, TX: Impetus Books.

Kollmayer, M., Schultes, M., Schober, B., Hodosi, T., & Spiel, C. (2018). Parents' judgements about the desirability of toys for their children: Associations with gender role attitudes, gender-typing of toys, and demographics. *Sex roles, 79* (5–6), 329–41. doi:10.1007/s11199-017-0882-4

Kurtz-Costes, B., DeFreitas, S., Halle, T., & Kinlow, R. (2011). Gender and racial favouritism in Black and White preschool girls. *British journal of developmental psychology, 29,* 270–87. doi:10.1111/j.2044-835X.2010.02018.x

Levin, D., & Kilbourne, J. (2008). *So sexy so soon: The new sexualized childhood and what parents can do to protect their kids*. New York, NY: Ballentine Books.

Limbé Dolls. (2013, July 27). A modest Muslim girl [Blog post]. Retrieved fromhttps://limbedolls.blogspot.com/2013/07/a-modest-muslim-girl.html

Malcom, N., & Sheahan, N. (2018). From *William's doll to Jacob's new dress*: Depiction of gender non-conforming boys in children's picture books from 1972 to 2014. *Journal of homosexuality, 66* (7), 914–36.https://doi-org.hbweb.lib.utsa.edu/10.1080/00918369.2018.1484635

Meyers, L. (2006). Dangerous dolls? *Monitor, 37*(8), 39.

Nelson, A. (2011). Gendered toy play as mediated action. *Psychologyical science and education. 2,* 71–77.

Nesbitt, A., Sabiston, C., de Jonge, M., Solomon-Krakus, S., & Welsh, T. (2019). Barbie's new look: Exploring cognitive body representations among female children and adolescents. *PLoS ONE 14* (6), e0218315 https://doi.org/10.1371/journal. pone.0218315.

Peck, E. (2017, March 3). Barbie's surprising comeback has everything to do with race: How diversity saved Mattel's iconic doll. *Huffington Post* Retrieved from https://www.huffpost.com/entry/barbie-diversity_n_58b5debde4b060480e0c7aa2

Rand, E. (1995). *Barbie's queer accessories*. Durham, NC: Duke University Press.

Schwarz, M. (2006). Native American Barbie: The marketing of Euro-American desires. *American studies, 46,* (3/4), 295–326.

Sherman, A., Zurbriggen, E. (2014). "Boys can be anything": Effects on Barbie play on girls career cognitions. *Sex Roles, 70*: 195–208. doi 10.1007/s11199-014-0347-y

Spinal Cord Team. (2019). Mattel is releasing first Wheelchair Barbie in 22 years. On line at https://www.spinalcord.com/blog/mattel-is-launching-its-first-wheelchair-barbie-in-22-years

Steinberg, S. (1997). The bitch who has everything. In S. Steinberg & J. Kincheloe (Eds.) *Kinderculture: The corporate construction of childhood,* pp. 207–18. Boulder, CO: Westview Press.

Stern, S. (1998). *Barbie nation: An unauthorized tour*. United States: El Rio Productions.

Stone, T. (2010). *The good, the bad, the Barbie: A doll's history and her impact on us*. New York: Viking.

Toffoletti, K. (2007). *Cyborg feminism, popular culture and Barbie: The posthuman body dolls*. London: I. B. Tauris.

Walsh, T. (2005). Timeless toys: Classic toys and the playmakers who created them. Kansas City, MO: Andrews McMeel.

Weisgram, E., & Bruun, S. (2018). Predictors of gender-typed toy purchases by prospective parents and mothers: The roles of childhood experiences and gender attitudes. *Sex Roles, 79*,(5–6): 342–57.

Yaqin, A. (2007). Islamic Barbie: The politics of gender and performativity. *Fashion Theory, 11* (2/3), 173–88. doi:10.2752/136270407X202736

Zolotow, C. (1972). *William's doll*. New York: Harper & Row.

8

PUPPETS AND PUPPETRY

Olga S. Jarrett

The hand speaks to the brain as surely as the brain speaks to the hand. (p. 59)

The desire to learn is reshaped continuously as brain and hand vitalize one another, and the capacity to learn grows continuously as we fashion our own personal laboratory for making things. (p. 295)
—Frank R. Wilson, *The Hand* (1998)

Puppets are inanimate objects that are animated for an audience by the hands of the humans who populate them (Baird, 1973). According to Jim Henson's daughter, Cheryl, "A puppet is an object that appears to be alive when manipulated by the human hand" (cited in Smith, 2019, p. 27). Puppets need hands. Neurologist Frank Wilson, author of *The Hand*, draws connections between hand manipulations and brain development and includes a chapter on marionettes (1998). In contrast to many children's toys and play equipment featured in this book, puppets are toys that did not start out as toys. Puppets are an art form and puppetry is a method of theatrical production long used by adults before becoming a children's activity.

Following are the many types of puppets: marionettes (string puppets), glove puppets (hand puppets without mouths that open), hand puppets (whose mouths move hence referred to here as hand/mouth puppets), finger puppets, ventriloquist dolls, rod puppets with the rods operated from either above or below, Japanese-style Bunraku puppets operated by two to three visible puppeteers, and shadow puppets (Bell, 2000/ 2005; Blumenthal, 2005; Currell, 1999). Aside from Bunraku puppets, all of these can be children's toys. There are also toy theaters, especially popular during Victorian times (Neff, 2011) but still available as cardboard cutouts that can be moved by rods to tell stories (for example the story of Peter Pan, by Tierney, 1983), finger puppet board books (e.g., *Curious George Pat-a-cake!* by Rey, 2011), flat puppets (two- dimensional images glued to craft sticks) (Smith, 2019), body puppets manipulated by the puppeteer from inside a costume (Sinclair, 1995), and over-life-size puppets such as those used for Macy's Thanksgiving Day parade.

The difference between puppets and some other toys is rather fuzzy. What about automata, jack-in the boxes, pop-up puppets that emerge from cones, and jumping jack toys, which children can move by pulling a string or moving a crank? What about flannel board figures moved around by a narrator (Exner, 2005)? Are they puppets? Perhaps. More likely to be considered puppetry are stop action techniques such as used in the production of *Wallace and Gromit* and *Shaun the Sheep,* children's creation of videos using digital puppetry (Wohlwend, 2015), and creation of animated dioramas and anim-atronic storytelling (Bull, Schmidt-Crawford, McKenna, & Choon, 2017).

Children can move dolls and stuffed animals in a way that makes them seem to come alive. Very young children often use their toys that way. Dolls get fed. They get put to bed. They interact with other dolls. However, puppets are generally manipulated for an audience, a peer, a parent, a teacher, or classmates. Puppets are generally not alive unless they are being animated by someone's hand.

Vetere and Vetere (2017) outline a framework for developmentally appropriate use of puppets with children. During birth to age two, they suggest that caregivers verbalize with babies using brightly colored puppets, giving the child "an infusion of rich language while promoting focus and attention" (Vetere & Vetere, 2017, p. 26) and promoting positive interactions between caregiver and child. From ages two to four, they recommend puppets be used in expressing the imagination characteristic of children at this age. Children speak for puppets, speak to puppets, act out favorite stories, and interact with other children and adults through puppets. Among four-to-six-year-olds, puppets are likely to be used for drama. Children this age can act out stories and use props with both peers and adults as their audiences. From age seven and above, children can develop formal puppet plays, creating their own puppets and writing their own narratives.

HISTORY OF PUPPETRY

Puppetry has a very long history in many parts of the world as one of the oldest forms of entertainment. However, early puppets were most likely considered sacred objects rather than toys. The forerunners of puppets may have been fertility dolls carved by the Cro-Magnon between 30,000 and 21,000 BCE, and Middle Eastern figurines with moving parts are thought to be 4,000 to 5,000 years old (Blumenthal, 2005). The first record of a performing puppet comes from the Nile Valley about 600 years before Tutankhamen.

Puppets were used for fertility rights in Greece (5,000 BCE, and by 300 BCE they were used at a theater at the Acropolis (Blumenthal, 2005). Puppetry was popular in the Roman circuses; but after the fall of the Roman Empire, such entertainment ended and puppeteers then wandered around Europe with their shows (Currell, 1975). In India 4,000 years ago, there was a religious taboo for people to impersonate other people, so it is likely that puppets existed before humans in their theater productions (Currell, 1999).

Traditional shadow puppets, carved from skins and operated by rods on their backs, are either left as silhouettes or are scraped so thin as to be translucent and colored with dyes or paints. In China, shadow puppets date back over 1,000 years and marionettes were used in the eight-century CE. Southeast Asia had its own ancient shadow puppet tradition (Blumenthal, 2005). Shadow puppets in Turkey date back to the fourteenth century and feature Karagöz and Hacivat, two popular, somewhat vulgar, and definitely satirical characters from the Ottoman capital of Bursa (Turkish Cultural Foundation, n.d.). Shadow puppets spread from Turkey to Greece where they are still popular today (Currell, 1975). Glove puppets of similar vulgar and satirical character spread through Europe becoming Pulcinello, Kasperl, and Petrushka in various countries and evolving into Punch and Judy in England (Bell, 2005). While glove puppets entertained the masses at carnivals and street parties, marionette operas, including one composed by Haydn, attracted other audiences.

In precolonial times, Africans had their own ancient puppet traditions using glove and body puppets for religious ceremonies, fertility rights, or social functions. Puppetry at least 700 years has been documented (Blumenthal, 2005). In the Americas, a pre-Columbian bas-relief found in Guatemala shows a man using a glove puppet and jointed burial figures in found in Mexico resemble puppets ready to help the dead in the afterlife. More recently, Native Americans from the Andes to Alaska have used puppets in ceremonies, including corn planting (Blumenthal, 2005).

In America, puppetry was imported by European immigrants and particularly flourished in the early twentieth century by itinerant puppet theaters and the formation of Little Theaters. It was kept alive during the depression by the Works Progress Administration (WPA), which supported hundreds of puppeteers who performed in many genres for adults and gradually more for children (Bell, 2005). Although various types of puppets, especially marionettes and glove puppets have long been available in toy shops, much of the current popularity of puppets as toys is an outgrowth of television programming. Early TV shows included the *Howdy Doody Show* (1947–1960), featuring Buffalo Bob Smith and Howdy Doody, a talking 11-stringed marionette. Howdy Doody marionettes and ventriloquist dummies can still be purchased.

Popular TV shows in the 1950s also included ventriloquism acts with Edger Bergen and his dummies, Charlie McCarthy and Mortimer Snurd, as well as Paul Winchell with

Jerry Mahony, a popular toy at the time. Other popular TV shows used glove and hand puppets. *Kukla, Fran, and Ollie* (1947–1957) featured Fran Allison (human) conversing with Kukla, a glove puppet, and Ollie, a hand/mouth puppet. Both were designed and performed by Burt Tillstrom, mentor to later TV puppet personalities, Shari Lewis and Jim Henson. Tillstrom did not want Kukla and Ollie to become toys, so he refused to release copyrights for toy production. However Shari Lewis's puppet, Lambchop, one of the stars of her TV show (1960–1963 and 1992–1997) is still available for purchase (MeTV Staff, 2017)

Two other popular children's programs featuring glove puppets were *Captain Kangaroo* (1955-1992) and *Mr. Rogers' Neighborhood* (1967–2001, plus reruns). On Captain Kangaroo's show, talkative Mr. Moose interacted frequently with taciturn Mr. Bunny Rabbit and was joined from time to time by other puppets. Puppeteer Kevin Cash worked with Captain Kangaroo before becoming Elmo on *Sesame Street* (Marks, 2011). *Mr. Rogers Neighborhood* was populated by many puppets including King Friday, Queen Sara Saturday, Lady Elaine Fairchilde, Henrietta Pussycat, and Daniel Striped Tiger, performed by Fred Rogers himself (Neville, 2018; *Mister Rogers Neighborhood*, n.d.). Occasionally, vintage puppets from this show can be found online.

The TV programs that most popularized hand/mouth puppets and made them available commercially were *Sesame Street* and *The Muppet Show*. Jim Henson designed and populated hand/mouth puppets whose arms were controlled by rods. He also invented ways in which his Muppets (a term combining marionette and puppet) interacted with humans without being on a puppet stage. Puppets like Kukla and Ollie interacted with Fran from their stage, and Fran became the primary audience. Without a stage, the Muppets appear to be interacting directly with the children and adults who enjoy watching with them (Underwood, 2009). This close interaction made the Muppets seem alive. Jim Henson and Kermit the Frog got up close and personal at the opening of the Center for Puppetry Arts in Atlanta in 1978.

Many of the Muppets on *Sesame Street* have become popular children's puppets, including Ernie and Burt, Big Bird, Elmo, Cookie Monster, and Oscar the Grouch. Although the latter two might have some negative though endearing characteristics, the Muppets in general, especially Elmo, represent caring and inclusiveness (Marks, 2011).

PUPPETS AVAILABLE FOR PURCHASE

Finger Puppets

The simplest and cheapest puppets are finger puppets. There seem to be four primary types of finger puppets: (a) sets of soft plastic characters, often from TV programs such as *Paw Patrol*, (b) soft cloth or crocheted figures of story characters, (c) realistic small birds and mammals from Folkmani, and (d) Magnetic Personalities, refrigerator magnet puppets of famous men and women including political leaders, artists, musicians, and authors for play and display.

Muppets

Many popular puppets currently for sale are based on the Muppet model. With soft heads and large mouths, they encourage children to puppet-talk with one another. Many companies make puppets, more than can be discussed here. Two companies making a large variety of hand/mouth puppets are Silly Puppets and Melissa and Doug. Silly Puppets sells hand puppets, marionettes, ventriloquist puppets, and large hand/ mouth puppets with legs that can be disconnected when performing at a hand puppet stage. Some include a rod for moving one of the arms. They feature children of different ethnicities and people in various jobs as well as biblical characters for puppet presentations of bible stories. Most seem designed for performances, being a bit large for early childhood classroom or home play.

Other Puppet Types

Melissa and Doug puppets tend to be smaller and more manageable for small hands and include glove puppets of animals and community workers as well as hand/mouth puppets, sometimes with rods for hand movement. Some of their hand puppets feature community workers such as police officers, firefighters, and surgeons, and many puppets could be used for storytelling by children in the classroom. Some of the most realistic animal puppets, including dogs, birds, turtles, frogs, sea creatures, and insects, are made by Folkmanis. Most of them have mouths that move, though not exaggerated large mouths.

Children can play with a Folkmanis skunk puppet after hearing a story that Curious George was sprayed by a skunk he mistook for a kitty. This puppet allows mouth movement with one hand while a finger of the other hand can raise its tail through a finger hole under the tail. Watch out! The Folkmanis puppets are realistically stuffed so they look like stuffed animals when not in action as puppets. Although Folkmanis produces nonrealistic puppets as well, their animal puppets are so realistic they could be used in classrooms to introduce science lessons.

Marionettes

Professional marionettes have many strings that control head movements, the back, the arms and hands, and the legs. These strings can easily become tangled, resulting in a lot of frustration. However, simple five string marionettes of figures like Pinocchio, clowns, or Chinese New Year lion puppets can give children the experience of using marionettes without too much hassle. Shadow puppets from China and Turkey can be purchased on the internet and used in teaching world history, culture, and geography. Toy theaters are available as booklets made of card stock to be cut out and assembled. These booklets include specific stories that can be acted out by pasting "characters" on sticks to use as rods for moving characters. Toy theaters are appropriate for older children who can read instructions and cut carefully.

Puppet stages for use of glove or hand/mouth puppets can be found in education supply catalogues for child care centers and Kindergartens. Stages establish a place in the classroom designed for puppet play and can stimulate puppet use. However, stages are not necessary. Children can interact directly with their audience or crouch behind a couch or a table lying on its side. Stages/theaters can also be created cheaply from large boxes.

Puppet Creation

In comparison to other toys that are almost always purchased, all types of puppets can either be purchased or made by a child or adult from junk materials. For example, a glove puppet can be made from a PediaSure bottle, a pom-pom, puffy fabric paint, and scraps of cloth. The thumb goes in one arm, two fingers reach into the head, and the other two fingers go in the other arm. There are many books with ideas for creating puppets, especially hand/mouth puppets. *Dressing the Naked Hand* (2015) by White, Pulham, and Blankenship includes instructions on making professional-looking hand puppets from cloth and scraps. The book includes a DVD and instructions on stage design and showmanship. *Puppet Mania!* (2004) by John Kennedy gives instructions for making hand and rod puppets from a variety of objects such as stuffed animals, paper plates, cloth scraps, bananas, photographs, and spoons. These ideas could be used at home, at school, or during summer programs and could result in imaginative puppet shows.

A book, *The Muppets Make Puppets!* (1994), by Cheryl Henson and the Muppet Workshop includes a wide variety of puppets, marionettes, glove puppets, hand/mouth puppets, and rod puppets made of junk materials including socks, spoons, cups, and spools and provides lessons in character building through hand movements and puppet voices. For adults and older children, *The Complete Book of Marionettes* (1948/1976) by Mabel and Les Beaton seems to be the classic on marionette creation and the production of marionette shows. Toy theaters can be produced simply in shoe boxes where characters can pop up on sticks (Exner, 2005). Or characters can be moved around by magnets underneath "the stage" because of paper clips on the feet of card stock characters (Palestrant, 1951).

Using Puppets in the Classroom

Puppets can be enjoyed similarly by boys and girls, though gender differences are seen among children in therapy, with more boys than girls choosing scary and aggressive puppets (Tilbrook, Dwyer, Reid-Searl, & Parson, 2017). In terms of age differences, young children interact with classmates and adults through puppets, while older children, including high school and college students, design their own puppets and put on sophisticated puppet plays (Wall, White, & Philpott, (1965). Professional puppeteers, as role models, come in all ethnicities, ages, and genders.

Several books include curricula on using puppets in early childhood education, arts education, and drama. In *Early Childhood Education* (Hunt & Renfro, 1982), the authors state that teachers can demonstrate puppet use during group time. Children can then make finger puppets, glove puppets, rod puppets, and flat puppets using easily available items such as paper plates, socks, and small paper bags. Flat puppets, drawings or cutouts glued to popsicle sticks are used for story telling by the children. The authors discuss the many ways simple puppets can be used in the classroom in story-telling and in classroom management and also recommend the use of commercial *Sesame Street* puppets, such as Kermit, Ernie and Bert, Cookie Monster, and the Count, whose familiarity tends to encourage involvement and cooperation.

Artist, puppeteer, and educator Karen Konnerth (2017), has developed a project-based puppet curriculum with ideas for kindergarten through fifth grade. Besides a helpful section on making puppets with instructions and templates, Konnerth includes activities on how humans express emotions, leading to how hands can express emotions and personality through puppets.

Puppetry in Education and Therapy: Unlocking Soors to the Mind and Heart (Bernier & O'Hare, 2005) is a worthwhile read for educators. It does not include how to make puppets or lesson plans. However, each chapter illustrates how a teacher or therapist used puppetry in their work, with many inspiring examples.

Highly recommended for teachers and teacher educators is *Puppetry in the Theatre and Arts Education* (2019) by Johanna Smith. Through her work in classrooms and summer programs, she has developed puppetry curricula for her teacher education course that includes the processes of puppetry, as a form of art and drama as well as how-to's of making and manipulating puppets. She claims, "if someone asks you why you use puppets in your classroom, you can tell them you are engaging sensorimotor processing to develop human cognition, generating knowledge from within an authentic milieu, developing empathy in your students, fostering brain development through the use of the hand, and integrating the arts in a transdisciplinary curriculum" (p. 7). Her lessons on making and manipulating puppets to show emotion and personality are appropriate for all students.

Purchased puppets are very popular both in the home and in the classroom. They can promote interaction and imagination, and can be employed effectively in the school curriculum. However, helping children make their own puppets can spark creativity and teach children more about construction and production.

Using Puppets in Healing

"Puppet therapy, puppetry in therapy, and therapeutic puppetry are terms which usually refer to the use of puppetry as an aid in physical or emotional healing, remediation, or rehabilitation" (Bernier, 2005, p. 109). Puppets are used to dispel prejudices against others; for example, against children with disabilities (Dunst, 2012) or people with mental illness (Pitre, Stewart, Adams, Bedard, & Landry, 2007), thereby helping to prevent discrimination. Also, puppetry is used to heal individuals and groups who suffer from physical or emotional problems. Children who will not talk with a therapist will often talk with a puppet (Kohler, 2018). According to clinical child psychologist Beth Onufrak (2012), children bond with puppets, especially puppets who seem to have the same problems they have, and children sometimes give therapeutic advice to the puppet.

The power of puppet therapy has been useful in getting trauma victims to speak (Mullen, 2018), preparing hospitalized children for frightening procedures (Greff, Sokolova & Slonimskaya (2018), coping with chronic illness (Nutting, 2015), and improving communication skills of special needs children (Carver, 2018). Puppetry has also had healing power with juvenile offenders (Telnova, 2018), prisoners (Astles, 2012), refugees in immigration detention (Smith, 2016), children at a Marine base coping with deployment of parents during the war with Iraq (Martin, 2003), and patients with dementia (Marshall, 2013). With the latter, puppets can promote communication between patients with dementia and family members even if the patient does not remember them.

Sesame Street is now fifty years old and as a tool for fighting poverty has long dealt with serious issues confronting children. Several new Muppets, including Lily, who is homeless (Ostrofsky, 2018); Julia who has autism (Kaplan-Mayer, 2019); and Karli, who is in foster care (Gonzalez, 2019) help children with special challenges feel less alone, and the encouragement provided by *Sesame Street* friends provide positive role models for other children. *Sesame Street*, with support from the International Rescue Committee, has programs around the world that have tackled difficult issues faced by children in refugee camps (Peters, 2016).

Other puppet companies have recently produced programs for adults and/or children to highlight issues faced by Palestinian refugee families who have inhabited a refugee camp in Lebanon for the past 70 years (Aftab, 2018), families who have tried to escape from Syria by ship (Varzi, 2016), refugees in England (Karmi, 2017), and challenges faced by Asian immigrants in the Unites States (Combs, 2017). The UN Refugee Agency has supported the use of puppetry to help refugee children heal from the trauma they have experienced.

Using Puppets in Research

Use of puppets has been popular in research in at least two ways: (a) examining the effect of puppets in teaching and (b) using puppets as aids in the research itself. An example of the first is a control group experiment on use of puppets in teaching that found that use of puppets increased student attention and involvement (Wallace & Mishina, 2004). Examples of the second involved telling children what two puppets preferred and then asking children which puppet is most like them (Dorie, Transby, Van Cleave, Cardella, & Svarovsky, 2013; Epstein, Stevens, McKeever, Baruchel, and Jones, 2007). In another example, children watched a puppet show on bullying and then were asked which puppet they wish to play with (the excluded puppet or the puppet that excluded others) (Hwang, Marrus, Irvin, & Markson, 2017).

CONCLUSION

Puppets are unusually powerful toys. In terms of *affordances*, a term coined by J. J. Gibson, to describe the links among perception, action, and meaning (Gibson, 1988), puppets provide many affordances that can provide benefits across the life span. They can stimulate language, promote empathy, encourage creativity in the arts, drama, and music, strengthen hand/brain connections (Wilson, 1998), and help to heal the body and mind. And they don't have to be expensive.

NOTES

Many thanks to Yanique Leonard, Collections Manager of the Center for Puppetry Arts, Atlanta, GA, for her assistance in locating some of the references in this chapter. She was extremely helpful. No product endorsements are intended.

REFERENCES

Aftab, K. (2018). The power of puppets brings the story of life in Lebanon's Burj el-Barajneh refugee camp to the world. (https://www.thenational.ae/arts-culture/film/the-power-of-puppets-brings-the-story-of-life-in-lebanon-s-burj-el-barajneh-refugee-camp-to-the-world-1.781233)

Astles, C. (2012). Puppetry for development. In L. Kroflin (Ed.), *The power of the puppet* (pp. 63–78). Zagreb; Croatian Centre of UNIMA.

Baird, B. (1973). *The art of the puppet*. New York, NY: Bonanza Books.

Beaton, M., & Beaton, K, (1948, 1976). *The complete book of marionettes*. Mineola, NY: Dover Publications.

Bell, J. (2005). *Strings, hands, shadows: A modern puppet history*. Detroit, MI: The Detroit Institute of Arts.

Bernier, M., & O'Hare, J. (Eds.) (2005). *Puppetry in education and therapy: Unlocking doors to the mind and heart*. Bloomington, IN: Authorhouse.

Blumenthal, E. (2005). *Puppetry: A world history*. New York, NY: Abrams.

Bull, G., Schmidt-Crawford, D. A., McKenna, M. C., & Cohoon, J. (2017). Storymaking: Combining making and storytelling in a school makerspace. *Theory into Practice, 54*, 271–81.

Carver, M. (2018). Access and therapy for the special needs (language) learner. *Puppetry International, 43*, 15–18.

Combs, M. (2017). Real immigrant stories, told with puppets. (https://www.mprnews.org/story/2017/08/04/mu-performing-arts-immigrant-stories)

Currell, D. (1975). *The complete book of puppetry*. Boston, MA: Plays, Inc.

Currell, D. (1999). *Puppets and puppet theatre*. Ramsbury, Marlborough, Wiltshire: Crownood Press.

Dorie, B. L., Tranby, Z., Van Cleave, S. K., Cardella, M., & Svarovsky, G. N. (2013). Using puppets to elicit talk during interviews on engineering with young children. School of Engineering Educaion Graduate Student Series. Paper 54. http://docs.lib.purdue.edu/enegs/54

Dunst, C. J. (2012). Effects of puppetry on elementary students' knowledge of and attitudes toward individuals with disabilities. *International Electronic Journal of Elementary Education, 4*(3), 451–57.

Epstein, I., Stevens, B., McKeever, P., Baruchel, S., & Jones, H. (2008). Using puppetry to elicit children's talk for research. *Nursing Inquiry, 15*(1), 49–56.

Exner, C. R. (2005). Practical Puppetry A-Z: A guide for librarians and teachers. Jefferson, NC: McFarland & Company.

Gibson, E. J. (1988). Exploratory behavior in the development of perceiving acting and the acquiring of knowledge. *Annual Review of Psychology, 39*, 1–41

Gonzalez, S. (2019). Meet Karli, the new "Sesame Street" muppet in foster care. https://www.cnn.com/2019/05/20/entertainment/sesame-street-karli-foster-care/index.html)

Greff, A., Sokolova, L., & Slonimskaya, E. (2018). Doctor-Puppet: An approach to psychological aid for sick children. *Puppetry International, 43*, 30–33.

Henson, C. & the Muppet Workshop. (1994). *The muppets make puppets! How to create and operate over 35 great puppets using stuff from around your house*. New York , NY: Workman Publishing.

Hunt, T., & Renfro, N. (1982). *Puppetry in Early Childhood Education*. Austin, TX: Nancy Renfro Studios

Hwang, H. G., Marrus, N., Irvin, K., & Markson, L. (2017). Three-year-old children detect social exclusion in third-party interactions. *Journal of Cognition and Development, 18*(5), 515–29.

Kaplan-Mayer, G. (2019). Why it's important that Julia, a muppet with autism, has a family. WHYY Philly Parenting. https://whyy.org/articles/why-its-important-that-julia-a-muppet-with-autism-has-a-family/

Karmi, O. (2017). British theatre company brings joy to refugee children. UN Refugee Agency (UNHCR). https://www.unhcr.org/news/stories/2017/2/58aff9e97/british-theatre-company-brings-joy-to-refugee-children.html

Kohler, M. (2017, Fall/Winter). Puppets for education and therapy. *Puppetry International, 24*, 22–23.

Konnerth, K. (2017). The sophisticated sock: Project based learning through puppetry. New Orleans, LA: PaperSunPress.

Kennedy, J. (2004). *Puppet mania!* Cincinnati, OH: North Light Books.

Marks, C. (2011). *Being Elmo: A puppeteer's journal*. DVD by Docuramafilms.

Marshall, K. (2013). *Puppetry in dementia care: Connecting through creativity and joy*. Jessica Kingsley Publishers. Philadelphia, PA.

Martin, H. (2003). Child's play has serious theme. *Los Angeles Times*, March 27, B12.

MeTV Staff (2017). 12 primetime television shows that featured puppets: From Kukla and Ollie to ALF and beyond. MeTV Atlanta. https://www.metv.com/lists/12-primetime-television-shows-that-featured-puppets

Mister Rogers' Neighborhood (nd). The puppets. https://www.misterrogers.org/puppets/

Mullen, K. (2018). "And then they spoke:" Trauma in Haiti, *Puppetry International, 43,* 4–7.

Neff, A. S. (2011). Toy theatre then and now. *Puppetry International, 29,* 4–7.

Neville, M. (2018). *Won't you be my neighbor?* DVD by Universal Pictures Home Entertainment.

Nutting, R. (2015). The strength of children externalizing the effects of chronic illness through narrative puppetry. *Journal of Family Psychotherapy, 26*(1), 9–14.

Onufrak, B. (2012). A child in mind: Reflections of a child psychologist on the preschool & primary years. https://achildinmind.wordpress.com/2012/09/24/you-can-tell-me-anything-im-a-puppet-why-play-therapy-works/

Ostrofsky, K. A. (2018). "Sesame Street" steps up to the biggest issues kids face. https://www.cnn.com/2018/12/14/opinions/sesame-street-homeless-muppet-mission-ostrofsky/index.html

Palestrant, S. (1951). Toymaking: 200 projects for fun and profit, New York, NY: Homecrafts.

Peters, A. (2016). Sesame Street is coming to refugee camps: When it comes to preschool education, Muppets speak a universal language. https://www.fastcompany.com/3060294/sesame-street-is-coming-to-refugee-camps

Pitre, N., Stewart, S., Adams, S., Bedard, T., & Landry, S. (2007). The use of puppets with elementary school children in reducing stigmatizing attitudes towards mental illness. *Journal of Mental Health, 16*(3), 415–29.

Rey, H. A. (2011). *Curious George Pat-a-Cake!* Boston, MA: Houghton Mifflin Harcourt.

Sinclair, A. (1995). The puppetry handbook. Castlemaine, VIC, Australia

Smith, J. (2019). Puppetry in theatre and arts education: Head, hands and heart. New York, NY: Methuen Drama.

Smith, M. (2016). Thinking through the puppet, inside and outside immigration detention. *Applied Theatre Research, 4*(2), 147–59.

Telnova, L. (2018). Adolescents in conflict with the law. *Puppetry International, 43,* 12–14.

Tierney, T. (1983). Cut & assemble a Peter Pan toy theater (models & toys) by Tom Tierney (1983-08-01). Mineola, NY. Dover Publications.

Tilbrook, A., Dwyer, T., Reid-Searl, K., & Parson, J. A. (2017). A review of the literature—The use of interactive puppet simulation in nursing education and children's healthcare. *Nurse Education in Practice, 22,* 73–79.

Turkish Cultural Foundation (n.d.). Turkish shadow theatre—Karagöz and Hacivad. http://www.turkishculture.org/performing-arts/theatre/shadow-theatre/karagoz-and-hacivad-90.htm?type=1

Unterwood, B. (2009). How to become a Muppet; or The great Muppet paper. In J. C. Garlen & A. M. Graham (Eds.), *Kermit culture: Critical perspectives on Jim Henson's Muppets* (9-24). Jefferson, NC: McFarland & Company.

Varzi, C. M. (2016). Puppet show casts spotlight on refugee crisis. https://www.aljazeera.com/news/2016/04/puppet-show-casts-spotlight-refugee-crisis-160425132600389.html

Vetere, M. J. III & Vetere, M. T. (2017, Fall/Winter). Creative puppet drama: A developmental framework for learning. *Puppetry International, 42,* 24–27.

Wall, L. L., White, G. A., Philpott, A. R. (1965). *The puppet book: A practical guide to puppetry in schools, training colleges, and clubs,* compiled by members of the Educational Puppetry Association.

Wallace, A., Mishina, L. (2004). Relations between the use of puppetry in the classroom, student attention and student involvement. Brooklyn College, M. Martinez-Pons Professor. http://citeseerx.ist.psu.edu/viewdoc/download?doi=10.1.1.492.2545&rep=rep1&type=pdf

White, A., Pulham, M. H., & Blankenship, D. (2015). *Dressing the naked Hand: The world's greatest guide to making, staging, and performing with puppets.* Sanger, CA: Familius.

Wilson, F. R. (1998). *The hand: How its use shapes the brain, language, and human culture.* New York, NY: Vintage Books.

Wohlwend, K. E. (2015). One screen, many fingers: Young children's collaborative literacy play with digital puppetry apps and touchscreen technologies. *Theory into Practice, 54,* 154–162.

9

CLIMBING TOYS AND STRUCTURE

Doris Bergen

In both indoor and outdoor settings, play equipment that have been popular over many years are structures that provide opportunities for climbing, moving in space, sliding down, hanging on, and observing the world from various heights. These structures range from relatively low-level ones, such as climbing steps and low-enclosed platforms, to high and challenging ones, such as towers, slides, and hanging gliders. While they vary greatly in appearance and configuration, these structures have some common features that have made them popular playthings for children of many ages.

Depending on the configuration of certain structures, they require children to use a variety of physical and perceptual skills, including balancing, stretching, stepping, climbing, jumping, grabbing, sliding, hanging, crawling, observing, and estimating spatial distances. They also initially call upon emotional strengths such as accepting challenges, performing carefully, conquering spatial incongruities, and gaining confidence about one's abilities to meet challenges.

Although appropriately designed types of climbing toys are of interest to most young children and particularly to those of preschool and elementary age, certain versions of these toys continue to be of interest to adolescents and to a certain segment of adults. For example, similar physical and perceptual skills to those required for young children's use and conquest are needed by adults for scaling climbing walls, using hanging gliders, crawling through tunnels, and engaging in many other activities that call upon mature versions of these skills.

TYPICAL TYPES OF CLIMBING TOYS AND STRUCTURES

Steps

These toys consist of a series of steps up, a platform, and a set of steps down. They are primarily designed for young children who are practicing fundamental motor movements. More complicated step series often are included in larger, more elaborate climbing structures as well, and they have many configurations.

Ladders

Ladders are a feature of most traditionally designed slides. Typically, a ladder must be climbed to reach the slide. There also are structures that consist of a ladder up, a ladder down, and a parallel ladder between the two. To navigate this type of ladder requires both dexterity and strength. Ladders are also usually part of more elaborate climbing and sliding structures. Some climbing structures primarily consist of ladder rungs in igloo-shape designs. Ladders may be made of wood, metal, or various other materials, such as rope.

Climbing Walls

These versions of ladders do not lead to other structural features but consist only of a series of climbing levels, often made of ropes, wooden or metal bars, or other materials.

Crawling Structures

These consist of tubes of various sizes and shapes that form "tunnels" that must be traversed. These range from short, on-the-ground configurations to sets of higher elaborate series included as part of elaborate climbing structures.

Hanging Structures

These are usually combined with some type of ladder or other climbing structure but require traversing space either by hanging on to a moving device as it moves or swinging the body across handles of various types.

Bouncing Structures

Inflated "houses" that require climbing, balancing, and bouncing are also of interest to children. These often are commercially available but not part of typical playgrounds. Trampolines, which involve bouncing on stretched canvas on a frame, also require both climbing and balancing skills.

Sliding Poles

These are often included in climbing structures for older-age children and they require climbing to a height and then grasping the pole to slide down. Good motor coordination and spatial skills are needed to be successful at this activity.

Tree Stumps, Hills, and Other Natural Materials

Children have always found natural materials in the environment to use for physical activity. Some of these structures are now deliberately provided in contemporary "natural" playgrounds that focus on the use of many natural structures rather than human-made climbing structures. For example, natural playgrounds have hills that can be climbed and rolled down and tree structures that can be climbed.

Other Structures

Depending on human ingenuity, many newer versions of such structures have been designed specifically for physically active play. Some of them have value and meet safety standards but others may have design flaws or be structurally unsound. For example, plastic "bounce houses" are available in some areas, but reports of winds destroying such structures have also been common.

Other Jumping or Physically Active Toys

Some types of toys also provide jumping or climbing experiences, but they are not actual structures. For example, jump ropes have been popular for many years and these can be used for individual child jumping, as a toy for group jumping activities (e.g., double dutch, circle jumping), and for many other competitive games. Hula hoops also provide physical skill development, as children swing their bodies to keep the hoops in motion.

FEATURES OF CLIMBING TOYS AND STRUCTURES

While the specific perceptual, motor, and emotional qualities vary across these structures, all of them require children to use their present level of these skills to be successful in manipulating and conquering the challenges of these structures. The low-climbing steps that are often present in infant/toddler settings encourage very young children to test and improve their crawling, stepping, and balancing abilities while the tall climbing structures, slides, and tunnels that engage older children test their coordination of motor skills, spatial judgement, energy levels, and persistence.

Specific types of play structures encourage a differentiated range of such skills that fit the perceptual and motor skills of young children. Physical skill development typically goes through four stages: reflex movements, rudimentary movements, fundamental movements, and sport-related movements (see Kaplan-Sanoff, Brewster, Stillwell, & Bergen, 1988). During infancy to about age two, children are learning rudimentary movements such as sitting, walking, running, and climbing. By about age two and continuing until about age seven, they are perfecting these various physical actions and gaining a range of fundamental skills. At about age seven, many children begin to specialize their movement patterns in relation to various physical sports on which they may focus. This pattern can be seen in the types of climbing toys and other constructions they enjoy at various ages.

AGE LEVEL DIFFERENCES

Infancy

Infants and toddlers enjoy opportunities to practice basic motor and perceptual skills (rudimentary movements) and often the ordinary home environment (e.g., sofas, tables, stairs) provide enough challenge. For example, infants use table edges or handles to grab on to and pull up to gain that first higher view of the world. Specific structures for young children are also very common, however. Low-climbing steps are often present in infant/toddler settings and these encourage very young children to test and improve their crawling, stepping, and balancing abilities. Specific climbing structures designed for infants include moderate inclines for crawling up and down, and wide, short steps that are study enough to crawl up or step on solidly and these often also have crawl spaces or platforms that are enclosed for safety.

Infants of about age seven or eight months begin to use such structures and over the course of their first year they may practice these emerging skills over and over on such materials. By toddler age, climbing structures that engage toddlers in crawling or walking up a series of steps and looking down from a deck (a "high" place), which is well enclosed and usually about three-to-four-feet high, are of great interest. Toddlers also enjoy openings to crawl into and out of, and they love "rocking" boats that give vestibular challenge. These structures may be made from wood or plastic materials, but the wood ones are usually sturdier.

Preschool

Preschool-age children, who are beginning to hone their fundamental movements, enjoy climbing structures that involve stepping up to greater heights and standing (and stomping) on "high" enclosed platforms. By this age, these structures also have a slide from the platform and children often can be observed "making the circle" of activities (stepping/climbing up, standing on top, sliding down to the floor, and then stepping/climbing, etc.). This is especially fun for them if other children are engaged in the same activity. Preschoolers also like to "hide" in structures and have parents, teachers, or other children look for them and finding them after they have looked in many unusual places!

Preschoolers also begin to challenge their vestibular motion skills with constructions such as rocking "boats" that they can operate with a friend, and, although some structures for infants have swings, these usually are more prominent in preschool constructions and twirling swings or going higher and higher also challenge these vestibular skills. Also, the addition of low level climbing bars on dome like structures or on ladderlike structures begin to be challenging and interesting to preschoolers.

Kindergarten

By kindergarten/elementary school age, children still enjoy the challenge of these types of physical and perceptual actions but, as they gain more competence in their fundamental movement skills, they enjoy structures that are larger and require perfection of many of these motor and perceptual skills. The constructions may be either in the indoor "gym" or be outdoors on playgrounds. Climbers become very diverse (due to the ingenuity of the playground designers!), and some are better designed than others to be safe but also challenging.

There also are many types of slides in higher structures with longer spans, varied levels and platforms in climbing structures, bars or rope slings to climb or hang on, and series of such hanging features for traversing space. A more recent addition to children's construction toys are "rock climbing" walls, which may be in use in school gyms or outdoors. Trampolines, which allow jumping and bouncing, are also popular, and spinning equipment that tests vertigo are of great interest to elementary-age children.

Gallahue (1982) has noted that if children have not had access and time to practice such motor and perceptual skills, they will not become well-coordinated and efficient in movement and thus, will have difficulty learning more complex motor skills and sport-related movements.

Elementary Age

Children of older elementary age sometimes also have access to "zip lines," which are accessed by higher ladders and then provide a downward ride with the child hanging on to handles. At later elementary age, children continue to enjoy such constructions and test their skills on more challenging versions, and they are more likely to select certain types of skills that they prefer and abandon others. Because the children have reached the age of sports-related movement skills, there is more challenge in these constructions and many issues have been discussed about the safety of such equipment.

In school gyms, these activities are supervised but there is often minimal supervision on school playgrounds and little supervision at public playgrounds so there has been much debate about the safety of such equipment (Frost, 1992; Frost & Woods, 2015). Guidelines for safety of such equipment have been developed by the Consumer Products Commission (see Hudson, Olsen, Thompson, & Olsen, 2004).

Adolescence

By adolescent age, such toys are not in much demand, although adult versions of equipment that test these same skills are popular and they are often require excellence in sport-related skills, thus, differentiating children into those who perfect one set of climbing-related skills (e.g., rock climbing) and those who perfect another set of such skills (e.g., climbing ladders for zip-line actions).

GENDER DIFFERENCES

In past eras, there were major differences in whether only males or only females participated in play on certain types of structures. For example, more strenuous or daring climbing or hanging activities were thought to be more appropriate for boys and activities that were less demanding or closer to home (e.g., jump rope) were encouraged for girls. In recent years, however, such differences have primarily disappeared, and the gender of the child is not usually a major factor in such play. There are, however, major differences in child personality that seem to affect which children find such activities of interest.

CHILDREN WITH SPECIAL NEEDS

A very important issue in relation to these types of play materials has been access problems for children with special needs, especially needs that involve physical (e.g., mobility, visual) or mental disabilities. Guidelines have been developed for making playgrounds with such structures accessible to these children (see Frost & Woods, 2015; Malkusak, Schappet, & Bruya, 2002). Suggestions include having wheelchair accessibility pathways, resilient surfacing, ways to access slides and crawl spaces, and sensory-rich materials. However, many climbing structures remain inaccessible to these children and more recent playground designers have stressed "natural" playground features be used rather than manufactured climbing-related structures.

AFFORDANCES OF CLIMBING TOYS AND STRUCTURES

The attraction of such playthings for all ages can be at least partially explained by consideration of the *affordances* they provide for all ages. These types of play materials can be examined by considering their *affordance* qualities, discussed by Eleanor Gibson (1969, 1997). Gibson has stated that affordances are perceived opportunities for action that various environmental features signal. Climbing structures are some of the most salient types of environmental features that signal physical actions to children (and very challenging versions also signal such actions to some adults!). Humans of all ages often like to test their skills on these types of structures by selecting ones that require skills that are slightly more difficult than those they already have mastered.

According to Carr (2000), there are three affordance factors that can be used to judge the effectiveness of various toys. These are *transparency, challenge*, and *accessibility. Transparency* refers to the ease of understanding the concepts inherent in the toy. That is, the toy affords options that the child can understand. Even very young children know almost immediately that steps and other structures of various levels are available for climbing. In fact, it is very difficult to prevent them from engaging in the physical actions that such structures afford. *Challenge* refers to what abilities are required (and perfected) for using the toy and, of course, the best challenge level is usually at the edge of the child's existing abilities. The challenge dimension thus increases the action possibilities rather than reducing action options.

Children's climbing toys and structures usually have affordances primarily related to the challenge and mastery of physical and perceptual skills. However, they also involve emotional skill development and present challenges that stretch children's abilities to take appropriate risks (e.g., going up higher), persevere in face of obstacles (e.g., trying over and over to make the higher perch), and show commitment to achieving a goal (e.g., not giving up until the higher level is gained). Thus, the affordance of challenge is very strong in these types of play materials. *Accessibility* refers to how convenient and available the toy is for children to use.

Because these climbing toys are usually study and somewhat complicated to set up, they are often readily present in the child's environment and so they immediately afford action. Also, because most climbing structures are relatively large, they are often accessible in both indoor and outdoor play environments. If such structures were difficult to unpack, set up, or maintain, they would rarely be used as playthings.

Research on these types of play materials has explored both the developmental value of such structures and the various concerns related to safety and use of them. For example, in one study, conducted in Norway, the researcher indicated that preschool children intentionally sought risk in their play by going to the greater heights and using higher speeds of performance (Sandseter, 2009). She noted that the children seemed to balance risk-taking decisions by evaluating the potential positive and negative outcomes of such play and they adapted if they thought the risk was too great. In every research observation period there were children climbing, balancing and jumping down from heights, and, although some children were more likely to take risks, in general most of the children sought out challenges through this risky play. The researcher noted that staff members also had to evaluate how much risk-taking they would allow.

This issue of acceptable risk has also been discussed by Stevenson (2003) in a paper focused on preschool children. She points out that, although children need these physical challenges, attention to safety requirements have implications for children's ability to experience physical challenges. McWilliam and colleagues (2009) have discussed guidelines for physical activity for young children, including the types of activity children encounter on many structures, and they suggest that this activity should be part of "best practices."

Much research has focused on public and school playground climbing and this body of research has generally found that such play was "essential to physical or motor development" (Frost & Woods, 2015, p. 339). Thus, most researchers and writers have concluded that playgrounds that include climbing structures can have developmental benefits for children (Frost, Brown, Sutterby, & Thornton, 2004).

RESEARCH ON STRUCTURE-RELATED PLAY EXPERIENCES

As noted earlier, although structures that invite children to engage in challenging physical and perceptual activities are extremely popular with children of many ages, in an age of high child supervision and many structured lessons, these types of play may be less available to many children. In general, these activities are highly supervised, but they can be very valuable play experiences if the equipment is designed for safety as well as challenge. A study in the Netherlands that investigate how various play equipment influenced the physical activity of two- and three-year-olds (Gubbels, Van Kahn, & Jansen, 2012) found that the children's outdoor physical activity levels were positively associated with the availability of portable jumping equipment and a structured track but negatively associated with slides, swings, and sandboxes.

Another study done in Australia (Coleman & Dyment, 2013) found that, although childcare providers stated that physical activities in play were desirable, the safety policies and practices of centers limited their facilitation of young children's physical activities on structures. In a US intervention study, however, researchers found that introducing portable active play equipment significantly increased three-to-five-year-old children's physical activity (Hannon & Brown, 2008).

Recently, research has been reported on rock climbing, a relatively new climbing activity for older children. Lower artificial rock climbing structures have been designed for these children and research on "bouldering," which involves continuous climbing on short distances off the ground or a floor surface, has been studied by Watts and Ostrowski (2014). They assessed children's oxygen uptake and energy expenditure during the rock-climbing activity and found that average and peak oxygen uptake values for children during both sustained and interval climbing were similar to that which has been reported for experienced adult climbers. The researchers note that whether the intensities they found would be sustainable for longer periods and lead to greater physical fitness among children is presently unknown.

RECOMMENDATIONS

There are many issues presently regarding the value and safety of various climbing toys and structures. However, in general this type of toy has been very much valued by children as well as by adults concerned about children's overall development. While these structures do require closer adult supervision that many other types of toys do not, and the safety of each type should be judged in relation to the children's age levels and skills, they also provide some very essential types of learning and thus should continue to be an important type of toy for children of all ages.

REFERENCES

Carr, M. (2000). Technological affordance, social practice and learning narratives in an early childhood setting. *International Journal of Technology and Design Education*, 10(1), 61–80.

Coleman, B., & Dyment, J. E. (2013). Factors that limit and enable preschool-aged children's physical activity on child care centre playgrounds. https://doi.org/10.1177/1476718X12456250

Frost, J. L. (1992). Playground guidelines for school systems. (Report No. PS-021-083). Austin: University of Texas at Austin (ERIC Document Reproduction Service No. ED353-082.

Frost, J. L., Brown, P. S., Sutterby, J. A., & Thornton, C. D. (2004). The developmental benefits of playgrounds. *Childhood Education, 81*(1), 42.

Frost, J. L., & Woods, I. C. (2015). Perspectives on play and playgrounds. In Fromberg, D. P. & Bergen, D. (Eds.) *Play from birth to twelve: Contexts, perspectives, and meanings* (3rd. ed). New York, NY: Routledge.

Gallahue, D. L. (1982). Understanding motor development in children. New York, NY: Wiley.

Gibson, E. J. (1969). *Principles of perceptual learning and development.* New York, NY: Appleton-Century-Crofts.

Gibson, E. J. (1997). An ecological psychologist's prolegomena for perceptual development: A functional approach. In C. Dent-Read & P. Zukow-Goldring (Eds.). *Evolving explanation of development: Ecological approaches to organism-environment systems* (pp. 23–54). Washington, DC: American Psychological Association.

Gubbels, J. S., Van Kann, D. H., & Jansen, M. W. (2012). Play equipment, physical activity opportunities, and children's activity levels at childcare. *Journal of environmental and public health.* https://doi.org/10.1155/2012/326520

Hannon, J. C., & Brown, B. B. (2008). Increasing preschoolers' physical activity intensities: an activity-friendly preschool playground intervention. *Preventive medicine, 46*(6), 532–36.

Hudson, S., Olsen, H., Thompson, D., & Olsen, M. S. (2004). Do the CPSC guidelines make a difference? *Today's Playground, 496,* 13–17.

Kaplan-Sanoff, M., Brewster, A., Stillwell, J., & Bergen, D. (1988). In Bergen, D. (Ed.), *Play as a medium for learning and development: A handbook of theory and practice* (pp. 137–62). Portsmouth, NH: Heinemann.

Malkusak, T., Schappet, J., & Bruya, L. (2002). Turning accessible playgrounds into fully integrated playgrounds: Just add a little essence. *Parks & Recreation, 37*(4), 66–70.

McWilliams, C., Ball, S. C. Benjamin, S. E., Hales, D., Vaughn, A., & Ward, O. S. (2009). Best practice guidelines for physical activity at childcare. *Pediatrics.*org/egi/doi/10.1542/peds 2009-0952

Sandseter, E. B. H. (2009). Risky play and risk management in Norwegian preschools—A qualitative observational study. *Safety Science Monitor, 13*(1), 2.

Stevenson, A. (2003). Physical risk-taking! Dangerous or endangered. *Early Years, 25*(1), 35–43.

Watts, P. B., & Ostrowski, M. L. (2014). Oxygen uptake and energy expenditure for children during rock climbing activity. *Pediatric exercise science, 26*(1), 49–55.

10

AIRPLANES, KITES, ROCKETS/DRONES

Jason T. Abbitt

The category of flying toys is extensive and includes simple toys from hand-held pro-pellers on a stick to complex remote-controlled aircraft that are capable of high-speed and high-altitude flight. The focus of this chapter is on the flying apparatuses that meet specific criteria associated with toys, such as: (1) commonly used for play, (2) relatively inexpensive. Within this more narrowly defined subset of flying toys are kites, airplanes, model rockets, and drones.

It is important to note, however, that for nearly all forms of these flying toys, there are versions that would be considered toys and used for children's play as well as more advanced versions used by hobbyist, enthusiasts, or in some cases, professionals. This wide range of complexity, both in design and function of the toys, provides a unique context in which to consider the affordances of the toy versions of these apparatuses through the lens of human development. Given this wide range of different versions of these toys, the forms of play can be explored from childhood to adolescence and adult-hood.

TYPICAL TYPES OF "FLYING" TOYS

Although many of these toys have characteristics that allow them to fly (or be flown) away from the ground, toys that also fit into this category are usually replica objects of planes or other flying objects that must be propelled (i.e., "flown" by the young child). Toys that are capable of flight are often such toys as gliders, kites, remote controlled airplanes, and so forth, whereas flying toys that are replicas of flying machines, such as airplanes and helicopters, do not fly, per se, but rather are used by children in pretend-play as if they were capable of flight.

Kites

There are multiple ways to consider the features of toys within this category, but kites would undoubtedly be among the least complicated flying toys in terms of design and function. In its most basic form, a kite is constructed from a sheet material (paper, plastic, fabric, etc.) attached to a lightweight frame of wood or plastic to form a shape that can be held aloft by the air movement in opposition to a tether to the individual flying the kite. Although there are various shapes of kites (diamond, delta wing, box, sled, etc.), the basic principle for the flight of these toys remains the same: the wind changes that shape of the kite material to become an airfoil, thus producing lift via differences in pressure above and below the kite.

A person flying a kite will have varying degrees of control and maneuverability of the kite, depending on the kite design. Simple kite designs will be limited to side-to-side maneuvering and altitudes controlled by the length of kite string, whereas more advanced designs (e.g., "stunt kites") may use multiple control tethers and allow for a higher degree of maneuverability.

Rockets

In terms of complexity, model rockets are similar to kites in that the design of model rockets can be quite simple. A basic form of model rocket will feature a hollow body tube with a pointed nose cone on one end and as few as three tail fins on the other end. Toy rockets may be powered by forces such as air or water that are used under pressure to provide rocket propulsion, while other forms of model rockets use solid-fuel rocket engines. Air- or water-powered toy rockets are typically either ready-made toys, such as Stomp Rockets (https://www.stomprocket.com), or homemade versions constructed from materials such as plastic bottles to which a child would affix a nose cone and tail fins. Model rocket kits, however, typically feature a hollow body tube in which a smaller tube is mounted to hold a solid-fuel rocket engine as well as a parachute or other device to allow for recovery and reuse.

A model rocket engine is a single-use cardboard-body tube that is manufactured with a clay nozzle on one end, propulsion from a propellant such as black powder, and a charge to eject the parachute and nose cone at the end of the flight. More advanced designs of model rockets may feature multiple stages, each with a separate body tube, recovery parachute, and rocket engine. For these model rockets, a first-stage engine is ignited to launch the rocket and then eject the first-stage body tube while also igniting the next stage, thereby propelling the model higher.

Launching a model rocket is quite simple and requires little more than connecting a small launch igniter to the solid-fuel rocket engine, attaching the rocket to the mast of a launch pad, and then pressing a firing button an electronic launch controller. The complexity in model rockets, however, is found in the assembly of the rocket and preparation for launch. Model rockets are most commonly available as kits that require assembly, commonly involving gluing tail fins, assembling the body tube with the engine mount, and packing the recovery parachute in a manner that will successfully deploy.

Children who would be assembling and launching a model rocket will, of course, usually wish to use decorative materials to customize the appearance of the model rocket before flight. Then, in preparation for the first flight, the flyer selects an appropriate launch site where the rocket can be launched and recovered successfully while also considering factors such as wind direction and other weather conditions. Although the simple launching of the rocket is a simple process, assembly and preparation for launch can be more complex.

Airplanes

Perhaps among the first types of flying toys that a child would play with at an early age are toy airplanes. Although the toy airplanes that infants and toddlers may play with do not actually have the capability to fly, these models of flying toys may range from those with exaggerated, cartoonish airplane designs to more realistic replica toys such as those that are found in nearly all airport gift shops that resemble real-world aircraft in great detail.

Toy airplanes that are capable of flight are found in a wide range of designs, some of which share design aspects with kites and model rockets and are controlled by the user to a small degree. A paper airplane is the simplest form of a glider-type toy airplane and can be made from almost any form of paper folded into a shape capable a remaining aloft following an initial launch by the user. Although there are also gliders made from materials ranging from balsa wood or other lightweight materials, the same basic form of play happens with any form of glider, paper or otherwise: launch the airplane by throwing or other manual propulsion, watch it fly, then repeat, perhaps after making minor adjustments or repairs.

More advanced versions of toy airplanes follow a different pattern of play, primarily because they add features such as a propulsion system or remote-control systems. These systems, however, can be very simple such as a propeller driven by a twisted rubber band and remote control by a tether string held by the user. They can also be more complex as well with propellers driven by either electric- or gas-powered motors and radio frequency remote controls for maneuvering. Nevertheless, this wide range of toy airplanes can appeal to a broad range of users through different stages of human development.

Drones

Another type of flying toy is what is commonly referred to as a "drone." The term *drone* is used to refer to a very wide array of machines ranging from simple toys to large-scale military aircraft, thus it is important to draw a distinction between the drone toys from other forms of drones. Perhaps the key distinguishing feature is the capability for autonomous flight. This feature is absent in most toy versions but is present in professional, commercial, or military drones that are also referred to as unmanned aerial vehicles (UAVs).

Most drones that are considered toys and used in forms of play are those that are directly controlled by a person using either a remote-control device or other forms of manual control. These toy drones may be designed with cameras and also are capable of flying either fast or to higher altitudes, but the user typically remains in control of a drone that would be considered a toy. The most common physical shape of a toy drone is the quad-copter design in which four propellers are attached to arms extending from a central body that houses the power supply and control systems for the aircraft.

Unlike other types of flying toys, all drones are powered, typically from a rechargeable battery, and a software-based control system translates user remote control input into changes in the rotational speed or pitch of each of the propellers to control speed and direction. In addition, many drones, even those that are considered toys, feature a camera system that can be viewed via a live streaming connection to smartphone or tablet display device attached to the remote control.

TOY INTERACTION WITH PLAYERS

All of these flying toys involve a form of user control, yet the manner in which a user, typically a child at play, will control the flying toy is quite different. Kites and gliders, for example, feature direct forms of control in which a physical movement by the child produces a direct effect of the flight of the toy. In this manner, the forms of play may revolve around the distance or altitude a glider or kite will fly or perhaps aerobatics that the toy is designed to do during flight, thus leading to repetitive trials of the flight with an increasing degree of difficulty.

By contrast to the relatively simple interaction with kites and gliders, user interaction with remote-controlled flying toys, including both airplanes and drones, requires fine motor skills as well as perceptual skills. These toys can be used either alone or in social groups and forms of play may feature increasing challenges (e.g., flying higher, faster, etc.) or competitive play such as racing or maneuverability challenges.

Recent advances in technology leading to lightweight cameras and wireless communications have led to a rather distinct change in user interaction with remotely controlled flying toys. First-person view (FPV) cameras are common on drones and provide the user a live "cockpit" view from the aircraft on a video display using a smartphone or tablet. These technological advancements have led to a unique change in the behavior of the remote pilot. Prior to the use of cameras, the user had no choice but to focus attention on the aircraft in flight. With an FPV camera, however, a user's focus may shift between visually tracking the aircraft and viewing the live FPV camera view on the video display.

An additional technological advancement that impacts user interaction are the software systems that are more prominent in drone toys that seeks to prevent what is perhaps the most devastating events when playing with flying toys: the crash. For most forms of flying toys, the ability of the user to successfully fly the toy will determine the likelihood of a crash. The technology available on drones, however, includes software that maintains a level flight position or automatically land the drone. More advanced versions of the toys may also feature sensors that automatically avoid other objects in order to prevent a crash.

TYPICAL ENVIRONMENTS

Flying toys are used in both indoor and outdoor environments, but a specific version of each toy may be suitable for use in each setting. For example, a small version of a quad copter drone, known as a nano-drone, can fit in the palm of most hands may have many similar features to larger-scale versions but is most suitable for indoor use. The limitations of the small form-factor drones to maintain flight in even slight winds will diminish their use outdoors. Conversely, larger-scale drones that are designed for outdoor flight often will have more powerful propeller motors and quick maneuverability, thus making their use indoors a significant safety concern.

In addition to drones that are intended for indoor use, there are flying toys of all types designed to be used in indoor spaces of varying sizes with many intended for larger spaces. Indoor kites are typically designed for use in larger indoor spaces where the flier can move slowly around a space in order to fly a wing/airfoil kite that is designed to maintain lift with minimal air movement. Rockets that are intended for indoor use typically use a small amount of air pressure or other substance like a seltzer tablet to develop the necessary propulsion for indoor flight. Indoor airplane toys are predominantly gliders, although some battery-powered indoor airplanes are designed to be tethered to a fixed point (e.g., ceiling) and fly a circular pattern.

The flying toys that are designed for outdoor use will typically feature a more durable, and potentially larger scale design. The design of outdoor kites can be from simple to extravagant and complex with seemingly endless variations on the basic design of frame, fabric, and string. Similarly, rockets are more commonly used outside where toy versions of rockets may be propelled by compressed air or solid-fuel rocket engines. The use of rockets in outdoor spaces will typically include recovery parachutes, streamers, or propellers that are deployed to slow the descent of the rocket and allow it to be used again and again. Outdoor airplane toys may be larger-scale gliders or more advanced battery- or gas-powered aircraft. Outdoor drones feature larger power sources and may also include global positioning system sensors and transmitters in order to locate the drone during longer-distance flights.

AGE LEVEL DIFFERENCES

Infant/Toddler Age

In general, "pretend" flying toys can be used by children according to the requirements of the toys with respect to the child's cognitive and physical development. Infants and toddlers at a sensorimotor stage of development are generally unable to play with most types of flying toys that require fine motor skills and may interact with flying toys simply as objects, rather than as an object capable of flight. For this reason, many flying toys with moving parts would be inappropriate around infants and toddlers due to safety concerns related to either the mechanical structure or small parts as the child. A young child who sees a drone taking flight, for example, is likely to want to touch or grab the aircraft without perceiving the danger of a moving propeller.

Preschool Age

Children at a preoperational stage of development (two to seven years old) during which they begin to be capable of symbolic thought and pretend play, flying toys such as kites and gliders will be increasingly appealing. Early in this stage, however, children are more likely to wish to hold a flying toy rather than releasing or launching it for flight. Children in this stage of cognitive development would begin to see a balsa wood glider as an actual airplane, recognize the similarity in design, and may call each of these items an "airplane." It is also common for children at this development to engage in pretend play with any object that resembles a flying machine and to hold the objects as high as they can reach while moving around a play space making audible noises to mimic the real-world machine.

As children progress through this stage, they may also begin to test the flight capabilities of toys, including both toy that can actually fly as well as those that cannot. In this manner, a child might throw any airplane-shaped toy with the full expectation it would fly, regardless of its actual flight capabilities. For toys such as balsa wood gliders, the actual flight of the toy will reinforce this behavior and often lead to repeated flight play in this manner. For replica toys that cannot fly, this behavior may be diminished when a test flight is unsuccessful, possibly resulting in a damage or broken toy.

Because children at the preoperational stage are most often limited to thinking about one aspect of a situation at a time, their response to seeing a kite fly, for example, may be that the kite is going away from them without understanding that the kite can be retrieved. As such, the simple activity of flying a kite may be perceived as a loss of their toy instead of its intended use. In general, at this early stage in development, the common forms of play with flying toys are more likely to be physical or manipulative play as the child may be highly curious and interested in flying toys, but this interest may be sparked more by the toys objective characteristics (color, shape, sound, etc.) rather than it's the ability of the object to fly.

Elementary Age

Children who are at the concrete operational stage (approximately seven to eleven years) will reach important milestones related to organized, rational, and logical thinking that influence the manner in which they may interact with flying toys. This organized thought, however, is centered on a physical object and children in this stage will begin to understand cause and effect and also to understand object permanence. Each form of flying toys (kites, rockets, airplanes, and drones) may be appropriate at this stage of development, but perhaps not all versions of these toys. For example, a small nano-drone used for indoor flight would be appropriate and allow a child to learn to fundamental operations. A more complex drone capable of flight beyond a user's line-of-sight would be less appropriate.

The important consideration for flying toys for children at this stage of development is the affordances of the toy for repetitive use and also tolerance for errors or mishaps. A paper airplane, for example, can be used repeatedly and adjusted, repaired, or rebuilt with little effort and cost. Similarly, a model rocket can be launched, recovered, and reused repeatedly within a fairly rapid succession. In both cases, the child's understanding of how the aircraft works can quickly evolve in a short time and maintain engagement in the activity. The repetitive play with flying toys by children at this stage may include solitary, associative, parallel, or cooperative play, perhaps including competitive games between children.

Adolescence

The formal operational stage of cognitive development follows the concrete operational stage and typically begins at approximately the age of twelve and extends into adulthood. A key milestone for adolescents in this stage is the capability for abstract thought. In other words, adolescents begin to be able to manipulate ideas about things that are not physically present. With respect to flying toys, someone entering the formal operational stage of development could mentally design a paper airplane and consider ways to design it prior to actually folding a piece of paper.

Because of this ability to think beyond one's physical environment, adolescents to adults are more adept at flying more advanced flying toys including the more advanced versions of these toys such as "stunt kites," multistage model rockets, and remote-controlled outdoor airplanes and drones. It is also during this stage that adolescents and young adults may develop an affinity for a particular form of flying toy that leads to different forms of play through participation in hobbyist or enthusiast groups that exist for all forms of flying toys.

Such groups vary widely in organization and could be loosely structured "club" that has an established place and time to fly an aircraft such as a model rocket and to interact with others who share a common interest. More organized groups also exist, such as drone racing leagues that may have regularly scheduled competitive events for members. In addition to the real-world affinity groups, online groups can be found in which members interact via social media services or websites.

GENDER DIFFERENCES

When considering the possible gender differences in play, toy airplanes have been examined most often with respect to gender roles. In general, gender differences in the play with flying toys are likely to emerge as children grow older with more boys preferring flying toys than girls. These differences, however, may be influenced by the design of the flying toy with respect to colors, shape, and similarity to other toys. Additionally, some differences exist between what adults and children perceive as masculine or feminine toys.

Miller (1987) examined a gender classification method and found that model airplanes were classified as a masculine toy by adults. Similarly, Bradbard (1985) compared toy requests for Christmas gifts and found that boys (ages one to six) requested more toy vehicles, including airplanes, than girls. However, Cherney and Dempsey (2010) observed three- to five-year-old children in a playroom setting that included a pink and purple toy airplane and found that the children classified the toy as feminine. Although both boys and girls played with the toy and that this play was likely to be a more complex than with other toys, the authors noted that the color of the toy was a factor in the gender classification.

ADAPTATIONS FOR CHILDREN WITH SPECIAL NEEDS

Within this category of flying toys, there exists multiple versions or adaptations to the design in order to be used by persons with a physical disability. More simplified flying toys such as kites have been adapted to allow a user to steer a kite with a set of tethers and control bar while the kite is anchored to a fixed tether, thus allowing a person with limited arm strength or mobility, for example, to maneuver the kite with less strength required.

For high-tech flying toys, innovations in technology such as head-mounted video displays with motion sensors and augmented reality features have been developed that allow a user to control a drone using a goggle-like device in which the FPV camera feed is displayed inside the head-mounted display and the aircraft is controlled via head movements instead of a more typical remote control device that would require more developed fine motor skills. In addition to modifications to the control device for a drone, the flight control software that is embedded in a drone can be adjusted to better suit the abilities of the user.

Although the design modifications may improve the accessibility of these types of toys, some activities involving flying toys also have a positive impact on other special needs such as autism. Founded in 2012, Talking Autism to the Sky (tatts.org) was created through a crowdfunded initiative to establish small- and large-group activities for children with autism to participate in order to foster social and employment skills ("Taking Autism to the Sky, Inc," n.d.). This volunteer-run organization provides group-based activities including building drones, flight planning, and flying drones in simulated real-world scenarios such as a search-and-rescue mission using drones. The activities are intended to allow individuals with autism to interact with each other and the volunteer staff in order to enhance social and communication skills while also developing knowledge and skills for flying drones that have real-world applications.

Educational Settings and Clubs

In addition to the many informal environments for play involving kites, rockets, airplanes and drones, each of these toys is commonly part of a formal or informal educational curriculum. For example, the 4-H youth development program has created curriculum and design competitions for rocketry (https://ohio4h.org/rocketry) and drones ("Youth to Explore Drones in World's Largest Youth-Led Engineering Design Challenge: 4-H," n.d.). Similarly, the National Aeronautics and Space Administration (NASA) has published many resources related to rocketry for use in K–12 and informal learning environments such as the Rocket Educators Guide (National Aeronautics and Space Administration, 2011) and Rocketry Lesson Plans (NASA, 2013).

Also, each of the flying toys discussed in this chapter is also the focus of affinity and competitive groups. Both formal and informal groups are commonly found that focus on different forms of play with flying toys and often hold public events for beginners in order to learn about a wide range of flying toys. Participation in such an affinity group may appeal to children who have an interest in a certain type of aircraft.

RECOMMENDATIONS

When selecting flying toys for children at any stage of development, there are important considerations that should be made in order to enable a safe, positive, and engaging experience. It is tempting to simply select flying toys for children based on age and complexity of operation of the toy. Thus, kites and gliders are for younger children and rockets and drones are for older children. Due to the wide range of different forms of these flying toys, however, the selection of flying toys is more nuanced. As such, it is recommended that toys be selected based on (1) the potential safety issues with the toy, (2) how the child will perceive and understand the toy, and (3) the motor and cognitive skills that are required to operate the toy.

The old adage that "everything that goes up must come down" certainly applies to flying toys and highlights the potential safety concerns as any of these toys can quickly become a falling or out-of-control projectile. Even the most simply flying toy can be a safety hazard, although some of the safety issues are matters of common sense. For example, a solid fuel rocket motor is not something that an infant or toddler should use under any circumstances, and an outdoor remote-controlled drone cannot be success-fully operated by a child who has not yet developed fine motor skills.

There are, however, safety issues that may be less obvious to many individuals that should also be considered. Although a quad-copter drone may seem like a reasonable toy for indoor play, many drone propellers are constructed of durable materials with sharp edges rotating at a high speed. When these toys are operated around younger children, who may simply view the devices as an object that makes an interesting sound, it would be reasonable to expect a toddler to move towards a drone as is starts to fly and try to catch it, thus possibly leading to injury from even low-powered drones.

In order to consider the safety issues as well as the engagement of the child, it is helpful to consider how the child perceives the device. For younger children who are more likely to most strongly respond to the visual or auditory characteristics of the toy, those toys that have few moving parts are more appropriate and allow the child to engage in physical, manipulative, or imaginative play with the toy will lead to a positive and engaging experience. As a child continues to develop, however, they are more likely to perceive other characteristics of flying toys and understand the fundamental concepts of flight and operation of the toy in a meaningful way. As such, when the perception of the toy by the child matches the intended use, safety concerns are minimized and the potential for engagement is optimized.

Finally, those selection flying toys for a child at a particular stage of development should carefully consider the cognitive and motor skills required to successfully operate the toy. For the successful flight of a relatively simple toy such as a balsa-wood glider, for example, a child will need to be capable of developing gross motor skills of arm movement as well as fine motor skills of releasing the glider from the child's hand. Because learning to fly these simple toys will require trial and error, the child must also be cognitively able to understand cause and effect.

To successfully operate more complex toys such as remotely controlled airplanes or drones, however, fine motor skills are necessary for construction, such as in the case of rockets, and operation, in the case of drones. Cognitively, however, the child must be able to think abstractly in order to predict how a movement of remote-control device will change the direction of a drone, or how to select a launch and recovery site for a model rocket. For both motor and cognitive skills, it may not be necessary that a child has fully mastered the skills that are required to operate a flying toy, but that those skills are emerging so that the activity of play may strengthen these skills through practice and repetition.

REFERENCES

Bradbard, M. R. (1985). Sex differences in adults' gifts and children's Toy Requests at Christmas. *Psychological Reports*, *56* (3), 969–70.

Cherney, I. D., & Dempsey, J. (2010). Young children's classification, stereotyping and play behaviour for gender neutral and ambiguous toys. *Educational Psychology Review*, *30*(6), 651–69.

Miller, C. (1987). Qualitative differences among gender-stereotyped toys: implications for cognitive and social development in girls and boys. *Sex Roles*, *16*, 473–87.

NASA. (2013, June 17). Rocketry lesson plans. Retrieved July 31, 2019, from http://www.nasa.gov/audience/foreducators/rocketry/lessonplans/index.html

National Aeronautics and Space Administration. (2011). *Rockets Educator Guide*. Retrieved from https://www.nasa.gov/sites/default/files/atoms/files/rockets_guide.pdf

Taking Autism to the Sky, Inc. (n.d.). Retrieved July 18, 2019, from Taking Autism to the Sky, Inc. website: http://tatts.org/

Youth to explore drones in world's largest youth-led engineering design challenge: 4-H. (n.d.). Retrieved July 31, 2019, from 4-H website: https://4-h.org/media/youth-to-explore-drones-in-worlds-largest-youth-led-engineering-design-challenge

11

BALLS, BEANBAGS, FRISBEES

Darrel R. Davis

Most adults have fond memories of play that involved throwing, including tossing rocks in the yard or playing a ball game. Playing outdoors with friends was typically a high-energy activity and throwing was usually an integral part of that activity. Although life is constantly changing, some things remain the same. Children still enjoy playing outdoors with friends and they still love to throw. In childhood, fun is synonymous with *motion*, and balls, beanbags, and Frisbees are toys for which *motion* is the primary purpose. These toys have entertained generations of children and they remain favorites despite the invention of more sophisticated toy options. Perhaps it is the uniformity of a sphere, the simplicity of a disc, or the flexibility of a polyhedron filled with beans, but these toys remain among the most common toys for children across the world. They are ubiquitous and, especially in the case of balls, they transcend time and culture.

THE SIGNIFICANCE OF THROWING TOYS

Balls, beanbags, and Frisbees are common throwing toys that might appear to be insignificant, but that is a limited view of these toys, given their role in enhancing the basic human act of throwing. Halverson (1940) broadly defined throwing as the "long-distance placement of objects" (p. 84) and noted the large number of anatomical systems involved in this complex action. Throwing is important because, along with language, it is a developmental skill that allows the individual to indirectly manipulate the environment (Burton & Rogerson, 2003). Throwing toys, like balls, allow the child to operate on the environment and receive feedback which, in turn, guides future action. The developmental implications of throwing are significant as the child acts to reconcile personal goals with the rules and requirements of the environment.

Throwing is also a basic human evolutionary tendency. Humans are the only species that can throw objects with speed and accuracy. Young (2009) stated that "Humans are the most adept throwers in the animal kingdom" (p. 19) and argued that the complexity of the throwing motion observed before the age of two, is beyond what an infant could quickly learn at that age. This shifts the act of throwing from learning and practice into the evolutionary and biological context. Further evidence for the evolutionary basis of throwing is found in fossil records which suggest that changes in the structure of the human hand resulted in specific adaptations for throwing and this provided an evolutionary advantage for the survival of the species (Lombardo & Deaner, 2018).

Finally, throwing of objects is an important developmental aspect of childhood that allows the expression of an evolutionary tendency. However, although almost any toy can be (and is) thrown, balls, beanbags, and Frisbees are particularly important because of the actions they afford. Affordance, according to Gibson (1969), refers to the information that the environment provides to the individual. Norman (1988) expanded the idea of affordances and suggested that objects have features that can be perceived, and objects suggest the ways in which interaction with them can occur. The real and perceived affordances of toys are important because each toy signals the ways that a child can play with it and this information can guide the child's actions. Thus, as Noman (2013) noted, "Balls are for throwing or bouncing" (p. 13) and that is exactly what a child does given the affordances of a ball.

CHARACTERISTICS OF THE TOYS

Balls

Balls are typically spherical objects, but they can also be oval, like the balls used in American football and rugby. Ball-like objects can be found in nature as a smooth round stone in a shallow creek or as the orange fruit picked from a tree. Balls can be crudely fashioned using backyard clay, or a perfect high-gloss ball can be made by following the Dorodango techniques, the Japanese art of molding earth and water into shiny spheres.

The significance of the ball is illustrated by Jaffe (2006) who declared, "A ball is the simplest and most basic toy" (p. 20). It has tremendous developmental implications for children and is an excellent toy at early ages. It is "the most important plaything of childhood" (Froebel, 1897, p. 32) and consequently, it is the first Froebel gift—a toy intended to allow the child to use direct senses to acquire knowledge about properties and motion in general. For adults, the ball is the basis for many games and sports that dominate life. And for all ages between birth and death, the ball is ever present and ubiquitous in play.

Modern balls come in many variations, most of which are designed around their potential uses. For example, cricket and billiards require balls that are internally solid, while soccer and tennis require balls that are filled with air. In a similar vein, there are a variety of materials used on the exterior of balls. In many cases, the selected material has specific properties that significantly impact the physical characteristics of the ball and its subsequent motion. For example, materials can be selected to minimize bounce (futsal ball) and friction (bowling ball), provide a certain texture or "feel" (basketball ball), or the material may be selected to help develop children tactile senses and motor skills (sensory ball for babies and toddlers). In all cases, the interior and exterior construction of the ball affects the characteristics of the ball.

Although balls are sometimes synonymous with organized games or sports, they are used for a variety of activities spanning educational props to teach physics concepts, ball pits to jump in, or even a simple game of marbles. Balls have limitless uses and they can entertain both the young and the old. A large beach ball can entertain a toddler at the beach for a long time and it can also entertain seniors playing chair volleyball. For those interested in higher levels of activity, dodgeball and wiffle ball are fun options. The ball used in dodgeball does not typically sting when it makes contact with the skin, and the wiffle ball is perforate to increase the unpredictability of its motion when thrown or hit with a bat.

Beanbags

Beanbags are small, sealed bags that are primarily used to play games such as cornhole or footbag (hacky sack). They come in various shapes, although they typically have a square base. Beanbags can be filled with various materials, such as dried corn kernels, beans, or synthetic materials. Similarly, the outer cover can be a variety of natural or synthetic materials. The components and overall construction of a beanbag is dependent on its intended use. Beanbags are not designed to be thrown great distances, but a heavier fill material could be selected to allow the beanbag to be thrown farther. Similarly, an outer cover might be selected to increase or decrease fiction and thereby altering the distance the beanbag travels upon contact with a surface.

Beanbags can be used for simple activities like juggling or in competitive sports like professional cornhole. They can also be used as therapeutic devices, where they are used to help individuals relax or concentrate. However, they are primarily associated with recreational games like the beanbag circle passing game, which is fun for any age group. In this game, players form a circle and pass a beanbag from one person to the next. The fun increases when multiple beanbags are introduced to the circle and some beanbags are passed in the opposite direction.

Frisbees

The Frisbee, a registered trademark for a flying disc, is a disc with an airfoil shape that is stable when thrown. Frisbees are typically between eight and twelve inches in diameter. They can be thrown great distances because of the lift generated by the disc's airfoil shape coupled with the stability that results from its spinning motion. This means that the disc must be constructed from a resilient material, typically plastic, that can withstand the impact forces present when the disc is caught or when it hits an object or the ground. Frisbees are typically solid, but there are many variations with internal spaces, an extreme example being the flying ring, which has a completely open center.

Frisbees are used in competitive games such as disc golf, disc dog, and ultimate, and they are also used recreationally by children and adults. Frisbees have other interesting uses, including a tool to shovel sand, a water container for pets, and a target to hit with a ball.

ORIGINS AND TRANSFORMATION OVER TIME

Balls, beanbags, and Frisbees have differing histories, but they are all very much a part of the fabric of play. The ball is a very interesting toy that has had a special place in life throughout human history. Evidence of balls as play objects has been seen in early civilizations, including the Egyptians, Romans, and Mayans (Fraser, 1966). Archeologists have unearthed small marbles and suggested that Egyptian children were playing marble games before 4000 BC. Similarly, Central America is the home to hundreds of ball courts that were used by the Mayans and other Mesoamerican civilizations for competitive and recreational ball games. Although the materials used to construct a ball has changed, the basic interactions of throwing, hitting, and kicking are still prevalent today. Children still play marbles, and ball games are still an important part of life.

The origin of the beanbag is unclear, with stories attributing its invention to Native Americans, Germans, Chinese, and individuals from the United States. In all likelihood, the origin of the beanbag is tied to games similar to cornhole and as the games increased in popularity, so did the use of the beanbag. Unlike beanbags, the Frisbee has a much clearer lineage. Humans have always thrown disc-like objects, beginning with disc-shaped rocks, for survival purposes and for play. But, the Frisbee did not exist until the 1950s when Wham-O trademarked and marketed a disc based on the ideas and designs of Walter Frederick Morrison. The Frisbee was subsequently marketed for use in both competitive and recreational games and it quickly became a favorite of young people at the time.

Balls, beanbags, and Frisbees have changed over time due to technological advances. New materials have improved the durability of balls and beanbags, while new disc designs have resulted in lighter and faster discs, such as the Aerobie flying ring, which was used to set several distance records for flying discs. However, technological change has not been limited to material and design. New features have been added to the basic shapes of the toys to enhance usability and entertainment. For example, radio frequency identification (RFID) sensors can be incorporated into beanbags to allow for electronic scoring of cornhole games. This reduces some of the discrepancies in scoring that sometimes leads to arguments. Similarly, flying discs can now be purchased with bluetooth speakers and light-emitting diode (LED) lights integrated into the disc itself.

Playing music through the speakers adds a layer of enjoyment to the toy, while LEDs have the practical value of making the disc easier to track in the air and easier to find after it has landed. Perhaps the most interesting technological change is in the area of interactivity. For example, Apple's Play Impossible Gameball uses advanced electronics to track the ball's motion (spin, speed, etc.) and it allows users to compete in various single or multiplayer games on their mobile devices. Although the Gameball incorporates significant electronic features, it still maintains the traditional functions of a ball, such as throwing, kicking, or rolling. Another example of an advanced ball is the Sphero Bolt, which is a programmable robot ball that can be controlled with a mobile device. The Sphero Bolt does not accommodate all the traditional functions of a ball like throwing because it is primarily focused on education and exploration. For both the Apple Play Impossible Gameball and the Sphero Bolt, the technological advances add value in terms of interactivity, but this may be at the cost of basic play with the toy. As Bergen and Davis (2011) discussed, there is a risk that the technologically-enhanced toy becomes the director of play, and thus reduces the generative and creative contributions of the child at play.

DEVELOPMENTAL IMPLICATIONS

The Relationship Between Age and Gender

There is a complex relationship between age and gender in terms of play with balls, beanbags, and Frisbees. There may be gender differences at infancy in terms of parental choices among the three toys, but there are clear gender differences at adolescence and adulthood as play preferences and activities diverge (Cherney & London, 2006). These differences may emerge due to social and cultural norms that define what acceptable play looks like and which toys are appropriate for each gender. Subtle differences in parental choices, for example choosing a princess-themed ball for an infant girl, might lay the groundwork for later play preferences. Thus, parental decisions might result in adolescent boys choosing organized sports as the preferred activity and girls choosing more sedentary activities like pretend play with dolls. These gender role stereotypes, particularly by parents (Eccles, Jacobs, & Harold, 1990), help to explain why the value of, and preference for, certain toys often differ by age and gender.

Individual differences in the level of physical activity might also help explain the overall decrease in play with toys like balls, beanbags, and Frisbees. Trost and colleagues (2002) found that physical activity rapidly declines with age, particularly at the elementary-school age level. Although the study found a gender component to the decrease in activity levels, age was the most important factor in the decline. Consequently, an age-based reduction in play with balls, beanbags, and Frisbees should be expected given the overall downward trend in physical activity. The parallel reduction in both overall physical activity and play with these toys may be due to the increasing play options available as children age. More options for nonphysical play, including television and video games, may contribute to the overall decline in physical activity, while more options for physical play, including organized sports, may contribute to a decline in overall play with balls, beanbags, and Frisbees.

The relationship between age and gender is also mediated by culture, which has a substantial effect on dimensions such the types of play available, time spent playing, and parental beliefs about play (Lillard, 2015). However, culture can change and in the United States there is currently an emphasis on increasing physical play opportunities for females, particularly in organized sports. This should have a net positive effect on the use of certain toys like balls.

Developmental Implications at Different Ages

Early Ages

There are clear differences in how balls, beanbags, and Frisbees are used during different ages and many of these differences are rooted in the affordances of each toy. For infants and toddlers, these toys help in the development of both gross and fine motor skills. For example, beanbags may be particularly useful for infants who need appropriate stimuli as they develop prehension. This is because a child between birth and three months of age can easily clutch a beanbag with a fist due to the suppleness and flexibility of the toy. From three to nine months, the child's reflexive grasping gives way to more purposeful reaching and grasping of the beanbag. It is during this time that haptic sensitivity emerges, so the texture and weight of the toy becomes even more important. Beyond nine months, bilateral coordination is established, and the child can manipulate the beanbag more precisely using a pincer grasp (see Adolph and Berger [2006]) for more on motor development).

Toddlers are stronger and more coordinated than younger infants. They have more advanced haptic perception and can manipulate objects with increasing ease. Toddlers can also throw objects with moderate coordination, thus a ball is a particularly interesting toy at this age. Not only does play with a ball improve timing and hand-eye coordination, but as Hewes (2014) noted, "the infant experiences a sense of agency, power and influence, simultaneously with unpredictability, uncertainty and lack of control of the movement of the ball. The result is fun" (p. 290). These contradictions add richness to a child's play with balls and provides ample opportunities for creativity and problem solving. Balls naturally provide dynamic feedback, which allows a child to practice important skills, such as making observations (ball bounces different height), forming hypotheses or predictions (ball will bounce higher on floor than bed), collecting data (bounce ball on floor and bed), and drawing conclusions (bouncing surface matters). Similarly, as symbolic thinking emerges, simple and versatile toys like balls become more important because they mirror natural or common objects. In this case, pretend play is enhanced when the ball becomes a pretend moon or when the child takes a bite from a pretend apple.

Elementary School Age

At elementary-school age, children have greater strength, endurance, and coordination. Toys like balls, beanbags, and Frisbees are still used, but the social aspects of play become increasingly important. At this age, play may be more structured around specific games, it may be more competitive in nature, and it is more likely to differ by gender. For example, friends might compete to see who can throw a Frisbee the farthest or make it return like a boomerang. At this age, developing affective characteristics like self-esteem and confidence are paramount given their relationship to later identity development (Erikson, 1963/1993). A simple game of Frisbee hot potato can be fun with friends or it can be aversive, and potentially destructive, if a player is always caught with the Frisbee (hot potato) when the timer ends.

Adolescence and Adulthood

Individuals reach maximum strength, endurance, and coordination somewhere in adolescence and adulthood and subsequently begin to see a decline in each at older ages. Adolescents and adults might play sports like lacrosse, or exercise and yoga using a Swiss ball. Similar to children at the elementary-school age, adolescents' and adults' use of toys like balls, beanbags, and Frisbees may center on the experiences derived via interactions with peers. For example, a ball and a Frisbee might only be interesting to a teen because they are used in handball or ultimate. Likewise, adults are more likely to be interested in the interactions with friends that result from playing cornhole, than they are to be interested in the beanbag itself. In both cases, membership in a group is important and it can have a great effect on the individual's identity development and subsequent expression of that identity (Erikson, 1963/1993). At this age, however, there may also be a well-developed intrinsic drive that motivates the use of a particular toy object. For example, a young rhythmic gymnast may be intrinsically motivated to perfect the throwing elements of her ball apparatus. In this case, the ball itself is the center of the experience.

ACCOMMODATIONS AND ACCESSIBILITY

There are a number of adaptations to balls, beanbags, and Frisbees that increase accessibility for individuals who need the accommodation. For example, the paralympic sport boccia (originally for athletes with cerebral palsy) is played with a ball that is soft enough for the athletes to grasp, but hard enough to roll for some distance on the court. General adaptations might focus on properties such as size and weight, which might make it easier for an individual with limited physical strength to, for example, play basketball. Where texture is important, focusing on the outer material of the toy makes sense. Thus, a beanbag with an appropriate outer material makes a game of cornhole more enjoyable for an individual with tactile sensitivity.

In many cases, adaptations to toys make them more accessible for everyone. For example, although a lighter or oversized ball makes volleyball accessible for those with limited strength or mobility, it also makes the game accessible for children. Similarly, paying attention to the color of a Frisbee makes access to disc golf more equitable for an individual with color blindness. However, the color might also make the Frisbee easier to find in the grass and that is useful to everyone.

Although adaptations to toys can make them more accessible to individuals with disabilities, special importance is given to toys that promote social behaviors. Kim et al. (2003) confirmed that social toys, like balls, promote social interaction for individuals with disabilities and this is important because social interaction is integrally linked to the development of many prosocial behaviors.

RESEARCH ON THROWING TOYS

There is a need for more research involving throwing toys like balls, beanbags, and Frisbees and the research can cover several areas. For example, research into the evolutionary origins of the human hand (Young, 2003; Lombardo & Deaner, 2018) could continue to add support for the importance of throwing and consequently the importance of throwing toys. Also, research should continue to examine these toys under varying contexts or within specific groups. For example, the implications of these toys could be explored within the scope of gender differences or among individuals with disabilities.

There is still much to learn about the implications of throwing toys on various aspects of development. For example, the Paidia theory of moral development (Bergen & Davis, 2013) explicitly connected playful activity and the development of moral emotions, behavior, and reasoning, but there is a need to explore specific play activities (such as play with throwing toys) and their contributions to moral development. In a different vein, Jirout and Newcombe (2015) focused on spatial development and their findings suggested that play with spatial toys is important for the development of spatial skills. But, similar to research in play and moral development, there is a need to explore spatial development and play with specific toys.

Another important area to consider is technology and its effect on children play. Bergen and Davis (2011) discussed technology-augmented toys and noted that these types of toys could alter a child's role as the *director* of play. This change, they argued, could have a significant effect on subsequent moral development. In a similar vein, Bergen, Davis, and Abbitt (2015) focused on the relationship among technology, cognition, and brain development and they discussed the importance of *representation modes* of toys. New research could continue to explore the developmental and social effects that occur when simple toys like balls, beanbags, and Frisbees, increase in technological sophistication.

SUMMARY

Balls, beanbags, and Frisbees are simple but consequential toys. They have significant developmental implications across all age groups and within various contexts. They have been an integral part of human history and, in the case of the ball, human evolution. These toys have been infused with technology and consequently they now challenge society to rethink the meaning and the role of toys in life. Despite the rich historical legacy and the many important traits that these toys possess, perhaps the most important characteristic is that they are fun. Given their tremendous value in terms of play, it is conceivable that balls, beanbags, and Frisbee will remain relevant toys for the foreseeable future.

REFERENCES

Adolph, K., & Berger, S. A. (2006). Motor development. In W. Damon & R. Lerner (Series Eds.) & D. Kuhn & R. S. Siegler (Vol. Eds.), *Hand-book of child psychology: Cognition, perception, and language* (pp. 161–213). New York, NY: Wiley.

Bergen, D., & Davis, D. R. (2013). Playful activity and thought as the medium for moral development: Implications for moral education. In B. J. Irby, G. Brown, R. Lara-Alecio, & S. Jackson (Eds.) & R. A. Robles-Piñā (Sect. Ed.), *The handbook of educational theories* (pp. 653–66). Charlotte, NC: Information Age Publishing.

Bergen, D., & Davis, D. R. (2011). Influences of technology-related playful activity and thought on moral development. *American Journal of Play, 4*(1), 80–99.

Bergen, D., Davis, D. R., & Abbitt, J. T. (2015). Technology play and brain development: Infancy to adolescence and future implications. London: Routledge.

Burton, A., & Rogerson, R. (2003). The development of throwing behavior. In G. Savelsbergh, K. Davids, J. van der Kamp, & S. Bennett (Eds.), *Development of movement co-ordination in children* (pp. 225–40). London: Routledge.

Cherney, I. D., & London, K. (2006). Gender-linked differences in the toys, television shows, computer games, and outdoor activities of 5-to 13-year-old children. *Sex Roles, 54*(9--10), 717.

Erikson, E. H. (1993). *Childhood and society*. W. W Norton & Company (original work published 1963).

Eccles, J. S., Jacobs, J. E., & Harold, R. D. (1990). Gender role stereotypes, expectancy effects, and parents' socialization of gender differences. *Journal of social issues, 46*(2), 183-201.

Fraser, A. (1966). *A history of toys*. London: Weidenfeld & Nicolson.

Froebel, F. (1899). *Pedagogics of the kindergarten* (J. Jarvis, trans.). New York, NY: D. Appleton & Co.

Gibson, E. J. (1969). *Principles of perceptual learning and development*. New York, NY: Appleton-Century-Crofts.

Halverson, H. M. (1940). Motor development. In A. Gesell (ed.), *The first five years of life: A guide to the study of the preschool child* (pp. 65–107). New York, NY: Harper and Row.

Hewes, J. (2014). Seeking balance in motion: The role of spontaneous free play in promoting social and emotional health in early childhood care and education. *Children, 1*(3), 280–301.

Jaffé, D. (2006). *The history of toys: From spinning tops to robots*. Charleston, SC: The History Press.

Jirout, J. J., & Newcombe, N. S. (2015). Building blocks for developing spatial skills: Evidence from a large, representative US sample. *Psychological science, 26*(3), 302–10.

Kim, A. H., Vaughn, S., Elbaum, B., Hughes, M. T., Morris Sloan, C. V., & Sridhar, D. (2003). Effects of toys or group composition for children with disabilities: A synthesis. *Journal of Early Intervention, 25*(3), 189–205.

Lillard, A. S. (2015). The development of play. In L. S. Liben & U. Mueller (Eds.), *Handbook of child psychology and developmental science: Volume 2: Cognitive processes* (pp. 425–68). New York, NY: Wiley-Blackwell.

Lombardo, M. P., & Deaner, R. O. (2018). Born to throw: The ecological causes that shaped the evolution of throwing in humans. *The Quarterly Review of Biology*, (1), 1–16.

Norman, D. A. (1988). *The psychology of everyday things*. New York, NY: Basic Books.

Norman, D. (2013). *The design of everyday things: Revised and expanded edition*. New York, NY: Basic Books.

Trost, S. G., Pate, R. R., Sallis, J. F., Freedson, P. S., Taylor, W. C., Dowda, M., & Sirard, J. (2002). Age and gender differences in objectively measured physical activity in youth. *Medicine and Science in Sports and Exercise, 34*(2), 350–55.

Young, R. W. (2003). Evolution of the human hand: The role of throwing and clubbing. *Journal of Anatomy, 202*(1), 165–74.

Young, R. W. (2009). The ontogeny of throwing and striking. *Human Ontogenetics: Aan International Journal of Interdisciplinary Developmental Research, 3*(1), 19–31.

12

REPLICA CARS, TRUCKS, TRAINS, OTHER VEHICLES

Annerieke Boland

A child lying on the floor with his face near a small toy car, intensely watching the wheels turn around when he pushes the car forwards and backwards will be a familiar image to many human beings all over the world. Children like to play with toy vehicles, from plastic boats to metal trucks or from wooden trains to electronic race cars. What attracts children to these toys? Such vehicles are very salient objects in the daily life of young children: their size, motion, colors and sound all draw the attention of children.

Toy vehicles present children with the opportunity to further explore of the characteristics they find fascinating by being in full control over the toy. Children can move and observe the toy vehicle at their own pace and experiment with all the affordances of the specific vehicle. Toy vehicles also present children with the opportunity to experience risk and danger, without being at risk themselves. High speed, jumping of ramps, crashes and falling are among the adventures that children act out with their vehicles.

Toy vehicles are often combined with other materials, like sand and water, parking garages, roads or railway tracks, blocks or small world play materials. These materials contribute to all the variations that can be witnessed in play with toy vehicles, from simple object-play to advanced pretend play. It is not only children who like such toys. There are also teenagers and adults who collect replicas, construct their own miniature vehicles or build railway tracks and sceneries for their model trains.

TYPICAL TYPES OF TOY VEHICLES

Cars and Motorcycles

Ride on cars or motorcycles are big enough for toddlers to sit on and make themselves go forward pushing themselves off with their legs against the floor. Most of these vehicles have a working steering wheel. Walking cars or go-carts are meant to be pushed around while the child is walking behind the car holding on to the grip at the rear side. They often contain a box with or without blocks that can be used for transport. Ride-on vehicles often have a grip at the back side so that children can also push the car around.

Wooden cars and other vehicles are in general not exact copies of real-world versions. They contain the most typical features of cars, truck or caterpillars, such as their general shape and wheels, but they are much less detailed and may have different proportions. Wooden vehicles are often meant for infants and toddlers as they have no tiny parts and most of them are bigger than other replica cars. Cars and trucks designed to be pulled around or carts (with blocks) to push around are often made of wood. Also, wooden parking garages that include rather small wooden cars, trucks or a helicopter are also available.

Typical toy cars are metal scale models that look very realistic. Scale models exist in many different types and shapes, including "regular" cars of all brands; buses, cabs, emergency vehicles like police cars and fire engines; trucks, transporters, construction equipment (bulldozers, dump trucks, excavators, backhoes, caterpillars, cranes, cement mixers, forklifts and other construction vehicles; agricultural vehicles such as tractors, ploughs, and harvesters; racing cars and other sports cars; military vehicles (army trucks, tanks, Jeeps), and "old-timer" vehicles. The toy vehicles selected for this chapter are cars, motorcycles, trains, and boats.

These scale models may be exact miniature versions of cars and other vehicles that exist in the real world, but they may also more remotely resemble real cars. In the twentieth century, replicas were typically made of metal (zinc or lead alloy), and scale models were relatively small (typical scales were 1:72 or even 1:144). During the last decades, more and more plastic model cars have been produced and models became larger. Scales of 1:28, 1:16, or sometimes even 1:8 have become much more common.

In particular, police cars, fire engines and trucks exist in larger versions, just like construction and farming vehicles. These two latter vehicles are often suitable for playing outdoors, such as in the sandpit. For smaller scale models, common accessories like parking garages, gas stations, a car wash, traffic lights and signs, or mats with "streets" and city-design add to the possible variations in play. Replica models can also count on the attention of adolescents or adults, who may be collectors of specific car brands or toy makes. Some replicas are true collector's items.

All-terrain vehicles and monster trucks are robust and have huge tires that can easily drive on uneven ground, indoors or outdoors. Monster trucks are specifically meant for crashes and stunting, like jumping off ramps. Vehicles that go "by themselves" include pull-back cars and motorcycles and vehicles with a windup mechanism or launcher sets. Racing cars with tracks come in a variety of styles. Different play sets are available to build tracks for cars. For toddlers, these are often prestructured plastic sets that make use of gravity or combine with battery cars. These sets save little room for imagination and creativity.

For preschoolers and older children there are different types of tracks such as flat wooden road pieces, small plastic shackles that can be connected to form roads, or streets, bends and crossings from LEGO. With these sets, children can use different types of toy cars and they push the car to make it go. Specific tracks belong to Hotwheels, the small fantasy racing car models; plastic tracks combined with ramps, loopings, slopes or turns are meant for spectacular stunts, crashes or race competitions. Launchers and gravity are used to make cars go.

For children in elementary school, there are electronic slot car racing sets. These sets resemble real-world racing sport circuits and are meant for race competitions between two cars. Children control the speed of the cars with remote control. Teenagers and adults often enjoy the spectacular stunts or race competitions.

There are many different cars with remote control, suitable for different age-categories, from preschoolers to adults. Preschoolers can have a hard time trying to make the vehicles go the way they want, but older children can be very skill full in controlling their toys. Remote control vehicles are also available in very sophisticated small and large-scale models for adults.

Trains

With toy trains much of the pleasure is found in building railways and sceneries. Preschoolers and older children play with wooden trains that consist of locomotives and wagons that are connected by hooks and eyes or by magnets. Children can build their own railway tracks with straight and curved parts. Tracks can be made more complex by adding bridges, switches, tunnels, or railroad crossings. The wooden train sets often combine with materials to create towns and other scenes, such as train stations, villages, and machinery for loading and unloading or harbors.

Different sets of electronic trains sets exist, with tracks that need to be built, and trains that move forward automatically. These systems often give little freedom and show limited variation in play compared to wooden train sets. Miniature electronic railways meant for older elementary school children, adolescents, and adults give opportunities to construct complex railway networks with working traffic lights and railroad crossings. The train sets exist in different scales and match with construction kits for creating miniature landscapes and villages.

Boats

Plastic or wooden bathtub boats for infants, toddlers and older children easily float on water. These toy boats have simplified shapes and contain no or few loose parts. Sometimes these boats have a wind-up mechanism. Wooden or plastic boats may resemble specific types of boats from real life, such as sailing boats, police boats, canoes, ferries, cruise ships, cargo ships, fishing boats, race boats, speed or torpedo boats, submarines, or pirate boats.

These boats often come with play figures or loading cargo, such as cars that can go on the ferry. The most famous boat might be the ark of Noah, which comes with animal and human figures. Remote control boats having electronic motors can be manoeuvred through water from a distance. They are designed for different age categories, running from simple boats for preschoolers to extremely advanced racing boats for adults.

Fantasy and Science Fiction Vehicles

Some vehicles have been fantasized to be "alive." There are many films and tv series for all age categories in which vehicles have faces or human characteristics, like being able to talk or act on their own behalf. Many toy vehicles for children are based on the character-figures from these movies or television series. Besides these humanlike vehicles, which still resemble vehicles of the real world, there are science fiction toy vehicles, such as those serving as the means of transport for action heroes, vehicles that transform into robots, dinosaurs or flying objects, and vehicles from or for outer space.

Vehicles in Play Sets

Building and play sets like Duplo, Playmobil, LEGO, Barbie, Little People, and Pet Shop regularly include vehicles that are "used" by the toy figures of these sets. Most of these vehicles have specific cultural functions, like an ambulance, a horse carriage, a police helicopter, or a camper. They stimulate pretend play.

Vehicle Building Kits

There are many different building kits for constructing 3D-vehicles. These kits can be made of cardboard, wood, plastic or specific building toys, for example K'Nex, Meccano, STEM-kits or PlusPlus. Some of these vehicles can drive or float after the children finish building them or they may have moving parts, while others are meant only to display. The complexity of construction kits ranges from few steps in building sets for toddlers and preschoolers (for example Duplo) to very advanced and detailed kits for teenagers and adults (for example LEGO Technic).

ADVANTAGES FOR DEVELOPMENT AT DIFFERENT AGES

Research on the developmental value of play with toy vehicles is scarce. But from observing children's play, inferences can be made on how this play promotes children's learning and development in many areas and at different ages. The development of play starts with physical play in infants. Play of older infants and toddlers is still very physical but now also focuses on objects. Children explore materials and experiment with the affordances of objects. At preschool age, simple symbolic and aesthetic play starts to develop but fully developed pretend play and goal-directed building and construction is only observed in kindergarten children and older (Leong & Bodrova, 2012).

Physical Skills

Children use their gross and fine motor skills by playing with toy cars and other vehicles. When infants and toddlers play with ride-on cars or walking cars, they need to find their balance stepping on, sitting on, or walking with the car. They use their muscles and strength to move the car forward and coordinate these movements with directing the vehicle in the proper direction. Children also use these vehicles for transporting objects; they put cargo in or on the vehicle and unload it later. Using toys, such as wheelbarrows for this purpose, is a real challenge for the coordination of large muscles. By moving smaller vehicles, children practice their gross motor skills as well. For example, while holding the vehicle, they crawl on the floor, walk, run or jump, or rotate their bodies. Reaching for and picking up vehicles that ended up under or behind chairs or cupboards, also makes children use their bodies in different ways.

Preschool children play with smaller vehicles, which require them to use fine motor skills for holding and orientating the vehicle when driving between or on furniture, in parking spots, or through tunnels. Small muscles are used to manipulate moving parts, like the doors of a car, the body of a truck, or the hoist of a crane. Also, parts that can be attached or detached, like train wagons or rail tracks require good hand-eye coordination, just like the construction of slopes and slides. Play with vehicles can also add to sensory experiences, in particular when vehicles are combined with other materials, such as boats in and under water or trucks in the sandpit.

SCIENCE, TECHNOLOGY, ENGINEERING, AND MATHEMATICS (STEM) SKILLS

Observing, Sorting, and Grouping

Toddlers and preschoolers observe their vehicles carefully; their shape, function, special features, color, size, speed, or material. They often distinguish (visual) details that are not noticed by adults. When children have two or more vehicles at their disposable, they often notice similarities or differences and they spontaneously sort and group vehicles according to one or more of their attributes. For instance, they select all the vehicles that belong to Superman, or they create categories of trucks, racing cars, and normal cars. Children also put away vehicles that do not belong to a certain category, like taking out a plane that happened to linger around in a box full of cars. Children put vehicles in logical orders, for example from small to big, from fast to slow or from most to least favourite. Often, preschoolers spontaneously start counting the objects in different categories.

Orientation in Space, Patterning

When preschoolers play with several vehicles, they like to organize them in space, by lining them up or putting them next to or on top of each other. Children may use patterns in their surroundings for organizing, like the tiles on the floor, or the parking spots on the toy parking garage or they may create their own patterns. Infants and toddlers already experiment with orientation in space, riding on or walking behind their cars and carts. Driving around with vehicles from different sizes makes children experiment with the width and the lengths of their vehicles, measuring whether they fit in a certain space, or can they go under, between, or through other objects?

Preschoolers and older children like to build their own tracks for vehicles to drive along, but constructing a railroad or a racetrack is quite a complex activity because pieces only fit together if they have the right orientation compared to the other piece, curved tracks change direction if turned upside down, pieces have different lengths and it requires logical thinking to make a continuing route. If children do not invent their own track but copy an example from pictures on the box, or from step-by-step guides, they need careful observation and understanding of the relation between the two-dimensional pictures and the three-dimensional tracks.

Tools and Technology

There are many types of mechanics and technology to discover in toy vehicles. Toddlers and preschoolers are often obsessed by small parts they can manipulate, such as the wheels that turn around, the steering wheel that changes the position of the wheels, doors that can be opened and closed, the pulley in tow trucks, levers to unload the cargo or to lift objects, magnets in train wagons to create longer trains or buttons that make the sirens and the flash lights go. Also, the mechanics of pull-back cars, wind-up boats, and launchers can be fascinating for children. Electronic vehicles or remote controls present different opportunities for discovering technology and hand-eye coordination for older children.

Science Concepts

When playing with vehicles, children as young as toddlers explore different concepts, like speed, distance, height, weight, and spatial dimensions. They like their vehicles to go fast and explore with driving on different undergrounds. This is how they learn about the effect of friction on speed. Preschoolers and older children more deliberately experiment with cause and effect. They explore what happens if they make their cars go down ramps: the higher the ramp, the faster the car. They also find out that the speed of the vehicle relates to the distance the car can cover. They experiment with their own strength by pushing away a car or with pull-back vehicles. They explore what works best and find out that their vehicle will follow a curved trajectory if it is not put straight at the start.

Children learn about width, height, and length if they want their vehicles to drive through tunnels or between walls that may be too narrow or wide enough; if they navigate their boats under bridges or if they let their planes and helicopters fly higher and higher. They learn about floating and sinking and the effect of balance and weight when playing with their boats in water.

Symbolic Representation

Designing, Building, and Crafts

Older preschoolers start building all kinds of objects and tracks for their toy vehicles. For example, with blocks they build train stations, bridges, tunnels, villages, parking garages or ramps, and slopes. With road tracks and railway tracks they design new routes for their race cars or trains. Children also create their own vehicles, using all kinds of materials and building toys. They may construct vehicles by following step by step instruction guides or copy examples from pictures or from others, but they often are very creative in bringing their own imagination to life when they are familiar with the characteristics of the materials. Sometimes younger children are building and coincidentally end up with a vehicle. Older children are more goal-directed and they plan ahead what and how they want to build.

Pretend Play

Vehicles can play an important part in pretend play. Even without toys or objects, young children imagine themselves to be a vehicle. They use their own body to represent a vehicle. For example, they stretch their arms and run around like a plane, they line-up with peers and hold on to each other to form a train, or they just run very fast and make noise of a car. When children are on a ride-on bike or a tricycle, or even just on the floor or on a chair holding (something that looks like) a steering wheel, they play what they know from their own experiences of being in a car with their parents: they go around corners, stop for (imaginary) traffic lights, they park, visit gas stations, and talk about their destination.

Children from about age three engage in more complex pretend play. Realistic toys help children to play out different scenarios and themes and use appropriate language (Pellegrini & Jones, 1994). Children often act out thematic play with realistic toy vehicles with specific cultural functions, such as emergency vehicles, a camper, a garbage truck, tractor, or sailing boat. Children act out the dialogues of the drivers, chauffeurs, captains, or pilots They may use real objects to represent these drivers, but they may also just imagine the drivers to be in and outside the vehicle, acting this out by moving the vehicle. Children in elementary school who play with automatic race cars or monster trucks, may identify with the chauffeurs and racers and often talk aloud as if they were the driver inside.

Language and Literacy

Oral Language

Toys stimulate parents to make conversation with their child, so that contingent conversations develop. This is very stimulating for language learning (Roseberry et al., 2014). When children play with toy cars, trains, and boats, their language learning mechanism is active. Even when playing on their own, children often make sounds for the vehicles and use private speech for commenting on what happens. "This one here." Children also act out dialogues. "Here I come." "Oh, wait, you are too fast."

When organizing and sorting their vehicles, children tend to share their observations, ideas and feelings: "Look, they are all red," "These are my favorites." Children talk about their explorations and experiments and start using more and more complex language structures: "If you push this button, then it makes noise." "Maybe if we put this one up here, it won't fall anymore." When playing, children are at the same time broadening their vocabulary and deepening their understanding of words and concepts.

Literacy and Numeracy

The symbols of different car brands are often fascinating for preschoolers. They memorize which symbol stands for which brand and may also try to read the name of the brand on the backside of the car. When playing with toy vehicles, children encounter these symbols and names again.

Older preschoolers recognize similarities in the sound of cars: short (Ford) and long names (Mitsubishi) that are sometimes difficult to pronounce, different brands that start with the same sound (Jaguar and Jeep). Furthermore, there may be letters, numbers and words on toy vehicles as a decoration or in number plates, or the name of a ship. Children in kindergarten often spontaneously want to draw symbols and write names of cars. Toy equipment for cars and boats often use signs or symbols, like "P" for parking or "H" for helicopter on toy parking garages; numbers for each different parking place; or the levels of the parking garage or symbols on traffic signs. They all help preschoolers to get acquainted with literacy and identify specific letters and numbers.

GENDER ISSUES

The first lines of this chapter give the impression that the child on the floor staring at the wheels is a boy. During the past decennia, small scale research in the Western world has shown that both for adults and for children, toy vehicles have very stereotyped gender associations. Miller (1987) found that college students considered toy vehicles to be masculine toys. In Green et al. (2004), six ECEC (Early Childhood Education and Care) professionals, equally male and female, unanimously chose six toys as typically masculine, of which four were vehicles (a fire engine, a dump truck, an ambulance, and a helicopter). Among the six toys that were chosen to be typically feminine, none of them was a vehicle. The four boys in this study showed high preference for the stereotypical masculine toys. They all played more than 90 percent of the time with these toys. The four girls only played 32 percent to 84 percent of the time with the stereotypical feminine toys.

In a small-scale study of Cherney et al. (2003), among the top three preferred toys of the boys (1:6–3:11), there were a tow truck and a car. For the girls, there were no vehicles included in their ten most favorable toys. Interestingly, girls tended to prefer the gender-neutral toys. They were least attracted to toys typically stereotyped as female. In another small-scale study, Jarret French-Lee, Bulunuz, and Bulunuz (2010) also found the preference of boys for vehicles. They examined play in the sandpit of 38 children (3- and 4-year olds). In general, girls were in the majority. When cars and trucks were added to the sandpit, this attracted more boys to the sandpit and fewer girls.

Although studies seem to indicate that boys like toy vehicles better than girls do, it is not clear why this is the case. Research has shown that children around two years of age start to be aware of differences between boys and girls (Kohlberg & Ullian, 1974) and by the age of five, they have strong ideas of which toys are appropriate for boys and which for girls (Sandnabba & Ahlberg, 1999). Furthermore, Freeman (2007) found that children think that their parents would highly approve play with stereotypical toys and that playing with the other-gender toy would be much less approved, in particular by their same-sex parent. This belief was stronger for five-year olds than for three-year olds and most strong for the five-year old boys, who believed that their fathers would only approve play with opposite-gender toys in 9 percent of the cases. The children had this belief even though their parents expressed a much more open mind to the choice of toys. The finding that preschool children are sensitive to social expectations of gender-related toy choice was consistent with an earlier study of Raag and Rackliff (1998).

Although girls seem to be rather open to play with neutral toys or stereotypical masculine toys (Green et al., 2004), they do play much less with toy vehicles than boys do. As vehicle play might stimulate so many areas of development, it would be worthwhile for girls' development if they felt freer to choose for toy vehicles. The findings of Cherney and Dempsey (2010) are interesting in this respect. Both the majority of boys (82 percent) and girls (75 percent) chose a pirate ship to be a masculine toy, but the *pink* airplane in their study was considered feminine by the majority of boys (76 percent) and girls (75 percent), due to the color. The school bus with both male and female figures was in general considered masculine by boys (59 percent) but girls had less strict opinions. Fewer than half of the girls (42 percent) thought the bus was a toy for boys, whereas 25 percent of them thought it was feminine and 33 percent thought it was both for boys and for girls. It seems that girls could be inspired to play with toy vehicles when they are presented with neutral accessories or with stereotypical feminine details.

ADAPTATIONS FOR CHILDREN WITH SPECIAL NEEDS

Children with special educational needs might not be able to move toy vehicles them-selves or to manipulate tiny parts. However, these children may like to play with the toys' electronic features that produce sounds or lights. When in a bed or a wheelchair, children may like to pretend they are in a vehicle. Objects, like a horn, siren, or lights, may support this imagination. Children may also like to sort and organize toy vehicles. Some toy vehicles have now been designed to show adaptations, such as wheelchair access.

History of Toy Vehicle Play

Archeological findings indicate that toy vehicles have existed for a long time. Small stone barrows and horses with wheels, made of stone from ancient Greek and Roman times have been found. In Turkmenistan, Mesopotamia, and North Kurdistan, there are some unique findings of earthenware toy cars that date back even thousands of years. During the Middle ages in western Europe, barrows, tow trucks, or wheelbar-rows were made of wood for children to play with. Not only toy cars and their precur-sors have stood the test of time, however. Many wooden toy boats have been found on archaeological sites and as soon as trains, trucks, motors, planes, and helicopters were invented, children enjoyed playing with these replicas.

Recommendations

More research is needed on play with toy vehicles in order to find out what the relations are between different toy vehicles and types of play. For example, Jarret et al. (2010) found in a preschool group that adding construction vehicles to the sandpit changed the type of play. Another question is how play with vehicles affects different areas of development. Is there evidence for the hypothesized relationships in this chapter? Another interesting topic is to examine how children of both sexes can be stimulated to play with vehicles. Thus, there is still much to learn about children's play with toy vehicles.

REFERENCES

Cherney, I. D., & Dempsey, J. (2010). Young children's classification, stereotyping and play behaviour for gender neutral and ambiguous toys, *Educational Psychology*, 30(6), 651–69.
Cherney, I. D., Kelly-Vance, L., GILL GLOVER, K. A. T. R. I. N. A., Ruane, A. M. Y., & OLIVER RYALLS, B. R. I. G. E. T. T. E. (2003). The effects of stereotyped toys and gender on play assessment in children aged 18–47 months. *Educational Psychology*, 23(1), 95–106.

Freeman, N. (2007). Preschoolers' perceptions of gender appropriate toys and their parents' beliefs about gen-derized behaviors: miscommunication, mixed messages, or hidden truths? *Early Childhood Education Journal*, *34*(5), 357–66.

Green, V.A., Bigler, R., & Catherwood, D. (2004) The variability and flexibility of gender-typed toy play: A close look at children's behavioral responses to counterstereotypic models. *Sex Roles*, *51*(7/8), 371–86.

Jarrett, O., French-Lee, S., Bulunuz, N., & Bulunuz, M. (2010). Play in the sandpit. A university and a child-care center collaborate in facilitated-action research. *American Journal of Play*, Fall 2010, 221–37.

Kohlberg, L., & Ullian, D. Z. (1974). Stages in the development of psychosexual concepts and attitudes. In R. C. Friedman, R. M. Richart, & R. L. Vande Wiele (Eds.), *Sex differences in behaviour*, 209–22. New York, NY: John Wiley & Sons.

Leong, D., & Bodrova, E. (2012). Assessing and scaffolding make-believe play. *Young Children, 2012*(1), 28–34.

Miller, C. L. (1987). Qualitative differences among gender stereotyped toys: Implications for cognitive and social development in girls and boys. *Sex Roles, 16*, 473–87.

Pellegrini, A. D., & Jones, I. (1994). Play, toys, and language. In J. H. Goldstein (Ed.). *Toys, play and child development* (pp. 27–45). Cambridge: Cambridge University Press.

Raag, T., & Rackliff, C. L. (1998). Preschoolers awareness of social expectations of gender: Relationships to toy choices. *Sex Roles, 38*(9/10), 685–701.

Roseberry, S., Hirsh-Pasek, K., & Golinkoff, R. M. (2014). Skype me! Socially contingent interactions help toddlers learn language. *Child Development, 85*(3), 956–70.

Sandnabba, K. N., & Ahlberg, C. (1999). Parents' attitudes and expectations about children's cross-gender behavior. *Sex Roles, 40*(3–4), 249–57.

WEBSITES

https://nspt4kids.com/parenting/developmental-skills-while-playing-with-cars/

https://www.telegraph.co.uk/cars/priceless-motorsport/playing-with-toy-cars/

http://www.bounty.com/toddler-1-to-2-years/development/development-stages/play

https://www.fatherly.com/play/child-development-benefits-toy-car-play/

13

SCIENCE TOYS

Shirley K. Morgenthaler

Science toys are a category of toys that have both intrinsic and extrinsic value. These toys may include chemistry sets, robot construction, microscopes with slides to explore; materials that can be used to explore concepts and theories; planting and growing materials, such as seeds or rhizomes; construction toys that challenge the thinking strategies of children at a variety of ages; broken items, such as clocks, motors, toy cars, and so forth; toys with multiple parts that require careful thought to assemble; and kites, drones, and other flying toys. This is not an exhaustive list. Rather, it is a list of examples that will inspire the thought processes of the reader.

In the past several years, there has been much discussion about STEM as a way of thinking about materials needed for science, technology, engineering, and mathematics. Often the STEM organization and ways of thinking are used to analyze and develop toys and experiences that will enhance children's exploration and understanding of STEM activities. It is this author's view that almost all STEM materials are also science materials, even though they have been labeled as technology toys, engineering toys, or mathematics toys.

Toys that utilize the scientific method are often highly specialized and involve experimentation. The scientific method includes observation, estimation, grouping, creating groups from a pile of objects, theorizing, testing theories, engineering materials to create objects for use or decoration, and creating objects from a multiplicity of pieces and parts.

THE SCIENTIFIC METHOD

Beginning with elementary school, the scientific method is in the planning guide of every science teacher across the country. That organizational structure is used to help teachers and students develop strategies that support learning in a very complex field.

This method begins with a question—What do I want to know?—continues with research to answer the question, then development of an hypothesis of what the answer to the question might be, goes on with collection and analysis of data to prove or disprove the hypothesis, and ends with a conclusion that can be communicated to others.

When children select toys with which to play, following the scientific method is far away from their minds. Rather, science toys are chosen for their interest, their playability, and the satisfaction of a result if one is wanted or promised by the toy. In the process of playing, however, the child begins to intuit the scientific method and moves from asking a questions to searching the available data to develop an hypothesis, saying to oneself, "Oh, I think this might be the answer!" to further testing to prove or disprove that hypothesis. Often that informal scientific method will lead to a shout of, "Look what I found out!" that is an example of drawing a conclusion and communicating it.

The point with science toys is that they need to be open-ended, having several ways in which they can be used. Many parents have had the experience of buying a toy that is advertised to do this and that. However, it is the toy doing the "doing," not the child. Such a toy will be played with for a day or two, then put aside. There is no exploration required or even supported for the child. Figure 13.1 shows an example of a visual map of the scientific method. Charts and maps such as this can readily be found on the internet for those interested in taking their understanding of the scientific method to a greater depth.

CATEGORIES OF SCIENCE TOYS

Science toys can be categorized in a variety of ways. For the purpose of this chapter, a specific set of categories will be described by the author and elaborated on in a later section. The categories are building/construction/engineering, chemistry, ecology/geology, physics, robotics, solar power, space exploration, toys that fly, and video games. These categories are not mutually exclusive. Rather, there is room for judgement regarding the classification. It matters little which category into which a toy is placed. What matters is whether the child is interested in the toy or activity in the first place.

MAKING SCIENCE TOYS AVAILABLE TO CHILDREN

It is a huge mistake to label something a science toy in the presence of children. Giving it that title limits its variability and the elasticity of implementation for the child. The purpose of science and science toys is discovery. If there is a "should" placed on a toy, that toy has just lost its usefulness as a toy for scientific discovery. Allowing the child to label a toy suitable for scientific exploration is an important strategy. But it is the child's

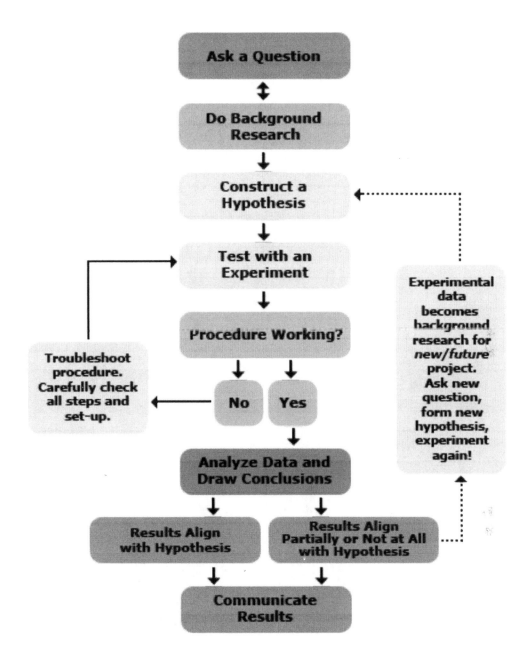

Figure 13.1. A Visual map of the scientific method Source: https://www.sciencebuddies.org.

task, not the parents or guardians, to do so. Some toys, such as drones, can be placed in two categories because they belong in each of those categories.

It is best to make a toy or activity available to a child based on that child's interests. The child will then take the toy or activity into their play and explore in ways that are important to that child's interests, temperament, and developmental level. Robotics and solar-powered toys, for instance, have a lot in common, given the toys that are currently available for purchase. How the toy is categorized in the mind of the child is what matters. A child interested in solar powering machines and objects will find a way to use that solar power with a wide variety of objects. The child who is more interested in creating robots and machines that can perform tasks will take solar-powered machines and building kits from the engineering category and apply them to their interest in robotics.

TYPES OF SCIENCE TOYS

The categories into which science toys have been placed for the purposes of this chapter can be organized in a variety of ways. This is one way that allows discussion and comparison.

Biology Toys and Resources

Biology toys include human body and anatomy kits, bones that can be put together to make a body, and stories of the blood stream and how it works. Also included are specimen kits, such as those of insects and butterflies. Butterfly hatching kits are a popular item in this category, especially for primary-age children.

Plants and animals also are a part of biology. Some of these resources include identification books of trees and of flowers. Both green plants and flowers are also available as seeds or rhizomes, ready for garden planting. Resources for garden planting also include child-size or adult-size gardening tools, such as rakes, trowels, and spades. Don't forget the garden hose and gardening gloves!

Building and Engineering Toys

Building and engineering toys include a variety of building blocks, and especially LEGO blocks. LEGO blocks can be made into buildings and cities. They can also become space stations or space shuttles or rockets or landing modules on other planets. Building toys also include kits of sticks and hubs that can be put together to make buildings, people, or whatever the imagination creates. In the past, these were made of wood and called Tinker Toys. Now, they are more likely to be formed of plastic, but they serve the same purpose in children's play.

A third type of building and engineering is the motor or engine kit. This material comes with specific directions on how to build the engine so that it will work. It still, however, is a toy even though its open-ended properties and uses are limited. Another toy in a similar category is the car-building kit, with or without the engine. Both engine kits can be miniaturized, no more than the size of an adult hand. They can also be almost life-size, giving the child-engineer a completely different experience.

Children will also use found objects for building and engineering. Indoor or outdoor forts can be made of blankets, cardboard, folding tables, or other similar materials that provide an enclosure that can be outfitted with the cooking or gardening or fighting resources to go along with the fort building.

Chemistry and Lab Toys

Chemistry toys, first of all, include the trappings of the chemistry lab, such as microscopes, beakers, and droppers. In addition, slides with specimens mounted are available for children to use with microscopes. Kits of solids, liquids, and gasses are available. For the older child, recipes for making gasses out of combinations of liquids can also be found. Slime, goop, and gunk also are a popular type of chemistry toy. They can be used to explore their properties and to make shapes and forms. Recipes for making slime and gunk are available, and especially appropriate for the older child.

Kitchen chemistry involves ingredients readily available in the kitchen, with recipes to make solids out of liquids, gasses out of solids, and the like. A similar resource is the kit for making and growing crystals of various colors and forms. Making bubbles out of water and liquid soap is an activity that is simple and engaging for children of all ages.

Finally, lava kits are the resource out of which eruptions and explosions are made. Small-scale explosions can be made of materials purchased in kit form or gathered from the kitchen or workshop. Care must be taken to ensure safety for the scientists and the observers of these activities.

Ecology and Geology Toys

Ecology and geology have to do with the earth, its resources, its topography, its chemical and mineral contents, its underground treasures, and its preservation and restoration. The toys included in this category are globes, maps, telescopes, terrarium or aquarium resources, and rocks and minerals. Rocks and minerals can be purchased for the older child and come with labels to identify and sort them.

Buried-treasure kits that imitate the archeologist can include dinosaur bones, pieces of shelter materials, and other items for which an archeologist would dig. Models of the earth in the form of globes can be purchased, along with models of the planets and solar system. Both types of models come with guides intended for exploration of the world and its position in the universe. Weather-observation resources include thermometers, barometers, rain gauges, and rain-gathering containers. For the older child, kits and recipes for making tornados are also available. These might include rain-making directions as well.

Ecology tips its hat to biology in that gardening tools and resources appear again here. For most children, garden play is an activity to be done alongside the adult gardener. For the highly interested child, giving over a small plot of dirt, or a dirt-filled planter box on an apartment balcony for planting and maintaining is a worthwhile strategy.

Physics Toys

Physics toys explore the physical environment and its properties. These include balance toys such as scales for weighing and balancing, clowns or objects to balance on the top of a pyramid, or blocks and boxes to balance on each other. Another toy in the physics category is the box of ramps and runways to build and design for use as runways for marbles, cars, and other wheel toys. Wheel toys can be constructed in different ways to experiment with speed and efficiency of the runway after it is built. In addition, sets of slot cars and runways are available for racing competitions between players.

Magnets and magnetized toys are another category related to physics. Magnetic tiles are available in a variety of shapes and in various levels of complexity. These can be used for arranging shapes on a surface, similar to puzzles. They can also be used to build towers and enclosures that challenge concepts of both balance and magnetic attraction. Electricity and circuitry kits are another element of the physical world. Circuitry boards with lights or motors are an effective toy for learning about electricity. In addition, using kitchen resources such as potatoes to create electricity can be an enjoyable toy for the primary child.

Finally gravity-experiment kits are another resource for exploring the physical world. Experiments involved in dropping objects of different sizes, different weights, and different shapes demonstrate the principles of gravity for children of a variety of ages.

Robots and Robotics

Robots and robotics have become a separate category of science toy in the past two decades. Robot-building kits are available at a range of complexities, making this concept available to a wide variety of ages and developmental levels. Making a robot implies some ability to make the robot do something, such as walk, turn, or move its head. Remote-control toys are a variety of robots, involving learning how to control the toy's movement rather than building it. This category can involve machines that move/ or walk or perform simple tasks.

Solar-Powered Toys

Solar-powered toys are a relatively new category of science toy. In some cases they are science toys only because they employ the technology of solar powering. That technology, however, since it also programs them to move, keeps them in the category of science toys. Machines and cars so powered may also be controlled remotely, as in the category above. They depend on sunlight for power, and so are primarily in use outside on sunny days. Drones, rockets, and airplanes can also be solar powered. They, too, would be dependent on sunshine to make them go and since they are flying objects, they may be remote controlled for convenience and safety.

Space and Earth Exploration

Space exploration toys are a popular new category. These toys often are acquired as a kit, with the trappings of Mars or the moon or the space station along with the spaceship or shuttle that would be needed to arrive at the destination. These toys can be simply powered by the imagination and running power of the child in charge. They can also be powered by small motors, making them remote controlled, or the small motor can be powered by solar energy, placing this toy in two or more categories beyond that of space exploration

Space exploration also includes planetary models. These may be built on an axis with a stand that allows display of the item. More than a toy, these models can be decorative in the home or child's room. Other planetary models come as kits that are put together by the older child who is learning about the relative size of planets as the construction goes along.

Earth-exploration toys begin with maps that show relative locations of cities, states, countries, or continents. Globes provide the larger, bird-in-the-sky view of the countries and continents as they are configured into the world. These can be as simple as showing continents and oceans around the globe or they can be as complex as using back-lighting and touchscreen technology to "speak" each time a child touches an area of the globe. This technology can be programmed to give names and locations, population for land areas and water depth for the oceans. More complex speaking globes will even include the capacity to identify cities and states, their populations, primary manufacturing targets, and sociological information, such as census data.

Toys that Fly

The most simple of flying toys are kites. These can be simple diamond shapes, built out of thin-but-strong paper held in shape by cross-bar strips of balsa wood. Most kites include tails made of string and ribbons. Kites can also be as complex as the kites originally found in Asian countries. These kites portray dragons or other animals and are usually round, with air being allowed to pass through the kite as well as over and under it. Some of these elaborate kites are held on long sticks of balsa wood and are flown by the actions of the person holding the stick in the air. Others are more like the more simple kites and are "fueled" by long lengths of string that is released to catch wind currents several feet above the earth.

Drones are a newer form of flying toy, or maybe they have just received a new label from the drones used in industrial applications. Most drones are shaped like a squashed orange, but are lightweight. They are powered by small motors that are either controlled remotely, or are thrown out to fly until they are caught by the player. Frisbees may be considered an older, simpler form of drone. However, they are intended to be thrown toward a target or toward another player who catches it and throws it back.

Another category of toys that fly are airplanes and catapults. Airplanes are models of real life flying vehicles and may fly by the use of small motors and remote controls that make then a part of another category. Catapults are usually hand controlled and are based on the designs and drawings of Leonardo da Vinci. These catapults often come as kits that, along with directions for construction, include information about da Vinci and the range of models he designed that still find application today.

Video Games Designed for Problem Solving

A final category in this listing of science toys is video games that are designed for the purpose of problem solving as well as playing the game. In a poll of young adults and their memories of science toys and activities, this category was a surprising addition. These young adults, primarily males, said that they did not consider these games to be related to science, but when asked to think about this, they identified games such as Minecraft, SimCity, and the Kerbal Space Program. They were included for different but related reasons of the need to build virtual objects that responded to the program in giving the player an advantage or disadvantage in the play. In some cases, the player moves to more difficult levels based on their solutions. In other cases, the player is moved toward their goal of building a city or a space station.

RESEARCH ON SCIENCE TOYS

The research directions for science toys tend to focus on toys that employ new technologies such as solar power, robotics, remote-controlled toys, and other similar toys. This research focus often takes a new development in technology that has real-world applications in order to determine ways that those technological developments might be applied to use in children's toys. However, it appears that the research tends to look backward rather that forward. Smimova, Salmina, and Tihanova evaluated the psychological esperiences of toys in 2008, and then in 2011, Smimova did a solo study of the psychological and educational values of toys. Both of these studies looked at what was, not what should be.

Children's toys often mimic adult activities. Examples of this are microscope and chemistry sets, telescopes, remote-controlled airplanes, and drones. Each of these examples help to take the child to a level beyond himself or herself (Rakoczy, 2005; Vygotsky, 1980). Other research regarding these mimicking toys tends to look at how these toys teach (Zubfowski, 1991; Rief-Ackerman, 2015; Albbdulaleva & Siminova, 2011).

One category of research promises to result in more dynamic information for both toy developers and educators. This is a category that might be entitled "exploration." It includes the use of LEGOs for children with spatial strengths (Mann, 2013), using toys to learn to pretend (Rakoczy, 2005), and exploration in engineering (Dare, Childs, Cannaday, & Roehrig, 2014). If exploration can include a focus on open-endedness, it bodes well for science play.

GENDER DIFFERENCES IN SCIENCE TOYS

Some differences in toys make them appeal to girls more than boys or to boys more than girls. However, the popularity and power of the STEM movement is that it gives messages to girls that toys with motors or solar control are for them as well as for boys. It is the author's opinion, based on more than fifty years of teaching, that toys appeal to individuals based more on the learning style or intelligence style/category than on their gender. Society lables toys as girl toys or boy toys, thus limiting their use.

It appears that part of the problem with gender-specific toys is that these are designed by manufacturers who are getting misinformation or mixed messages from marketing realms regarding what is popular and what will sell. Manufacturers have not caught up with the research that indicates the desire for more gender-neutral toys. Shannon Paulus (2012) had written an article demanding that a moratorium be placed on gender-specific toys in the manufacturing world.

Groups other than manufacturers are also being blamed for children developing gender-specific interests at a young age. Parents are blamed (Jacobs & Bleeker, 2004). Peers are blamed (Downs & Langiois, 1977; Desous & Czerniak, 2002). Early experiences in the culture are also blamed (Banse, Gawronski, Rebetez, Gutt, & Morton, 2010; Paz-Ablbo, Cvencek, Herranzl-Jacer, Hervas Escobar, & Metzoff, 2017; Weisgam

& Dinella, 2018). It appears, however, that whether the opinion of the researcher is that gender differences should be acknowledged and studied or whether the opinion of a research team is that gender-neutral is the way to go, there are studies with a range of results that will satisfy both ends of the thought spectrum.

The voice of reason within the gender-difference research community is the voice that asks for more research on engineering activities for girls. Also, there should be more research on play materials that do not telegraph a message of "I'm a girl toy" or "Boys play with me." The STEM movement is a step in the right direction.

Science as a Part of STEM

Throughout this chapter, the acronym STEM, so named for science, engineering, technology, and mathematics, has been referenced. The category of science obviously belongs in this nomenclature. Technology, on the other hand, is not a separate category of toy or item. Rather, it is the field of study that allows us the power to harness solar power for toys, to design video games that include science-related experiences and challenges. Engineering, too, does not have its own chapter in this book and finds its way to science by default. Mathematics as a field of study and application is more complex. It does have its own category of toy. But much of mathematics applies to science and other areas. Complex mathematics have applications to many types of science toys, in that the solutions that have led to solar-powered objects or to engine-powered toys often are based on mathematical formulae that most persons do not understand.

EFFECTIVENESS OF SCIENCE TOYS

Many of the young adults in the author's poll (Morganthaler, 2020) are current university students or very recent graduates. The questions probed not just their memories of science play, but also their science play as it relates to their current courses of study or careers. All of them avoided that second line of questioning, with responses that indicated that they saw little relationship. However, in most cases these young adults are in science-based or science-related fields. While their play did not visibly demonstrate a connection to their current fields of study, their play did, in fact, encourage scientific thinking in both obvious and obscure ways.

One young adult, a female in a bioengineering program, tells the story of washing the hair of her Barbie dolls in the sink with various soaps and shampoos. She was trying to discover the type of soap or shampoo that would make the dolls' hair the softest, the easiest to comb, or similar hypotheses. While she may not always have gotten the results she sought, she was learning to develop and test hypotheses, an important skill for her field of study.

Another young adult, a male in a neuroscience major, tells a story of using LEGOs, cars and trains, video games, and his own ingenuity to create challenges and solutions in his play. He built cities, both virtual and in model form, that were limited only by his imagination for the complexity they included. As a child, he was more interested in how people and things get from place to place than in the destinations to which the travel led. Thus, the airplane and the airport, the ship and the loading dock, the car and its mechanisms led to the formation of hypotheses that he both identified and tested.

In both of these examples, the scientific fields of study may have been inspired by their choices of toys and of ways to use those toys. On the other hand, their predilection to thinking like a scientist may have led to the toys and activities they chose. As with gender studies, it is important to allow for the interest to drive the play, rather than the other way around. It is important to intentionally make complex and scientific toys available to children for just those times and cases that the toy will identify an interest that will become a passion.

RECOMMENDATIONS

There are a number of things to recommend regarding science toys. Many of these recommendations sit in juxtaposition to each other because both extremes are needed. For instance, there should be more technology applications to children's toys. At the same time, there should be toys with greater simplicity. Technological applications in toys readies the next generation for the technology-filled world they will live in as adults, but simplicity in science toys encourages more creativity in the child, creating the nimble mind that will be so needed in the future.

Science toys need to have more parts to put together. As engineering toys, these are critical experiences for children. In addition, the ability to add moving parts to an engineering toy adds the complexity that challenges the brain and possibly works on a part of the brain that needs development at that tune. Above all, science toys need to be discovery toys. There need to be challenges that can be solved in a variety of ways for a variety of results. In addition, these discovery toys need to have problem solving as their central challenge. It is through the thinking of discovery that children will engage more readily in science toys and, at the same time, enhance their learning capacities in all areas

One concerns related to these recommendations for more moving parts, more complexity, more parts to put together and more technology, is that the adults interacting with children and selecting the toy in the first place will be put off by the potential mess of this more, more, more. It is, however, this complexity, these moving parts, and parts to put together that are exactly what children need now in order to be ready later for the complexity of the world they will inherit.

REFERENCES

Abbdulaeva, E. A., & Smimova, E. O. (2011). The role of dynamic toys in child's development. *Psychological Science & Education, 16*(2), 30–38.

Banse, R., Gawronski, B., Rebetez, C., Gutt, H., & Morton, J. B. (2010). The development of spontaneous gender stereotyping in childhood: Relations to stereotype knowledge and stereotype flexibility. *Developmental Science 16*(2), 298–305.

Bleeker, M. M., & Jacobs, J. E. (2004). Achievement in math and science: Do mothers' beliefs matter 12 years later? *Journal of Educational Psychology, 96*(1), 97.

Dare, E. A., Childs, G. T., Cannaday, E. A., & Roehrig, G. H. (2014). Engineering encounters: Blasting off with engineering. *Science and Children, 52*(3), 60–64.

Desouza, J. M. S., & Czerniak, C. M. (2002). Social behaviors and gender differences among preschoolers: Implications for science activities. *Journal of Research in Childhood Education, 16*(2), 175–88.

Langlois, J. H., & Downs, A. C. (1980). Mothers, fathers, and peers as socialization agents of sex-typed play behaviors in young children. *Child Development*, 1237–47.

Mann. R. (2013). Got LEGO bricks?: Children the spatial strengths. *Parenting for high potential, 3*(2), 4–8.

Morganthaler, S. K. (2020). *Grandchildren's memories of science play*. Western Springs, IL.

Paulus, S. (2012). Science fair(er): Can we quit it with the gendered toys? *Bitch Magazine*, 55, 10.

Paz-Albo Prieto, J., Cvencek, D., Herranz Llácer, C. V., Hervás Escobar, A., & Meltzoff, A. N. (2017). Preschoolers' mathematical play and colour preferences: A new window into the development of gendered beliefs about math. *Early Child Development and Care, 187*(8), 1273–83.

Rakoczy, H. (2005). On tools and toys: How children learn to act on and pretend with "virgin objects." *Developmental Science, 8*(1), 7–73.

Reif-Acherman, S. (2015). Toys as teaching tools in engineering: The case of Slinky. *Ingenieria Competitividad, 17*(2), 111–22.

Smimova, E. O. (2011). Psychological and educational evaluation of toys in Moscow Center of Play and Toys. *Psychological Science and Education, 2*, 5–10.

Smimova, E. O., Salmina, N. G., & Tihanova, I. G. (2008). Psychological expertise of a toy. *Psychological Science & Education*, (3), 5–19.

Vygotsky, L. (1980). Cole, M. (Ed.). *Mind in society*. Boston, MA: Harvard University Press.

Abdulaeva, E. A., & Smirnova, E. O. (2011). The role of dynamic toys in child's development. *Psychological Science and Education, 16*(2), 30–38.

14

CRAYONS AND PAINTS

Tracy Settleberry

Crayons and paints are present all around us. It would be hard to go to a restaurant without seeing a child coloring in the next booth, or walk on a sidewalk that hasn't been decorated with imaginative chalk drawings. On both the big and the small screens, children's paintings and crayon drawings adorn every family's refrigerator or parent's office desk. As these artistic experiences are commonplace wherever children reside, toys such as crayons and paints are widely available and can vary greatly. When studying crayons, one must consider quality, shape, size, and color, among other aspects such as personal preference. When looking at paints, one must think about the tools used to apply the paint and the type of paint being used.

Beyond understanding the physical qualities of crayons and paints, part of differentiating countless paints and crayons on the market requires an understanding of the history of these tools, as well as, access to them through home and school life. Other important considerations with crayons and paint relate to child development in terms of cognitive, physical, and socioemotional growth. Crayons and paints are an important aspect of child development as they help with brain development (e.g., learning colors, patterns, and symbols), fine motor skills, self-expression, and emotional processing.

The physical attributes of crayons and paints, as well as, the developmental opportunities they provide give insight into the significance of these toys for young children. However, when studying these toys, it is also important to acknowledge accessibility, gender differences among products, opportunities for growth, historical issues, and current research.

FEATURES OF CRAYONS AND PAINTS

Crayons

Crayons can be purchased at any grocery, drug, big-box, or art store, as well as, through numerous vendors online. Although crayons are a commonplace item, there are so many variations that it can be overwhelming to decide what a child a might need or want, and how much it should cost. The following are some important aspects to consider.

Quality

Crayons are made of wax and pigment, with the pigment being the most expensive part. Therefore, cheaper crayons often have less pigment, and as a result, are not as bright or easy to use. The type of wax and the process used in making the crayon can also influence how well the crayon transfers color onto the paper, as well as, the durability of the crayon. In terms of use, some crayon companies glue the label onto the crayon, which can make it tricky to peel as a child uses the crayon. If price is a factor for the person purchasing the crayons, remember that because crayons are considered "back to school" supplies, higher quality crayons are often more affordable just before the school year starts.

Shape and Size

Crayons come in many shapes and sizes, but are most commonly seen in the form of 3.5" sticks in a traditional pack of 8, 16, or 24. For younger children, there are jumbo crayons that are thicker, and also, egg-shaped and pyramid-shaped crayons that allow children to use a palm-grip while holding. For children who are looking for variations of crayons, there are finger-tip crayons that resemble claws, but draw just like traditional crayons, as well. For elementary-aged children, twistable crayons are sometimes more desirable (some were erasable, at one point) as they have plastic casing around them which takes away the issue of peeling the paper and can also withstand more pressure from a stronger grip. Finally, there are homemade crayons, which are made by melting pieces of used crayons down in muffin tins (shapes and sizes vary based on the bakeware). Keep in mind that homemade crayons, although easy to conceptualize, do require some attention to detail regarding bake time and oven temperature in order to keep the wax from separating from the pigment.

Color and Other Considerations

The crayon boxes with a smaller quantity often consist of the primary and secondary colors. Boxes add tertiary colors, pastels, and darker colors as they become bigger. In addition, there are specialty boxes such as glitter crayons, construction paper crayons, scented crayons, metallic crayons, washable crayons, single-color boxes, or crayons colors that revolve around specific movies or toys.

Paints

In terms of paint, it is important to consider the tools used to create a painting, the type of paint used, and the surface upon which the paint is spread. Although there are many variations of crayons, the category of "paints" is even more broad.

Painting Tools

When it comes to painting, the tools used to create a piece are endless. Similar to crayons, specific tools can be more or less appropriate depending on the child's age. Finger painting is often the first step in a child's artistic development as it gives more opportunities for physical movement such as "pressing, rubbing, scratching dotting, stroking, and drawing" (Blum & Dragositz, 1947, p. 93). Beyond fingers, children often use stamps, which can consist of sponges, potatoes cut in half, or even daubers (such as the kind used for bingo). Today, assortments of sponges can be purchased which include rollers, stamps, brushes, and wands that resemble small mops. As children age, they move toward large brushes with coarse bristles, and then onto finer brushes, although the process is not completely linear as there is often a use for various brush types at many ages.

Paint Types

Most important, paints need to be nontoxic when used with children, although nearly all children's paints would meet this requirement. Finger paints—which are often tempera paints—are usually the building blocks for many young artists. Finger paints are available in primary and secondary colors, but usually not a larger variety as children make their own colors while using movement to mix the paints together. While in preschool or kindergarten, children transition to tempera paints with brushes which are the standard for most child art. Tempera paints come in individual sizes, but also in gallon jugs for classroom use.

In addition, there are also paint mediums that can be added to provide texture (e.g., sand) or to change finish (e.g., matte, gloss, glitter). Easels help children to move from finger paints to paint brushes, as well. In elementary school, there are even more options for children to aid in their artistic development. Watercolors are often the next step as children progress to smaller and finer brushes. Watercolors can be found in liquid form, or in pans where children add the water themselves.

Other Options

Although tempera and watercolors are most common for children, there are many other options for someone designing a paint-based project for children. For example, print-making can be a great option for young artists. This art form can be as simple as dipping cut vegetables or sponges into paint and pressing them onto paper or canvas. There is also an opportunity for children to create their own stamps using printmaking tools (e.g., linoleum). As children progress in printmaking, they move from paints toward ink. Outside of printmaking, other painting opportunities include spin art, throwing paint-filled balloons, or even using a drinking straw to blow paint across a surface.

The surface being painted upon is also an important aspect of the painting process. Large paint pads are common for young children who use larger movements to create their pieces. The weight (or strength) of the paper needs to be considered when working with paints, as well. There are specific papers for certain types of paint (e.g., watercolor paper); however, traditional paint pads or construction paper are most common, and tend to work well in most situations. In addition, using glaze (which acts as a paint, but consists of ceramic material) is a wonderful way for children to "paint" onto a three-dimensional ceramic surface before firing the piece in a kiln (making the piece glassy and more professional looking).

THE EVOLUTION OF CRAYONS AND PAINTS

Drawing and painting can be traced back to as early as 30,000 B.C., predating even written history (Mules, 2019). Both mediums have helped historians tell story of humankind although the materials used to create these pieces have changed significantly throughout time.

History of Crayons

Crayons began in ancient Egypt with the birth of encaustic painting, which combined hot beeswax with pigment (Wilkinson, 1847). It was not until the 1500s that pastels were made with pigments and binders (often chalk or talc) in Europe, and then produced as sticks in the 1600s (Beeny, 2017). Following the birth of pastels, Conte crayons (which contain clay and graphite, and draw more similarly to crayons today) were developed in Paris (Taws, 2016). Even more like current crayons, industrial crayons were used in the late 1800s; however, the crayons known in classrooms and households around the world today were invented in 1903 when the company Binney & Smith made the first Crayola box (The History of Crayons, 2019). Throughout the twentieth century, many crayon companies capitalized on these toys introducing new colors, shapes, and products such as built-in crayon sharpeners and at-home crayon makers for reusing leftover crayons.

In 1903, there were eight crayon colors: red, orange, yellow, green, blue, violet, brown, and black. Today, the colors are endless, with companies producing boxes with more than 150 colors in one box (these boxes often include "specialty colors" that have additives, such as glitter or metallic ingredients). One area of controversy, however, is the naming of these colors. For example, Crayola has retired names, such as "Flesh" (now Peach), and "Indian Red" (now Chestnut), based on consumer concerns throughout the 1900s (Boboltz, 2015). Colors can be retired or renamed at any time.

History of Paints

The history of paints is vast and much more detailed than the history of crayons as painting encompasses more types of paints and styles of painting than the category of crayons. Painting existed in nearly every culture whether it was found formally on canvas or less formally on cave walls. Although paints have been available for centuries, it was not until the twentieth century that nontoxic paints were created for child's play. To understand the rigor versus freedom associated with painting (and drawing, for that matter), take a brief look at the historical and sociological implications of this medium.

AGE LEVEL DIFFERENCES

Children of varying ages need different tools to accommodate their ideas and self-expression. Just as there is some disagreement about whether children's growth is through stages or continuous, the same argument holds true for a child's artistic growth. Much of this development is directly related to their fine motor skills and their attention to detail, and therefore, their development as outlined by Piaget, Skinner, Erikson, and other prominent researchers.

Although some argue that stage-wise development is too generalized and linear—often not giving enough weight to cultural influences (Kindler & Darras, 1997)—Lowenfeld's (1957) stages of artistic growth are still widely known and recognized today. For the purposes of discussing crayons and paints, and their use throughout childhood, Lowenfeld's stages (scribbling, preschematic, schematic, gang, and pseudo-naturalistic stages) will be reviewed.

Before discussing the stages specifically, it is important to note that Lowenfeld stressed the significance of allowing children time to move through stages at their own pace, and for teachers to follow the interests of the children. For example, if a teacher wants students to draw animals found in the woods, the teacher should provide opportunities for growth, exploration, and play in that area. These opportunities could include a nature walk where students may find animals, have time to hold or observe animals, or imitate animals. These experiences would influence the child's visual representation of the animals they were asked to draw and would provide them with more information as they visualize and plan what they want to put on paper.

Infant/Toddler (The Scribbling Stage)

In this stage, the scribbles on the paper represent movement, and the process of creation, rather than portraying objects in the child's world. Toward the end of the stage, children begin to label their scribbles which marks the beginning of a transition to the next stage.

Preschool Stage (The Preschematic Stage)

Rather than representing kinesthetic motion used to create the piece, in this stage, a child's artwork starts to represent what he or she is seeing. Often, their first artistic attempt is a person that consists of a circle for the head with arms and legs (lines) that attach directly to the circle. This is sometimes referred to as a "tadpole" drawing (Jolley, 2009). Development happens quickly as children are constantly learning and understanding more about their world.

Early Elementary (The Schematic Stage)

During the schematic stage, children begin to draw with more appropriate proportions and start to use a base (or "ground") line. Colors become more representative of what they see (e.g., the sky is blue), and stories emerge about their pieces. The word "schematic" is used as children often have a "schema" that can be seen in many drawings (e.g., a car may look the same in every drawing or painting). Often, the largest symbols are the most important to the child (Barnes, 2015).

Later Elementary (The Gang Stage or "Dawning Realism")

This stage is considered a "dawning" for children as they realize that their schema from the previous stage does not represent reality. This can lead to frustration and children thinking that they "can't draw." However, even as self-confidence may decline, ability (e.g., fine motor skills, attention to detail) continues to improve. During the dawning realism stage, children overlap objects in their artwork and strive for realism in their pieces. This stage can be a turning point regarding children's interest and confidence in their art, overall.

Early Adolescence (The Pseudonaturalistic Stage)

Similar to the dawning realism stage, during the pseudonaturalistic stage, children become more critical of their artistic skills. At this time, children also demonstrate an understanding or spatial awareness using perspective (objects that are further away are drawn/painted smaller in the artwork). Children also continue to grow in their use of detail and shading.

GENDER DIFFERENCES IN USE

When it comes to controversial gender-specific toys, crayons and paints tend to transcend those stereotypes. Although there can be a push for boys to participate in more rough and tumble activities, there are numerous traditionally masculine jobs that require a person to know and understand drawing and painting, as well as, the fundamentals of art (e.g., architecture, engineering, advertising and graphic design). However, there are companies that have capitalized on gender in hopes of selling more crayons and paints. For example, crayon packs that are sold with superhero coloring books, or watercolor paints sold with princess painting pads do cater to traditional stereotypes.

ADAPTATIONS FOR CHILDREN WITH SPECIAL NEEDS

Because crayons and paints are so widely available (and often cheap), there are many adaptations of these tools for children with special needs. Some of these adaptable tools are available from manufacturers, but often, they are made by teachers and parents to suit the specific needs of a child. For example, crayons are sold in different shapes for children who have a difficult time gripping crayon sticks. However, palm-grasp crayons can be made at home using old crayons, a muffin tin, and an oven.

In terms of painting, children have been known to paint with extended brushes, brushes that attach to an elbow or a foot, or even by putting a brush in their mouth. Many teachers have training in creating adaptable tools; however, the majority use creative thinking to problem solve when there is a child in need.

As stated previously, school can be an access point for many when it comes to drawing and painting. For children who cannot attend schools due to illness or injury, they often have teachers or tutors assigned to visit them, but these children can be at a disadvantage as they miss out on both the social and the artistic experiences at school *especially* when they are going through a difficult time. Fortunately, there are certified child life specialists (CCLSs) who are experts in improving patient and family care for children in healthcare settings through interventions such as therapeutic play. These experts often use drawing and painting as a tool as they are both very accessible for nearly all children.

Research has shown that children can often draw what they are feeling more easily than they can articulate it (Koppitz, 1984). Although CCLSs are not art therapists, they are trained to help children cope with trauma and can be found in hospitals and hospice programs, camps, community programs, bereavement groups, and many other places helping children through art and other means (Association of Child Life Specialists, 2018).

OPPORTUNITIES FOR GROWTH

Although drawing and painting are important aspects of a child's artistic development, these skills and experiences have an even stronger influence when used in an interdisciplinary setting. As education continues to revolve around science, technology, engineering, and math (STEM), often taking the emphasis away from the arts, art advocates have argued that art is more important than ever pushing a new acronym, STEAM (which includes an "A" for art, as well). Art tools—even those for young children—reflect that emphasis with specific products that encourage the use of crayons and paint along with science, math, and technology (e.g., design challenges, play-based learning, other interdisciplinary activities).

HISTORICAL/SOCIOLOGICAL ISSUES

History of Art Education and Access to Art

It is relevant to consider the history of art education when discussing the history of crayons and paints, as much of the access to these supplies (especially for children living in poverty) has been through schools. In addition, it is also important to know that art education has been thought of as a pendulum in terms of how it is taught (rigor versus artistic freedom), and how important it is to society (funding and access versus cutting programs).

Art education started with humble roots: in the 1920s, children were educated with "picture study," which taught students how to appreciate art in hopes that their appreciation would spread around the community and garner support for neighborhood and city beautification (Smith, 1986). This continued throughout the decades, and it wasn't until after World War II that students were encouraged to enter into visual arts training post–high school (Oakes, 2006).

In the 1970s, Viktor Lowenfeld arose as a prominent researcher and encouraged adults to teach art using a playful "hands off" approach allowing for complete freedom of the student (Lowenfeld, 1957). In 1987, the Getty Center for Education in the Arts published an essay by Dr. Elliot W. Eisner (1987) regarding the importance of discipline-based art education, which encouraged instructors to teach art using four academic disciplines: art history, art criticism, aesthetics, and studio. This approach outlined what children should learn at various ages taking into consideration physical, cognitive, and socioemotional developmental milestones. This approach also became the basis of the National Standards.

Although "arts and crafts" had been a part of schooling for decades, it wasn't until the National Standards were created that the arts were taught using competencies. To many administrators, these competencies legitimized the subject of art next to the "core" subjects (e.g., math, science, reading, writing, history), and helped school districts prioritize the arts in a new way. Although, for most of history, education (including arts education) was only attained by the elite, most schools today provide arts education.

Current Issues in Access to Art

Again, the access point for crayons and paints for many children is school. Children of a lower socioeconomic status, children who are homeless, or even children in foster care often do not have art supplies readily available. Although most school districts have an art curriculum, when funds are tight, it is often one of the first programs to see major cuts.

Because schools cannot always provide a strong arts foundation, and because the arts should not be held only for those children who can afford it, community partnerships have provided a bridge for many arts programs. These partnerships offer schools funding, unique resources, creative ideas, and guidance from professionals in the field (Bowen & Kisida, 2017). Community funding is not necessarily an answer to purchasing consumable resources such as crayons and paint, but it is a temporary solution that provides children supplies and support. In addition, grants and funding exist for children whose families do not have access to supplies at home. Some foundations offer free after-school arts programs, and many art museums offer funded field trips for Title I schools. In addition, there are organizations that offer art supplies for educational purposes free of charge. Lastly, even for expensive art camps, there are often generous donors who will sponsor a child's tuition.

RESEARCH ON THE DEVELOPMENTAL VALUE OF CRAYONS AND PAINTS

Much of the research on crayons and paints revolves around the therapeutic aspects of art for specific populations or the role of drawing and painting in child development. In terms of specific populations, for children dealing with war or in refugee camps, Shulsky and Kirkwood (2015) found that drawing and painting helped children better recognize and understand their emotions, and even encouraged happiness during difficult times. In addition, Lima and Santos interviewed children facing cancer, and several participants identified the opportunity to play (specifically paint) while in the hospital as an activity that brought them joy.

Lastly, Morgenthal (2015) found that her participant who was diagnosed with autism would play with paints and crayons in a nontraditional way giving the tools personalities and identities while acting out scenes from everyday life. This is notable as children with autism often use scripts (or social stories) to practice for social encounters or new experiences. Despite studies focusing primarily on paints and crayons being few and far between, crayons and paints are ever-present in child development, and were important themes in each of these studies.

Although art—in general—can be inherently isolating, researchers have found that it is an important part of a child's social development. For example, Hosea (2007) found that mothers who used paints in playing with their infants had an improved emotional connection with them. In terms of slightly older children, Parten (1933) studied preschool children, and found that although they did not engage in drawing and painting together, these art activities offered an important chance for parallel play. As one of the pioneer researchers of parallel play, she describes the phenomenon of parallel play as the act of playing with the same toy or activity beside another child, but not engaging together. This may not appear to be inherently social, but this type of play is widely understood to be a building block of language and social development.

The study of crayons and paints extends to teaching styles, as well. Douglass and Jaquith (2018) studied the importance of teachers using teaching artistic behavior (TAB), Reggio Emilia, or a Montessori pedagogy to offer a child-centered curriculum giving way to more artistic choice for children. To understand why creative choice is important, one must look back to the research of Amabile and Gitomer (1984) who found that creative choice in materials yields more creative artwork. Alternatively, Amabile and Gitomer found that constraining the options for children in an artistic setting could even be damaging.

In keeping with teaching, Karmiloff-Smith (1990) studied how teacher prompts and consequent redirection can change a child's drawing as he or she ages. She found that when younger children were asked to alter their pieces, they did so by changing its size, shape, or by deleting part of it completely whereas older children tended to change a subject's orientation or position. This research supported the idea older children have greater flexibility in thinking, and also recognized that these tasks was mirrored by the way they tackled other relevant challenges in their lives (e.g., seriation in children, phonological awareness in adults).

RECOMMENDATIONS

This chapter covered many aspects of crayons and paints including how they came to be, how they are used by children, and the importance of access to these toys; however, there is a need for more research. Considering the number of children who will use crayons and paints within their lives (in school, at home, or in another setting), there are ample opportunities to conduct more research around how children make decisions regarding these toys, as well as, how they decide whether to use these toys at all.

In addition, another recommendation would be to encourage parents, teachers, and others who work with children to have crayons and paints accessible for all children whether for structured learning or free play. Not only is the act of creating important for self-expression, but the byproduct of creating—the resulting piece of art—is an important tool that adults can use to better understand children. After all, a child's artwork provides adults the window through which the child sees the world. Finally, take time to draw and paint with children and to observe in person what was covered in this chapter. Don't be afraid to get messy.

REFERENCES

Amabile, T. M., & Gitomer, J. (1984). Children's artistic creativity: Effects of choice in task materials. *Personality and Social Psychology Bulletin, 10*(2), 209–15.

Association of Child Life Professionals (2018). *The evolution of the profession of Child Life in North America*. Arlington, VA.

Barnes, R. (2015). *Teaching art to young children*. Philadelphia: Routledge.

Beeny, E. (2017). The birth of pastel. Retrieved from https://blogs.getty.edu/iris/the-birth-of-pastel/.

Blum, L. H., & Dragositz, A. (1947). Finger painting: The developmental aspects. *Child Development, 18*(3), 88–105.

Boboltz, S. (2015). A brief yet complex color history of Crayola crayons. Retrieved from https://www.huffpost.com/entry/crayola-crayon-color-history_n_7345924.

Bowen, D. H., & Kisida, B. (2017). The art of partnerships: Community resources for arts education. *Phi Delta Kappan, 98*(7), 8–14.

Douglas, K. M., & Jaquith, D. B. (2018). *Engaging learners through artmaking: Choice-based art education in the classroom (TAB)*. Teachers College Press.

Eisner, E. W. (1987). The role of discipline-based art education in America's schools. *Art education, 40*(5), 6–45.

Hosea, H. (2006). "The Brush's Footmarks": Parents and infants paint together in a small community art therapy group. *International Journal of Art Therapy, 11*(2), 69–78.

Jolley, R. P. (2009). *Children and pictures: Drawing and understanding*. Hoboken, NJ: John Wiley & Sons.

Karmiloff–Smith, A. (1990). Constraints on representational change: Evidence from children's drawing. *Cognition*, *34*(1), 57–83.

Kindler, A. M., & Darras, B. (1997). Map of artistic development. *Child Development in Art*, 17–44.

Koppitz, E. M. (1984). *Psychological evaluation of human figure drawings by middle school pupils.* New York, NY: Grune & Stratton.

Lima, K. Y. N. D., & Santos, V. E. P. (2015). Play as a care strategy for children with cancer. *Revista Gaucha de Enfermagem*, *36*(2), 76–81.

Lowenfeld, V. (1957). *Creative and mental growth* (3rd ed.). New York: Macmillan.

Morgenthal, A. H. (2015). *Child-centered play therapy for children with autism: A case study* (Doctoral dissertation, Antioch University).

Mules, H. (2019). The History of Drawing. Retrieved from http://www.scholastic.com/browse/article.jsp?id=3753864.

Oakes, J. W. (2006). How the Servicemen's Readjustment Act of 1944 (GI Bill) impacted women artists' career opportunities. *Visual Culture & Gender*, *1*, 23–31.

Parten, M. B. (1933). Social play among preschool children. *Journal of Abnormal and Social Psychology*, 28 (2), 136–147.

Shulsky, D., & Kirkwood, D. (2015). Beyond tempera paint: authentically exploring visual art in early childhood. *Childhood Education*, *91*(5), 363–369.

Smith, P. (1986). The ecology of picture study. *Art Education*, *39*(5), 48–54.

Taws, R. (2016). Conté's Machines: Drawing, Atmosphere, Erasure. *Oxford Art Journal*, *39*(2), 243–66.

The History of Crayons (2019). Retrieved from https://www.crayola.com/-/media/Crayola/About-Us/History/CrayolaTimeline_2016.

Wilkinson, J. G. (1878). *The manners and customs of the ancient Egyptians* (Vol. 2). J. Murray.

15

KITCHEN AND HOUSEHOLD REPLICA TOYS

Dorothy Sluss

Kanisha sets the table, Pete sets out glasses for everyone, and Haley pretends to put food on each plate. They all sit down to eat as Sierra pours tea for everyone. They talk, agree and disagree as they laugh and play together. Adults who observe the play see a variety of scenarios. Some may enjoy watching the children laugh and play. Others may see a reflection of their own play and may even be observed serving a pretend pizza as they join in the play. Professionals examine this play scenario in terms of their own stated goal. They may focus on the child's language, pretend play, social interaction, play level, or fine motor skills. Others may look at the foods that are offered, the culture reflected in the interactions, or the gender roles. Regardless of the rationale for the observation, one thing is obvious, when children play with kitchen and household toys they are having fun. This scenario is important because it could have occurred one hundred years ago or yesterday, which speaks to the enduring nature of play with kitchen and household toys and it could have occurred in America, Italy, or Korea, which speaks to the commonality of play with kitchen and household toys around the world.

Pretending to "pour" juice into a toy glass from a toy pitcher or to "drink" tea from a toy teacup is one of the very first types of pretense commonly seen in toddler-age children, especially if their parents have encouraged this type of play and have provided replica kitchen and household toys as early play materials for their young children. As children grow, they can plan tea parties, cook pretend meals, and host celebrations with their friends and family members. These toys can also be found in high-quality preschool classrooms, which usually have areas devoted to pretend food preparation, cleanup, and other household activities. Kitchen and household toys may vary in appearance from nation to nation, state to state, and area to area, but their commonality is that they reflect the reality that children experience daily in their own home and community. In this way, kitchen and household toys stimulate high quality dramatic and sociodramatic play as children play with others, interact with other children in a variety of settings, or transition from home to school (Sluss, 2005, 2018; Pucket & Vail, 2018).

TYPES OF KITCHEN AND HOUSEHOLD REPLICA TOYS

Kitchen toys are those used to store, prepare, and serve food to a person or family. They include toys such as a play stove, refrigerator, sink, cabinet, dishwasher, microwave oven, table and chairs, or highchair. They also include small versions of dishes, glasses, plastic utensils for eating, tea or coffee pots, a toaster, blender, and food containers. Other kitchen play materials may include shopping carts and bags, or other culturally relevant items.

Household, home, or living room replica play items include items such as a small couch or chair, television, bed, dresser or chest, mirror, broom and mop, vacuum cleaner, lamps, coat rack, and doll beds. Other materials may include a phone, doll clothes, books, and magazines. In home settings, these materials will reflect the family cultural practices and in preschools they typically reflect the geographical and cultural area that surround the area.

General Characteristics

Kitchen and other household toys vary in terms of durability, safety, and quality. Perhaps the most durable toys of this type are those made of wood. Wooden kitchen sets have been used in home, preschool, and kindergarten settings for fifty years or more. These sets are made of a hard wood such as birch or oak that have a natural finish that can be renewed by using linseed oil to restore the beauty and durability of the equipment.

Plastic sets are less durable than those made of wood. These may a single set or individual items such as a stove or refrigerator. When these are contemporary single units, they may have many new technological innovations that mimic current technology, such as microwave ovens that beeps when it is finished, stove timers that can be set, or sinks that can be plumbed to a water source.

In terms of safety, sets made of wood and plastic are equally safe if they are cared for and inspected on a regular basis. Quality may be linked to both material and cost. Wood sets are more expensive but have greater durability.

Kitchen Replica Toys

There are a wide variety of such toys and the come in simple "home play" versions as well in more elaborate versions. They include the following types.

Cabinets

Cabinets have been found in kitchen areas since Montessori first developed these materials. They can be wood or plastic. They can be used to store dishes, cooking ware, or food. Some of these will look like the other kitchen equipment and some will look more like a dining room table and chair set. Be careful to ensure that the cabinets are not too large for the child. If a toddler is playing with the cabinet, they should not be able to turn it over.

Coffee Pots/Coffeemaker

This equipment ranges from a simple pot for a beverage to a machine with a place to add and brew coffee, add water and stand where the coffee cup is placed and that actually creates a beverage.

Cookware

A set of pots and pans generally looks similar to those used by parents in that they are made of stainless steel, round, and have a handle. Good sets will include lids that fit the pots and pans. Some sets may be made of a hard plastic. Better sets are replicas of the cookware used in their own home.

Dishes

A set of dishes usually includes plates, bowls, saucers, and glasses that look similar to those used by their parents. These can be glass or plastic. As a rule, glass dish sets are not as safe as plastic dishes.

Dish drainer

A child-sized dish drainer can be plastic or metal. It is a square container for dishes that are wet. This is always used with a sink but it can be used with and without a dishwasher.

Dishwasher

A child-sized dishwasher looks exactly like an adult-sized dishwasher in that it is a square piece of equipment with a front door that opens forward. A control panel on the top of the door or above the door on the cabinet. Control knobs are either painted on or created out of molded plastic. These frequently have a sound effect that accompanies turning the machine on by pushing one of the buttons or knobs on the control panel. Some machines will have a door painted on the front of the dishwasher, others will have a door that opens with a dishrack that is painted on the opening, while some may have a dishrack inside that can hold dishes and moves in and out of the machine.

Food

Plastic food that resembles food found in the local community is included in the kitchen area. Foods generally include common vegetables that children like.

Groceries

Replicas of the boxes, cans, and cartons that are found in kitchens should be included. Note: If used in a group setting, adults should check for child allergies (e.g., peanut butter). Even an empty container that housed peanut butter or peanuts can affect some children.

Microwave

A child-sized microwave made of wood or plastic and is a box with a door that opens. The microwave will generally have plastic buttons on the front of the box that will mimic the sound of a real microwave.

Refrigerator

A child-sized refrigerator is generally represented by a cabinet that has two doors: the top being smaller than the lower door. Shelves are generally found in the refrigerator and some may have a drawer or two. Wooden refrigerators typically have wood shelves, but plastic refrigerators will have shelves and drawers for vegetables that rival their counterpart in the kitchen.

Scales

A child-sized scale for measuring food and/or beverages may be included. These are generally made of steel and plastic or only plastic.

Shopping Basket or Cart

A plastic basket to carry fruits, vegetables, and groceries from the "store" to the "kitchen" or a metal or plastic shopping cart allows the child to transport groceries from a pretend vehicle to a kitchen where they can be placed on clearly labeled shelves.

Silverware

This generally includes knives, spoons, folks, and other utensils such as large spoons and may be steel or plastic.

Sink

A child-sized sink is usually housed in a cabinet. It will have a single or double bowl where dishes can be washed and knobs that move realistically. Two doors are generally placed beneath the sink area for storage. Some sinks are plumbed so that water comes out of the faucets and can be caught in the sink and then released through pipes.

Stove

A child-sized stove is usually housed in a cabinet with a cover that has a place to set pots and it has an oven inside the cabinet with an oven door that may or may not open. Wooden stoves may have electrical units/eyes painted on, knobs for turning, and a shelf. Plastic stoves will have knobs, shelves, timers, and other features that resemble a modern oven.

Table and Chairs

A child-sized table and chairs will have four table legs that keep it level so that it is stable and secure. Tables are usually sized to the age group for which it will be used. Thus, a table and chair set for a toddler will be a different size than one for a four-year-old.

As kitchens and food-preparation methods change, the hardware and machines change in the same way. There are few appliances found in any kitchen that are not also found on the local toy shelf.

Household Replica Toys

These toys also are commonly found both in children's homes and in preschool classrooms, but they are more elaborate in group settings.

Beds

A child-sized bed is similar to a large bed in that it has a headboard and a mattress on boards that are located between the headboard and the footboard. Some will be outfitted with a blanket, bedspread, or pillows.

Clothes Dryer

A child-sized dryer resembles an adult-sized dryer in that is a box with a door on the front that opens and closes to allow clothes to be placed inside the box. It may have knobs and make sounds that sound like a dryer in the home.

Couch and Chair

A child-sized couch or sofa where children can sit and socialize with other children looks similar to ones that adults use and may be composed of cloth or plastic. Single chairs will seat only one person.

Doll Beds

Beds for dolls vary according to the doll's size and the child's age. Large doll beds (20 –30") are made for large dolls that are used by very young children and small doll beds (10"–20") are made for smaller dolls that are designed for older children. Blankets, quilts, bedspreads, and pillows align with the size of the doll.

Doll Carriage/Stroller

A child-sized doll carriage is a box that is placed on wheels that can move the doll from one place to another. It has a handle that can be used to guide the movement of the carriage. It may have a mattress, pillow, and cover for the doll. A stroller is a replica of those used by adults.

Ironing Board

A child-sized ironing board looks similar to an adult ironing board and it has a way to placed it upright and take it down easily. Many wooden sets have a small iron, laundry basket, or additional laundry equipment.

Iron

A child-sized iron may accompany an ironing board. An iron may be made of wood, steel, or a combination of both. It typically has a flat surface on the bottom and a handle on top that can be used to hold the iron. A steamer may be preferable as fewer and fewer people are ironing clothes and more are beginning to steam clothes.

Mop and Broom

A child-sized broom generally has straw or plastic reeds that are bundled tightly together. A mop has a set of strings or strips of cloth bundled tightly together, though these are also evolving into mechanical mops.

Television

A child-sized television set looks like a model television set and replicates the television sets found in many homes.

Vacuum Cleaner

A child-sized vacuum cleaner is a version of vacuum cleaners that adults use in the home. They have a hose and brush for picking up dirt, a canister for holding the dirt until emptied, and a switch to turn it on and off. Some will have bells that ring or sound effects.

Washing Machine

A child-sized washing machine resembles an adult washing machine. Clothes can be placed inside the box to replicate the washing machine process. The replica may have knobs and make sounds that resemble an adult-sized machine.

ROLE IN PROMOTING CHILD DEVELOPMENT

Maria Montessori was among the first to recognize the value of kitchen or household replica equipment and materials for child development. She believed that children should be prepared "by addressing the strengths and needs of the whole person and teaching life skills and independence" (Matthews & Jewkes, 2009, p. 396). To accomplish this goal, she created materials and equipment that were smaller versions of adult equipment and materials. These were designed to teach specific skills and to provide a space and place to develop skills needed to assume a productive role in society. For Montessori, interactions in the kitchen and household area prepared children for life.

Piaget also recognized the value of kitchen and household replica equipment and materials. He found that when children played in an area filled with replicas from the adult world, they engaged in pretend or symbolic play (1962). Replicas of objects from the adult world helped children carry out pretend play that included symbolic narratives and imagery. For example, a child might pretend that a plain box is a television set, but a box that looks like a television set will facilitate the transformation of the object into mental imagery. Younger children need more realistic models than older children. Symbolism which is the substitution of a real object for a symbol and imagery is necessary for higher order thinking skills and is facilitated when the child plays with replicas of materials in their world. For Piaget, high-level pretend play occurs when materials from the real world are used and this is crucial for cognitive development.

In the same way, Vygotsky valued play with materials, but for a different reason. Vygotsky believed that when children play, they act more mature He supported the notion that children learn through play. In this scenario, the television set would serve as a pivot to scaffold symbolic thinking or cognitive growth. As children talk to each other, they move through what Vygotsky called the zone of proximal development (ZPD; Vygotsky, 1932/1978). When children move through the ZPD, their cognitive skills grow and develop. As children talk about their meal, they develop language and higher order thinking skills. Language development needed for cognitive growth and development is a key outcome of play in the kitchen and home areas.

Recent neurological studies have found that when children engage in pretend play in kitchen and HR areas, they utilize the executive functions of the brain (Sluss, 2017). That is, they plan what they are going to play, what they are going to cook, who and how they will serve it, and who and how they will clean the area after the feast is over. This thinking process occurs in the prefrontal lobe and involves executive functioning skills. As they play in the kitchen area, they may stop in the middle of the conversation and switch gears. "You can't be the Mommy. I am the mommy. OK, you be the mom, and I will be the doggy." This requires flexible or fluidity of thought. This skill is crucial for problem solving.

Because development is not the only benefit of play with kitchen and household replica materials, some researchers have investigated outcomes related to playing with kitchen and household materials. One notable study was conducted by Morrow and Rand (1991) on the relationship between literacy and play in the kitchen area. The results indicate that when children use props to promote literacy in the kitchen and house centers, they increase their preliteracy skills. Research continues to support these initial results.

EVOLUTION OVER TIME

Play at and with food-preparation materials or kitchen themes may be among the oldest and most basic type of play. Materials for food-preparation play were first found in the tombs of Egypt. Because girls from wealthy families were viewed as delicate, their activities were limited to those that supported this perspective. It is unclear if other children had materials to use as few artifacts survived. During the Medieval Period, girls might play with "miniature jugs, ewers, cups, and plates made out of lead–tin alloy" (Sayer, 2009, p. 274). This view of girls playing with food-preparation materials persisted into the Renaissance period when child-sized furniture was created for the children of Queen Victoria and Prince Albert (Sayer, 2009). The eighteenth century saw a focus on how children grew and developed. John Lock and Rousseau believed that children were innocent and must be protected and this was viewed as a reason to separate boys and girls. Boys play involved rough and tumble play while girl's play was synonymous with small versions of tea sets and other materials designed to maintain the pure and innocent state of the child. This idea persisted into the twentieth century.

During the early twentieth century, Maria Montessori, the first female physician in Italy, established the first *casa die bambini* (children's house) in Rome. The school was designed to develop the child's creativity and intellect through the use of "practical live exercises and sense-training materials." (Carlisle, 2009, p. xxxviii). This was the impetus for the creation of child-sized equipment and household materials that are now referred to as kitchen and household toys. However, she did not value play and did not view the use of these materials as play. Schools that use this philosophy include many of the same kitchen and home replica or real-life materials that were originally used in Montessori's 1907 classroom.

In contrast, Patty Hill, Carolyn Pratt, and Harriet Johnson (Sluss, 2019) believed that play is a powerful learning tool and that children learn best when they are actively using toys and materials. Pratt spent a large part of her life creating materials that are still used today. Johnson's work occurred at the Bank Street Schools, which were a part of the Columbia University in New York City. In this center, children may visit a restaurant or have a chef visit the school. When they return to school or the person leaves, they discuss the trip, write letters about the trip, draw pictures, and build a restaurant in their dramatic play center which houses kitchen or household toys. The restaurant may influence play in the house area for a month. A visit to a pizza shop may inspire the study of pizzas. The kitchen area can be used for pizza preparation and tables can be used for serving. Prop boxes are filled with materials that enrich the play. For example, a pizza play prop box might have menus, aprons, pizza boxes, plastic drink cups, miniature money, cash register, a pad for recording orders and paying for the pizza. These toys are added to the kitchen and household area as needed and many centers still use this approach.

The Schools of Reggio Emelia are constantly changing the materials to enhance the theme that is being used in the classroom. The real difference is that instead of putting the theme materials away at end of the day, they may leave their materials intact until the next day. One such theme involves grapes that are grown in the area. They use some of the equipment that their grandparents used, but they also use modern equipment, and this is reflected in their kitchen and home areas. The philosophy of the community, school, teachers and parents guide the selection of kitchen and home equipment.

Today, many schools have kitchen and household toys, but the emphasis is placed on the type of play that occurs. Most of these areas are called dramatic play areas or pretend centers, but they include kitchen and household toys. Given that toys have been called tools for learning, it is difficult to understand the hesitancy in using the term. Thus, they create the context for play, but toys are invisible in much of the scholarly writing about pretend or dramatic play.

Modern trends in real-life equipment affect the types of such toys in homes and preschools. For example, when Montessori started her centers wood or gas stoves were used and now microwave and convection ovens are popular. Similarly, refrigerators look different and phones have changed to cell phones. Also, televisions have turned into computers and mops have been replaced with automatic cleaning tools.

ADAPTATIONS FOR CHILDREN WITH SPECIAL NEEDS

Children may have disabilities that range from hearing impaired to autism. To ensure the child's success, individual adaptations in kitchen and household replica materials must be made that are specific to the child's disability. When adaptations are made, children can be successful in the kitchen or house area. Adaptations may include drawing outlines of where to place a plate, silverware, and glass on the menus that are used on the table. This provides a template that allows the child to be more successful. Stacking bowls and pots that are graduated in size help the child to understand size, shape, and seriation. As the child uses these materials, they can develop an array of skills.

GENDER DIFFERENCES AND SEX ROLE MESSAGES

Differentiation of gender roles have long been observed in the play that occurs in kitchen and home areas. As noted earlier, miniature jugs, and cups made of lead-tin alloy were first found in the tombs of the early Egyptians. These were probably used by girls to mimic activities at home. At this time, girls were not allowed to play with materials set aside for boys and boys were not allowed to play with those materials considered appropriate for girls.

Today, gender is still the major factor affecting how these toys are used in home and group settings. For example, parents or grandparents may buy certain toys of this type to give to girls but will not give these toys to boys. The feminist movement and current recognition of the impact of the strict separation of boys and girls for many centuries has had some effect on how the kitchen and household areas rooms are viewed. One recent article in the popular *National Geographic* magazine article featured a story entitled, "How today's toys may be harming your daughter" (Daly, 2017). Though it was retracted and rewritten, few will read the amended article and the impact of the article may cause some parents to doubt the value of kitchen toys for their daughters and to be concerned that their brains are not developing as quickly as those of some of the boys.

The controversy has moved to the web. One site, *Think or Blue*, featured an article with the title, "5 Reasons Why Every Kid Needs a Play Kitchen." The author noted that kitchen toys should be included so that *all* children play together in the kitchen and home area. She noted that today's child-sized kitchens can be purchased in gender neutral colors and that every child deserves the play and fun that occur in kitchen and household areas. She also mentioned that social skills, fine motor skills, and imaginative play that would benefit all children. Ultimately, it is up to parents and to teachers to break gender stereotypes and this can occur by actions such as placing pictures that show both men and women in the kitchen and selecting books to read that show men and women in the kitchen. Given that both men and women today cook and clean their own homes, a kitchen or household area must reflect this reality.

ADDITIONAL RESEARCH NEEDED

Additional research is needed on the impact of kitchen and household toys on young children. Much of the research that has been conducted focused on play that occurs within the dramatic play area. However, the types of toys (e.g., kitchen and household) are not mentioned in most of the studies. A great deal of research by sociologists and the business community focuses on gender roles and marketing. Advertisements are mentioned prominently in these ads. Those who purchase and maintain kitchen and household toys will find little in the scholarly literature that will assist them in the selection, purchase, and maintenance of the area. This chapter has tried to create space for the importance of kitchen and household toys and refute the idea that it is only a place for girls. All children eat and most adults prepare food, so all children should play with kitchen and household toys.

REFERENCES

Bailey, C. (2020). Why every kid needs a play kitchen. *Think or Blue*. Retrieved from https://www.thinkorblue.com/play-kitchen/

Carlisle, R. P. (2009). *Encyclopedia of PLAY in today's society, Vol.1*.Washington, DC: Sage.

Christie, J. F., Johnsen, P. E., & Peckover, R. B. (2009). The effects of play period duration on children's play patterns. *Journal of Research in Childhood Education* (3) 2, 123–31.

Daly, N. (2017). How today's toys may be harming your daughter. *National Geographic,* Retrieved from https://www.nationalgeographic.com/magazine/2017/01/gender-toys-departments-piece/

Lillard, A. (2007) *Montessori: The science behind the genius*. New York, NY: Oxford University Press

Matthews, E., & Jewes, A. (2009). Montessori. In R. P. Carlisle (Ed.), *Encyclopedia of PLAY in today's society, Vol. 1*. Washington, DC: Sage.

Morrow, L., & Rand, M. (1991). Preparing the classroom environment to promote literacy during play. In James F. Christie's (Ed.). *Play and early literacy development*. Albany, NY: State University of New York Press.

Piaget, J. (1952/1962). *Play, dreams, and imitation in childhood*. New York, NY: Basic Books.

Puckett, G., & Vail, M. (2018). Meeting learning standards through dramatic play. *Dimensions of Early Childhood, 46*(2), 29.

Sayer, K. A. (2009). Girl's play. In R. P. Carlisle (Ed.), *Encyclopedia of PLAY in today's society, Vol. 1*.Washington, DC: Sage.

Sluss, D. J. (2019). *Supporting play: Environment, curriculum, assessment*. New York, NY: Cengage.

Sweet, E. (2014). Toys are more divided by gender than they were 50 years ago, *The Atlantic*.

Vygotsky, L. (1932/1978) *Mind in society: The development of higher psychological processes*. Cambridge, MA: Harvard University Press.

Wohlwend, K. (2018). Child's play: Reading and remaking gendered action texts with toys. In B. Guzzetti, T. Bean, & J. Dunkerly-Bean's (Eds.) *Literacies, sexualities, and gender: Understanding identities from preschool to adulthood*. New York: Routledge.

16

REAL-LIFE/FANTASY DRESS-UP CLOTHES AND MATERIALS

Brooke R. Spangler Cropenbaker

Developmental psychologists support diverse play experiences across childhood to strengthen physical, cognitive, and social-emotional development. Sociodramatic imaginary play, involved in dress-up play, has been a well-respected and supported opportunity for young children to practice adult roles, regulate emotion, resolve conflict, and navigate new terrains. Allowing children to have the option to experience a character while playing promotes deeper engagement in the play experience, granting the opportunity for even greater developmental gains. Dress-up play can involve real life characters (e.g., putting on a pair of mom's high heels and pretending to be a business professional; wearing an apron and a chef's hat while pretending to be a chef) or more fantasy-based (e.g., donning a superhero suit to help save the day).

Prop-based play allows for children to explore new worlds and become physically immersed in someone else's clothes, which may help with cognitive perspective taking. Physical development can result from the fine motor control of buttoning buttons to balancing in a pair of dad's clunky work boots. Socioemotional development occurs when playing dress-up with peers who want access to the coveted materials or want to play the same role promoting negotiation, conflict resolution, and problem solving. In a short session of make-believe pretend play, all developmental domains are supported.

Dress-up play requires access to materials, which can range in cost and availability, limiting the opportunity for some children to engage in this type of play. Though many children may simply wish to wear their own parents' clothes and shoes, some parents may be reluctant to share these larger sized items considering safety concerns or lack of clothes they feel they can willingly give to their children. In modern times, creative play clothes are mass-produced in child-sized dimensions, allowing many safety concerns to be eliminated, but increasing the financial resources needed to purchase these items.

Having children engage in imaginary play has many benefits. Recently, researchers have reported that engaging in fantasy-based make-believe play results in greater cognitive skills (Thibodeau, Gilpin, Brown, & Meyer, 2016). They found that a five-week fantasy play intervention promoted improved executive functioning when compared to nonfantasy-play-based activities (Thibodeau et al., 2016). Pretend play interventions also have demonstrated increased creativity in a sample of elementary-aged girls (Hoffmann & Russ, 2016). Divergent thinking, a process executed in problem solving, was fostered for those children in the pretend play group. The children engaging in imaginary play also showed higher rates of positive affect, illustrating an additional emotional benefit to this type of play.

Promoting cognitive and emotional development in children relates to better educational outcomes as well as later life outcomes, as advanced cognitive and emotional processing are considered valuable modern skills for the workforce (Hoffman & Russ, 2016). Pretend play is a common pastime for children, yet as children spend more time in school, imaginary play opportunities become limited. It becomes essential for caregivers to promote imaginary play at home to help children gain the developmental gains needed to be successful in the modern world.

TYPICAL TYPES OF DRESS-UP CLOTHES

Dress-up clothes have evolved over time. In years past, the only child-sized dress-up clothes were typically costumes used for Halloween or theatrical plays. More recently, toy manufacturers have noticed a market in creating more "everyday" costumes for children available outside of the trick-or-treating season. These outfits can be found at local retail stores and range from tutus and princess dresses to superhero masks and popular movie character get-ups. Also, the range of options increases exponentially if someone shops through online marketplaces.

Real Life

Real-life dress-up involves realistic outfits for children to be able to emulate their favorite professions. These materials are typically the uniforms of professional roles, where children can put on these outfits and pretend they are engaging in the activities typical of that adult. They can extend from the uniforms of service professionals (such as police, fire, or medical personnel) to the use of prop-based tools of the trade (such as having a painter's palette and a paint brush to pretend to be an artist, a cardboard sword and a colander to be a knight, or a notepad and some plates to pretend to be a restaurant server).

Fantasy Based

Fantasy-based dress-up involves the opportunity to be a mythical character or animal and typically involve more costume-based material. Common fantasy-based dress-up experiences may include being an alien from outer space, a colorful unicorn exploring the forest, a daring superhero rescuing the city from a villain, a brave dragon slayer, or a movie or literary character familiar to the child. Though using accurate representations of the character a child is attempting to portray is exciting, it is not the only way. Fantasy based materials can also involve using generic materials to represent the experience. If children are given access to more open-ended items, the richness of the play experience could increase. For example, the child wearing a colander on his head as a knight could easily change roles to become a construction worker wearing a hard hat to stay safe on the job site.

INTEREST ACROSS THE LIFESPAN

Infancy

While infants from birth to two years of age, are not yet able to cognitively process advanced concepts related to make-believe play, there is a natural progression to engage in this type of play as children progress through early childhood, ages three to six years. Make-believe play requires cognitive perspective taking that develops as the brain grows throughout these early years.

Early Childhood

During early childhood, the drive to engage in pretend play increases, and dress-up play is one type of this imaginative realm. Therefore, this type of play becomes a common child-centered experience for preschool aged children. It is important when caregivers promote this type of play, the child is the driver in this play setting. When children make decisions about their play, they gain competence and confidence in practicing these unique roles. Children who engage in dress-up play with other children reap socioemotional and language benefits during a time when social skills are strengthening. Research shows that when children play with other children, language skills improve, as they need to communicate more to have the other children understand the parameters of the play experience (Coplan, & Arbeau, 2009). When playing with adults, children do not have to be explicit, because adults come with preconceived notions about the context of play that other children do not have. This limits the need for children to explain the context to adults, and adults may not ask the questions other children may ask to navigate the play space.

As previously mentioned, social dress-up play with others can promote cognitive and social gains in childhood. When multiple children in a play-based setting want to be a fire marshal and there is only one fire hat, the children need to work out the conflict. In order for social play to be successful, children need to understand the wants and desires of their peers, which supports theory of mind development, the ability to understand that other people have unique desires, beliefs and wishes. Theory of mind develops throughout early childhood allowing children to increase their successes in interacting with others. Promoting social-based dress-up play can provide the richest context for development for children across early childhood.

This is not to say that imaginary play must be supported with dress-up materials. Imaginary play is a type of play that once emerges may be difficult to stifle in a pre-school aged child. Thinking back to one's own childhood, it is easy to remember times lost in imaginary narratives—no costumes needed. This can be comforting to families without the resources to support elaborate props, as a cardboard box and a marker can provide an inexpensive canvas for creating many objects that can be used in fantasy play experiences without the higher price tag of more formal and mass produced fantasy-based play materials. Adults can help children create an airplane, racecar, or a space-ship with the simple drawing of some wheels and/or windows on the box! Better yet, they can ask the child what type of vessel the box is preferred to be and take his or her lead in order to provide the most developmental support.

Middle Childhood

As children age into middle childhood, pretend play may become more advanced as brain growth relates to gains in thinking about the world in richer, more complex ways. School-aged children are commonly found playing fantasy-based imaginary games on the playground during recess, though access to dress-up clothes typically stays behind in preschool classrooms. For some children, this does not cause a decrease in imaginary play, but requires more creative descriptions and narrative storytelling to describe the play experience without the props. Communication across friend groups continues to provide a venue for negotiation, questioning, and problem solving.

As one ages through the elementary school years, the later ages of this developmental period brings along a decline in this type of play. This may be because of an increased interest in team-based sports and cooperative play, as well as advanced knowledge of rules and a heightened draw to board game-based play activities.

Adolescence and Adulthood

Adolescents may continue to dress-up in the context of theatrical plays or costume-based holidays. Even adults may find joy in these recreational activities, though labeling the experience as dress-up may no longer be socially acceptable without impact on how one is viewed. As one ages, the context for dress-up activities may be tied to recreational parties or events where special outfits may be ceremonial (e.g., weddings, galas) or planned and purposeful yet informal (e.g., Halloween, Day of the Dead festivals, Renaissance fairs, historical reenactments, cosplay, costume parties, live action role playing [LARP]).

Adolescents and adults may engage in these activities allowing for dress-up play to continue. There may be fantasy-based play under the guise of video game engagement where an adolescent or adult immerses as a character in the digital context. Fron, Fullerton, Ford Morie, and Pearce (2007) argue that dress-up play is rooted deeply in human culture and the rise in massive multiplayer online games allows for adults to continue with this rich interactive and expressive experience long beyond childhood in a socially acceptable sphere.

CHILDREN WITH SPECIAL NEEDS

Dressing up and engaging in make-believe play does not present striking differences between children with special needs when compared to typically developing children. While some children with physical limitations (such as motor control issues or visual impairments) may be physically unable to manipulate the items or dress into the outfits unassisted, pretend play experiences engage cognitive processing when fully immersed in the experience. If children with special needs have a limited ability to engage in make-believe play, the experience may be hindered, but children with cognitive impairments may not be interested in this type of play to begin with. Because this type of play is child-centered, taking the cues from the children themselves allows caregivers to know if this type of play would be enjoyed by developmentally diverse individuals as there is a typical trend to engage in make-believe play as children progress throughout early childhood.

GENDER DIFFERENCES

Having interest in make-believe play and engaging in dress-up or using props while playing does not differ between genders, though the types of characters the children may want to emulate may differ. Gender-based stereotypes may prevent caregivers from thinking that young boys can be princesses or young girls can be male superheroes, but this is not the case. Children's unique interests should be supported, and the opportunity to engage in pretend play promotes positive developmental outcomes regardless of the alignment with gender ideals.

While preschool-aged children may self-segregate into female and male separate groups, the opportunity for dress-up play should be made available to both. In a school setting, starting as young as preschool classrooms, fantasy play may be a sphere where integrated groupings may occur as there is opportunity for larger numbers of players (Edwards, Knoche, & Kumru, 2001). Despite the opportunity for mixed gender groups, female-initiated dress-up experiences may relate more to family and domestic life (e.g., playing house and dressing up like the members of the family), while the male-initiated dress-up experiences may relate to more physical types of exploration (e.g., actively saving the town from the fire as the fire chief) (Edwards et al., 2001). It is important to remember, however, that a children's preferences for what activities they engage in while playing are also influenced by parents and caregivers as well as the children themselves. Parents may foster sex-stereotyped roles of fantasy play subtly or more overtly (Edwards et al., 2001), through purchasing toys for their children that promote gender ideals or limiting access to opposite-gendered items. It is important to note that media may have an influence on the types of fantasy play that boys and girls engage in as well, promoting attitudes and ideas that map on to what is expected or valued in our society.

Differences emerge in early childhood between boys and girls and how they use objects as symbols in play. As Edwards and colleagues (2001) describe, a boy may use the same object as a girl in a completely different imaginary way. For example, a boy may imagine a scrap of cloth is a cape for the superhero they are emulating, while a girl may imagine the scrap a cloth is a blanket for an imaginary baby. Children across genders do not differ in the amount of time they engage in fantasy play, though the themes and content may differ (Edwards et al., 2001).

DEVELOPMENTAL OUTCOMES

As previously mentioned, imaginary play provides opportunity for many developmental gains. Open-ended fantasy engagement allows for players to move beyond scripted and calculated experiences, promoting growth in rich cognitive contexts. A child who dresses up as an adult-role character (i.e., a parent, a firefighter) uses existing schemas to organize his or her play, there are no rules to follow or handbooks to read. Not only does this allow for exploration in the adult role, it allows for practice in a developmentally safe environment.

For example, if a child is pretending to be a firefighter, it is safe for the child to forget safety gear. This would not be the case in the emergency setting an adult firefighter finds him- or herself in. This practice play can also allow for exploration of adult roles that may later relate to career interests or other adult roles that will be actually carried out in the future. If dressing up in the character's outfit or gear promotes stronger alignment with the role, then the benefits are ripe for the picking.

Not only does dress-up play promote adult role exploration, often imaginary play is engaged in by multiple children together promoting socioemotional development. Collaborative play allows for problem solving, negotiation, and conflict resolution. These skills promote childhood socioemotional gains which benefit the preschool aged child as he or she becomes an older child. Socioemotional skills promote friendships, allowing for support systems to begin to develop in the early educational years. These early friendships can allow for greater exploration and engagement in school settings promoting even greater positive outcomes. Physical development can be fostered through dress-up play when children need to use fine motor skills to assemble the outfits, button the buttons, and lace the work boots. If dress-up play promotes greater exploration and exaggerated movements, then physical development may also be evident in gross motor muscles as well.

RESEARCH ON DRESS-UP PLAY

Recently, developmental experts have started to state explicitly how important play is for children, and suggesting that adult-provided support for promoting such play not be considered separate from learning (as many teachers may erroneously believe) but to be conceptualized as "play equals learning" (see Singer, Golinkoff, & Hirsh-Pasek, 2009 for details). In this vein, dress-up play needs to be considered a developmentally purposeful and worthwhile endeavor.

There are several categories of play that experts believe are fundamentally important for proper development. Object play, physical play, outdoor play, and social or alone pretend play are considered the hallmark experiences that children should engage in and parents and caregivers should foster (Yogman, Garner, Hutchinson, Hirsh-Pasek, & Golinkoff, 2018). While there are benefits for development across these play modalities, fantasy play may provide a context to promote cognitive growth in ways the other types of play promote physical growth at the forefront. For example, "Dress-up, make believe, and imaginary play encourage the use of more sophisticated language to communicate with playmates and develop rule-based scenarios" (Yogman et al., 2018, p. 3). Object play, physical play, and outdoor play may include others, but the focus is on the movement and manipulation of an object or the child, creating an opportunity for physical development of fine and gross muscles.

Pretend play with props (such as dress-up play) promotes language development, because of the practice with representation. As the colander represents the knight's helmet, a word represents a concept (Weisberg, Zosh, Hirsh-Pasek, & Golinkoff, 2013). Allowing children to have experience with the object-symbol relationship may allow children the opportunity to explore and practice these complex cognitive processes. If children are playing dress-up with their parents, this relationship may be even greater, as adults are more likely to scaffold language development growth for their children (Weisberg et al., 2013; Yogman et al, 2018). Interactions in creative play spaces with other children (without adults) also promote positive language outcomes.

When children are playing with peers, communication is necessary, otherwise the play experience would be considered unsuccessful. Children must communicate the concepts and ideas within their minds, to be on the same page as the other players. Without communication, these fantasy experiences would be solitary and isolating. Moreover, when children are engrossed in a play experience, which fantasy play often requires, they are more likely to stay engaged and this engagement promotes better language outcomes due to the richness of the play (Weisberg, et al., 2013).

It has long been understood that creating enriched environments for children allows for better cognitive growth (Wolff & Feinbloom, 1969). Wolff and Feinbloom encourage parents to create these enriched environments by promoting fantasy play, allowing for a child to explore the novelty of the experience, and the creativity that results. When fantasy play is discouraged, there can be lasting negative effects on cognitive growth. No parents want to set their children up to have hindered cognitive processing. Promoting fantasy play, such as providing dress-up clothes, can be an inexpensive and convenient way to present a blank canvas for creativity and innovation, communication, and problem solving.

In a world dominated by technology, popular toys for children are often battery operated and digital. While interacting with modern electronics is helpful for children to gain understanding and comprehension of these platforms for future success, this should not be a priority during early childhood. As described by Healey and Mendelsohn (2019), parents perceive electronic toys as being "necessary for developmental progress" (p. 2) yet there is no evidence to support this commonly held misconception. Digital toys do not promote interactive play, while socioemotional play, such as dress-up play, does.

When parents promote imaginary play, children play with others, whether children or parents, promoting social interactions and socioemotional growth (Healey & Mendelsohn, 2019). Not only does imaginative play promote social interactions, language gains are evident in this type of play as well. Children must describe the imaginary experience to their playmates, create narratives, and communicate intentions (Healey & Mendelsohn, 2019). This does not need to happen with digital and technology play experiences.

Children are developmentally ready to engage in fantasy play throughout early and middle childhood. Paley (2004) claims that fantasy play is the activity that children are the *best* prepared to engage in. There is no risk to the player, as the imaginary play space is safe from real world consequence. This allows children to engage in calculated risk, to explore new ideas, and new roles without the critique of others.

RECOMMENDATIONS

It is recommended that all caregivers promote real-life/fantasy-based dress-up play in children. Providing enriched environments for children, including access to costumes and props, allows for greater developmental growth; something that all supportive care-givers want to foster. Children will naturally be interested in make-believe play and promoting this type of engaged play only leads to better outcomes for the youth partici-pating in this creative type of play across all developmental domains.

REFERENCES

Coplan, R. J., & Arbeau, K. A. (2009). Peer interactions and play in early childhood. In K. H. Rubin, W. M. Bukowski, & B. Laursen (Eds.). *Handbook of peer interactions, relationships, and groups* (1st ed.). New York: Guilford.

Edwards, C. P., Knoche, L., & Kumru, A. (2001). Play patterns and gender. In J. Worrell (Ed.). *Encyclopedia of women and gender, 2,* (pp. 809–15), San Diego, CA: Academic Press.

Fron, J., Fullerton, T., Ford Morie, J., & Pearce, C. (2007). Playing dress-up: Costumes, roleplay, and imagina-tion. Paper presented at the *Philosophy of Computer Games Conference*, January 24–27, 2007. Retrieved January 15, 2019 from https://pdfs.semanticscholar.org/131d/13916ba062717e45efea0a5e81b4bd372830.pdf

Healey, A., & Mendelsohn, A. (2019). Selecting appropriate toys for young children in the digital age. *Pediatrics, 143*(1), 1–10.

Hoffmann, J. D., & Russ, S. W. (2016). Fostering pretend play skills and creativity in elementary school girls: A group play intervention. *Psychology of Aesthetics, Creativity, and the Arts, 10*(1), 114–25.

Paley, V. G. (2004). *A child's work: The importance of fantasy play*. Chicago, IL: The University of Chicago Press.

Singer, D. G., Golinkoff, R. M., & Hirsh-Pasek, K. (Eds.) (2009). *Play = learning: How play motivates and enhances children's cognitive and socioemotional growth*. Oxford, England, UK: Oxford University Press.

Thibodeau, R. B., Gilpin, A. T., Brown, M. M., & Meyer, B. A. (2016). The effects of fantastical pretend-play on the development of executive functions: An intervention study. *Journal of Experimental Child Psychology, 145,* 120–38.

Weisberg, D. S., Zosh, J. M., Hirsh-Pasek, K., & Golinkoff, R. M. (2013). Talking it up: Play, language develop-ment, and the role of adult support. *American Journal of Play, 6*(1), 39–54.

Wolff, P. H., & Feinbloom, R. I. (1969). Critical periods and cognitive development in the first two years. *Pediatrics, 44*(6), 999–1006.

Yogman, M., Garner, A., Hutchinson, J., Hirsh-Pasek, K., & Golinkoff, R. M. (2018). The power of play: A pediatric role in enhancing development in young children. *Pediatrics, 142*(3), 1–18.

BOARD GAMES

James E. Johnson and Sonia Tiwari

Although board games go back to much earlier times, modern technology-augmented games—those in the digital realm—have existed for only a few decades, not evolving over centuries like chess and backgammon. Nevertheless, this chapter covers both because many games exist and are popular in both formats, analog and digital. These games are usually played indoors, vary greatly, sometimes have age-appropriate specifications, and typically involve more than one player. Winning the game can be based purely or mostly on skill and strategy (e.g., chess), or on chance or luck (e.g., Candyland). Most board games (the term used in this chapter for physical board games and screen-augmented reality versions) in their playing and outcome contain elements of player skill and random events (spinning stops unpredictably, with spun teetotums, number disc or dice showing its face value independent of the player's will or effort).

Favorite board games found across nations include backgammon, checkers, Parcheesi, Go, among others in addition to chess. Of the world games, chess is by far the most well-known. Throughout history there have many players and readers and writers of chess books. The Library of Congress lists 4,767 books under the key word "chess" (checkers had 452); the John G. White Collection at the Cleveland Public Library houses more than 32,000 volumes of chess literature (Fine, 2015). The United States Chess Federation promotes scholastic chess that aims for using the game to help child development. Hence, this board game will receive further coverage in the chapter. First, other board games and the topic in general are discussed, because they are also fun to play, and because they, too, are playing a roll (pun intended) in promoting child development and education.

Board games can be grouped based on common characteristics in the means and ends of play. The means are the materials and procedures used in following games rules to reach a winning situation. The end or purpose of playing a board game is to prevail, to win. The Greek word for game is *agon*, referring to contest or competition. Players usually are pitted against each other, but in the case of solitary or cooperative play the player(s) are, in a sense, competing with the game itself. Winning is the purpose and the termination of the game. Board games for children are discussed in terms of age-level differences and gender and special needs considerations. The aim is to define types of board games, describe their characteristics, and summarize what is known concerning the relationship of playing board games with development and learning during child-hood. Some recommendations are offered in conclusion.

KINDS OF BOARD GAMES

More than one system exists for discussing types of board games. Parlet (1999) covers five kinds, which include the following:

- **Race games**. The aim is being first to get one's pieces or piece "home" by casting dice or spinning a numbered wheel or teetotums.
- **Space games** . The purpose is getting all of one's pieces in a line or specified area (e.g., Chinese checkers).
- **Chase games** . The goal is for side with dominance in number of pieces to immobilize the weaker side (e.g., Fox & Geese).
- **Displace games**. Like war, as in chess, the goal is to capture or displace the opponents' pieces; or as in Mancala to capture a majority of neutral pieces (beans, seeds, etc.).
- **Theme games**. Many modern games have thematic content such as property trading (Monopoly) or crime detection (e.g., Clue). These games are invented and protected by copyright. As such they are proprietary as opposed to traditional or evolved games, like backgammon and chess.

Below is a second example of a classification system for board games suggested by the chapter authors.

- **Strategic.** Strategic board games involve structured rules, planning, anticipation, predictions and other nuances of playing strategically against opponents. These board games offer higher social interaction as they tend to run long and are often played best as a group, such as Monopoly, Life, Risk, and Settlers of Catan. Other strategic board games may require specific number of players, such as four players playing as doubles in carom, or two players in chess.
- **Educational** . Educational board games focus on specific learning goals such as counting and sorting in Hi-Ho! Cherry-O, or forming simple equations using Mathable. For younger children, the learning goals are often limited to one pri-

mary and one secondary, while for older children an educational board game can be more complex and have multiple learning goals.

- **Mysterious.** Mysterious games rely on deduction within a fictional narrative, such as ruling out suspects in the game of Clue or Outfoxed, or guessing each other's mystery person in Guess Who? The game progresses based on a series of clues that help players rule out suspects.

- **Luck-centered.** Luck-centered games such as Chutes and Ladders or bingo do not require any strategizing or deduction and are purely based on luck. A dice/spinner would direct players to move their game pieces to a particular segment of the board. The simplicity of this genre makes it accessible to a wider age range.

- **Creative.** Creative board games offer a unique spin on traditional strategies, such as combining memory-matching and luck to remember and seek hidden treasures in Enchanted Forest, or the ability to switch/flip sections of the board to reveal new pathways in Peppa Pig surprise slides.

- **DIY.** Do-it-yourself board games offer children the ability to use their choice of images, texts, rules, and contexts by using available resources and their own imagination. With the rise of the Maker Movement (i.e., learning by making), children can also make use of fabrication technologies such as 3D printing or laser cutting to create customized board games on demand.

FEATURES OF BOARD GAMES

Physical Components of Board Games

The *board* in a board game typically comprises of a paper or textile flat surface with several sections. There is a clear beginning and end marked on the board. Some are linear tracks, while others circular or looped. The length of track can vary. Folding in layers can increase its length, as can creating reticular boards that have grids for the appearance of nets or networks. Board games have many possible patterns.

Game-pieces is an umbrella term for all the small bits and pieces used to play on the board.

Units (also called token, figurines, pawn, marker, chit, trophy, etc., depending on the game) are the small objects that represent each player on the board game.

Progression tools, such as dice, spinner, or teetotum, is used to direct players to move their units to a particular section on the board.

Currency of the game could be objects such as coins, figurines, cards, and so forth, that act as a measure of gains or losses in some board games.

Conceptual Components of Board Games

Rules provide board game players a clear beginning, progression, end, possible outcomes, alternatives, and possibilities of gameplay.

Rewards and penalties help some players move further close or away from the goal, making the board game interesting.

Scope of competition refers to whether the board game allows players to go against another team, or to work cooperatively against the game itself. Gameplay's scope of competition is a continuum on which players may try to improve from previous performance, as well as winning over others, to varying extents.

Social Components of Board Games

Social interactions with players on the same or opposing teams during gameplay, such as taking on roles within the narrative of the game, planning, conspiring, or deceiving to get ahead in the game are all engaging social components of a board game.

Live feedback or physical cues given by our bodies during gameplay, such as nervously touching our faces or moving our feet underneath the desk or smiling at a victorious progression on the board are all instant, live feedback for players.

Players as people first is a defining social component of board games where players are often people from everyday life (family, friends, neighbors) and are not dehumanized—unlike in digital games where it is easy to hide behind a screen and misuse anonymity.

Communities for board games offer players support in finding help on gameplay or finding games by themes or interests, such as the online forum Board Game Geek or social media fan pages of individual games. Events such as GAMA's Origins, GenCon, and Germany's Essen Spiel bring about board gamers from across the globe to share ideas and seek feedback. Toy libraries offer board game players the opportunity to discover, borrow, and explore different board games without spending a fortune on buying them.

AGE AND DEVELOPMENTAL APPROPRIATENESS

Preschool and Early Elementary Age Board Games

Board games designed for young children (ages three to five) often have one or two simple rules and take a shorter amount to finish the game, such as games that ask players to race till the end based on luck (e.g., Race to Planet X, Chutes and Ladders).

For slightly older children (ages five to seven years), board games such as Outfoxed or Race to the Treasure can be more engaging.

Later Elementary and Adolescent Age Board Games

For older children (ages eight years and older), board games such as Monopoly or Life, which are more complex and take longer to finish are better suited. Age recommendations by Game Designers may not be a true indication of developmental preparedness to handle a game with ease. Play should come naturally; and there is not a one-size-fit-all age level for enjoying any board game.

DEVELOPMENTAL APPROPRIATENESS

Characteristics of quality games designs that are developmentally appropriate are listed below:

- *Clarity.* Design board games with clear rules, guidelines, rewards, penalties, or any other contingencies.
- *Versatility.* Define if there only one way to play the board game or is it possible to configure the board in different ways each time.
- *Social setup.* Design board games for maximum possibility of social interaction; make use of the players being right next to each other
- *Apt art.* Consider relatable characters, storylines, and visual style for that age group
- *Level the playing field.* Allow players to try on different personalities such as to be more open or guarded, polite or aggressive in strategy.
- *Nature.* Design to support a specific nature of the board game. Is it ridiculously simple and straightforward for casual playing, or more complex in rules and game-play for a deeper, longer social interaction?
- *Definitive conclusion.* Engaging board games progress not so quick that they end right after they begin, and not so complex that they go on for too long. Ideally, a victor should emerge in less than an hour.

GENDER DIFFERENCES

While there is a push for "gender neutral" themes for board games such as animals, multicultural children, objects, aliens, or abstract characters that may appeal to all genders, there are still stereotypically distinct themes of board games for girls and boys.

Common themes for board games designed for girls include fairies, princesses, uni-corns, mermaids, bugs, and butterflies in shades of pink, purple, and pastels. For boys, popular themes are super-heroes, Vikings, dinosaurs, robots, and battles in shades of blue, green, and red.

Research suggests that gender-typical color preferences are often acquired over time with exposure to environment, and that it is possible to create equal learning opportu-nities by removing such color coding (Wong & Hines, 2015). Gender typical characters such as superheroes for boys (Coyne, Rasmussen, Nelson, & Collier, 2014) are often seen in board games such as Marvel's Chutes and Ladders. Even though the game explicitly says it is for "boys and girls," there still exists a very visible "pink aisle versus blue aisle" of toys in the stores, a popular term used in the parenting-blogs community.

As the world's largest online marketplace, Amazon does not categorize its board games based on gender overtly, the search term "board games for boys" returns games such as Battleship and Monopoly and the search term "board games for girls" returns games such as Pretty Pretty Princess and Mermaid Island. A similar search on Google returns highly gendered results, which shows that although on the surface there is no clear segregation of gendered games, the algorithms driving these searches are stereo-typical in nature, often referred to as "data bais" (Perez, 2019). Gendered games for girls also end up being more expensive because of the "Pink Tax," the tendency of products and services for females costing higher. Authors recommend the use of gen-der-neutral characters, colors, and themes to avoid these stereotypical biases and en-courage equal learning opportunities.

ADAPTATIONS FOR CHILDREN WITH SPECIAL NEEDS

Given their tactile nature, board games can be redesigned to support play experience of children with special needs. For example, for children with low vision, Braille versions of classic Monopoly and a tactile version of chess are available. In the redesigned chess, darker squares are raised, pieces have a dowel to hold them in place, and the dark pieces have the required spike to indicate their color.

Since early 2000s, there has been a rise in the availability of tactile versions of popular games such as bingo, Chinese checkers, Monopoly, Parcheesi, Sudoku, chess, or Scrabble. Majority of the games are currently exclusively available online through specialized toys and games websites such as maxisids.com, braillebookstore.com, or Amazon. Accessibility to these games remains a challenge due to almost exclusively having to rely on online stores. The term *adaptive toys* has gained popularity in the last decade, focusing in design and distribution of more inclusive toys that serve children with disabilities. Many nonprofits and universities that have toy adapting programs, such as RePlayforKids.org, DIYability.org, the Toy Adaptation Program (TAP) at The Ohio State University, or the HuskyADAPT at University of Washington. The goal of these programs is to teach students, teachers, parents, engineers, designers, and other members of the community to create adaptive toys and games. making play accessible to all.

RESEARCH ON BOARD GAMES

Play and toy use during the formative years, including playing a board game, is generally considered the "work" of children, helping them develop and prepare for school. An *Exceptional Parent* article put it in these terms: "When children play . . . *Candy Land*, they have to wait their turn, follow the rules, negotiate when to end the game and learn to deal with losing and winning" (Murphey, 1996, p. 32). Parents are urged to help their children to become good players, building social relations and forming friendships. Board games that afford choices and thoughtful decision making while following the game rules foster social and emotional skills and behaviors important for academic success.

Researchers have used board games in educational contexts to promote academic attainments in areas such as math and to facilitate cognitive functioning such as concentration and persistence (executive functioning). For example, years ago, Kamii (1985) employed the board games Sorry! and Double Parcheesi, formatively assessing how first graders cooperatively and profitably engage in play with these board games while covering (reinventing) the math curriculum. Recently, Good and Ottley (2019) stated, "Throughout life, games can be a wonderful way to develop mathematics knowledge and skills. From *Chutes and Ladders* to chess, many games use and build math abilities" (p. 73).

Considerable research has been completed on the relation of board game play with early math development (Elofsson, Gustafson, Samuelsson, & Traff, 2016; Ramani & Siegler, 2008; Ramani, Siegler, & Hitti, 2012; Stebler, Vogt, Wolf, Hauser, & Rechsteiner, 2013). The research is partly motivated by the desire to better understand and to design remedial or preventative interventions concerning the achievement or opportunity gap problem in school readiness. Ramani & Siegler (2008) reported that 80 percent of middle-income families but only 47 percent of lower-income ones play board games involving their preschoolers, while 66 percent of lower income but only 30 percent of the middle-class families did video games with their young children. Low-income five-year-old children who played board games at school with the researchers increased their proficiency in comparing quantities, number line estimation, counting, and identifying numerals. Effects were sustained over nine weeks when delayed post-intervention assessments were taken. In a later study, these gains were found when low-income children played board games with trained paraprofessionals in small group learning activities (Ramani et al., 2012).

Elofsson et al. (2016) explored further the value of playing board games for emergent numeracy by comparing the effects of playing board games with a linear number board line versus a circular one. Intervention was over 3 weeks, with 114 preschoolers playing board games 6 times each about 10 minutes. The investigators were testing their representational mapping hypothesis that posited the importance of linearity going left to right on the board game, not in circles, for helping young children form a mental number line, a core factor in early math competence. The reported results in favor of their hypothesis—linear numbered board games are helpful but not circular ones.

Playing board games have been linked to early literacy as well as numeracy. Hassinger-Das et al. (2016) used board games with individual children who had heard a book read and were asked by the adult questions of recall (simpler) to making inferences (more complex). These questions were asked when the child landed on the particular target word on the board game; target words came from the story in the book. Such board game play yoked to a book increased children's expressive and receptive vocabulary. Lenhart, Brueck, Liang, and Roskos (2019) also found that board game play is advantageous for word learning and memory. Using certain books together with board game play related to the books is a promising new method currently being research. Roskos (forthcoming) in contrasting board game interventions with traditional sociodramatic play methods notes, "Board game play has several advantages. It has clear rules and boundaries; it focuses talk around game content; it has clear goal (to win); it incentivizes learning; it is efficient. It, in short, gamifies learning words from books" (2021)

Research from cognitive psychology does not usually directly study child development and learning, but nonetheless, has produce some findings that are noteworthy. Cognitive psychology literature suggests that playing board games influence general cognitive functioning and development. Playing them may enhance players' "perception, memory and thinking" (Gobet, de Voogt, & Retschitzki, 2004). Expert players acquire and strengthen thinking mechanisms and actions similar to experts in disciplines such as mathematics, medicine, and physics. Other skills board game play have the possibility to offer players include computational thinking involving conditional logic (involves if-then-else), algorithm (making an action plan that can be repeated and used in the future), debugging (detecting errors), and distributed computation (thinking with coplayers' contributions to problem solving opportunities inherent in games) (Berland & Lee, 2011).

Research Emphasis on Chess

In the website of the United States Chess Federation (www.uscf.org) under research articles, information can be found supporting the value of chess in education. Consensus exists that serious chess playing can positively impact the child's cognitive development. Every year, more and more children enter scholastic chess programs in their schools and play in local, state, and national tournaments. Parents see chess now as providing their children with cultural capital, to include in their "concerted cultivation" (Lareau, 2003). Families are reported to spend as much as $50,000 per year for their child's chess talent development (Kiewra, 2019).

The number of children playing in scholastic programs is especially high among third and fourth graders, and in elementary school 40 percent are girls. Young people 14 years old and under make up a sizable percent of membership in the United States Chess Federation, as much a 40 percent based on one estimate (Fine, 2015). As arguably humanity's greatest board game, chess enthusiasts and activities are found across a wide array of settings, with communities and homes being very common locations. Further, the internet has added new dimensions for chess play and talent development. Technology has expanded and enriched play opportunities for other games as well.

TECHNOLOGY INFLUENCES ON BOARD GAMES

Modalities of board games vary. Tangible board games refer to tactile boards often made from laminated cardboard or wood, along with all tactile units and materials needed for gameplay.

Digital board games can be played completely digitally, such as online in a browser, as an application in a mobile device, such as a mobile phone, tablet, or using a gaming console.

Multimodal board games utilize a mixture of tangible and digital interaction for gameplay, such as an augmented reality or virtual reality board game where some portions of the board or units can be scanned to reveal animated graphics. An example is Star Wars: Jedi Challenges, which allows users to play Dejarik, Star War's version of chess, with animated holographic creature game pieces. The game can be scanned through a phone or an AR headset. Most classic board games now have a VR alternative, such as Catan VR, or Checkers VR.

Augmented reality games attempt to extend an aesthetic game experience and accompanying enjoyment in order to compensate for what is lost by not playing board games the usual way with a physical setting and real persons in place for social interaction. Solitary game experience behind a monitor is not the same as the intimate game experience in board games with coplayers in close proximity. Andersen, Kristensen,

Nielsen, and Gronbaek (2019) studied the BattleBoard 3-Dimensional (3D) experience of children and noted that children enjoyed perceiving animation from all angles and were fascinated when examining characters close up using goggles. The children shifted looking at the screen and the actual board and appreciated the chance to view animated 3D warriors. They came to expect a large amount of stimulus variation as typically found in computer games but not found in ordinary board games, which by definition are always static in comparison to reality augmented games. However, classical board game play with real life opponents allows players to read the reactions of others while playing.

RECOMMENDATIONS

Although it cannot be denied that board game play has been affected by competition from computer and video games over the past few decades, the gaming habits of children still make room for traditional board games. Since board games are played up close and produce interpersonal and personal experiences, they should be encouraged for their value to children who need to develop psychological and social skills and have experiences self-regulating and cooperating with others. Adults in school, community, and family settings need to help children with their play and recreational time budgets through offering amble opportunities for various board game play. Depending on their ages and experiences, adults should co-play and scaffold the play of children. Traditional board games play can be quality time for children and adults to pay attention to each other and what they are playing together. They can and should welcome taking a break from social media and the digital realm in general, and be unplugged from what can perhaps best be described as the internet "attention industry."

As a major genre of toys, board games warrant more attention and evaluation by parents, educators, and researchers. By surface appearances, it seems that the cognitive form of play typically engaged in while playing board games is constructive play, and the sociality of it is cooperative (Johnson, Christie, & Wardle, 2005). The quality depends on the game itself and the ages and developmental levels and background experiences of the players. The play that unfolds varies and can be an indicator and mediator in the developing child's social, creative, and intellectual competence or performance. Although board games were not analyzed, Trawick-Smith, Russell, and Swaminathan (2011) observed children playing with different kinds of playthings (i.e., blocks, paints, pretend props, math games, and puzzles). They developed a measuring instrument with scales for creativity/imagination, social interaction, and thinking/learning.

Useful information about specific games and play could be generated by applying this instrument or similar ones to various board games. The affordances of board games are likely to range considerably across these social and psychological dimensions and in their educational benefits. Board games can be used effectively in classrooms because they have embedded within them potentialities for learning and for the practice of important skills.

Board games come in all varieties and types suitable for many situations and good for meeting the needs and interests of children who vary considerably from one another. Board games can be and should be used flexibly, supporting and scaffolding the growing child and his or her siblings and peers. It is also fun to invent and design and construct and then play one's own board game, as many teachers and children have done in classroom settings. Numerous sources exist on the internet that demonstrate and instruct how to make educational board games. Bank Street College of Education has an online article that is helpful (http://www.readingrockets.org/article/six-games-reading).

Also, teachers and parents should modify the rules of commercial games and assist children in inventing their own games. For example, a group of primary grade children with the help of the teacher can make a rain forest–themed game when studying this topic in social studies. They can design the game board and game pieces and cards and rules. Perhaps the game will require movement over large areas of the classroom. Practicing social and psychological skills occur along with mastering academic content.

Board games fit well for their value to play and gaming per se, and also for their instrumental value. Scholastic chess programs have spawned across the globe for this reason. They help children develop intellectually and do well at school and have become "cultural capital" at face value. Learning about a board game or board games, in addition to playing them for their intrinsically and relationally motivated reasons, is a worthy avenue to follow, especially if it leads to finding out about the games of other cultures (Bayeck, 2018), and thus increasing recognition of indigenous and shared knowledge and understandings. Board games, like play itself, can be a great cultural ambassador and bridge for different peoples, providing valuable learning for all children and adults across home, community, and school settings.

REFERENCES

Andersen, T., Kristensen, S., Nielsen, B., & Gronbaek, K. (2019). Designing an augmented reality board game with children: The BattleBoard 3D experience.

Bayeck, R. (2018). A review of five African board games: Is there any educational potential? *Cambridge Journal of Education, 48*(5), 533–52.

Berland, M., & Lee, V. (2011). Collaborative strategic board games as a site for distributed computational thinking. *International Journal of Game-Based Learning, 1*(2), 65–81.

Donovan, T. (2017). *It's all a game: The history of board games from Monopoly to Settlers of Catan.* New York, NY: Thomas Dunne Books.

Coyne, S. M., Linder, J. R., Rasmussen, E. E., Nelson, D. A., & Collier, K. M. (2014). It's a bird! It's a plane! It's a gender stereotype!: Longitudinal associations between superhero viewing and gender stereotyped play. *Sex Roles*, 70(9–10), 416–30.

Elofsson, J., Gustafson, S., Samuelsson, J., & Traff, U. (2016). Playing number board games support 5-year-old children's early mathematical development. *The Journal of Mathematical Behavior, 43*, 134–47.

Fine, G. (2015). *Players and pawns: How chess builds community and culture.* Chicago, IL: University of Chicago Press.

Gobet, F., de Voogt, A., & Retschitzki, J. (2004). *Moves in mind: The psychology of board games.* New York, NY: Psychology Press.

Good, S., & Ottley, J. (2019). Learning mathematics through everyday play activities: Enhancing exposure and mastery. *Young Children,* July, 73–78.

Hassinger-Das, B., Ridge, K., Parker, A., Golinkoff, R. M., Hirsh-Pasek, K., & Dickinson, D. K. (2016). Building vocabulary knowledge in preschoolers through shared book reading and gameplay. *Mind Brain Education, 10*, 71–80.

Johnson, J., Christie, J., & Wardle, F. (2005). *Play, development, and early education.* Boston, MA: Allyn and Bacon.

Kamii, C. (with DeClarke, G.) (1985). *Young children reinvent arithmetic: Implications of Piaget's theory.* New York, NY: Teachers College Press

Kiewra, K. (2019). *Nurturing children's talents: A guide for parents.* Santa Barbara, CA: ABC-CLIO, LLC.

Lareau, A. (2003). *Unequal childhoods: Class, race, and family life.* Berkeley, CA: University of California Press.

Lenhart, L., Brueck, J., Liang, X. & Roskos, K. (2019). Does play help children learn words?: Analysis of a book play approach using an adapted alternating treatment design. *Journal of Research in Childhood Education, 33*(2), 290–306.

Murphey, K. (1996). Toys: The tools of play. *Exceptional Parent,* October, p. 32.

Parlett, D. (1999). *The Oxford history of board games.* New York, NY: Oxford University Press.

Perez, C. C. (2019). *Invisible Women: Data Bias in a World Designed for Men.* Abrams.

"Pink Tax" forces women to pay more than men. (2017, March 27). Retrieved from https://www.usatoday.com/story/money/business/2017/03/27/pink-tax-forces-women-pay-more-than-men/99462846/

Pink Tax in Toys. (2019, April 27). Retrieved from https://nycdatascience.com/blog/student-works/pink-tax-in-toys/

Ramani, G., & Siegler, R. (2008). Promoting broad and stable improvements in low-income children's numerical knowledge through playing number board games. *Child Development, 79*(2), 375–94.

Ramani, G., Siegler, R., & Hitti, A. (2012). Taking it to the classroom: Number board games as a small group learning activity. *Journal of Educational Psychology, 104*(3), 661–72.

Roskos, C. (forthcoming). The book-play paradigm in early literacy pedagogy. In M. Han & J. Johnson (Eds.). *Play and literacy, play & culture studies, vol. 16.* Lanham, MD: Hamilton Books.

Stebler, R., Vogt, F., Wolf, I., Hauser, B., & Rechsteiner, K. (2013). Play-based mathematics in kindergarten. A video analysis of children's mathematical behavior while playing a board game in small groups. *Journal Math Didakt, 34*: 149–75. doi:10.1007/s13138-013-0051-4.

Trawick-Smith, J., Russell, H., & Swaminathan, S. (2011). Measuring the effects of toys on problem-solving, creative and social behaviors of preschool children. *Early Child Development and Care,* 181(7), 909–27.

Wong, W. I., & Hines, M. (2015). Effects of gender color-coding on toddlers' gender-typical toy play. *Archives of Sexual Behavior, 44*(5), 1233–42.

18

CRAFT/WORKSHOP REPLICAS

Sandra J. Stone

Craft and workshop replicas include toys that provide children with broad opportunities to create, design, and imagine, as well as develop physical and cognitive skills. Defined as handmade crafts made with tools and equipment, workshop replicas include a woodworking bench, sewing and craft areas, and tools. They provide the equipment, tools, and a designated space for woodworking, sewing, and craft making to unfold. Children work and play with various materials such as wood, paper, glue, fabrics, yarn, and clay, along with tools such as hammers, scissors, and needles.

From early civilization to the present, children play with crafts toys as representations of adult roles at home or skilled workers in the community. Craft and workshop replicas are a type of project-play that is particularly popular with kindergarten through adolescence. Many of the skills developed through playing with these toys and materials lead children to continue their passions for creating, building, and designing into their adult years, as they become experienced woodcrafters, quilt makers, or clothes designers.

TYPICAL TYPES OF CRAFTS AND WORKSHOP REPLICAS

Woodworking Workshop

The woodworking workshop is often an outside place. However, indoor workshops often accommodate younger children with plastic workbenches and tools. Outdoor workshops accommodate older children with metal or wooden workbenches and actual tools and wood for wood working projects. Typical woodworking tools include hammers, nails, drills, screws, screwdrivers, saws, vices and clamps, wrenches, nuts and bolts, tape measures and rulers, and safety goggles (glasses) (Larson, 2018).

Typical Types of Woodworking Projects

Woodworking Toy Replicas

Toy workbenches for infants and toddlers provide children with experiences with plastic handheld tools and workbenches. Children use a toy screwdriver and wrench to turn nuts and bolts or a wooden hammer for pounding the pegs into holes on a wooden bench.

Functional Wooden Structures

These handmade wooden projects result in a structure to serve a purpose such as birdhouses. Often these structures come in precut pieces or patterns for children to cut, nail, or glue together. Children can also design their own projects. Other structures can include wood boxes, workbenches, or wilderness shelters.

Play Wooden Structures

Wood working kits can be purchased to create play fairy houses, dollhouses, or race-tracks to assembly with glue or nails. Some kits also include small wooden furniture, fairies, or cars. Patterns can be simple or elaborate depending on the age and skill of the child.

Play Wooden Toys and Games

Craft kits, ready to assemble or cut from wood, range in skill level and include toy cars, boats, planes, animals, and creatures. Some require the use of saws, scroll saws, and assembly with nuts and bolts. Some toys are simple cutout animals such as a cat or giraffe, to more complex moving toys such as an animated wooden dinosaur that can walk, wobble, and roll. Games include puzzles and giant wooden yard dice.

Making Wooden Furniture

Older children and adolescents begin making simple furniture such as a stool, chair, book holder, table, or plant stand from patterns or their own designs.

Woodcarving

Woodcarving is a hand skill of whittling that uses a sharp knife to transform a piece of wood into a boomerang, walking stick, or a carved bear.

Woodworking Age-Level Differences

Infants and Toddlers

Younger children, age eighteen months to three-year-olds, play with plastic or wooden hammers to pound the pegs into holes on the bench. The tools and workbench are for playing and exploring, not for actual building or creating. Children can use these tools for enjoyment or to pretend they are carpenters.

Older toddlers through age five use a child-sized standing workbench with tools made from durable plastic. Wood-looking foam is used instead of real wood products. Children use plastic tools instead of metal tools. Children can pretend to saw and hammer the wood-like pieces, and they can actually use a plastic screwdriver, screws, and vise to assemble precut trucks, planes, and animals. Children can build from predetermined models or combine pieces to make their own creations.

Preschool and Early Elementary

Children, age five to eight, are introduced to child-sized metal constructing tools such as a hammer, vise, and screwdriver. With adult supervision, these children will use actual soft wood to build their own projects. Along with a metal or wooden workshop bench, toolsets provide children with various types of actual tools. The metal tools are ergonomically fitted for smaller hands.

Later Elementary

Older children, age 8 to 12, begin using adult size tools, including power tools (with adult supervision). Workshops for woodworking continue through adulthood as a hobby or profession. Adults create furniture, art, wooden toys, and even actual houses (Larson, 2018).

Sewing Workshop

The sewing workshop is usually an indoor experience. Inclusive with sewing is weaving, needlepoint, knitting, crocheting, and quilting. Tools for sewing crafts include lacing forms and threading tools, a variety needles, thread, and yarn, scissors, straight pins and pincushions, thimbles, measuring tapes, frames and looms, a variety of fabrics and sewing machines (Lisle & Plumley, 2010).

Typical Types of Sewing Projects

Lacing Toys

Lacing toys provide young children with experience of lacing colorful beads and shapes together, or lacing around forms of animals, dinosaurs, or monsters. Lacing cards are made from wood or thick, sturdy cardboard and designed for small hands to hold. Lacing toys are emerging sewing skills for young children.

Sewing Projects

Beginner sewing projects for primary children involve the use of a large plastic needle and thread. Craft kits include precut felt patterns of various objects, animals or creatures, tools, and visual instructions. For example, children can hand sew together unicorns, stars, dogs, elephants, monsters, dinosaurs, and even hand puppets. After the toys are stuffed, sewed or glued closed, the sewing project becomes a toy for further sociodramatic, imaginative play.

Older children, age 8 to 12, begin using patterns to cut out their toy characters or objects and may use a sewing machine with adult supervision. Sewing projects include making a felt bag or purse, backpack, headband, pillows, phone case, or designing clothes or costumes for dolls or for themselves.

Needlepoint

Needlepoint kits provide young children, age five and up, with a plastic frame, canvas, and needle, all designed for young hands. A pattern is preprinted onto the framed canvas, and children loop the thread around and through the large open holes. Pictures for children to make commonly are simple butterflies, flowers, and animals.

For children, age eight and older, the pattern is printed on cotton fabric and is more intricate. The thread is thinner for the less coarse fabric. Common pictures are detailed scenery and pictures of people, plants, and animals.

Knitting or Crocheting

Knitting or crochet kits provide children age eight and up with projects to create items, such as hats, scarves, bracelets, mittens, pillows, toys and even clothes, such as sweaters or baby clothes and blankets. With either a loom or needles, children can follow the directions for the project and use varied types of stitches suggested for knitting and crocheting (Anderson, 2019).

Weaving

For young children, age five and up, simple weaving kits provide a frame made from paper, cardboard, or foam, where the child weaves different colors of yarn through the slatted frame. More advanced looms, table or standing looms, provide children who are eight and older, with opportunities to weave larger items, such as scarfs, pillow covers, placemats, or blankets, using varied yarn to design their own project (Weil, 2018).

Quilting

Preschoolers and kindergarteners often make paper quilt crafts by cutting out paper pieces to create a design, and then gluing the paper pieces onto a sheet of paper. Children, age six and above, can make easy fabric quilts by tying together fabric squares with fringed sides.

Quilting for older children and adolescents, is usually a project where an adult-size quilt or baby quilt is made from smaller cloth squares sewn together by hand or with a sewing machine. Children can make quilts from kits, which provide the necessary components (Plumley & Lisle, 2018).

Sewing Age Level Differences

Stringing beads and lacing toys as presewing skills are usually prominent for 18 months to toddlers. Children, age five to eight, actually begin to sew. They use large, easy-to-thread, plastic needles to avoid frustration. Threads are usually yarn or thick threads to fit into the large needles. Precut felt patterns are most often used for sewing. Scissors for young children are smaller in size, have stainless steel, blunt blades, and plastic handles. Scissors, ergonomically fitted, should accommodate both right-and left-handed children. The scissors should be of good quality, designed for cutting fabric rather than paper, so they do not frustrate the children and their emerging cutting skills.

Primary children, age six to eight, can begin using a sewing machine made for children, which is lightweight, simple to turn off and on, and portable. It should have a safety cover surrounding the needle.

Older children, age eight and up, are not only hand sewing, but are capable, with adult supervision, of using actual sewing machines. When sewing by hand, children use steel needles with smaller eye openings, patterns, pins, thimbles, and tape measures. Older children use adult-size scissors. This age group begins using patterns to cut out their projects and also to create their own patterns. They are learning how to use different types of hand stitching.

Needlepoint, knitting, crocheting, weaving and quilting usually begin for children around age five. Younger children begin with simple kits or adult instruction. Older children use more elaborate kits and tools. Sewing crafts can continue as an enjoyable hobby or profession through adulthood.

Crafts Workshop

The crafts workshop is usually an indoor experience. Craft making sets the stage for children to create and design (Aerila & Ronkko, 2015). Tools include scissors, kilns, and metal and jewelry tools. Scissors should be for both paper and cloth and should have some that have different blades for distinct edging and borders. Supplies include different types of paper, fabric, boxes, clay, metal and glue along with decorative items, such as glitter, buttons, fabrics, rickrack, gems, confetti, rocks, nature items, and paint.

TYPICAL TYPES OF CRAFT PROJECTS

Nature-based Crafts

Rock Art

Flat smooth rocks, washed and painted with a clear acrylic paint, can be painted to look like ladybugs, butterflies, snails, or even simple designs. They then may be used as toys, garden or house decorations, or paperweights.

Sand Crafts

Colored sand can be used to create scenery, pictures, or layered into glass or plastic containers.

Rubbings

Rubbings can be made from tree trunks, leaves, and rocks with paper and crayons or chalk.

Fruit or Vegetable Stamping

Fruit and vegetables, such a potato or apple, can be cut in half and a design cut into the bottom. They are dipped into paint and then used for stamp painting to create pictures and designs.

Seed and Bean Mosaics

Dried seeds and beans of different colors can be glued to wood or heavy cardboard to create a design, an animal, or scenery.

Nature Collages

Nature collages can be made from pinecones, leaves, pebbles, seeds, seashells, eggshells, and wood pieces.

Wood, Bark and Fiber Crafts

Wood and bark can be used in decoupage or building stick houses. Birch bark can be used for making paper. Driftwood can be used to make artwork or furniture. Fiber dolls can be made from sisal, raffia, long grass, or yarn.

Basket Weaving

Baskets can be woven from pine needles, bamboo, reed, raffia, fiber rush, grasses, palms, yucca, or flax—any fibrous materials that can bend and be formed into a shape.

Paper Crafts

Fans, Pinwheels, and Paper Dolls

Paper crafts include making paper fans, pinwheels, paper dolls, and mosaics. Colorful paper can be cut into strips for weaving, or folded to make a drinking cup, hat, boat, or airplane.

Origami

Origami is a paper folding art. Paper can be folded into simple or complex objects and creatures.

Papier-mache

Paper can be used to make papier-mache pulp, which can be modeled into figures, puppet heads, animals and various imagined creatures, then dried and painted.

Papier-mache is made from strips of newspapers or other paper and dipped into thin starch paste and then smoothed on the outside of a container mold such as a small box, a balloon, or bowl. When the paper dries, the container can be removed. This paper process can be used to make masks, planets, or decorative containers.

Clay and Glass Crafts

Clay crafts can include play dough, clay, or even adobe mud. Clay can be crafted into creatures, animals, ornaments, or pottery. Some clay can be painted and fired in a kiln.

Glass crafts can include glass bead making, glass blowing, stained glass mosaics, or glass etching.

Box Crafts

With construction paper, paints, and markers, small and large boxes can be changed into interesting and creative crafts. Animal creations can be made from boxes by adding ears, eyes, tails, and feet to make a lion, a hippo, tiger, or a monkey.

Boxes can be made into cars, tractors, trucks, boats or trains by gluing on cardboard wheels and features. Boxes can also become a banjo, xylophone, or drum just by adding rubber bands or craft sticks.

Boxes can be made into costumes such as clown feet or turned into a tiny world or dollhouse for action figures or dolls. A large box can be made into a puppet stage.

Box games are not only a craft but can become a fun-filled toy such a basketball hoop, a miniature soccer field, or as a maze for marbles (Siomades, 1998).

Cardboard, Styrofoam, and Plastic Crafts

Tubes and plastic cups can be made into octopus, penguins, fairy houses, and trees. Cardboard tubes can become pretend telescopes or butterflies. Cardboard egg cartons can be transformed into caterpillars. Styrofoam can be used in a variety of crafts including adding chenille wire to create a spider or lion. Flat Styrofoam can be used to create buildings, games, or art displays. Plastic lids can become the base of a sailboat, the form for glass mosaic or a bird feeder.

Puppet Crafts

Puppets can be made from Popsicle sticks, paper bags, socks, gloves, mittens, boxes, and cardboard tubes.

Book Making

Book making involves paper, cardboard, scissors, yarn, stapler, and glue. Simple books can be made from folded paper, stapled along the edge, or hole-punched and tied together with string or ribbon. Book types can include accordion, step, pop-up, bound, scroll, comic, and paper bag books.

Mobiles

Hanging mobiles can be made from a variety of materials. Beads, buttons, feathers, pinecones, or clay creations are hung with string, wire, or chenille sticks from a hanger, plastic lid, or paper plate.

Craft Sticks, Clothespins, Plastic Spoons, and Straws

Popsicle sticks, craft sticks, clothes pins, plastic spoons, and straws can be used to make houses, doors, puppets, sharks, whales, dolls, monsters, and mermaids.

Metalwork Crafts

Metalwork kits provide sheets of craft steel or aluminum sheets or foil along with tools such has hammers, engravers, stencils, knives, and metal cutters to make engravings, etchings, jewelry, or carvings.

Leatherwork Crafts

Leather craft kids provide leather and tools, such as needles, threads, scissors, an awl, and thimbles, for making clothing, shoelaces, and handbags.

Science Crafts

Science crafts can involve children in building and inventing from multiple materials (wood, metal, glass) objects that can be used for scientific observation, such as a toad-house, thunderstick, or solar oven (Diehn & Krautwurst, 1994).

Craft Kits and Workshops

Craft kits provide children with all the needed materials to create toys, vehicles, masks, and jewelry. Build-A-Bear Workshop is a national chain of stores, rather than a kit, which offers children the opportunity to use their products to design and build their own stuffed bear.

CRAFT AGE-LEVEL DIFFERENCES

Crafts for toddlers, age 18 months to 3 year olds, are usually simple such as painting rocks or making play dough snakes or balls. For young toddlers, the process and the play is predominant, not the product.

For children, age five to eight, the process is still a priority, but products now become more detailed as the children's skills are becoming refined. For example, a rock painting now looks like an actual creature.

Older children, age eight and up, still enjoy the process, but now begin to see the product of their craftwork. These ages begin using more decorative items, such as confetti, gems, and glitter. Children are beginning to use more advanced crafts such as making pottery or jewelry. Adolescents and adults take crafts to another level of the creative process, for example, weaving usable baskets and working with metal and leather.

ROLE IN PROMOTING CHILD DEVELOPMENT

Physical Development

The coordination of gross and fine motor skills becomes more integrated and defined as the child moves and interacts with the environment in woodworking, sewing, and handcrafts. Gross motor development occurs mainly with woodworking when young toddlers pound pegs with a wooden hammer. Elementary children through adolescents use their large arm muscles for hammering, drilling, sanding, or sawing while developing strength, endurance, flexibility, and agility (Copple & Bredekamp, 2009; Feeney, Christensen, & Moravcik, 2006).

Small motor development and eye-hand coordination occur in woodworking, sewing, and handcrafts. When infants play with a soft plastic hammer, they develop their grip capacity. Toddlers and preschoolers continue using their pincer grasp to secure large plastic nuts and bolts or for stringing beads. Elementary children use their hands to saw wood, paint a project, glue wood or crafts together, knit, or cut with scissors. As older children begin sewing and using craft tools and materials, small motor muscles, eye-hand coordination, and dexterity are refined (Isenberg & Jalongo, 2000).

Cognitive Development

Infants, toddler, and preschoolers begin the journey of the brain's sensory development as they enjoy experiences of banging with a hammer or hearing the noise of nails as they hit the bottom of the can (Weiser, 1991). Craft tool use also fosters brain development by increasing children's conceptual and perceptual awareness. Children are developing abilities of concentration, depth perception, distance, discrimination, judging space, judging length and distance, weight and pressure, judging amounts, measuring, concept of change, concepts of size and shape, concepts of balance and gravity, concepts of sounds, concepts of texture, cause and effect, and whole-to-part relationships (Day, 1975; Green, 1998). Children are using mathematical concepts of number, symmetry, patterning, quantity, and equivalence (Isenberg & Jalongo, 2000; Hildebrand, 1997). Children use cognitive skills to measure, estimate, and plan.

Social-Emotional Development

Crafts provide children opportunities to enhance their independence, autonomy, and self-esteem as they begin to understand and control their physical world. A broad range of craft making encourages positive attitudes toward trying new things, persistence, a sense of physical competence, and taking risks. As children develop craft skills, self-confidence promotes self-worth as indicated when children exclaim, "Look what I made!"

Working with crafts also increases attention span, concentration, releases tension, reduces stress, anger and anxiety, and promotes relaxation. Socially, woodworking, sewing, and crafts provide children with opportunities to talk, make decisions, negotiate, solve problems, laugh, create, and imagine together as well as develop friendships through hours of fun.

Fostering Curiosity, Imagination, and Creativity

Crafts provide children with maximum opportunities to use open-ended materials with the focus on process rather than product. Crafts invite children's curiosity to unfold as they build, take apart, and create (Hildebrand, 1997). As children have choice and investigate different ways to use materials and equipment, imagination, creativity, and divergent thinking naturally unfold (Isenberg & Jalongo, 2000). Each craft project becomes the child's original and unique invention or creation.

WOODWORKING, SEWING AND GENERAL CRAFTS FOR CHILDREN WITH SPECIAL NEEDS

In meeting the needs of every child, including children with special needs, adults focus the toy environment, so it is personalized to meet the varied needs of each individual child (Hildebrand, 1997). For example, in woodworking, children with poor muscle control might need equipment adapted to their special needs such as using attachment straps so children can use a sandpaper block.

For crafts, a stretchable hair band can be attached to the tools or materials and the child's hand (Carpenter, 2007). A universal art tool holder, which fits the child's hand to hold craft tools, such as felt pens or art brush, could be provided. Adaptive technology such as large plastic tools with large handles also provide for an easier grip.

For children with intellectual disabilities, skills in using tools for woodworking and crafts may take more time, so breaking down the skills into smaller parts will support the child in having a sense of accomplishment (Seefeldt & Barbour, 2000). Children with varied hearing impairments may need visual aids or modeling gestures to facilitate tool use and project design whether for carpentry, sewing, or general crafts as these crafts help develop visual and tactile sensitivity (Yuan-shih, 1984).

Children with visual impairments may enjoy tactile exploration, which can be facilitated through woodworking and handcrafts. Fabric collage, weaving, and object printing all provide children with tactile experiences. For woodworking or craft tools, sandpaper dots can indicate the correct orientation or type of tool.

For children with emotional disabilities, craft experiences can be overwhelming, so provide simple explanations or modeling as appropriate, allow the child time to adapt and problem solve, and provide choices and ownership of the process (Schwabe, 2018). The tactile nature of woodworking, sewing, and crafts lowers anxiety and promotes a sense of calm.

Research has shown that woodworking is therapeutic for children with autism and children with speech disorders, giving them the ability to communicate and have opportunities for personal expression, as crafts become a holistic therapy (Brudern & Zellerhoff, 1995). For children with speech and language delays, the concrete nature of craft experiences will enhance their opportunities to learn by doing through handling tools and creating projects (Paweni & Rubovits, 2000).

The interactive nature of woodworking, sewing, and craft toys heightens every child's positive capabilities and skills, increasing a child's overall sense of independence, confidence, and competency (Brodin, 1999).

GENDER ROLES: WOODWORKING, SEWING AND GENERAL CRAFTS

From earliest times in society, both men and women engaged in a variety of crafts. Women engaged more in specific homemaking crafts such as making clay containers, weaving baskets, or quilting bed covers. Men engaged in specific crafts such as carpentry or metal works.

Woodworking crafts as toys were often seen as something of interest for boys such as building cars, planes, dinosaurs, and pirate ships. Woodworking kits marketed for children are most often depicted with boys holding or playing with the kits. However, woodworking kits now include projects that appeal to both boys and girls. Diverse woodworking crafts include toy animals, puzzles, dollhouses and furniture, and elaborate castles and fairy villages as well as cars and planes. Tool belts for children are now marketed in blue and pink. All children are encouraged to enjoy woodworking crafts and to choose how and what they wish to do without designating gender stereotypes, thus limiting their choices (Kollmayer et al., 2018).

Similarly, sewing crafts were often depicted with pictures of girls. However, they are now marketed to a variety of interests to engage both boys and girls. For example, young children can lace a variety of animals, toys, and monsters. Boys and girls can choose to sew felt patterns of elephants, unicorns, or dinosaurs. *Choice* in crafts dictates the direction each child, whether a boy or a girl, will engage in for his or her own personal enjoyment as all children enjoy creating and making things with a variety of materials.

CRAFT TOYS: PAST, PRESENT, AND FUTURE

Past: History of Crafts

The history of crafts begins with human life. Artifacts have been found which show children used craft tools, such as miniature toy hand axes, as toys (Spikins, Hitchens, Needham, & Rutherford, 2014). Other toys have been unearthed in ancient civilizations. For example, Egyptian children played with dolls made from stone, glass and wood—all handcrafted, of course. Quilting crafts have been traced back to Stone Age Mongolia and Ancient Egypt. A quilted jacket dating to 3400 BC was found in an Egyptian tomb (Ray, 2019). Basket weaving is also an old craft with a place in early human civilization. Some baskets have been dated as 10,000 and 12,000 years old.

Tools became the essence of craft making as adults used tools to make the things they needed for basic survival such as wooden or pottery bowls, furniture, or baskets. In time, the Industrial Revolution replaced many artisans by producing manufactured rather than handmade goods. In spite of manufacturing, crafts continued to engage adults and children across time as parents passed down craft skills to their children. Crafts, for parents and educators, became a tool for building character, intelligence, and industriousness in children as well as supporting positive child development. Adolescents began taking craft or vocational education programs in school (Thorsteinsson &

Olafsson, 2014). As time advanced, handcrafts became a hobby for many adults and for some a sought-after profession as seen in quilt making, woodworking, and pottery.

Crafts also embodied the culture of a given time, becoming the carrier of the culture (Mark, 2019). For example, one can see the metalsmiths' craftsmanship in gold cups, bracelets, and death masks found in ancient Egyptian tombs. One can enjoy the baskets, rugs and clay pots of the cultural heritage of native Southwest peoples (Langham, 1997). Crafts became a window to historical and current cultures.

Present Research

Educational researchers advocate for a more holistic approach to learning which includes play-oriented toys and crafts (Ernest, et al, 2019). The benefits for whole child development are well documented (Bodrova & Leong, 2005; Brown & Vaughan, 2009; Fromberg & Bergen, 2006; Piaget, 1962; Stone, 2017). In recent years, the trend for parents and educators is to limit play and creative toys and crafts in favor of academic pursuits. However, research shows that play with toys and crafts advantages children in many more important ways than narrow academic pursuits can provide.

Future Recommendations

For parents and educators, the creative interaction of children with crafts produces immediate and long lasting benefits for children including the gifts of creativity and imagination. One of the values of crafts is its remarkable focus on the individual. While the handcrafted product adds beauty or usability for others, it is the inherent value of the creative process within and for the child that makes advocacy for craft making an inclusive undertaking for all children of all ages.

REFERENCES

Aerila, J., & Ronkko, M. (2015). Integrating literature with craft in a learning process with creative elements. *Early Childhood Education Journal, 43*, 89–98.

Anderson, S. (2019). *Kids' knitting workshop: The easiest and most effective way to learn to knit!* Muskogee, OK: Artisan.

Bodrova, E., & Leong, D. (2005). Why children need play. *Early Childhood Today, 20*(1), 6–7.

Brodin, J. (1999). Play in children with severe multiple disabilities: Play with toys—A review. *International Journal of Disability, Development & Education, 46*(1), 25–34.

Brown, S., & Vaughan, C. (2009). *Play: How it shapes the brain, opens the imagination and invigorates the soul.* New York, NY: Penguin Group.

Brudern, R., & Zellerhoff, R. (1995). Working with the living material wood as a means of making contact with handicapped and nonhandicapped youth. *European Education, 27*, 59–68.

Carpenter, C. (2007). Play and the child with special needs: 25 reminders. *Exceptional Parent, 37*(10), 45.

Copple, C., & Bredekamp, S. (Eds.) (2009). *Developmentally appropriate practice in early childhood programs serving children birth through age 8* (3rd ed.). Washington, DC: National Association for the Education of Young Children.

Day, B. (1975). *Open learning in early childhood*. New York: NY: Macmillan.

Diehn, G., & Krautwurst, T. (1994). *Science crafts for kids: 50 fantastic things to invent & create*. New York, NY: Sterling.

Ernest, J., Nicholas, A., Vardanyan, S., Hafiz, F., Alazemi, M., & Dixon, D. (2019). Childhood remembered: Reflections on the role of play for holistic education in Armenia, Kuwait, Saudi Arabia, the USA, and Wales. *International Journal of the Whole Child, 4*(1), 5–19.

Feeney, S., Christensen, D., & Moravcik, E. (2006). *Who am I in the lives of children?* (7th ed.). Upper Saddle River, NJ: Pearson/Merrill Prentice Hall.

Fromberg, D., & Bergen, D. (2006). *Play from birth to twelve: Contexts, perspectives, and meanings*. New York, NY: Routledge.

Green, M. (1998). *Not! The same old activities for early childhood*. Albany, NY: Delmar Publishers.

Hildebrand, V. (1997). *Introduction to early childhood education*. Upper Saddle River, NJ: Merrill/Prentice Hall.

Isenberg, J., & Jalongo, M. (2000). *Creative expression and play in the early childhood curriculum*. Englewood Cliffs, NJ: Prentice Hall.

Kollmayer, M., Schultes, M., Schober, B., Hodosi, T., & Spiel, C. (2018). Parents' judgments about the desirability of toys for their children: Associations with gender role attitudes, gender-typing of toys, and demographics. *Sex Roles, 79*(5–6), 329–41.

Langham, B. (1997). Native art of the Southwest. *Texas Child Care, 20*(4), 22–31.

Larson, M. (2018). *Wood shop*. North Adams, MA: Storey Publishing,

Lisle, S., & Plumley, A. (2010). *Sewing school: 21 sewing projects kids will love to make*. North Adams, MA: Storey Publishing.

Mark, J. (2019). *Crafts*. Accessed 4-25-2019 from https://www.ancient.eu/crafts.

Paweni, S., & Rubovits, D. (2000). The power of play. *Exceptional Parent, 30*(10), 36–38.

Piaget, J. (1962). *Play, dreams and imitation in childhood*. London: Routledge & Kegan Paul.

Plumley, A., & Lisle, A. (2018). *Sewing school quilts: 15 projects kids will love to make*. North Adams, MA: Storey Publishing.

Ray, A. (2019). *Quilting for beginners*. Fountain Valley, CA: Valley of Joy Publishing Press.

Schwabe, J. (2018). Empowerment and fun through play. *Exceptional Parent, 48*(10), 42–45.

Seefeldt, C., & Barbour, N. (2000). *Early childhood education* (4th ed.). Upper Saddle River, NJ: Merrill.

Siomades, L. (Ed.) (1998). *Look what you can make with boxes*. Honesdale, PA: Boyds Mills Press.

Spikins, P., Hitchens, G., Needham, A., & Rutherford, H. (2014). The cradle of thought: Growth, learning, play and attachment in Neanderthal children. *Oxford Journal of Archaeology, 33*(2), 111–34.

Stone, S. J. (2017). The essential role of play in school contexts for the well being of children. *LEARNing Landscapes, 10* (2), 305–18.

Thorsteinsson, G., & Olafsson, B. (2014). Otto Salomon in Naas and his first Icelandic students in Nordic Sloyd. *History of Education, 43*(1), 31–49.

Weil, A. (2018). *Weaving within reach*. New York, NY: Clarkson Potter/Publishers.

Weiser, M. (1991). *Infant/toddler care and education*. New York, NY: Merrill.

Yuan-shih, P. (1984). The effects of arts and crafts education on hearing-impaired children. *Art Education, 37*(6), 15–17.

19

INDIGENOUS TOYS

Jean-Pierre Rossie

Looking for definitions of indigenous toys one finds several different and overlapping concepts referring to geographical, historical, technical, economic, and social points of view such as non-Western toys, Indian toys, traditional toys, handmade toys, child made toys, or popular toys. The indigenous toys referred to in this chapter are toys belonging to the tangible heritage of children living in rural areas and popular quarters of towns of non-Western countries. However, attention is not only paid to tradition and continuity but also to evolution and change.

In all continents, but especially in Africa, Asia, Australia, and Middle and South America, regions and populations exist where children, adolescents, family members, elderly people, and craftspeople create a wide range of toys and play materials. In areas where natural and waste materials are available, children have the possibility to continue the local play and toy heritage, a tradition that is more and more subject to the influence of the consumption societies.

The author's research relates to the toys and games of Amazigh (Berber)-speaking and Arabic-speaking communities in North Africa and the Sahara. His fieldwork took place among children in the Tunisian Sahara (1975, 1977) and in Morocco (1992–present). The indigenous children whose toys and games are mentioned belong to Amazigh populations of northern Africa, namely the Amazigh of the Moroccan High, Middle, and Anti-Atlas Mountains and the Tuareg from the Sahara and Sahel.

Because this chapter discusses toys, less attention is paid to the games of make believe, skill, and chance in which they are used and receive their sociocultural meanings and roles. After all, it is only in the hands of playing children that toys become meaningful material items. The transformation of empty sardine tins into a table, a bed, a sand filter, or a percussion instrument shows that the intention of the player is fundamental and that the used object is secondary. Girls and boys can bestow on an object whatever concept they have in mind and replace a given object by several other objects that for them represent the same concept.

FEATURES OF NORTH AFRICAN– AND SAHARAN CHILD–MADE TOYS

Using Natural and Waste Material in Toy Creation

In rural areas and popular quarters of towns, indigenous children, and possibly also adults, create, since immemorial times, toys with natural material. These natural materials are from mineral origin (e.g., sand, clayish earth, stones, pebbles), vegetal origin (e.g., flowers, plants, leaves, branches, sticks, reed, bark, ear of maize, nuts, dates, summer squash, potatoes), animal origin (e.g., bones, horns, snail shells, hair, skin, intestines, dung) and human origin (hair).

The oldest toys in northern Africa seem to be clay animal figurines dating back about two thousand years. They were excavated in 1981 by Susan and Roderick McIntosh at the Inland Niger Delta in Mali located near the southern border of the Sahara (Rossie, 2005/2013). North African and Saharan children have used waste materials for making toys for a long time. Indeed, in the collection of Saharan toys of the Musée de l'Homme in Paris (now in the Musée du Quai Branly) there is a 1935 collected toy car made by a Tuareg boy living in the Algerian Sahara. The car's body is a piece of wood and four round tin cans are the wheels. Two keys to open these cans serve as axles and champagne corks pushed on the axle fixe the wheels (Rossie, 2013). These waste materials include earthenware, wooden, fibrous, paper, cardboard, glass, plastic, rubber, metal, paint and make up products but also parts of toys, furniture, bicycles, cars, and polystyrene packaging.

These children are masters in designing toys with natural and waste materials taken from their natural and human environment. However, in these last decades, waste materials have become more important than natural materials. Moreover, natural and waste materials are quite often combined (e.g., when girls make dolls with a cross-shaped structure of two reeds or sticks and dress this structure in rags) (Rossie, 2005a) or pieces of shiny packaging (Rossie, 2019) and when boys build tractors with a chassis cut out of a cactus, wheels cut out of soles and bottle stoppers serving as steering wheel or headlights (Rossie, 2013).

Technical Know-How in Building Toys

Making toys necessitates material but also technical know-how. Indigenous children use hand tools they mostly find themselves, such as stones or other heavy objects to hit with, the child's own teeth or other sharp objects to cut or make holes, but they seldom have adult tools at their disposal. A technological aspect to be solved by toy making children is movement; movement of parts of the toy or movement of the whole toy. Some toys such as toy vehicles, windmills, and toy weapons have movable parts.

However, child-made toy animals or dolls with movable parts were not found, in contrast to this imported type of toys. The fact that self-made dolls and toy animals do not have movable parts cannot be attributed to a lack of technical know-how because North African and Saharan children undoubtedly demonstrate this know-how when making all kinds of toy vehicles. Therefore, these children could have given movable parts to their dolls and toy animals if they chose to. An explanation for this situation could be that the children see no need to do this because they themselves manipulate these toys, regard them as short-living objects, and create new toys as part of many play activities. Many toys from these regions can move by having wheels and axles (Rossie, 2013). The construction of such axles and wheels certainly necessitates some apprenticeship whereby older children serve as masters for younger ones.

Self-made toys are mostly assembled from different parts, such as the frame, clothes, hair and ornaments in the case of dolls; the chassis, cabin, steering wheel, axles, and wheels, in the case of toy vehicles; the pickets, threads, and shuttle in the case of a toy weaving loom. Assembling all these parts into well-functioning toys is something young children gradually learn to master.

CHILDREN'S INTERPRETATION OF ADULT LIFE IN TOY AND PLAY CULTURE

Child made toys in indigenous North African and Saharan communities but also in other indigenous communities all over the world, relate to the adult world, to female and male obligations and activities, and to feasts and rituals. However, this should not be seen as an imitation of the lives of adults because this toy making is not a repetitive work but a continuous recreation of models. In this context, Brian Sutton-Smith wrote, "Play schematizes life, it alludes to life, it does not imitate life in any very strict sense . . . it is a dialectic which both mirrors and mocks reality but never escapes it" (1986, p. 141).

Indigenous toys are highly symbolic objects intentionally designed for children by children, rarely by adults. Girls and boys alike, create dolls mostly representing adults in socially esteemed roles (e.g., Tuareg warriors, Amazigh brides or bridegrooms, mothers). They also make valued items such as household items, musical instruments, vehicles and high tech products (e.g., cars and trucks and more recently airplanes, helicopters, and digital phones).

Recontextualization of Toys and Objects

The Moroccan examples of recontextualization of toys and objects refer to children reinterpreting imported dolls and materials, giving new meanings to traditional toys, and changing these into touristic items. Imported plastic dolls are regularly subjected to local recontextualization. Already about 1980 when other girls still made dolls with a frame of reed, a nine-year-old girl of Amazigh origin and from a poor quarter—now a specialist in putting henna designs on hands and feet—turned a cheap undressed plastic doll into a nicely decorated bride of the historical city Marrakech in which she lived. Another example comes from a small High Atlas village where in 1996 self-made dolls with a frame of reed coexisted with imported plastic dolls. The girls, however, adapted the plastic dolls to local customs by dressing those in hand-sewn outerwear and underwear (Rossie, 2005a). Polystyrene packaging of refrigerators and TVs has become an appreciated material to cut out doll frames, weapons, and cars.

New meanings are also attached to traditional toys as when a reed toy with a turning blade becomes a helicopter. Moreover, an important functional change occurs when traditional toys lose their playful role to become a pecuniary object children sell to occasional tourists. This is what happened in the 1990s in the Moroccan pre-Sahara to toy animals boys wove with palm leaves and in 1997 to girls' dolls from Merzouga in the Moroccan Sahara (Rossie, 2005b).

Elucidating Indigenous Children's Point of View

In a book review published in 2019, Artemis Yagou quotes Lynette Townsend's definition of "children's material culture," namely "items that have been made, adapted, or created by children themselves' or even 'items from the adult world or commercially produced items" that "have been appropriated, adopted, or adapted by children for their own means" (p. 1). She also stresses "the historical invisibility of children and the neglect of their lived experiences" (p. 1), an invisibility certainly more pronounced in relation to Saharan and North African children and indigenous children in general than to Western children. The author's fieldwork on Tunisian and Moroccan children's play and toy-making activities has stimulated taking into account children's agency and children's perspectives in a clearer way. The toys and other objects generated and adapted by these children and used in games of make believe, skill, or chance not only offer useful information and insight on the world of indigenous children but also on their viewpoints regarding the adult world and the communities in which they grow up.

When indigenous children engage in toy making and play activities they not only conform to the cultural, social, and moral rules of their families and communities, but at the same time resist, adapt, change, and subvert the rules imposed by adults or comment and even criticize local situations. This becomes visible in recent Anti-Atlas girls' doll play when they dress skinny industrial dolls in European, belly dancing, gym, sun bathing, and beach fashions, as influenced by TV programs and female tourists' behavior, or make remarks on the rape of a girl and the situation of handicapped girls (Rossie, et al., 2020).

CHILDREN'S RELATIONSHIP TO TOYS

In the regions under discussion, creating and using toys is seldom an isolated activity and seeing a girl or a boy playing alone is rare. Moreover, these children show in their play activities also much emotion, non-verbal and verbal behavior, singing and dancing. As far as the available data suggest, Saharan and North African children use their dolls and toys related to the animal world, domestic life and technical activities for enacting events they observe in the life of family members, neighbors and other adults in their community.

The children's affective relation to the toys they make is more directed toward the represented model than to the material realization of that model. Therefore, they are used as objects that only remain valuable as long as the play activity continues. The function of such a toy is limited to the game and it only comes to 'life' when manipulated by a player. When toys are activated they become part of a series of representations and relationships accepted and enacted by the members of the playgroup. As soon as the play activity stops, the toy becomes a material item treated with indifference, left on the spot or thrown away. However, such a general statement should be relativized because Saharan and North African examples show children have a stronger relation to well-made dolls, toy animals, toy vehicles or musical instruments and reused them for later play activities (Rossie, 2005/2013; 2005b; 2019).

CREATIVITY IN TOY MAKING AND PLAY ACTIVITIES

As an anthropologist researching cultural and social aspects of children's socialization and play, the author only got interested in the topics of creativity and individuality when being invited to two congresses on creativity in Turin (Italy, 1988) and in Hameenlinna (Finland, 2002).

It is important to stress that every self-made toy and play activity, although taking place in a given ecological and sociocultural context, also is a manifestation of children's individuality. That is, some children play more often than other children, they not only show fidelity to traditional canons but develop personal designs and are eventually recognized by others as specialized toy makers (Rossie, 2005/2013; 2008). Frank and

Virginia Salamone express the relationship between the individual and social aspects of play as follows:

> But what the child does with the material of everyday life—how it plays with it, the joy it takes in that activity—is its concern as it constructs, destructs, and reconstructs its environment . . . As such . . . pure play has social and cultural functions as well as psychological ones. (Salamone & Salamone, 1991, pp. 136–37)

Therefore and because of the primordial importance of Amazigh children's playgroups and—according to the author's limited information—also in several other indigenous communities, it is important to stress that this children's creativity in making toys and in playing should be rather seen and investigated as an interactive and collective creativity than as a solitary and individual one.

THE ROLE OF INDIGENOUS TOYS AND PLAY IN PROMOTING CHILD DEVELOPMENT

Earlier the author prepared a booklet on *Games and Toys: Anthropological Research on Their Practical Contribution to Child Development* (Rossie, 1984). Using this information, two themes were noted: A. Play as a source of insight into the child and the society (p. 19–24) and B. Play, education, and child welfare (p. 24–32).

In a document on the play and toy cultures of Moroccan Amazigh children in relation to their development, the author suggested possibilities for using the local Amazigh play and toy culture by Amazigh cultural and social movements and for its integration in the Moroccan school system where Arabic is the language of education (Rossie, 2011). This online publication has continued to be useful and has received both verbal accolades and respect for its practical applications. Due to the limited scope of this chapter, the interested reader is directed to these two documents and to recommendations hereafter.

INDIGENOUS CHILDREN'S TOYS IN NORTH AFRICA AND THE SAHARA

Dolls

Usually, self-made dolls have a cross-shaped frame of reed or sticks. Girls, more seldom boys, start to make such dolls from the age of three years and dress them with rags following the local fashion. Once they get more experienced, the children add hair and decorations. Facial features are possibly added, but dolls without or with facial features coexist since long ago. In the literature, in a large museum collection and during field-work the author did not find traditional dolls with movable parts like arms and legs but a few times the lower part of the vertical reed has been cut out or two sticks are used to create legs.

The analysis of how indigenous children use these dolls, and also the imported plastic dolls they adapt to their needs, shows that they mostly refer to adult life. The female doll becomes a bride, spouse, mother; a divorced, old, rich, or poor woman; a wedding specialist, midwife, or doctor. The male doll represents a bridegroom, herds-man, cook, trader, warrior, horseman, and camel or mule-driver. Children anticipate their future life as adults, at least in communities where the lifestyle changed slowly, a cultural stability that disappeared in most regions after World War II. These last decades, adult roles related to the outside world as seen on TV, videos, smartphones and through tourism, galvanize indigenous children's interests (e.g., through Egyptian and Turkish movies and soaps, news programs, publicity, music, athletic, car and avia-tion championships, European tourists).

Toy Animals

All the above mentioned materials are used to make animal figurines, but children particularly like to use clay or clayish earth to model animals being dried in the shadow or baked in an oven, something already done in prehistoric times on the southern border of the Sahara.

Creating toy animals representing, birds, cats, cows, dogs, donkeys, dromedaries, fish, goats, horses, lizards, sheep, snakes, tortoise, and so forth, and using these in make-believe play seems to be more an activity of boys than girls. That is, boys use them for acting out male activities such as herding, breeding, organizing a Saharan encampment, being a warrior or hunter, plowing and organizing transport, or for caring and using domestic animals in the case of girls (Rossie, 2005b).

Toys Related to Domestic Life

Indigenous girls of the concerned regions prefer making toys representing items of their home environment, and they often play with them in small houses delimited by stones or mud. A special way to make such toys and figurines is by modeling them in clay mostly during the raining season when older girls sometimes build ovens to bake the clay toys. Argyris Fassoulas' detailed description of how Anti-Atlas Amazigh chil-dren today make, dry, bake, and decorate clay toys can be read in Annex 1 of *Make-Believe Play among Children of the Moroccan Anti-Atlas* (Rossie et al., 2020).

Toys and play activities related to dwellings, dinner and household tasks, and danc-ing are typical for girls, although boys occasionally engage in these. On the other hand, games and toys related to breeding, agriculture, trade, and playing self-made musical instruments are often boy games. Some games are girl games as well as boy games, but normally, they play these separately. Specific toys and play activities are linked to feasts and rituals (Rossie, 2008). In Morocco, the most important feast in this context is Ashura, a ten-day festive period in the beginning of the first month of the Muslim lunar calendar, during which it is customary to spray water on each other, play with fire, sing and hit drums, and to receive sweets, new clothes, and presents from adults.

Toys Related to Technical Activities

This category includes toy weapons, toys related to transport, and toys related to com-munication (Rossie, 2013). These toys typically belong to the play world of boys and they are meant to prepare them for adulthood and professional life. Since several decades, the influence of foreign ideas and materials and of the media, toy, entertain-ment, and communication industries stimulates boys more often than girls to create toys referring to vehicles, airplanes, digital cameras, and smartphones.

Toys for Games of Skill

Although several of these games do not need toys, children create toys for games of physical and intellectual skill using several materials, such as, tops made with small fruits, waste materials, and clay. Such modeling of tops with clay require fine manual skills. These toys are made and used for games of physical skill played with or by babies, tots, and toddlers, for games of dexterity, aiming, equilibrium, suppleness, speed, strength, and fighting, and for games related to the natural elements. Games of wit and intellectual skill refer to learning about the body, to insight, concentration, strategy, and word-painting, such as designing riddles (Rossie, 1984; 2015).

TRADITIONAL GAMES OF SKILL FOR CHILDREN WITH MOTOR DISABILITIES

In December 2009, the author came into contact with the Safi Centre of the Mo-hammed VI Foundation for the Disabled. During this contact with the center's director and one of the physiotherapists, the problem of using expensive equipment for chil-dren's therapy was discussed. These specialists stressed that parents lack means to buy such equipment and continue the therapy at home. In a seminar for parents with motor-handicapped children, the author proposed some local toys for physical games and discussed how they could be used to continue the therapy. These were toys these parents knew as children and could make without costs. Although the creation of a working group to analyze toys for games of skill useful in developing therapeutic applications and to test their functionality was of interest to some parents. Unfortunately, the proposal did not go further than good intentions.

SOCIOCULTURAL ASPECTS OF INDIGENOUS TOYS IN NORTH AFRICA AND THE SAHARA

Next to the material, technical and typological aspects of indigenous children's toys, the sociocultural aspects have great importance. An analysis of these sociocultural aspects is proposed in the collection of books Saharan and North African Toy and Play Cultures mentioned in the bibliography.

Relations Between Children

Rural Amazigh children of school age are largely in charge of making their own toys and the role of adults in children's play activities is minimal. Observing children, the author noted the importance of playgroups and the relationship between players based on family and neighborhood. Affectional and long-time relations are crucial in integrating and elaborating local toy and play cultures. The number of children in these communities offers a multitude of players of same and different age and sex that can serve as playmates. When going to primary school, befriending other children becomes possible. Older girls, sometimes older boys, take care of tots and toddlers and may make a toy for these younger children.

Play areas in villages and popular quarter streets in towns are real laboratories for interaction and creativity. There small children mix with same age children, older children, and adolescents, whereby same-sex peers and older children become crucial in transmitting toy making techniques and games (Rossie, 2008).

Gender

Toys made by girls are largely inspired by family life (e.g., dolls, dwellings, toy utensils, miniature tools for female crafts). Boys prefer to create toys inspired by economic activities, vehicles and technology. Girls and boys eventually collaborate in play activities (e.g., when constructing children's villages), but then they engage in parallel play, enacting typical male or female roles and using gender-specific toys.

Sexual differentiation is unimportant for small children, but from the age of six years it becomes very obvious in play activities. Then boys leave the playgroups controlled by older girls to form only boys' playgroups in which they enjoy more freedom than girls in their playgroups, (e.g., boys can go further away from home this way escaping adult control). Normally, girls should stay in their home's vicinity to help in the household or to look after little ones, but also to remain under closer supervision. Nevertheless, one must remain cautious about the separation of girls and boys as there are indications that it can be surmounted in play activities (Rossie, 2005/2013; 2008).

CONTINUITY AND CHANGE

In the sections above, some remarks have been made about the evolution of Amazigh children's play and toy culture. Although research on traditional children's cultures is really necessary, one should always strive to gain insight into the evolution of this tradition. Change is caused by internal factors, such as moving from village to town, going to school where Arabic is the used language and the increasing adults' habit to donate toys to children, and external factors, such as mass media, digital communication, and cheap Asian plastic toys (Rossie, 2005/2013; 2008; 2019). Although the influence of these external factors in North Africa and the Sahara became more prominent these last forty years, it is not a recent phenomenon as Castells mentions in 1916 that toy guns manufactured in Europe were sold to Moroccan town children.

INDIGENOUS CHILDREN'S CULTURES AND SOCIOCULTURAL AND EDUCATIONAL DEVELOPMENT

Being trained first as a social worker, the author believes that studying indigenous children's play and toy cultures should not remain an academic occupation only. On the contrary, eventual applications in which using this heritage can be valuable are child welfare, formal and informal education, the adaptation of the school to local conditions, the relationship between children, adults and children, and parents and teachers, of community development and the promotion of intercultural understanding. The author has been active in writing about these topics, of promoting interest in indigenous children's tangible and intangible heritages through expositions, lectures, seminars, and workshops. Interested readers will find information on all this in two sections, one related to an African context and another to a European and South American context (Rossie, 2005/2013; 2013).

RECOMMENDATIONS

An excellent book to start further reading is *The Anthropology of Learning in Childhood* (Lancy, et al., 2010) as it offers a detailed cross-cultural analysis of the contextualized development of indigenous children. Two books, by Rogoff et al. (1993) and Göncü (ed.) (1999) refer to children's participation and engagement in their environment. Those interested in handmade toys created for developmental and educational purposes may look at the work of Sudarshan Khanna and Arvind Gupta. Two important sources on indigenous peoples are: the United Nations Permanent Forum on Indigenous Issues (https://www.un.org/development/desa/indigenouspeoples) and the Center for World Indigenous Studies that publishes the *Fourth World Journal* (https://www.cwis.org/fourth-world-journal). In 2019, Artemis Yagou wrote:

> A breakthrough in the history of childhood would require more substantial proof of the children's perspective. Extensive archival or material evidence of children's actions and points of view should come to the fore to support the revisionist reading of childhood and to document the agency of children in a truly solid manner . . . This collective, interdisciplinary effort would aim at written sources . . . but also material objects made and used by children, as well as traces of use, misuse, or abuse of playthings; additionally, it would require the cross-fertilization of all available evidence. (p. 2)

Because children's agency and creativity prevails in toy making and play activities, more fieldwork on indigenous children's cultures is really needed. Moreover, if the situation of these children must improve and if the desertion of rural areas should diminish a better understanding of their world and of the changes affecting it will be indispensable.

Indigenous children play an active role in transmitting and adapting local knowledge, skills and beliefs so I believe we should not only promote their rights but also recognize their contributions.

REFERENCES

The publications of the author are available on

Academia.edu: https://ucp.academia.edu/JeanPierreRossie
Scribd: https://www.scribd.com/user/63524386/Jean-Pierre-Rossie

Béart, Ch. (1955). *Jeux et jouets de l'Ouest Africain*. Mémoires de l'IFAN.
Bellin, P. (1963). L'enfant saharien à travers ses jeux. *Journal de la Société des Africanistes*, 33.
Brandow-Faller, M. (ed.) (2018). *Childhood by design: Toys and the material culture of childhood. 1700-Present*. Bloomsbury Visual Arts.

Burnett, C., & Hollander, W. J. (2004). The South African indigenous games research project of 2001/2002—https://www.ulwaziprogramme.org/2016/10/indigenous-games-project

Castells, F. (1916/1987). Note sur la fête de Achoura à Rabat. *Les Archives Berbères*.

Edwards, K. (s.d.) *Bibliography of the traditional games of Australian Aboriginal and Torres Strait Islander peoples*—http://travelsdocbox.com/Australia_and_New_Zealand/71870013-A-bibliography-of-the-traditional-games-of-australian-aboriginal-and-torres-strait-islander-peoples.html

Ferrarese Capettini, S. M. (2006–2011). *El Sembrador. Juegos étnicos de América y documentos sobre educación física intercultural*. 3 volumes.

Göncü, A. (Ed.) (1999). *Children's engagement in the world: Sociocultural perspectives*. Cambridge, UK: Cambridge University Press.

Gupta, A. (1999). *Toy Treasures*, 4th ed. New Delhi: CAPART.

Haagen, C. (1994). *Bush toys: Aboriginal children at play*. National Museum of Australia.

Herrera Velásquez, M. I., et al. (2018). *Juegos y Deportes Autóctonos, Tradicionales y Populares*. Editorial Académica Española—https://www.dropbox.com/s/pz7smz6nb22yozu/Libro%20juegos%20autoctonos.pdf?dl=0&fbclid=IwAR1tSMwJWQAItDKpY9Kk2z6EyxrR5e9rnaTEExcXC9YWdj5gYKqZ3ny8Eeg

Khanna, S. (1992). *Joy of making Indian yoys*. National Book Trust India—https://archive.org/details/JoyOfMakingIndianToys-English-SudarshanKhanna/page/n57

Khanna, S., Wolf, G., Ravishankar, A. & Sundram, P. (2018). Toys and play with everyday materials. India: Tara Books Pvt. Ltd.

Klepzig, F. (1972). *Kinderspiele der Bantu*. Verlag Anton Hain.

Kubik, G. (1997). Children, child education and "children's furniture" in the cultures of sub-Saharan Africa. *kid size. The Material World of Childhood*. Skira editore/Vitra Design Museum.

Lancy, D. F. (1996). *Playing on the mother-ground. Cultural routines for children's development*. New York: Guilford Press.

Lancy, D. F., Bock, J., & Gaskins, S. (Eds.) (2010). *The Anthropology of Learning in Childhood*. Lanham, MD: Altamira Press.

Lombard, Ch. (1978). *Les jouets des enfants baoulé. Essais sur la créativité enfantine dans une société rurale africaine*. Quatre Vents Editeur.

Mawere, M. (2012). *The struggle of African indigenous knowledge systems in an age of globalization: A case for children's traditional games in South-Eastern Zimbabwe*. Langaa RPCIG—partially available on https://books.google.com.ph/books?id=XH35Y3A6rGEC&printsec=frontcover&dq=south+african+indigenous+toys&hl=en&sa=X&ved=0ahUKEwjT3ZX305ThAhXk6XMBHfwcCVc4ChDoAQhPMAg#v=onepage&q&f=false

McQuiston, D., & McQuiston, D. (1995). *Dolls and Toys of Native America*. San Francisco: Chronicle Books.

Pinto Cebrián, F. (1999). *Juegos Saharauis para Jugar en la Arena. Juegos y Juguetes Tradicionales del Sáhara*. Miraguano S.A. Ediciones.

Rogoff, B., Mistry, J., Göncü, A. & Mosier, C. (1993). *Guided participation in cultural activity by toddlers and caregivers*. Chicago, IL: University of Chicago Press.

Rossie, J.-P. (1984). *Games and toys: anthropological research on their practical contribution to child development*. Unit for Co-operation with UNICEF & W.F.P., UNESCO.

Rossie, J.-P. (2005/2013). *Toys, play, culture and society. An anthropological approach with reference to North Africa and the Sahara*. SITREC.

Rossie, J.-P. (2005a). *Saharan and North African toy and play cultures. Children's dolls and doll play*. SITREC.

Rossie, J.-P. (2005b). *Saharan and North African toy and play vultures. The animal world in play, games and toys*. SITREC.

Rossie, J.-P. (2008). *Saharan and North African toy and play cultures. Domestic life in play, games and toys*. SITREC.

Rossie, J.-P. (2011). La cultura lúdica de los niños amazigh marroquíes y las cuestiones del desarrollo. Ferrarese Capettini, S. M., *El Sembrador 3* (also available in French).

Rossie, J.-P. (2013). *Saharan and North African toy and play cultures. Technical activities in play, games and toys*. Braga: CEFH.

Rossie, J.-P. (2015). *Games of skill from the Tunisian Sahara and Morocco: Anthropological research and physical education for peace*. SITREC.

Rossie, J.-P., Jariaa, Kh., Daoumani, B. & Fassoulas, A. (2021). *Saharan and North African toy and play cultures: Make-believe play among children of the Moroccan Anti-Atlas*. Braga: CEFH.

Salamone, F. A., & Salamone, V. A. (1991). Children's games in Nigeria redux: A consideration of the "uses" of play. *Play and Culture*, *4*, Human Kinetics Publishers Inc.

Sbrzesny, H. (1976). *Die Spiele der !Ko-Buschleute*. White Plains, NY: Piper.

Sutton-Smith, B. (1986). *Toys as culture*. Cincinnati: Gardner Press.

Yagou, A. (2019). Book review *Childhood by design: Toys and the material culture of childhood, 1700–present*. The Design Journal. https://www.academia.edu/38493223/Book_Review_Childhood_by_Design_Toys_and_the_Material_Culture_of_Childhood_1700-Present_?email_work_card=view-paper

20

THIS BOOK IS MAGIC . . .
EXPLORING THE BOOK AS TOY

Kathleen Roskos

It's snack time in Ms. Madrid's preschool class. Three-and four-year-old children are seated at tables around the room. They have just been served a carton of milk and graham crackers, when the following conversation takes place between two boys.

Jeb: Hey, where's my chocolate milk?

Luka: A little boy in China drinked it.

Jeb: China?

Luka: 'Cause I readed that Chinese book and it did this: "Abra-cadabra—poof!" and then your chocolate milk just disappeared!

Jeb: It disappeared?

Luka: Yup, everything just disappeared. Everything 'cept this book. This little book is magic . . .

Technically speaking, a book is not a toy in the traditional sense. It is not an action figure, a miniature, a puzzle, a construction piece, a doll, a ball or the like. A book (as a real object) is not something children typically play with, per se, unless they are very young and like to hold it, hit it, chew it, stack it, or throw it. But in a more abstract sense, a book is a toy found on the playground of the mind. Its contents transform the book (like magic) into a toy, making it into something to "play with" in many ways. Like all good toys, a good book can challenge the mind, support development, attract interest, be safe for play and not cost too much—all criteria of a good toy (Green, 1983; Wardle, 1993).

This chapter explores the book as toy—that is to say as an object in the child's world that invites action. This investigative journey is limited to young children, preschoolers primarily, and explores what the book as toy affords early learning, especially in early literacy development. The chapter starts on firm ground with books that are especially playful in and of themselves, namely pop-up books and more recently digital picture books. Then looking back at the historical link between books and dramatic play, research that supports book-related play in early literacy pedagogy is explored. Finally, the toy-like qualities of the book as a launch pad for the imagination, building foundations of higher order language and thinking skills, such as narrative competence, are discussed. The chapter closes with a parting glance at the lasting toy-like qualities of books as imaginary friends that become lifelong sources of entertainment and pleasure. Some early childhood toys, happily, are not left behind in dusty attics.

BOOK AS TOY

It is September 30, 2018, in Kansas City, Missouri, and the Movable Book Society has announced its 2018 Meggandorfer Prize winner for the Best Paper Engineering for a Trade Publication at its biennial conference. This award honors Lothar Meggendorfer (1847–1925), a legendary nineteenth-century illustrator and movable books paper engineer. The 2018 award winner is: Simon Arizpe who engineered an amazing pop-up book entitled, *Zahhak: The Legend of the Serpent King* (Rahmanian & Arizpe, 2018). Arizpe's paper engineering feat rests on 250 years of pop-up book history that began with Richard Sayer's *metamorpheses books* in the late eighteenth century, which offered children much-needed amusement through illustrations that changed and kept pace with the story. The basic pop-up techniques used then, like pull, tilt, spin, and lifting elements, remain the foundations of good pop-up design today that are enhanced by motion that animates the way a pop-up folds out and moves in increasingly complex ways. Kelli Anderson's *This Book is a Planetarium: And Other Extraordinary Pop-up Contraptions* (2017), for example, transforms into six functional tools: a real working planetarium projecting the constellations, a musical instrument complete with strings for strumming, a geometric drawing generator, an infinite calendar, a message decoder, and a speaker that amplifies sound.

From relatively simple to complicated paper designs, the pop-up engineering goal is one of interactivity—to pull tabs, tug strings, lift-up flaps, turn revolving discs (volvelles), view three-dimensional illustrations, unpack paper folds—so as to actively *play along with* the story. The result can be intense physical interaction with the storyline that may support narrative comprehension of the story elements (or not). The primary purpose of the pop-up book, after all, is "to give children spontaneous pleasure, and not primarily to teach them, not solely to make them good, nor to keep them profitably quiet" (Darton [1770] in Montanaro). Thus, it is to this purpose that the pop-up book is a genuine toy. One of the best places to learn about the wonderful world of pop-up books (book toys) is the Best Pop Books website (https://www.bestpopupbooks.com). It provides pop-up information, pop-up news, video reviews, a store, book rankings and much more.

At an early age, the pop-up book and its close relatives (e.g., accordion books) invite children to comprehend their world through experiential handling of the book object, creating an embodied meaning-making experience. A core theoretical concept at work here is that of materiality, (i.e., the influence of physical materials on the young child's behavior), which via object play are hypothesized to support behavioral flexibility in early childhood (Pellegrini, 2019; Sorenson, 2009). The book design goal is one of active, multimodal engagement on the part of the reader that affords individual meaning making and consequently learning. When five-year-old Luka explores David Carter's *Hide and Seek* (2012), for example, he immediately sees colorful visual worlds of three-dimensional sculptures, pulls and flips tabs, turns wheels and searches for images and letters hidden within the art. In the exploratory act, he learns about shapes, colors, and structures through embodied actions that integrate perception and action in experience (Borghi & Caruana, 2015).

In paper book toys, the focus is on physical materiality—attributes that make us aware of an object or image occupying physical space, whether it be texture, color, dimension, and so forth—and in picture book apps, discussed next, on digital materiality—the attributes that make us aware of an object or image having been created or manipulated in digital space (Choi, 2017). Materiality involves the child as player in the interplay between the book's content, its visual displays and as object in time and space. The resulting playful interactions between eye, hand and mind synergize meaning making to build conceptual knowledge and guide comprehension of new information (National Academies of Sciences, Engineering, and Medicine, 2018).

Version 2.0 of the pop-up book is the digital-age picture book app, which expands verbal and visual modes to include auditory, tactile and performative dimensions. It differs radically from the materiality of paper pop-ups (as toys): an app exists as an intangible on a two-dimensional screen, not as a tangible object in three-dimensional physical space. Its materiality is more virtual than real. Its playground is the screen. So far educational research of picture book apps focuses primarily on their effects in adult-child book reading contexts versus paper books and on young children's language and early literacy development (e.g., vocabulary) (Bus, Takacs & Kegel, 2014). Less attention has focused on their materiality as play objects, although apps offer a wider spectrum of toy-like interactivity than paper books, which are limited largely to page turning (pop-ups and movable books aside). Rather, attention focuses on the sense of touch, which makes the picture book app especially toy-like for children. Its most salient form is the physical interaction with the story using multitouch gestures (e.g., tap, swipe, pinch) that allow *extra-text interactivity*: touch the hotspot/button for an outcome (action-reaction sequence) (Zhao & Unsworth, 2019). This design supports exploratory play of the book app toy. Touch gestures can also trigger highly interactive, multimedia experience (e.g., helping out the main character) and personalized engagement (e.g., recording/replaying one's voice), referred to as *intratext interactivity*, which affords pretense with the book app; that is, participating *as if* in the story (Zhao & Unsworth, 2019). It is the touch design of a book app, then, that makes it more of a toy for playing with that may lead to learning outcomes, such as narrative comprehension skills or vocabulary.

Whether paper or digital, it is children's physical interaction with a book that turns it into a toy where the goal or intention is object use. This orientation can support the book as story and should be considered as such. In some respects, it is a case of Bateson's metacommunication concept, *this nip is not a bite* (Bateson, 1972/2000). Book as toy is play, not serious book reading. The playful nip denotes book reading, but it does not denote what would be denoted by true storybook reading. Book toy play, in short, is not about the story told.

BOOK TOY PLAY AND DIVERSITY

While books afford play for all children, there are some books that appeal to young children's distinct differences and enhance their playful interactions with books. Books, for example, can relate to children's specific culture and language, helping them to identify with familiar concepts, topic, and themes that encourage play. Titles can reflect special needs and contain good stories about disabilities that inspire playful experiences (e.g., *Just Because*, which describes two siblings' pretend play, one of whom is in a wheel-chair [Elliot, 2010]). Assistive technologies, such as enlarged print, audio and book construction (e.g., hard/soft cover) can support children's engagement with books as objects as well as their content. Book apps, in particular, provide accommodations for children with special needs, such as print highlighting, narration (in different voices and languages), music, and animation.

At an early age, children demonstrate few gender differences in book preferences with most youngsters finding great pleasure in the overall read-aloud experience with a parent. According to the Scholastic Kids and Family Reading Report (2017), more than 80 percent of both children and parents across all income levels and child's age love or like read-aloud time a lot, which creates many opportunities for book play as a result.

Bricolage

Books provide one of richest sources of complex language for young children, and storybook reading creates an equally rich opportunity for language learning. Book language, a necessary prerequisite for literate thought (Paul & Wang, 2006), is more complex and diverse than everyday talk (Montag, Jones, & Smith, 2015). On average, there are 16.3 sophisticated words per 1,000 words in preschool books (Hayes & Ahrens, 1988), five times the amount of sophisticated vocabulary words that are used in oral conversations (Snow, 1983). Book reading fosters active, social, and meaningful involvement with ideas, words, and emotions; it helps children make connections between the known and the new; and it organizes information into meaningful patterns, or text structures that help children remember story lines and facts.

It is not unusual for the characters and events of children's favorite books to find their way into children's play. Book-play sets consisting of a book plus props (e.g., a stuffed animal) blur the boundaries between book as story and book as toy, creating a tangible play space for action. Rowe's descriptive account of book-related play among preschoolers provides a stellar example (Rowe, 1998). In the preschool setting, book-related props were at hand in the book and block play areas, and children brought book-related toys to hold and spontaneously play with in conjunction with story reading, at times assuming a role or engaging in pretend actions. Four-year-old Steve, for example, made sound effects, *dop, dop, dop* as he made a toy alligator bite at the picture of the farmyard dog in the book *The Farmyard Cat* (Anello, 1987).

At home, Rowe's young son, age three, created and enacted book-related dramatic play, assembling toys and props to retell favorite stories, especially for the book *Mike Mulligan and His Steam Shovel* (Burton, 1939). He pretended to use a wooden spoon, for instance, to shovel coal into the door of the bathroom, which was transformed into Mary Anne's boiler. Rowe's thick description of book-related play in the preschool and home setting reveals the synthesis of book plus props to produce a bricolage (new plaything) that is at once ideational and real—which, she argued, helped young children to realize the literate potentials of books.

Capitalizing on the bricolage arising from book-prop interactions, Saltz and Johnson (1974) introduced thematic fantasy play (TFP) as "a type of dramatic play somewhat akin to Smilansky's (1968) sociodramatic play" training (p. 624) that organized play around themes and plots of folk tales or favorite books. Children are provided opportunities to enact story sequences and required to imagine and perform behaviors with book-related props following along with the story narration. The TFP, in sum, reins in the spontaneity of book-prop play by applying a clear story structure that more deliberately taps its literate potentials—and simultaneously shifts its focus from toy play to educational play (linking learning outcomes to play features) (Johnson, Christie, & Wardle, 2005, p. 199).

In terms of playfulness, TFP resembles story drama made popular by David Booth in the 1980s (Kukla, 1980). Story drama is anchored in a story read whole or in part, discussed and then enacted with props by the players as the story is read. Similar to TFP, it is driven by a shared story, but different in that story drama, after repeated reading, encourages improvisation on the story elements whereas in TFP children are guided to enact scenes and roles as described in the story (i.e., to transition from "symbolic story form into behavior form"; Saltz & Johnson, 1974, p. 624). The TFP's ultimate purpose, in brief, is more academic than playful and it gets results. The historical line of TFP research demonstrates its value in increasing young children's cognitive functioning and in particular their story comprehension. (See Roskos, 2019, for a review.)

Recent book-play research further advances the theory that book-related play is beneficial for achieving early childhood language and early literacy outcomes. In their Read-Play-Learn project (increasing vocabulary of low-income preschoolers), Hadley, Dickinson, and colleagues (2016), for example, describe a book-guided play method conducted by intervention specialists. Each book reading is followed by a 10-minute play session with replica toys that match book characters and other props. Intervention specialists use play scripts to scaffold the play activity toward usage of target vocabulary words. Analyses of pre-/posttest data from 240 preschoolers showed significant increases in depth of knowledge for all word types. Along these same lines, Han, Moore, Vukelich, and Buell (2010) and more recently LaGamba (2018), provided teachers with scripts to help them "play with" children after book reading to enact pretend play scenarios using book-related props associated with target words. Both studies showed the benefits of guided play for increasing children's vocabularies on target words. Across these studies, two design features of the book-play paradigm are consistent with prior TFP research: book-based props and scripts as scaffolds to achieve educational goals. It's also important to note here a distinct shift in research perspective from either/or to both/and; that is, not the historical either adult or play, but rather both adult facilitation and play as agents of change.

But, while this line of research is fascinating, showing the evolution of book-related play from Rowe's descriptive account of spontaneous book-related play to literacy-oriented experimental studies, it is far afield from exploring the book as plaything—as an assembly of story ideas and related objects that are played with for the sheer fun of it. So, returning to this purpose, let's explore how books provide a launch pad for the imagination where the stories told are transformed into *toys of the mind*.

Launchpad

Princess Elsa to Anna: Wanna play with me? Wanna play with me in the castle? I'll go in the castle and hide.

Anna to Princess Elsa: Wanna play "uppies"? Up, up, up. Up the other side (of the castle).

Anna to Cinderella: You're so pretty. Wanna play in the park?

Princess Elsa to Cinderella: Beautiful! So down, down the slide.

Princess Elsa to Cinderella: Wanna talk with us? Up there?

Anna to Princess Elsa and Cinderella: Go in the castle . . . go to sleeping.

Sofia, almost three years old, has seen the movie *Frozen* multiple times and the book is an old favorite, shared often with mom and dad, and browsed alone. She owns several replica dolls from the story, and her favorite is Princess Elsa (the heroine). As the vignette illustrates, the storybook is a launch pad for her imagination as she transports the story into pretend talk involving her miniature princess dolls in their doll-sized castle. Her "flight of fancy," so to speak, allows her to improvise on the book story (i.e., to play with its elements on her own terms, and to create a kind of virtual mind-toy for play).

That a book has this power to evoke "toying" with stories is not trivial; rather it nurtures narrative competence, which goes to the core of literate thought. Bruner (1984) reminds us that it is dramatic story that keeps "firm hold on the constitutive function of language—the warnings, threats, promises, and spells that create social and personal reality" (p. 199). And it is this premise that brings us to the importance of replica play in developing children's narrative skills for future learning. Replica play is play with animate figures that involves storytelling grafted on to a storybook stem (another kind of prop) (Rubin & Wolf, 1979). So we have an abstract prop (the story) supported by real props (replica toys) that allow the child to be both actor giving voice to story events and director providing justifications and explanations for these events.

This is challenging mental work that produces longer, more complex narratives than play without props, and access to more personally meaningful props, in fact, it (like Princess Elsa to Sofia) results in even better stories (Fein, 1995; Sawyer & DeZutter, 2007). Fein's early study illustrates this finding. She investigated three hypotheses: (a) replica figures enhance the structural qualities of stories (Wright, 1992); (b) figures serve as script markers of story theme (Hudson & Shapiro, 1991); and (c) figures evoke universal problem-response story types around a threat or lack (Botvin & Sutton-Smith,

1977). Using two sets of replica props—one designed to elicit stories about daily life (canonical set) and the other to elicit problem-based stories (breach set), she collected four-year-olds' replica play stories. Analyses showed that props do make a difference: the breach set outperformed the canonical set in the children's production of tales, complex story structure, villainy themes, and story length. Sets of props that include incompatibilities—an alligator with family figures, for instance—increases the chances for structurally more complex narratives in both solitary and collaborative pretend play, drawing not only on children's background knowledge, but also their emotions.

A more recent study coincides with Fein's earlier observations. Investigating how storybooks and story-related replica props with realistic and fantastical themes affect children's vocabulary learning, Weisberg, et al. (2015) found that children in the fantastical theme condition showed significantly more gains in their productive knowledge of new words than those in the realistic condition, although positive gains were observed in both conditions. But why the value-added of fantasy? The fantastical story plus replica props, the authors conjecture, encourage children to think more flexibly, explore word meanings more deeply, and use higher order cognitive processes, such as inferencing, for story comprehension. It is possible, too, that fantastic stories plus related replica props add suspense, as Fein (1995) suggested, and it is the emotional meanings evoked that make story content particularly memorable. Experimental studies, however, are mixed on this matter, suggesting that pretending with props helps storytelling, but role play may be the more salient variable in young children's narrative development (Lillard, et al., 2013).

Perhaps (and more research is needed) having lots of *book as launch pad* play activities does do something quite wonderful for the young mind, and that is to prime the mechanisms of narrative development, such as awareness of story structure, word meanings, syntactic awareness, inferencing, and memory (Lillard, et al, 2013; Nicolopoulou, 2019). Toy-like at the onset, the active manipulation of story elements with story-related props may help children to create mental models of story events that ultimately aid narrative comprehension (Kintsch & Kintsch, 2005), and in the process, advance their own language skills. Some research, in fact, suggests that this may be the case. Correlational evidence shows a positive relationship between language elements used to engage in pretending (generally) and those useful in learning literate language (e.g., syntactic awareness, vocabulary, endophora) (Pellegrini, 1985; Vedeler, 1997; Wasik & Jacobi-Vessels, 2016).

Previous sections described the toy-like qualities of a book as a bricolage where diverse objects are assembled around the book, ranging from stuffed animals to board games, that are played with together. This section explores the book as a launch pad that when "fueled" by replica props that are closely related to story elements creates an imaginary play space in the mind where the challenging skills of pretense, role play, and object use are coordinated by the child to use language and to tell stories. Researchers do not fully understand what this means for the young child's developing cognitive and emotional abilities, but it is evident that it is integrally involved with other capacities, including language, narrative competence, empathy, and self-regulation (Bodrova & Leong, 2007; Nicolopoulou, 2019; Pellegrini & Van Rysin, 2007; Weisberg, 2014).

The book as toy of the mind develops tools of the mind that are needed for future learning under certain play conditions, including at the very least (a) familiarity with storybooks, (b) a place and time to play, and (c) a few story-related replica props. Playing with books in this way is situational, spontaneous, multimodal, and improvisational yet constrained by story elements and replica props. It can be three-dimensional in space (real embodiment) or two-dimensional on a mobile tablet (virtual embodiment) (e.g., Puppet Pals [WeeSchool, n.d.]). But it is always engaging, personally meaningful, pleasurable and fun.

Imaginary Friend

In the panoply of early childhood toys, the book *is* magic because it can make things happen that seem impossible. It begins as an object to hold, to explore and to read with another, but—abracadabra poof!—it becomes a plaything for the mind that can be shared with others or alone. The toy qualities of books, from pop-ups to apps to constructed play worlds, can morph into imaginary companions with age. One of the most engaging examples of this toy-like feature of books is the short-animated film, *The Fantastic Flying Books of Mr. Morris Lessmore* (Joyce & Oldenburg 2011). The story starts—*Morris Lessmore loved words. He loved stories. He loved books*—and so he did. Applying the basic design elements of the pop-up in film-like animated form, the story creates an imaginary world where books can move, talk, have feelings, share thoughts, and befriend. The story recounts Morris' life cycle with books that begins in a rough and tumble way (a dark and windy day) to an encounter with a *festive squadron of flying books* and a flying lady who gave him a favorite book (*an amiable fellow*) that led him into days and then years lived with books. He tried to keep the books in order; he cared for them; he got lost in them; he shared them with others; he wrote in his own book. And as he aged the books—his friends—took care of him until it was time for him to move on. The story ends as it began—with a book. A small girl opens Morris' book *of all he knew and everything that he hoped* and starts her own lifelong journey with books. Books, you see, are our imaginary friends—they are the early childhood toys that last.

REFERENCES

Bateson, G. (1972/2000), *Steps to an ecology of mind: Collected essays in anthropology, psychiatry, evolution, and epistemology*. Chicago, IL: University of Chicago Press.

Bodrova, E., & Leong, D. (2007). Play and early literacy. In K. Roskos & J. Christie (Eds.), *Play and literacy in early childhood* (pp. 185–200). New York, NY: Lawrence Erlbaum Associates.

Borghi, A., & Caruana, F. (2015). *Embodiment theories*. In J. Wright (Ed.), *International encyclopedia of the social & behavioral sciences*, 2nd Ed. (pp. 420–26). doi: 10.1016/B978-0-08-097086-8.56025-5.

Botvin, G. J. & Sutton-Smith, B. (1977). The development of structural complexity in children's fantasy narratives. *Developmental Psychology, 13,* 377–88.

Bruner, J. (1984). Language, mind and reading. In H. Goelman, A. Oberg & F. Smith (Eds.) *Awakening to literacy* (pp. 193–200). Exeter, NH: Heinemann Educational Books.

Bus, A. G., Takacs, Z. K., & Kegel, A. T. (2014). Affordances and limitations of electronic storybooks for young children's emergent literacy. *Developmental Review,* doi: 10.1016/j.dr.2014.12.004

Choi, J. (April 10, 2017). *Theory of visual communications: Materiality in design TED talk.* Retrieved from https://rampages.us/janachoi/2017/04/10/materiality-in-design-ted-talk-write-up/ April, 2019.

Fein, G. (1995). Toys and stories. In A. D. Pellegrini (Ed.) *The future of play theory,* (pp. 151–64). Albany, NY: SUNY Press.

Green, D. H. (1983). What makes a good toy? Retrieved from http://www.parents-choice.org/article.cfm?art_id=303

Hadley, E. B., Dickinson, D. K., Hirsh-Pasek, K., Golinkoff, R. M., & Nesbitt, K. T. (2016). Examining the acquisition of vocabulary knowledge depth among preschool-aged children. *Reading Research Quarterly, 51*(2), 181–98.

Han, M., Moore, N., Vukelich, C., & Buell, M. (2010). Does play make a difference? How play intervention affects the vocabulary learning of at-risk preschoolers. *American Journal of Play, 3,* 82–104.

Hayes, D. P., & Ahrens M. G. (1988). Vocabulary simplification for children: A special case of "motherese"? *Journal of Child Language, 15,* 395–410.

Hudson, J. & Shapiro, L. R. (1991). From knowing to telling: Children's scripts, stories, and personal narratives. In A. McCabe & C. Peterson (Eds.), *Developing narrative structure* (pp. 89–134). Hillsdale, NY: Lawrence Erlbaum & Associates.

Johnson, J., Christie J., & Wardle, F. (2005). *Play, development and early education.* New York, NY: Pearson.

Kintsch, W., & Kinstch, E. (2005). Comprehension. In S. G. Paris, & S. A. Stahl (Eds.), *Children's reading comprehension and assessment* (pp. 71–92). Mahwah, NJ: Ablex. http://dx.doi.org/10.1002/9780470757642.ch12

Kukla, K. (1980). David Booth: Drama as a way of knowing. *Language Arts, 64*(1), 73–78.

LaGamba, E. (2018, April). *An investigation of read alouds, classroom interactions, and guided play as supports for vocabulary learning in preschool.* Unpublished doctoral dissertation, University of Pittsburgh. Pittsburgh, Pennsylvania.

Lillard, A. S., Lerner, M. D., Hopkins, E. J., Dore, R. A., Smith, E. D., & Palmquist, C. M. (2013). The impact of pretend play on children's development: A review of the evidence. *Psychological Bulletin, 139,* 1–34.

Montag, J. L., Jones, M. N., & Smith, L. B. (2015). The words children hear: Picture books and the statistics for language learning. *Psychological Science, 26*(9), 1489–96. doi:10.1177/0956797615594361

Montanaro, A. *A concise history of pop-up books and movable books.* Retrieved from https://www.libraries.rutgers.edu/rul/libs/scua/montanar/p-intro.htm April, 2019.

National Academies of Sciences, Engineering, and Medicine. (2018). How people learn II: Learners, contexts, and cultures. Washington, DC: The National Academies Press. doi: https://doi.org/10.17226/24783.

Nicolopoulou, A. (2019). Pretend and social pretend play: Complexities, continuities and controversies of a research field. In P. K. Smith & J. L.Roopnarine (Eds.) *The Cambridge handbook of play: Developmental and disciplinary perspectives* (pp. 183–99). New York, NY: Cambridge University Press.

Paul, P., & Wang, Y. (2006). Multiliteracies and literate thought. *Theory into Practice, 45*(4), 304–10.

Pellegrini, A. D., (1985). The relations between symbolic play and literate behavior: A review and critique of the empirical literature. *Review of Educational Research, 55,* 207–21.

Pellegrini, A. D., & Van Rysin, M. J. (2007). Commentary: Cognition, play and early literacy. In K. Roskos & J. Christie (Eds,), *Play and literacy in early childhood* (pp. 65–82). New York, NY: Lawrence Erlbaum Associates.

Pellegrini, A. D. (2019). Object use in childhood: Development and possible functions. In P. K. Smith & J. L. Roopnarine (Eds.) *The Cambridge handbook of play: Developmental and disciplinary perspectives* (pp 165–82). New York, NY: Cambridge University Press.

Roskos, K. (2019). Play-literacy knowns and unknowns in a changing world. In P. K. Smith & J. Roopnarine (Eds.) *The Cambridge handbook of play: Developmental and disciplinary perspectives* (pp. 528–45). New York, NY: Cambridge University Press.

Rowe, D. (1998). The literate potentials of book-related dramatic play. *Reading Research Quarterly, 33*(1), 10–35.

Rubin, S., & Wolf, D. (1979). The development of maybe: The evolution of social roles into narrative role. In E. Winner & H. Gardner (Eds.), *New directions for child development, No. 6: Fact, fiction, & fantasy in childhood* (pp. 15–28). San Francisco, CA: Jossey-Bass.

Saltz, E., & Johnson, J. (1974). Training for thematic-fantasy play in culturally disadvantaged children: Preliminary results. *Journal of Educational Psychology, 66*, 623–30.

Sawyer R. K., & DeZutter, S. (2007). Improvisation: A lens for play and literacy research. In K. Roskos & J. Christie (Eds,), *Play and literacy in early childhood* (pp. 21–36). New York, NY: Lawrence Erlbaum Associates.

Scholastic Kids and Family Reading Report, 7th Edition. https://www.scholastic.com/readingreport/home.html

Smilansky, S. (1968). *The effects of sociodramatic play on disadvantaged preschool children.* New York, NY: Wiley.

Snow, C.E. (*1983*). Literacy and language: relationships during the preschool years. *Harvard Educational Review, 53*(2), 165–89.

https://doi.org/10.17763/haer.53.2.t6177w39817w2861

Sorenson. E. (2009). *The materiality of learning: Technology and knowledge in educational practice.* Learning in Doing series, New York, NY: Cambridge University Press

Vedeler, L. (1997). Dramatic play: A format for literate language. *British Journal of Educational Psychology 67*, 153–67.

Wasik, B. A., & Jacobi-Vessels, J. L. (2016). Word play: Scaffolding language development through child-directed play. *Early Childhood Education Journal, 44*(6), 769–76.

Wardle, F. (1993). Criteria for selecting toys. *Exchange.* Retrieved from https://www.childcareexchange.com/article/criteria-for-selecting-toys/5009443/

Weisberg, D. S., Ilgaz, H., Hirsh-Pasek, K., Golinkoff, R., Nicolopoulou, A., & Dickinson, D. K. (2015). Shovels and swords: How realistic and fantastical themes affect children's word learning. *Cognitive Development, 35,* 1–14.

Wright, J. L. (1992). *Correlates of young children's narrative competence: Maternal behaviors and home literacy experiences.* Doctoral dissertation. University of Maryland, College Park.

Zhao, S., & Unsworth, L. (2019). Touch design and narrative interpretation: A social semiotic approach to picture book apps. In N. Kucirkova & G. Falloon (Eds.) *Apps, technology and younger learners: International evidence for teaching.* (pp. 89–101). New York, NY: Routledge.

Children's Books/Apps

Anderson, K. (2017). *This book is a planetarium: And other extraordinary pop-up contraptions.* Chronicle Books.

Anello, C. (1987). *The farmyard cat.* New York, NY: Scholastic.

Burton, V.L. (1939). *Mike Mulligan and his steam shovel.* Boston, MA: Houghton-Mifflin.

Carter, D. (2012). *Hide and seek.* London: Tate Publishing, Pop Edition.

Elliott, R. (2010). *Just because.* Oxford, UK: Lion Hudson.

Joyce, W. & Oldenburg, B. (2011). *The fantastic flying books of Mr. Morris Lessmore.* Shreveport, LA: Moonbot Studios.

Rahmanian & Arizpe, (2018). *Zahhak: The legend of the serpent king.* Seattle: Fantagraphics Books.

WeeSchool, Inc. (n.d.). Puppet Play. https://itunes.apple.com/us/app/puppet-play/id665031692?mt=8

PUZZLES AND MUSICAL TOYS

Doris Bergen and Gail Burnett

This chapter discusses two different types of toys, both of which involve the practice and further development of physical, cognitive, and social skills. Puzzles primarily engage children's problem solving and cognitive comparison abilities, while musical toys build on children's early sensitivity to musical sounds and rhythms, but both types of toys also involve exercise of children's fine motor and cognitive abilities. Also, both types of toys initially involve periods of exploration and, after an exploratory period, they then result in a set of very purposeful child actions.

Both puzzles and musical toys have been present in human history for a very long time and versions of them have been found in excavations at sites of many ancient civilizations. Also, both puzzles and musical toys exist in very simple to very complex versions. Although they are often part of very young children's play experience, these early and simple toy versions become very complex at later ages, and both continue to be of interest as playful experiences to many adults. That is, puzzles and musical devices are both types of "toys" that many adults use!

PUZZLES

Play with puzzles includes two elements: (1) a manipulation of objects and/or thoughts, and (2) a testing of one's knowledge and ingenuity. Although puzzles can be nonconcrete and entirely verbal or just focused on internal thought, the type of puzzles used in children's play typically are concrete objects with clear solutions that can give the player the satisfaction of "solving" the puzzle. Types of puzzles designed for children have been found in the remains of early civilizations, and they continue to be a type of plaything that most children find both challenging and enjoyable.

Puzzle as Playthings

Most current children's puzzles are a type of "jigsaw" puzzle, which became prominent in the seventeenth and eighteenth century. John Spillsbury is usually credited with providing early examples of this type of puzzle, which were mainly based on European map designs (Sheffrin, 1999). Such puzzles were considered educational and thus they became popular at boarding schools and for the education and amusement of children of wealthy families (Norgate, 2007). In fact, such puzzle play was considered a means of shaping the future generation of leaders (Norcie, 2009). Puzzle maps of the United States became popular in the mid-nineteenth century and those for children were made from heavy cardboard so they were less expensive and thus, their popularity grew. Today, children's puzzles may be made of wood, cardboard, or plastic, and they are a staple play item for young children. The topics imprinted on puzzles have expanded and include animals, houses, outdoor scenes, historical settings, and many other scenes. There are a wide variety of types of puzzles for children of various ages.

TYPES OF PUZZLES

Wooden or Plastic Boards Cut in the Shape of Puzzle Pieces

This type of puzzle is commonly used in puzzles designed for very young children as the shapes of the cutout places give the child help in solving the puzzle. They may have one or more cutouts (usually not more than six), and sometimes the pictures of the objects are in the slots. Often the pieces have "handles" so they can be easily grasped by young children. The shapes are usually complete objects (e.g., dogs, fruit).

Large Puzzle Pieces of Wood, Plastic, or Cardboard

These puzzles do not have a board to guide them, but they are usually accompanied by a same-size picture on the box. The puzzle pieces range from about six to twelve or fifteen and, instead of complete objects, the pieces of an object may be two to five parts. The puzzle topics are related to young children's interests (e.g., trucks, cars, farm or zoo animals, people of various types).

"Jigsaw" Puzzles

The typical jigsaw type of puzzle may range in difficulty from about 20–30 pieces to over 200. The ones with lower number of pieces are of interest to kindergarten/elementary age children, but older child players and many adults enjoy puzzles with many pieces. Both the size of pieces and the number of pieces vary widely, depending on the age level focus. The topics of the puzzles also are extremely varied, depending on the age-level audience and interests of the players. For example, everyday topics and many children's stories are topics of puzzles for younger players, while puzzles for older players cover a wide range of topics.

Other Types of Puzzles

In addition to the "jigsaw" type, there also are many other types of puzzles, and they can be made of metal, wood, or other concrete materials. They also can be drawings, diagrams, or just word puzzle problems that result in thought puzzle solving. Most of these puzzle versions are designed for older children, teens, or adults. Typical examples are crossword and other word puzzles, Rubik's cube types, and logic puzzles. In contrast to many playthings of children—because they can vary greatly in the complexity of the cognitive—language, and social knowledge required to solve them, puzzles are one type of play material that continues to be of interest to players of all ages.

AGE LEVEL DIFFERENCES IN PUZZLE PLAY

Infant/Toddler

Very young children use puzzles that have a sturdy base with one to three or four cutout items that the child can insert in the cutout shape. Infants of about nine months or so (when the infant is beginning to have some eye/hand coordination) can begin to use very simple puzzles of one or two pieces, after seeing the process demonstrated by an adult. Toddlers who have had "puzzle practice" may be able to handle four- to six-piece puzzles, with some initial adult help. Once the child has experienced success in "solving" these puzzles, they can do puzzles with ten to twenty pieces and they often go through a period of dumping and redoing the same puzzle over and over, showing great satisfaction with their prowess. The topics of the puzzles for this age level are typically familiar objects that the children have seen in picture books, in the household environment, street, backyard, zoo, park, or other places where children have had first-hand experiences.

Preschool

The preschool age is one in which puzzles are of very greatest interest to many children, and they often enjoy their growing prowess in puzzle solving. Preschoolers can handle both wooden and heavy cardboard puzzle pieces, and they can do puzzles with a greater number of pieces. As the children become more adept at doing puzzles, they may "binge" on them, demanding ever increasingly difficult puzzles to solve. They may also make their puzzles more complex by dumping two or more together and sorting them as they solve the combined puzzles. Although not all preschoolers have a focused "puzzle solving" period, many do so, and often after this focused puzzle play time period, they may then seem to be "finished with puzzles." That is, they then go off to other play pursuits, leaving their puzzles behind.

Kindergarten and Early Elementary

Children of this age are adept puzzle solvers, and they are interested in more types of puzzles and more complex puzzles. The topics also change to meet the interests of this age level and the types of puzzles begin to include "word puzzles" (often expressed in verbal riddles). However, in contrast to the behavior of preschool puzzle enthusiasts, the amount of time children spend in puzzle play is not as extensive. Thus, their puzzle play is often a solitary "at-home" activity. Recently, puzzle play has become a virtual activity, with a range of puzzle types now being available on iPad and other virtual platforms. As would be expected, the topics and complexity of puzzle solving also change, and many themes come from television or other virtual settings. Also, children of this age like to create puzzles for others to solve and they enjoy verbal puzzles, puzzles involving humor, and puzzles that might have "shocking" elements.

Late Elementary and Adolescence

The puzzles that are of interest at this age are rarely concrete ones. Most often they are virtual, purely verbal, or made up by the player to try to "fool" others. However, word puzzles and concrete puzzles of many pieces that take days to complete remain of interest to some children of these age levels (and to many adults).

GENDER DIFFERENCES

At younger age levels, play with puzzles is interesting and challenging for both boys and girls. However, as children grow older, some of the topics of the puzzles that are of interest changes to meet the supposed interests of girls and boys. For example, male/female stereotypical puzzle topics based on movies or other popular sources may be of more interest to one gender or the other. However, puzzles usually have not been as divisive for gender differences as many other playthings are. Researchers have reported some gender differences in puzzle skill and interest, but these differences are primarily related to time spent in certain types of puzzle play. In one study, children of age four and a half showed greater skill on a spatial task involving mental transformations of shapes if they were also frequent puzzle players, and boys were judged to have had experience with slightly more difficult puzzles, as well as more parent involvement (Levine, Ratliff, Huttenlocher, & Cannon, 2012). However, when puzzle play of toddlers was examined, girls in one study showed slightly better skill at puzzle construction of two- and three-piece puzzles than boys (Cannon, Levine, & Huttenlocker, 2007).

PLAY OF CHILDREN WITH SPECIAL NEEDS

For children who have physical difficulties or other special needs, there are some adaptations that have been made to puzzles to enable them to participate in such play. Some puzzles have sounds that help in matching, cutout spaces that can be easily felt, or knobs to hold when placing pieces. Most special educators encourage puzzle play because they know that it can be satisfying and both cognitively and emotionally enriching play for these young children. Also, research has indicated that children with certain types of disabilities may be especially interested in puzzle play. For example, research has indicated that young children diagnosed with autism (Thiemann-Bourque, Brady, & Fleming, 2012) and those with Prader-Willi syndrome (Dykens, 2002, Verdine, Troseth, Hodapp, & Dykens, 2008) perform relatively well on simple puzzles.

RESEARCH ON PUZZLE PLAY

Researchers who have studied puzzle play generally note that children of a variety of ages who engage in such play show stronger abilities on some learning processes. They have reported a relationship between puzzle performance and spatial skills of elementary age children (Verdine et al., 2014). Preschool children's puzzle play also has been linked to their development in various learning areas (Aral, Gursoy, & Yasar, 2012). Also, researchers who have studied the developmental trajectory of young children's puzzle skills have reported that providing co-speech gestures and spatial language can assist them in doing puzzles independently (Young, 2014).

MUSICAL TOYS

Since music is such a basic interest of humans of all ages, toys that make music or engage children in making music have long been popular. Such toys can be used to enhance learning of not only music, but other brain areas that music seems to positively affect. There are, however, great differences in children's musical experience, depending on the types of musical toys that they have. Some are geared more toward play and enjoyment while others focus more on music learning and increasing other skills. Some of these differences are explored here.

TYPES OF MUSICAL TOYS

Three types of musical toys are part of most children's play experiences. They include basic musical toys, technology-enhanced musical toys, and toys that encourage a "beat" rather than musical note sounds.

Basic Musical Toys

What might be called "basic musical toys" are ones that help young children learn that when they strike a toy that has musical keys, hit buttons on various musical devices, or blow into particular sound-enhanced toys, that they will cause a musical sound. The children can learn that the musical tone of the sound may change when they strike a different key or button or blow in a different way. Some of the toys in this category are xylophones with colorful keys, toy pianos that have keys that make musical sounds, plastic or metal horns and kazoos that can be blown to make sounds, and replica musical instruments like guitars with strings that play sounds.

Technology-Enhanced Musical Toys

The basic types of musical toys are now often technology-enhanced so instead of children being able to make a simple sound through a plucking or blowing action, they can just push a button or pull a lever and the toy plays music and lights up, hit a piano key and hear an entire song, or "play" a guitar by pushing a button rather than strumming. Thus, although this second type of musical toy creates more musical sounds, the child's musical actions are more limited because the music plays with only minimal effort by the child. Some of these toys play music even if the player does not do any activation. That is, the sounds are built into the toy and occur whenever the toy is played with. This type of musical toys does not really teach children about making music but just teaches cause-effect connections. That is, when the child strikes a button or pulls a lever, songs, lights, and other types of noises or actions will occur. Often adults like to give these toys to children because the music and accompanying actions help keep the children's attention. However, the repetitive nature of these sounds can become irritating to both child and adult.

"Beat" Toys

The third type of musical toy is an "instrument" that encourages keeping a "beat" or playing a basic "tone" when it is being struck or shaken. These musical toys include small drums that can be struck with hands or sticks and various objects that can be shaken to make musical sounds, such as tambourines, triangles, bells, finger cymbals, castanets, or rhythm sticks. These "child-safe musical instruments" serve to help children learn to keep a steady beat or engage their musical movement and they are often used in group play settings because the children then are using a "real" (but also a simple) musical instrument. Usually these toys are activated when songs are being played (either recorded or in person) because they are designed to accompany the rhythm of music initiated by an adult.

AGE LEVEL DIFFERENCES

Infant/Toddler

Because young children come into the world already attuned to musical sounds and rhythms, even very young children respond positively to toys with musical elements. At first, they are responsive only, but by age one, they seem to enjoy moving to musical beats and listening to (and sometimes even initiating) the simple melodies embedded in toys. If the toys have a key or lever to initiate musical sounds, older infants have the developing fine motor skills to do that over and over. Also, by toddler age, they enjoy "playing" toy pianos, blowing toy horns, and beating on toy drum-like objects. With models provided by older children or adults, they begin to engage in other actions that musical toys elicit. For example, toddlers "dance" to recorded or played music, and they are very active in initiating the musical sounds that various toys make. At later toddler age, some children also begin activating the sounds of recorded music on electronic tablet devices, especially if there are images that are created when the music plays.

Preschool

Preschoolers are great toy music makers and often enjoy marching to music or playing in a "band." Toy drums and shakers are of great interest as are devices that make musical sounds when blown, such as horns. Marching to toy instruments that have a sustained "beat" is also an enjoyable preschool activity. At older preschool age, the children may begin to use a variety of enhanced and interactive technology-augmented musical toys. Also, electronic tablets may have games that can introduce musical factors such as simple notation and music principles (e.g., time signatures, rhythm). Especially if the adults in the child's environment enhance the children's interest with occasional questions (such as how many beats does a half note get) their music play can increase their musical abilities.

Kindergarten and Early Elementary

By kindergarten or early elementary age, some children are already beginning music "lessons," and so the elements of play with music may be transformed into "learning musical performance." However, music invention is still a major interest of these children, especially if "beat" or "shake" musical instruments are available. Xylophone and other simple instrument play is enjoyed by these children and simple songs can be invented by children of this age. Kindergarten and early elementary children can use a wider variety of enhanced and interactive technology music toys and music tablets/ games as well. Even when used for play, these devices assist children in learning music principles. For those children already taking "music lessons," their play time still may include listening or dancing to songs or playing with a favorite toy instrument.

Late Elementary and Adolescence

At this age, "original" songs using a digital keyboard, guitar, or other instruments is a favorite "play" activity. However, these activities are not considered playing with "music toys" because they are using real musical instruments. Also, with music training, students can enjoy creating playful "music inventions." By this age, there is a division between those who just enjoy listening to music made by others and those who continue to make music on a variety of musical devices, such as guitars or drums. Inventing musical sounds, listening to songs and "playing" in "bands" with other young people are common playful activities.

GENDER DIFFERENCES

Young children do not seem to have differences in music play related to gender and, until elementary age, most children enjoy similar types of songs and other music types. However, at later ages, the music preferences may be different for girls and boys, and the instruments they think are appropriate for girls or boys to play may differ. For example, in one study both elementary age girls and boys though girls would be more likely to play the flute and boys more likely to play the drums (Harrison & O'Neill, 2000).

ADAPTATIONS FOR CHILDREN WITH SPECIAL NEEDS

With the exception of children who are deaf or have intense emotional reactions to sounds, music toys can be enjoyed by most children who have special needs. Many musical toys that require physical action to activate have been adapted for children with physical disabilities. (Simpson & Lynch, 2003). Also, for children with special needs, "child-safe" musical toys that would normally be geared to younger age children may work effectively for many of these children. Because music is such a basic aspect of human experience, most children who have special needs will respond well and will enjoy initiating play with musical toys.

RESEARCH ON MUSIC TOY PLAY

Although there is mounting evidence that children who receive music training have earlier brain development in some areas related to language, sound, and speech (Habbi, et al., 2008), there are not many studies of how children's self-chosen musical toy play may affect their development. A recent parent interview study regarding the musical experiences of very young children found that, although some music play involves young children and their parents, "digitized" music was predominant and some of that was generated by "musical toys." The author (Young, 2016) concluded that, because of digitized musical experiences, children of today may be gaining very different musical skills and knowledge from that of previous generations. However, parent–child active music play continues to be advocated as an important experience for infants, toddlers, and preschoolers (e.g., Guilmartin & Levinowitz, 2017).

One study that observed infant play with a Munchkin Mozart Magic Cube (Merkow, 2013) found that the infants engaged in many different interactions with the toy, responding to its tactile, visual, and auditory features. Although some educators suggest digital toys that engage young children's imaginative attention can be valuable for their development (e.g., Young, 2007), others are concerned that these toys limit young children's creativity and detract from social interactions (Levin & Rosenquest, 2001). Kersten (2006) suggests one criteria for digital instruments or toys that play music is that they be in the singing range of the children (2006).

Preschool children often choose to engage in musical toy play, as Berger and Cooper (2003) observed in a study of children's free choices of musical play in a preschool. They noted that when musical toys were available in the preschool setting, many children engaged in free musical toy play. However, they also found that time constraints for free choice play were so limited that the children who chose musical toy play had very short sessions of such play.

SUMMARY

There is mounting evidence that musical toys can help brain development, improve cognitive skills, enhance memory, and help with not only musical, but other types of creativity. Musical toys should be included in any classroom or home environment beginning with infants. When a child begins formal music training, having previously used musical toys allows them to music as both fun and challenge. They will have made some musical brain connections related to rhythm and pitch along the way. Certainly, in addition to musical toys, other musical experiences, such as a parent-child music class and exposure to all kinds of music and dancing are important. However, the right kinds of musical toys can give children a meaningful sensory and musical foundation.

SUMMARY

Both puzzles and musical toys are important playthings for fostering brain development, as they draw on early sensorimotor skills of young children and provide them with hours of pleasure. As children grow older, these toys, in more complicated versions, continue to be enjoyed, and in adolescence and adulthood puzzle play and musical play continue to be important. That is, because these toy types have older child and adult versions, they continue to be playthings throughout life.

REFERENCES

Aral, N., Gursoy, F., & Yasar, M. C. (2012). An investigation of the effect of puzzle design on children's development areas. *Procedia-Social and Behavioral Sciences*, 51, 228–33.

Berger, A. A., & Cooper, S. (2003). Musical play: A case study of preschool children and parents. *Journal of Research in Music Education*, 51(2), 151–65.

Cannon, J., Levine, S., & Huttenlocher, J. (2007). A system for analyzing children and caregivers' language about space in structured and unstructured contexts. *Spatial Intelligence and Learning Center (SILC) Technical Report*.

Dykens, E. M. (2002). Are jigsaw puzzle skills "spared" in persons with Prader-Willi syndrome? *Journal of Child Psychology and Psychiatry*, 43(3), 343–52.

Habibi, A., Damasio, A., Ilari, B., Veiga, R., Joshi, A. A., & Leahy, R. M., . . . & Damasio, H. (2018). Childhood music training induces change in micro and macroscopic brain structure: Results from a longitudinal study. *Cerebral Cortex*, 28(12), 4336–47.

Harrison, A. C., & O'Neill, S. A. (2000). Children's gender-typed preferences for musical instruments: An intervention study. *Psychology of Music*, 28(1), 81–97.

Guilmartin, K. K., & Levinowitz, L. M. (2017). *Music and your child: A guide for parents and caregivers.* Princeton, NJ: Music Together LLC.

Kersten, F. (2006). Inclusion of technology resources in early childhood music education. *General Music Today*, 20(1), 15–28.

Levin, D. E., & Rosenquest, B. (2001). The increasing role of electronic toys in the lives of infants and toddlers: Should we be concerned? *Contemporary Issues in Early Childhood*, 2(2), 242–47.

Levine, S. C., Ratliff, K. R., Huttenlocher, J., & Cannon, J. (2012). Early puzzle play: A predictor of preschoolers' spatial transformation skill. *Developmental Psychology*, 48(2), 530.

Merkow, C. H. (2013). Measurement of infants' behaviors with electronic music toys. *Texas Music Education Research*, 14, 26.

Norcia, M. A. (2009). Puzzling empire: Early puzzles and dissected maps as imperial heuristics. *Children's Literature* 37, 132. doi:10:1353/chl.0.0807

Norgate, M. (2007). Cutting borders: Dissected maps and the origins of the jigsaw puzzle. *The Cartographic Journal*, 44(4), 342–50.

Shefrin, J. (1999). "Make it a pleasure and not a task": Educational games for children in Georgian England. *Princeton University Library Chronicle*, 60(2), 251–75.

Simpson, C. G., & Lynch, S. A. (2003). Adapting and modifying toys for children with special needs. ERIC Document, ED 481 092

Thiemann-Bourque, K. S., Brady, N. C., & Fleming, K. K. (2012). Symbolic play of preschoolers with severe communication impairments with autism and other developmental delays: More similarities than differences. *Journal of Autism and Developmental Disorders*, 42(5), 863–73.

Verdine, B. N., Troseth, G. L., Hodapp, R. M., & Dykens, E. M. (2008). Strategies and correlates of jigsaw puzzle and visuospatial performance by persons with Prader-Willi syndrome. *American Journal on Mental Retardation*, 113(5), 343–55.

Verdine, B. N., Golinkoff, R. M., Hirsh-Pasek, K., & Newcombe, N. S. (2014). Finding the missing piece: Blocks, puzzles, and shapes fuel school readiness. *Trends in Neuroscience and Education*, 3(1), 713.

Young, S. (2008). Lullaby light shows: Everyday musical experience among under-two-year-olds. *International Journal of Music Education*, 26(1), 33–46.

Young, C., Cartmill, E., Levine, S., & Goldin-Meadow, S. (2014). Gesture and speech input are interlocking pieces: The development of children's jigsaw puzzle assembly ability. In *Proceedings of the Annual Meeting of the Cognitive Science Society*, 36(36).

TECHNOLOGY-AUGMENTED DOLLS, ANIMALS, AND VEHICLES

Sohyun Meacham and Myae Han

Technology has a great deal of influence on the toy industry and technology-based toys are among children's most preferred options in today's world. There are many different terms to refer to technology-augmented toys, such as *electronic toys, smart toys, computer toys*, and *digital toys*. Johnson, Christie, and Wardle (2005) define *technology-enhanced toys* as battery-operated toys and toys with computer chips installed that make the toys talk or act in certain ways. Bergen and Davis (2011) explained technology-augmented toys as follows: "Technology-augmented toys contain computer chips that enable the toy to exhibit a variety of actions, languages, and sounds during play. They range from relatively simple toys—such as a bear that laughs when its ear is pulled—to more complex robots designed to offer numerous actions or sounds that guide play" (p. 85). Technology-augmented toys have become increasingly sophisticated over the years.

Technology-augmented toys are part of new technologies that have altered the nature of play (Bergen & Davis, 2011). Although play is hard to define, researchers agree that play has certain characteristics in common: intrinsic motivation, free choice, process over product, and nonliterality (Johnson et al., 2005). Peter Gray (2009) defines play as self-chosen and self-directed, intrinsically motivated, guided by mental rules, and an imaginative activity. Play with technology-augmented dolls, animals, and vehicles shares these common characteristics of play.

It is important to separate video games and virtual communities/reality from technology-augmented toys, as video games and virtual communities/reality do not involve physical, real-life objects. This chapter focuses on technology-augmented toys excluding video games, virtual communities, and virtual reality. This discussion does not include pretend high-tech toys that resemble adult hand-held devices such as iPads, tablet PCs, and smartphones. If they target infant toddlers, they simply generate sounds when buttons and keys are pressed. If they target preschoolers, these pretend hand-held devices are often designed to be used for e-books or online learning games.

Also, technology-based toys that have instructional purposes such as writing also are excluded in this chapter because their goal is not on play as we defined above and they have little to do with dolls, animals, or vehicles. This chapter focuses on the types and features of technology-augmented toys, such as technology-augmented dolls, animals, robots, vehicles, and buildable toys. It also reviews the research literature that examines use of technology-augmented toys.

TYPES AND FEATURES OF TECHNOLOGY-AUGMENTED TOYS

Most of these toys are various types of "action figures," but they also include vehicles and buildable toys.

Technology-Augmented Dolls, Animals, and Robots

Humanoid/animaloid robots, such as Kismet (Breazeal & Scassellati, 2000), Robosapien (Behnke, Müller, & Schreiber, 2005; WowWee, 2005), Robovie, Nuvo (ZMP, 2005), Aibo (Sony, 1999), and Golden Pup (Hasbro, 2018) interact with the players by using speech/vocalization, facial expression, gaze direction, and/or gestures in a free-play situation (Bartneck, Suzuki, Kanda, & Nomura, 2006). There also are small, simple, creature-like interactive robots like Keepon (Kozima, Michalowski, & Nakagawa, 2009), which is less sophisticated than the other humanoid/animaloid robots. It differs from humanoid robots because it is nonverbal.

The developers of this robot sought to keep it simple to minimize distractions in an effort to establish joint attention between Keepon and child players with autism. Keepon displays not only attentive but also emotive expressions. Most of these types of robots appear only in research literature, so are unavailable for the public. Therefore, the following section focuses on technology-augmented dolls, animals, and robots available in the market. They include the following:

Robosapien has been one of the frontier technology-augmented robots marketed at an affordable price (Behnke et al., 2005; WowWee, 2005). Although is not autonomous, its upright walking and humanlike attitudes make it more humanoid than animaloid. It is somewhat responsive to the player's action. It can be programmed to make designate movements.

An interactive animaloid robot, Sony's (1999) AIBO (artificial intelligence robotic pet), "was designed to look like a dog, walk like a dog, and act like a dog" (Sinatra, Sims,

Chin, & Lum, 2012), although its movement and appearance without dog fur are still robotlike.

Joy for All Companion Pets Golden Pup (Hasbro, 2018) is an interactive dog that does look like a dog even having dog-like fur. It makes realistic dog sounds. Its interaction with a human is quite authentic, as it barks back at human's invitation to interact (e.g., saying "hi" to Golden Pup). Its heartbeats can be detected with a gentle pressure on its back. Motion sensors on the head, cheek, back, and mouth will activate Golden Pup's reaction such as blinking and wagging tails to the player's petting behaviors. The same company later released companion pet cats that look, feel, and sound like real cats. Similar to the pup, the companion cat responds to the player's petting and hugging.

There are programmable/codable dolls, animals and robots, such as Bee-Bot (Terrapin Software, 2016), Blue-Bot (Terrapin Software, 2016), Code-a-pillar (Mattel, 2016), Dot and Dash (McCoy-Parker, 2017; Wonder Workshop Inc., (2017), Botley (Learning Resources, 2017), Programmable Robot Mouse (Learning Resources, 2016), Cube, Anki, Codi, Sphero, Ozobot, Probo, and CHERP (Creative Hybrid Environment for Robotic Programming). These programmable/codable dolls, animals, and robots are not necessarily interactive with the players until they are programmed to be. Their acts can be programmed and controlled by the players.

For example, Bee-Bot resembles a bee's appearance with a round body and black–yellow pattern of stripes. Its movement is not quite bee-like, however. It doesn't fly, as it doesn't have wings. Using several buttons with assorted colors on top, the player can move the toy either forward, backward, right or left (90 degree rotation) and pause by programming those movements in a series of instructions (Di Lieto et al., 2017).

Blue-bot is a sister product of Bee-bot developed by the same company. Its functions are similar to Bee-bot. It has the same layout of buttons for programming (four arrows for forward, backward, right, or left; go, cancel, and pause) as Bee-bot's. However, Blue-bot can be remotely connected with a tablet device such as iPad via Bluetooth for programming transmitted through the device.

Programmable Robot Mouse marketed by Learning Resources (2016) seems to be the most affordable robot designed for young children (age four and up) to learn coding. Similarly functioned as Bee-Bot, it allows the player to program it to move forward, backward, and right or left (90-degree rotation). In addition, random actions such as moving forward and back, making mouse noises (e.g., squeak, chirp) and lighting up eyes can be also programmed. Because the Robot Mouse also gives random actions, a young player can feel this feature resembles a live animal's behavior.

Code-a-pillar (Mattel, 2016) resembles a caterpillar. It is designed for preschoolers to separate and combine segments of the caterpillar body. Each segment is designated for an action: one for sound, three for a straight move, two for right turns, and two for left turns. Its head is motorized. Depending on how each segment is combined with one another, the Code-a-pillar's movement can vary.

Botley (Learning Resources, 2017) is marketed as a coding robot for children age five and up. It has two eyes in front on the boxy, vehicle-looking body, and its two arms are detachable. The remote programmer that transmits coding to Botley has four buttons for directions: forward, backward, left turn, and right turn. As Botley has a sensor that detects obstacles in front of it, the player, using the object detection button, can program an alternative movement (left turn or right turn) when it confronts an obstacle. Botley also has a sensor underneath that follows a black line so the player can draw a path for it to follow.

Dot and Dash (Wonder Workshop, 2017) consists of four blue spheres (three on the bottom and one on top) and one eye on the top sphere, and was originally designed to teach children's basic coding skills. It can be programmed to move, dance, and sing with handheld devices.

Technology-Augmented Vehicles

KIBO is a robotics kit for young children's coding and programming. It resembles a vehicle with four wheels. The player uses tangible programming blocks to control its actions, such as spin, shake, and blue light on, so that a computerized screen environment is not involved. KIBO can be customized by the player. The player can add embellishments on the main body of KIBO (Sullivan & Bers, 2017). In 2015, another company (WowWee) developed robotic enhanced vehicles (R.E.V.), which are remote controlled racing cars. REV cars can also be controlled with smart phone using an app.

Technology-Augmented Buildable Toys

There also are technology-augmented, buildable toys. These toys consist of manipulable and/or buildable bricks, a receiver of programming, and sensors that detect motions, which allow versatility for play. The player can build imaginative animals, vehicles, and/or robots using the bricks, which can be connected with the programming receiver and sensors. A computer or a handheld device is needed to program the object built by the player. LEGO Mindstorms EV3 is a robotics kit designed for children aged 10+. The player can build a robot that drives, shoots, slithers, walks, slams, and spins. LEGO WeDo 2.0, while similar to LEGO Mindstorms EV3 in functions and features, is for younger children (Meacham & Atwood-Blaine, 2018).

USE OF TECHNOLOGY-AUGMENTED TOYS

These technology-augmented toys can be used for different types of play, such as problem-solving play, competition-based play, games, and imaginative play. Teachers or other adults who provide guidance might suggest preset goals. For instance, the players may have to code the robot correctly for it to arrive at the location designated by the provider. In free-play contexts, however, the players can be creative by making their own problems or setting their own goals for the robot to arrive at. Multiple players can engage in competitions.

In addition, these toys can be used as dolls, animals, and robots by the players. The toys also can be used for imaginative play (Meacham, 2017; McCoy-Parker et al., 2017). Use of such toys can engage children in elementary grades in pretend play. McCoy-Parker and colleagues (2017) reported that participating children used fantasy aspects (e.g., evidence of story characters, famous people, a holiday event, pretending, performances) when using Dot and Dash robots. For example, they described that the fifth-grade students created a dormitory for their Dot and Dash robot.

GENDER AND TECHNOLOGY-AUGMENTED TOYS

In several studies, researchers found that females reported a greater number of negative attitudes toward educational robots than their male counterparts did (European Commission, 2012; Kuo et al., 2009; Nomura, Kanda, Suzuki, & Kato, 2008; Reich & Eyssel, 2013; Reich-Stiebert & Eyssel, 2015; Tsui, Desai, Yanco, Cramer, & Kemper, 2011). However, some conflicting observations of gender differences have also been reported regarding different responses to attributes of robots and interactivity with robots.

Tan and the colleagues (2018) developed a multimodal interactive social robot and examined the gender differences in interacting with this robot. They found that female participants rated the social robot more highly than the male participants with regards to anthromorphism, animacy, likeability, perceived intelligence, and attentiveness. Meanwhile, the perceived safety of the robot was rated more positively by male participants than the female participants. However, the researchers note that these findings do not necessarily confirm that women perceive robots to be more human-like. There have been conflicting results from other studies.

For instance, Schermerhorn, Scheutz, and Crowell (2008) found that female participants saw a robot as more machine-like while their male counterparts saw a robot to be more human-like. Bartneck and Hu (2008) examined the ways players' might abuse robots and found differences in behaviors of males and females. They also found that females perceived the robots to be intelligent more than their male counterparts did. Also, Kennedy, Baxter, and Belpaeme (2015) found that female participants outperformed male participants in the learning outcomes when a social robot was actually used for educational purposes.

CHILDREN WITH SPECIAL NEEDS AND TECHNOLOGY-AUGMENTED TOYS

Technology-augmented toys can also be used as manipulation tools allowing children with disabilities to participate in play and therapeutic activities (Komendzinski et al., 2016).

Children with severe motor impairment such as cerebral palsy or muscular dystrophy can use toys like Robo Nino (POB Technology, 2005) to explore the surroundings and get involved in a play. Children can use the robot as an extension of their bodies, allowing them to indirectly modify the environment.

Affordances of humanoid/zoomorphic interactive robots is a predominant topic among the literature about technology-augmented toys for children with autism. Children with autism showed positive prosocial behaviors such as touching, vocalizing, and smiling at the humanoid interactive robots (Scassellati, 2005). François, Powell, and Dautenhahn (2009) studied the effectiveness of use of a zoomorphic, dog-like robotic pet in a nondirective play therapy that encouraged proactivity and initiative taking of children with autism. They found the participating children with autism progressed toward higher levels of social engagement, play and reasoning. These children even expressed some interest and affection toward the robot.

Other researchers have focused on different features of technology-augmented toys for children with autism. Robins, Dautenhahn, and Dubowski (2006) found that children with autism seem to engage more easily with more simple and non-human-looking robots without needing as many social cues than when engaging humanlike robots. Kozima and his colleagues (2009) similarly discovered simple design was effective for children with autism in eliciting a motivation. They also found an important role of rhythm of robots for engaging these children in interaction. They noted that rhythmic interactional synchrony is an important nonverbal aspect of interpersonal coordination.

REVIEW OF RESEARCH: EXPERIENCES WITH TECHNOLOGY-AUGMENTED TOYS

This section reviews empirical articles about children's play with technology-augmented toys. Both articles that use technology-augmented toys for play purposes and those that use them for didactic purposes are reviewed. As explained earlier, players should be the owners of play and they direct and choose their own behaviors within the play (Bergen & Davis, 2011; Gray, 2009). Thus, motivation to play should be intrinsic and there should not be goals imposed on children by others. Goals, if set by the player, are secondary to the activity itself (Bergen & Davis, 2011; Fromberg, 2006).

Based on this guiding principle regarding play, this review distinguishes articles about technology-augmented objects designed to simply replace teachers (e.g., articles which used robots that narrate specific information with buttons for the player's cueing; training studies that controlled the players' goals for certain learning outcomes) from those focused on play. However, it is hard to clearly distinguish some studies that handled technology-augmented toys in terms of didactics rather than play. Those were included for a rich discussion regarding *playing with* technology-augmented toys rather than focusing just on those toys as objects.

Bergen and Davis (2011) reviewed the literature to investigate how new technology-augmented toys have influenced recent changes in playful activities and children's moral development. Discussing earlier scholars' theories such as Freud, Erikson, Winnicott, Piaget, and Vygotsky, these authors delineated strong theoretical backgrounds regarding associations between play and moral development (e.g., relief of guilt and shame through play-therapeutic activities; justice and cooperation learned through engagement in game play; self-regulation developed through play).

According to these authors, play becomes a safe medium for moral development because individuals can test roles, boundaries, and possibilities while taking risks without real-world consequences when they play. Inquiring about consequences of technology-based play on empathy development, good behaviors, and reasoning about moral issues, they reviewed studies with technology-augmented toys such as Sony's AIBO (Artificial Intelligence Robotic pet; studied by Kahn, Friedman, Perez-Granados, & Freier, 2006) and the Gesture-Activity Recognition System (GARS; Westeyn, Brashear, Atrash, & Starner, 2003). While these systems allow a certain level of characteristics of play (e.g., self-motivating, not goal oriented, nonliteral, dynamic, risk-free), the researchers of AIBO and GARS observed a lack of self-regulation and empathic behaviors, as the player merely becomes the reactor while AIBO or GARS was the actor.

Therefore, the relationship between play and these toys was vague. In many interactions with technology-augmented toys, play was not necessarily sustained or elaborated, although interactions with technology-augmented toys positively affected social, physical, and language interactions (Bergen, Hutchinson, Nolan, & Weber, 2010). For instance, both talking and nontalking technology-augmented toys elicited caring behaviors (Bergen, 2004). However, when a robotic toy and a typical toy were compared in Kahn and colleagues' study (2006), children's physical being, mental states, social rapport, or moral sense were in a better shape when playing with a typical toy than with a robotic toy.

Bergen and Davis (2011) concluded that there are conflicting findings whether play with technology-augmented toys promotes moral development regarding empathy, caring, honesty, and higher-order moral reasoning. They raised a concern that the market and the technology developers "shape the play preferences of children through technology" (p. 94) to commercialize the products and constraint the authenticity and quality of play.

In the same vein, many research studies involving technology-augmented toys use didactic approaches to investigate the learning outcomes that are channeled through the pre-determined ways of play with the toys. Sullivan and Bers (2018) studied how a KIBO robotics curriculum in Singapore affected preschoolers' knowledge of programming concepts and found positive results. While KIBO can be potentially used as an object for children's play, Sullivan and Bers (2018) apparently focused on the children's achievement in understanding of programming concepts measured by Solve-Its. They did not neglect the players' positive engagement with the technology-augmented toy. However, they did not analyze quality or depth of children's play, as they focused on learning outcomes in terms of programming concepts.

Di Lieto and her colleagues (2017) studied whether educational robotics intervention with Bee-bot was effective for preschoolers' executive functions. They found a positive short-term effect of 13 robotics sessions on the 12 preschoolers' visuo-spatial working memory, inhibition skills (self-control and selective attention), and robot programming skills. Goals and aims in the intervention sessions were controlled by the researchers.

Following the "error-less learning" method (Warmington, Hitch, & Gathercole, 2013), the difficulty levels of activities proposed were controlled from easier to more difficult as the sessions progressed (e.g., one to three sessions: Familiarization with Bee-bot; 4–7 sessions: Visuo-spatial planning; 8–13 sessions: Inhibition). Even the first three sessions for familiarization with Bee-bot, the players were asked to move the Bee-bot on the given city map to reach a specific aim point (e.g., Bee-bot reaching the restaurant on the map).

Meacham's (2017) study about use of robotics for young children focused on authentic play rather than didactics. She qualitatively analyzed her data of PK–3 children's spontaneous literacy practices in an after-school LEGO robotics club. While play aspects were not her initial focus in the research, she found that the play ecology was an important aspect for the children's engagement in spontaneous literacy practices. The data were coded as play when there were giggles, laughs, and imaginative play aspects (e.g., using pretense).

In addition, when the children were negotiating to make decisions based on their interests, as adults' inputs are minimized, the portion of the data was also coded as play. The coverage of the play code segments within a randomly selected 15-minute-long video data was 8.58 percent. While other portions of the data were not necessarily coded regarding play/fun aspects, there still was no evidence of "pedagogical violence" (Matusov, 2009, p. 315; e.g., a mandatory work was imposed on children; children expressing intentions to leave the group to play: "Now I want to play").

Meacham and Atwood-Blaine (2018) reported how PK–3 children played with LEGO WeDo 2.0. Initially in the LEGO WeDo 2.0 application that the player needs to use for programming, there were guided goals for the player to pursue, as the tutorials for desirable robot models and coding were introduced in the iPad application for coding and instructions. It was entirely possible that this technology-augmented build-able toy could be used for didactic purposes if teachers only allowed the children to build and code the model robots with instructions given in the iPad application.

However, when the children were controlling LEGO WeDo 2.0 and the iPad application for coding, they started modifying the robot models to build similar but different robots. In addition, the children created imaginary stories about the robot that they created, which was apparently *playful thoughts* that Bergen and Davis (2011) conceptualized for indicating engagement in play.

McCoy-Parker, Paull, Rule, and Montgomery (2017) used Dot and Dash robots to compare elementary students' (first and fifth grades students) learning and attitudes during free play and direct instruction. Through a repeated measures design, all participating students went through both free play and direct instruction sessions. During the direct instruction sessions, the teachers directly taught coding skills. During the free play sessions, the students, while they could engage in free play with Dot and Dash robots, were encouraged to challenge themselves to solve their own problems. These researchers found that technical scores for robot performances (e.g., varied movement, sensory event coding, creation of visual image, variety and combination of coding skills, programming loops, attachments or accessories, met specific performance needs) were higher during the direct instruction sessions, whereas the creative score for robot performances (e.g., uniqueness, humor, emotional expressiveness, word play, elaboration, fluency, flexibility, abstract ideas, fantasy, unusual movement) were higher during the free play sessions.

RECOMMENDATIONS

Technology-augmented dolls, robots, animals, and vehicles are newer than other traditional toys, which allows numerous opportunities for creative practices and new lines of research. These toys provide some developmental benefits in different areas: sociomoral, creativity, language, and cognitive development. Research on the usability of this type of toy for didactic purposes (e.g., teaching scientific or engineering concepts; teaching reading or social skills), however, does not necessarily emphasize play quality or playfulness. The studies that used didactic approaches with the technology-augmented toys explain customizability, repeatability and interactivity as important features that can impact the learning outcomes (Saadatzi, Pennington, Welch, & Graham, 2018). There is a lack of available research regarding how differences in technology-augmented toys (e.g., features and types) affect the quality of play. More careful observation and research are required to endorse the use of this type of toy.

REFERENCES

Bartneck, C., & Hu, J. (2008). Exploring the abuse of robots. *Interaction Studies, 9*(3), 415-433.

Bartneck, C., Suzuki, T., Kanda, T., & Nomura, T. (2006). The influence of people's culture and prior experiences with Aibo on their attitude towards robots. AI & Society–*The Journal of Human-Centered Systems, 21*(1–2), 217–230.

Behnke, S., Müller, J., & Schreiber, M. (2005). Playing soccer with Robosapien. *RoboCup 2005: Robot Soccer World Cup IX, 36–48.*

Bergen, D. (2001). Learning in the robotic world: Active or reactive? Technology in the Classroom. *Childhood Education, 77,* 249–50.

Bergen, D. (2004). Preschool children's play with talking and non-talking rescue heroes: Effects of technology-enhanced figures on the types and themes of play. In J. H. Goldstein, D. Buckingham, & G. Brougère (Eds.), *Toys, games and media* (pp. 195–206). Mahwah, NJ: Lawrence Erlbaum.

Bergen, D., & Davis, D. (2011). Influences of technology-related playful activity and thought on moral development. *American Journal of Play, 4*(1), 80–99.

Bergen, D., Hutchinson, K., Nolan, J., & Weber, D. (2010). Effects of infant-parent play with a technology-enhanced toy: Affordance related action and communicative interaction. *Journal of Research in Childhood Education, 24,* 1–17.

Breazeal, C., & Scassellati, B. (2000). Infant-like social interactions between a robot and a human caretaker. *Adaptive Behavior 8,* 49–74.

Champion, E. (2011). *Playing with the past.* London, UK: Springer-Verlag.

Di Lieto, M. C., Inguaggiato, E., Castro, E., Cecchi, F., Cioni, G., Dell'Omo, M., Laschi, C., Pecini, C., Santerini, G., Sgandurra, G., & Dario, P. (2017). Educational robotics intervention on executive functions in preschool children: A pilot study. *Computers in Human Behavior, 71,* 16–23.

Esposito, N. (2005). A short and simple definition of what a videogame is. *Proceedings of DIGRA 2005 Conference: Changing Views—Worlds in Play.*

European Commission (2012). Public attitudes towards robots. Special Eurobarometer, 382. Retrieved from http://ec.europa.eu/commfrontoffice/publicopinion/archives/ebs/ebs_382_en.pdf

François, D., Powell, S., & Dautenhahn, K. (2009). A long-term study of children with autism playing with a robotic pet: Taking inspirations from non-directive play therapy to encourage children's proactivity and initiative-taking. *Interaction Studies: Social Behaviour and Communication in Biological and Artificial Systems, 10*(3), 324–73. http://dx.doi.org/10.1075/is.10.3.04fra

Fromberg, D. (2006). Play's pathway to meaning: A dynamic theory of play. In D. Fromberg & D. Bergen (Eds.), *Play from birth to twelve* (pp. 159–66). New York, NY: Routledge.

Gray, P. (2009). Play as a foundation for hunter-gatherer social existence. *American Journal of Play, 1,* 476–522.

Hasbro (2018). Golden pup. Retrieved from https://joyforall.com/

Johnson, J., Christie, J., & Wardle, F. (2005). *Play, development, and early education.* Boston, MA: Allyn & Bacon.

Juul, J. (2003). The game, the player, the world: Looking for a heart of gameness. *Proceedings of the 2003 Digital Games Research Association Conference*, 30–45.

Kahn Jr., P. H., Friedman, B., Perez–Granados, D. R., & Freier, N. G. (2006). Robotic pets in the lives of preschool children. *Interaction Studies, 7*, 405–36.

Kennedy, J., Baxter, P., & Belpaeme, T. (2015). The robot who tried too hard: Social behavior of a robot tutor can negatively affect child learning. In 10th ACM/IEEE International Conference on Human Robot Interaction, Portland, 67–74.

Komendzinski T, Mikołajewska E, Mikołajewski D, Dreszer J, Bałaj B (2016) Cognitive robots in the development and rehabilitation of children with developmental disorders. Bio-Algorithms Med-Syst, 12(3), 93–98

Kozima, H., Michalowski, M. P., & Nakagawa, C. (2009). Keepon: A playful robot for research, therapy, and entertainment. *International Journal of Social Robotics, 1*(1), 3–18.

Kuo, H., Rabindran, J. M., Broadbent, E., Lee, Y. I., Kerse, N., Stafford, R. M. Q., & MacDonald, B. A. (2009). Age and gender factors in user acceptance of healthcare robots. In 18th IEEE International Symposium on Robot and Human Interactive Communication, Toyama, 214–219.

Learning Resources (2016). Programmable Robot Mouse. Retrieved from https://www.learningresources.com/stem-robot-mouse?gclid=EAIaIQobChMItrrOvNL27QIV0FPVCh1TDAnLEAAYASAAEgKpQPD_BwE

Learning Resources (2017). Botley. Retrieved from https://www.learningresources.com/botley-2-the-coding-robot-classroom-bundle

Mattel (2016). Code-a-pillarTM. Retrieved from https://fisher-price.mattel.com/shop/en-us/fp/think-learn/think-learn-code-a-pillar-dkt39

McCoy-Parker, K., Paull, L. N., Rule, A. C., & Montgomery, S. E. (2017). Challenging elementary learners with programmable robots during free play and direct instruction. *Journal of STEM Arts, Craft, and Constructions, 2*(2), 100–129.

Meacham, S. (2017, December). *Young children's literacy practices in a K-8 after-school LEGO club*. Proposal for the LRA 2017 Annual Conference, Tampa, FL.

Meacham, S., & Atwood-Blaine, D. (2018). Early childhood robotics with inspirations from Reggio Emilia educators. *Science & Children, 56*(3), 57–62.

Nomura, T., Kanda, T., Suzuki, T., & Kato, K. (2008). Prediction of human behavior in human–robot interaction using psychological scales for anxiety and negative attitudes toward robots. *IEEE Transactions on Robotics, 24*(2), 442–51.

Reich, N., & Eyssel, F. (2013). Attitudes towards service robots in domestic environments: The role of personality characteristics, individual interests, and demographic variables. *Paladyn: Journal of Behavioral Robotics, 4*(2), 123–30. doi: 10.2478/pjbr-2013-0014

Reich-Stiebert, N., & Eyssel, F. (2015). Learning with educational companion robots? Toward attitudes on education robots, predictors of attitudes, and application potentials for education robots. *International Journal of Social Robotics, 7*(5), 875–88.

Robins, B., Dautenhahn, K., & Dubowski, J. (2006). Does appearance matter in the interaction of children with autism with a humanoid robot? *Interaction Studies, 7*(3), 479–512.

Saadatzi, M. N., Pennington, R. C., Welch, K. C., & Graham, J. H. (2018). Small-group technology-assisted instruction: Virtual teacher and robot peer for individuals with Autism Spectrum Disorder. *Journal of Autism and Developmental Disorders, 48*, 3816–30. Doi: 10.1007/s10803-018-3654-2

Scassellati, B. (2005). Using social robots to study abnormal social development. In *Proceedings of the 5th International Workshop on Epigenetic Robotics*, 11–14.

Schermerhorn, P., Scheutz, M., & Crowell, C. R. (2008). Robot social presence and gender: Do females view robots differently than males? In 3rd ACM/IEEE International Conference on Human–Robot Interaction, Amsterdam, 263–70.

Sinatra, A. M., Sims, V. K., Chin, M. G., & Lum, H. C. (2012). The effect of physical appearance on human interaction with robots and animals. Interaction Studies, 13(2), 235–62. Doi: 10.1075/is.13.2.04sin

Sony (1999). *Aibo*. Retrieved from http://www.aibo.com

Sullivan, A., & Bers, M. U. (2018). Dancing robots: Integrating art, music, and robotics in Singapore's early childhood centers. *International Journal of Technology and Design Education, 28*(2), 325–46.

Tan, Z., Thomsen, N. B., Duan, X., Vlachos, E., Shepstone, S. E., Rasmussen, M. H., & Højvang, J. L. (2018). iSocioBot: A multimodal interactive social robot. *International Journal of Social Robotics, 10*(1), 5–19.

Terrapin Software (2016). Bee-Bot. Retreived from https://www.bee-bot.us/

Tsui, K., Desai, M., Yanco, H. A., Cramer, H., & Kemper, N. (2011). Measuring attitudes towards telepresence robots. International Journal of Intelligent Control and Systems, 16, 113–23.

Warmington, M., Hitch, G. J., & Gathercole, S. E. (2013). Improving word learning in children using an errorless technique. *Journal of Experimental Child Psychology, 114*(3), 456–65.

Westeyn, T., Brashear, H., Atrash, A., & Starner, T. (2003). Georgia Tech Gesture Toolkit: Supporting experiments in gesture recognition. In ICMI 03.

Wonder Workshops, Inc. (2017). *Meet Dash and Dot*. Retrieved from https://www.makewonder.com

WowWee (2005). *Robosapien*. Retrieved from http://www.wowwee.com/robosapien/robo1/robomain.html

ZMP (2005). *Nuvo*. Retrieved from http://www.nuvo.jp/nuvo_home_e.html

23

OTHER TECHNOLOGY-AUGMENTED PLAY MATERIALS

Lena Lee

Children in contemporary society frequently use interactive technologies (i.e., digital media such as iPads, iPhones, computers, and televisions) as one of their dominant play materials (Bergen, Davis & Abbitt, 2016; National Association of the Education for Young Children, 2012; Rideout, Lauricella, & Wartella, 2011). Of the various technology play toys and materials, many children use technology-augmented play (TAP) materials. TAP materials are the toys, or the play tools, in which technologies (e.g., online and digital media) are integrated and enhanced. TAP materials often have physical objects (e.g., a book, a tablet, a wheel) with technological components (e.g., internet, apps, online programs).

CHILDREN'S DEVELOPMENT AND TECHNOLOGY-AUGMENTED PLAY MATERIALS

It is still not definitively clear in research studies about the precise impacts that TAP materials have on children. Some positive perspectives indicated that TAP materials enhance children's development, including various ways of imaging, problem solving, and active coping skills in virtual bullying (e.g., Dye, Green, & Bavelier, 2009; McLoughlin, Spears, & Taddeo, 2018; Resnick, 2006). When TAP materials are used to teach specific contents and concepts such as science and literacy, in particular, children can learn more effectively (e.g., Kara, Aydin, & Cagiltay, 2012; Laurillard, 2014). Furthermore, according to Lim and Clark (2010), TAP materials offer children physically safe home environments as they are online, which let parents and adults in contemporary societies and communities have no concern about unknown environments that they cannot control. TAP materials such as iPad app games can also support positive learning outcomes and efficiency (e.g., Flewitt, Messer, & Kucirkova, 2015; Lee & Tu, 2016; Miller, 2018) when the games are designed with, and are used for educational concepts.

However, several other studies have presented the opposite perspective, particularly as it is related to children's social skill development with human interaction and real-world experiences. For instance, some researchers (e.g., Freed, 2018; Kardaras, 2016; Lillard & Peterson, 2011; Small & Vorgan, 2008) discussed children's insufficient or low-quality human relationships and interaction (e.g., those with parents and peers) and their unusual and "dulling" brain development during children's TAP (Kardaras, 2016, p. 33). As is well-known in early childhood education, the lack of enriched social environments in which children have adequate human interactions can cause young children to experience negative impacts on their social, emotional, and cognitive development (e.g., Bruner, 1975; Bronfenbrenner, 1979; Trevarthen, 1980; Vygotsky, 1981).

This perspective suggests that, if children's time is limited for experiencing social relationships and involvement due to their time in TAP, this can negatively influence not only young children's development but also adolescents' development, including their emotional and physical abilities to be empathetic, gain sufficient communication skills and self-knowledge, and develop physical coordination and control (e.g., Palmer, 2015; Wakefield, 2018).

TAP Material Usage and Variations by Ages

The uses of TAP vary significantly depending on children's ages, socioeconomic status (SES), racial and ethnic groups, and sociocultural contexts (e.g., American Academy of Pediatrics Council on Communications and Media, 2016a; Rideout & Hamel, 2006). For instance, high-SES schools invest more in technology support, instructions, and staff, while low-SES schools have less technology support in general, and personnel in these schools also frequently demonstrate less confidence in using technology (Melhuish & Falloon, 2010; Warschauer, Knobel, & Stone, 2004). Children from low-SES families, minority children, and children whose parents have a lower level of educational attainment have more exposure to television and are less likely to have a computer at home (Rideout, Foehr, & Roberts, 2010). Taking these variations of children's TAP uses into consideration, the next section briefly reviews different types of age-dependent TAP materials.

AGE LEVEL DIFFERENCES

Infants/Toddlers and Preschoolers

Very young children's uses of TAP materials have been increasing rapidly. TAP materials for these children typically have an input-output connection between children's action (e.g., sitting on a toy chair and pushing a button as input) and the toy's responding function (e.g., playing a song and saying a word as output). Many TAP materials for these ages are for educational purposes. An example of popular TAP toys is the Fisher-Price Laugh & Learn. It has several the interactive buttons to press to light up or/and hear the sounds that help children learn shapes, numbers, letters, animals, and so on. Some of these toys have a role play feature and can introduce basic Spanish.

There are three different stages to play for each age group of 6 to 18 months and 18 months to 36 months. There are similar types of toys from Vtech and Leapfrog. The Fisher-Price Think & Learn Smart Cycle, which is for preschoolers focusing on educational concepts, provides a physical playing experience (cycling) on a tablet, and allows children to have control of racing and learning games. As a technology-augmented (TA) mobile, Nurture Smart Mobile, provide a projector for starlight images on the ceiling, sound machine, nightlight, and mobile. It has several different sounds, visually stimulating images, a large domed mirror, and a button pad that offers up to an hour of interactive play.

As for apps, many of them aim to have educational purposes like the other toys discussed above. The apps are played on iPads or on the iPhones most likely given to children by their parents or other caregivers. This aspect implies that the first initiative of using TAP materials can be from caregivers even though children's later continual requests for and interests in playing with such TAP materials might occur after this initial stage of adult-initiated TAP material uses (Bergen et al., 2016). These materials do not necessarily require an adult or a peer to guide, interact, and/or play with the young children. Thus, younger children's contemporary TAP environment differs from the traditional one where a caregiver often had to be with them to play or interact.

Typically, as young children—who have had a limited time period for learning about human interactions and attachments—develop sound social skills and lives, their "how-to" plays into this type of material. However, if their major form of play is in interacting with these TAP materials that may have a role in their interpersonal attachments as the children's attachments may shift to objects instead of to their caregivers. If younger children play with the TAP materials more than with typical and traditional toys, then their future interaction patterns might be very different from those of the existing generations.

Elementary-Age Children

TAP materials for elementary-age children are more diverse and complex than those for very young children reflecting their more developed skills and abilities in general. With these developmental advantages, elementary-age children can complete more complicated tasks. One of the most popular examples of TAP materials for this age is online gaming with consoles, such as Xbox, PS4, and Wii. These types of TAP materials are mostly used in children's homes with a connection to a screen like a television or a computer. Although these materials can be used by elementary children, they are played widely from this age to adults—the age-level differences are in what game programs or levels they play. Similarly, such games also have some programs for preschoolers. Because of the characteristic of games, children can share the opportunities with adults to gain access to and play with technology that was only in the adult domain before (Bergen et al., 2016).

Some TA books remain for these older children, particularly for early-grade children (K–3). *LeapReader Books* started its basic TA-featured books a few decades ago with Leapfrog's books. It developed a "system" for each age level to connect virtual components. The books of the LeapStart 3D interactive learning systems have "3D-like" video animations to download and a stylus pen to use. All of these books develop reading or/ and writing skills with visual, auditory, and sensory functions. *Smart Book* has similar features for older children, along with an interactive augmented and virtual reality by downloading a 4D app. It does not have a certain age recommendation. However, several books with scientific concepts are likely to need the children to have more advanced reading skills (ages eight and up), although the graphics with the 4D app can be used for children ages six to eight.

A different technology-enhanced example is *Smart Puzzle*, which is an interactive augmented and virtual reality puzzle. It is mostly designed with different scientific themes such as the solar system, human anatomy, and undersea environs to help children enhance creative perceptions, learn about spatial and temporal concepts, and build listening comprehension. This puzzle connects each theme's contents and concepts through animations, puzzling, educational read-alongs, and an app to play. There are some similar TAP materials to support educational concepts and learning for young children (ages five to six and up): *BEST LEARNING i-Poster* and Interactive Talking *USA Map for Kids*.

Another example is *Merge Cube*, a holographic cube to learn STEM concepts and play games with augmented reality. There are many Cube apps to download on a smartphone or a tablet, and this shows the Cube transformation. By using their sense of touch to hold the Cube, children can experience and interact with virtual objects, such as the solar system, works of art, geometric shapes, and objects they create. The other example of the cube game is Cube-Tasitic Puzzle Cube. It is a 3D-puzzle cube with a feature of a free app to help children scan and solve the puzzle. Like a traditional Rubik's Cube, it helps to develop problem-solving skills, hand-eye coordination, and memory.

Adolescents

As for adolescent age, many TAP materials are designed with more complicated virtual components. Online games with consoles such as Xbox and PS4 are still in demand. Moreover, a newly developed portable online game system, Nintendo Switch, allows children to have more access to playing regardless of time and place. One of the salient characteristics in playing this online gaming is its collaborative simulation play. For instance, children often create a group to battle, build, or complete a story in *Fortnite* and *Call of Duty*. This pattern of collaborative simulation play seems to be transitioned from *StarCraft* and *Minecraft*. The previous popular examples of simulation online games are *Super Mario Brothers*, *Pokemon*, and *The Sims*, all of which were designed mainly for solitary play.

They are grouped according to their levels and they can choose their group members only from the same "lobby" of levels in *Call of Duty* while players choose any friends of the players or random people online regardless of the levels in *Fortnite*. Children can play by themselves with a specific program of each game (e.g., "Save the World" for *Fortnite* and "Campaign" for *Call of Duty*), but the collaborative play is dominant. Children can talk to each other via a headset with a microphone for winning strategies, important information about the opposing teams or enemies, and support team members or seek help from team members. Comparing this collaborative online play, one of the popular online gaming for solitary play is *NBA 2K*, which is a series of basketball sports simulation video games. Children can control an entire team or a select player from actual NBA teams and players in the past and at present. Children can also create fictional players and teams to play.

Despite some positive impacts of the online gaming such as spatial skill development and cooperative and diverse interaction skills (e.g., Brockmyer, 2015; Damour, 2018; Granic, Lobel, & Engles, 2013; Kühn et al., 2018), there have been more serious concerns, such as having fewer social skills than people who have more face-to-face interactions, and negative impacts on parent-adolescent relationships and positive adolescent development, including social competence (Lei & Wu, 2007; Ramsey, Gentzler, Morey, Oberhauser, & Westerman, 2013). Like the issues of very young children's attachment patterns with TAP materials discussed earlier in this chapter, the greater amount of time adolescents' spent watching television or computer was associated with low attachment to and more problems with parents (Davou & Sidiropoulou, 2017; Richards, McGee, Williams, Welch, & Hancox, 2010).

These two games are considered riskier for adolescents due to their "virtual violence" as the main theme (AAP Council on Communications and Media, 2016b). This may lead children to have potential desensitization, which is the reduction of cognitive, emotional and/or behavioral responses to stimulus (Brockmyer, 2015). There is also the linkage between virtual violence and aggression, which is described as "any behavior intended to harm another person who does not want to be harmed (AAP Council on Communications and Media, 2016b; italics in original).

A different example of the recent TAP materials for adolescents is *Star Wars: Jedi Challenges* is an augmented reality experience smartphone game based on the Star Wars movie series. The game includes an app to start and a headset. A player progresses through various levels of difficulty across six planets. Players can play by themselves or engage with other players. The augmented-reality (AR) play materials are relatively new and often used to teach educational concepts and ideas. For instance, adolescents learn with a location-based AR forms, which are GPS-enabled smartphones, tablets, or an app, *Google's SkyMap*, to present digital media to students as they move through a physical area or use a QR code with their smartphones (Dunleavy, 2014).

APPLICATION FOR CHILDREN WITH DIVERSE BACKGROUNDS AND NEEDS

Although study findings have been mixed on the use of TAP materials, there has been a more positive possibility for use of these materials for young children from diverse backgrounds and needs during the last few decades. For example, using digital media for young English language learners (ELLs) and children with special needs increases their attention, concentration levels, and understanding of knowledge and content (e.g., Faux, 2005; Flewitt, Kucirkova, & Messer, 2014; Lee & Tu, 2016). In addition, some studies point out that assistive technology tools supported adolescents with special needs, including those with autism and physical disabilities (e.g., King et al., 2014; Odom et al., 2015; van der Meer, et al., 2011). A study also showed the positive results of video game play that involved perceptual, attentional, and cognitive skills especially for children with disabilities (Eichenbaum, Bavelier, & Green, 2014).

As for the online games, however, there have been ongoing critiques of gender and racial bias and violence (Beasley & Standley, 2002; Burgress et al., 2011; Park, Gabbadon, & Chernin, 2006; Royse et al., 2007). For instance, certain minorities such as Latina women and native American men were never present; black men were often portrayed as aggressive, violent, and athletic; and Asian characters were mostly shown in physical fighting games (Dill, Gentile, Richter, & Dill, 2005; Glaube, Miller, Parker, & Espejo, 2001). Some studies found that only 14 percent of characters in video games are women and even those female characters are ten times more likely to have nudity comparing to the counterparts (Beasley & Standley, 2002; Shu-Fang, 2010). In addition, over 25 percent of female characters have unrealistic body proportions, even in E-rated online game, which everyone can play regardless of age.

The majority of online simulation sports games such as *NBA 2K*, *Madden NFL 19*, and *NHL20* do not have female characters. This leads to a situation in which girls must play a game with male characters that they must identify with, unlike Wii games where each child can create his or her own avatar. Therefore, in the simulation sports games, girls are more likely to have a limited virtual environment than boys where they are not allowed to fully create virtual representations of the game characters that present and share their own self-identity, which is so-called "projected identity" (Gee, 2007).

Although research has identified some issues with TAP materials, the numbers and types of game apps are rapidly increasing. A statistical data source estimates there were 2.6 million apps for Android users, 2.2 iOS apps in the Apple app store, and 38.3 billion game downloads made through Google Play Store and iOS App store in 2018 (App Annie, 2019). As a result, there is not a reliable or research-based significant analysis on game apps due to this fast-moving, large volume of apps.

REFLECTIONS AND RECOMMENDATIONS

TAP materials are powerful in influencing children's ways of thinking, learning, communicating, and living. Moreover, children can have the immediate and interactive experiences of digital content and information that are more and more similar to real situations and environment, which is called, "augmented reality (AR)" (e.g., Chian, Yang, & Hwang, 2014; Martin-Gutierrez & Fernandez, 2014; Lu & Liu, 2014). In this play, virtual objects can coexist and combine in the same space with the real world with multimodes of experience. These TAP materials with AR are used in school settings promising an ample possibility for children including those with special needs and diverse backgrounds to explore and learn things and worlds they cannot physically do (e.g., Bacca et al., 2014; Correa, Ficheman, Nascimento, & Lopes, 2009).

Interestingly, however, one study pointed out that children had fewer opportunities to manipulate the AR experience and to ask questions, and were even less engaged than they were in typical teaching methods including role-play and printed materials because they were often asked to watch teachers for demonstration and tell what they learned (Kerawalla, Luckin, Seljeflot, & Woolard, 2006). From these points of view, these types of TAP materials will be positive in children's learning experiences only when they are used in appropriate and relevant ways. In a similar vein, the other types of TAP this chapter discussed can support children's interests, motivation, and learning with the important consideration of how to use them. As Bergen and her colleagues (2016) indicated, children's development can be more enriched if children can use both typical and traditional play materials and TAP materials as well as without replacing one for another.

This view has been supported in studies (Lee, 2015; Lee & Tu, 2016) on the effects of iPad uses for low-income children with and without special needs and ELL status. These studies found positive results because the iPad uses were conducted with significant meaningful and playful interaction with pre-service teachers. (See Vygotsky's the concepts of More Knowledgeable Others in his work, *Mind in Society* [1978]). That is, when children use TAP materials, parents, teachers, and other adults in society should make sure that the children are sufficiently exposed to and interacting with real-life people and environments.

As for online gaming, online games offer a third space for children to represent who they want to be. However, this space closely reflects and connects to real life and world. As Rorty (1989) argued, such a cultural apparatus is not often considered moral or aesthetic, and thus is put in "a subordinated position within culture" (p. 82). Thus, young children might unconsciously acquire stereotypes of what being a boy or a girl means or how a black man, an Asian girl, or a Latina woman should behave by means of the biased media representations and experiences (e.g., Hall, 1977, Kellner, 2003). It is important not only to critically analyze current games but also develop socially just and culturally appropriate games so that every child can play without any bias or disadvantage.

There is still a huge need to do more in-depth and longitudinal studies of the various impacts of TAP materials on children. TAP materials should have more diverse language supports and reflect more individual differentiation. Lastly, it is important to provide more serious parent education and professional training for teachers and boost public awareness concerning TAP materials' pros and cons for children.

REFERENCES

AAP Council on Communications and Media. (2016a). Media and Young Minds. *Pediatrics, 138*(5). Retrieved on May 25, 2019 from https://pediatrics.aappublications.org/content/138/5/e20162591

AAP Council on Communications and Media. (2016b). Virtual Violence. *Pediatrics*. 138(1). Retrieved on May 25, 2019 fromhttps://www.ncbi.nlm.nih.gov/pubmed/27940893

App Annie. (2019). Report: *The state of mobile 2019*. Retrieved on May 14, 2019 from https://www.appannie.com/en/go/state-of-mobile-2019/

Bacca, J., Baldiris, S., Fabregat, R., Graf, S., & Kinshuk. (2014). Augmented reality trends in education: A systematic review of research and applications. *Educational Technology & Society, 17*(4), 133–49. Retrieved February 27, 2018 from http://disde.minedu.gob.pe/handle/123456789/5029

Beasley, B., & Standley, T. C. (2002). Shirts vs. skins: Clothing as an indicator of gender role stereotyping in video games. *Mass Communication & Society, 5*, 279–93

Bergen, D., Davis, D., & Abbitt, J. (2016). *Technology play and brain development: Infancy to adolescence and future implications.* New York, NY: Routledge.

Bronfenbrenner, U. (1979). *The ecology of human development.* Cambridge, MA: Harvard University Press.

Brockmyer, J. (2015). Playing violent video games and desensitization to violence. *Child Adolescent Psychiatric Clinics of North America, 24*(1), 65–77.

Bruner, J. (1975). The ontogenesis of speech acts. *Journal of Child Language, 2*, 1–19.

Burgess, M., Dill, K., Stermer, S., Burgess, S., & Brown, B. (2011). Playing with prejudice: The prevalence and consequences of racial stereotypes in video games. Media Psychology, *14*(3), 289–311.

Chian, T. H., Yang, S., & Hwang, G. (2014). Students' online interactive patterns in augmented reality-based inquiry activities. *Computers & Education, 78*, 98–108.

Correa, T., Hinsley, A. W., & Zuniga, H. G. (2010). Who interacts on the web? The intersection of users' personality and social media use. *Computer in Human Behavior, 26*, 247–53.

Correa, A. G. D., Ficheman, I. K., do Nascimento, M., & de Deus Lopes, R. (2009). Computer assisted music therapy: A case study of an augmented reality musical system for children with cerebral palsy rehabilitation. IEEE International Conference on Advanced Learning Technologies, New York, pp. 218–20.

Damour, L. (2018). Parenting the Fortnite Addict. *New York Times.* Retrieved January 2, 2019 https://www.nytimes.com/2018/04/30/well/family/parenting-the-fortnite-addict.html?action=click&module=PopularOnFacebook&region=Lists&pgtype=collection

Davou, B., & Sidiropoulou, A. (2017). Family life around screens: Some thoughts on the impact of ICTs on psychological development and the development of relationships. *Contemporary Family Therapy, 39*(4), 261–70.

Dill, K. E., Gentile, D. A., Richter, W. A., & Dill, J. C. (2005). Violence, sex, and age in popular video games: A content analysis. In E. Cole & J. H. Daniel (Eds.), *Featuring females: Feminist analyses of media* (pp. 115–30). Washington, D.C.: American Psychological Association.

Dunleavy, M. (2014). Design principles for augmented reality learning. *TechTrends, 58*(1), 28–34. Retrieved on September 16, 2016 from https://link.springer.com/article/10.1007/s11528-013-0717-2

Dye M., Green C., & Bavelier, D. (2009). Increasing speed of processing with action video games. *Current Directions in Psychological Science, 8* (6), 321–326.

Eichenbaum, A., Bavelier, D., & Green, S. (2014). Video games: play that can do serious good. *American Journal of Play, 7*(1), 50–72. Retrieved on June 12, 2016 from https://archive-ouverte.unige.ch/unige:84313

Faux, F. (2005). Multimodality: How students with special educational needs create multimedia stories. *Education, Communication & Information, 5*, 167–81.

Fiewitt, R., Messer, D., & Kucirkova, N. (2015). New directions for early literacy in a digital age: The iPad. *Journal of Early Childhood Literacy, 15*(3), 289–310. Retrieved on July 31, 2017 from https://pdfs.semanticscholar.org/e217/932428f9ee2f1af2f40f821be23b9cad9dbd.pdf

Flewitt, R., Kucirkova, N., & Messer, D. (2014). Touching the virtual, touching the real: iPads and enabling literacy for students experiencing disability. *Australian Journal of Language & Literacy, 37*(2), 107–16.

Freed, R. (2015). Wired child: Reclaiming childhood in a digital age. North Charleston, SC: CreateSpace Independent Publishing Platform.

Gee J. (2007) Pleasure, learning, video games, and life: The projective stance. In Lankshear C., Knobel M., Bigum C., & Peters M. (eds.), *New Literacies and Digital Epistemologies* (pp. 95–114). New York, NY: Peter Lang.

Glaube, C. R., Miller, P., Parker, M. A. & Espejo, E. (2001). *Fair Play? Violence, gender and race in videogames: Report.* Oakland, CA: Children Now. Retrieved on October 15, 2010 from http://www.childrennow.org/uploads/documents/fair_play_2001.pdf

Granic, I., Lobel, A., & Engels, R. (2013). The benefits of playing video games. *American Psychologist, 69*(1), 1–13. Retrieved on May 22, 2019 from https://ecirtam.net/autoblogs/autoblogs/wwwpsyetgeekcom_b5b05cdb291029679998f4bbf13bf6d0c1b27186/media/affa8d7f.amp-a0034857.pdf

Hall, S. (1977). Culture, the media and the ideological effect. In J. Curran, M. Gurevitch, & J. Woollacott, *Mass Communication and Society* (pp. 315–48). London: Arnold.

Kara, N., Aydin, C. C., & Cagiltay, K. (2012). User study of a new smart toy for children's storytelling. *Interactive Learning Environments, 22*(5), 551–63.

Kardaras, N. (2016). *Glow kids: How screen addiction is hijacking our kids—and how to break the trance*. New York, NY: St. Martin's Press.

Kellner, D. (2003). *Media spectacle*. New York, NY: Routledge.

Kerawalla, L., Luckin, R., Seljeflot, S., & Woolard, A. (2006). "Making it real": Exploring the potential of augmented reality for teaching primary school science. *Virtual Reality, 10*(3–4), 163–74.

King, M., Takeguchi, K., Barry, S., Rehfeldt, R., Boyer, V., & Mathews, T. (2014). Evaluation of the iPad in the acquisition of requesting skills for children with autism spectrum disorder. *Research in Autism Spectrum Disorders, 8*, 1107–20.

Kühn, S., Kugler, D., Schmalen, K., Weichenberger, M., Witt, C., & Gallinat, J. (2018, March). Does playing violent video games cause aggression? A longitudinal intervention study. *Molecular Psychiatry, 24*(8), 1220–34. Retrieved on June 16, 2019 from https://www.nature.com/articles/s41380-018-0031-7.pdf?origin=ppub

Laurillard, D. (2013). *Teaching as a design science: Building pedagogical patterns for learning and technology*. Philadelphia: Routledge.

Lee, L. (2015). Young children, play, and technology: Meaningful ways of using technology and digital media. In D. P. Fromberg & D. Bergen (Eds.) (3rd ed.), *Play from Birth to Twelve: Contexts, Perspectives, and Meanings* (pp. 217–24). New York, NY: Routledge.

Lee, L., & Tu, X. (2016). Mathematical learning with digital media for low income preschool children: A case study of ELL and non-ELL. *International Journal of Early Childhood Learning, 23* (3), 1–10.

Lei, L., & Wu, Y. (2007). Children' paternal attachment and internet use. *Cyber Psychology and Behavior, 10*(5): 633–39.

Lillard, A., & Perterson, J. (2011). The immediate impact of different types of television on young children's executive function. *Pediatrics, 128*(4). Retrieved on July 1, 2019 from https://pediatrics.aappublications.org/content/128/4/644.short

Lim, S. S., & Clark, L. S. (2010). Virtual worlds as a site of convergence for children's play. *Journal of Virtual Worlds Research, 3* (2), 2–19.

Lu, S., & Liu, Y. (2014). Integrating augmented reality technology to enhance children's learning in marine education. *Environmental Education Research, 21*(4), 525–41.

Martín-Gutierrez, J. M., & Fernandez, M. D. M. (2014). Applying augmented reality in engineering education to improve academic performance & student motivation. *International Journal of Engineering Education, 30*(3), 625–35.

Martín-Gutierrez, J., & Fernandez, M. (2014). Augmented reality environments in learning, communicational and professional contexts in higher education. *Digital Education, 26*. Retrieved on May 4th, 2015 from https://revistes.ub.edu/index.php/der/article/view/11581/pdf.

McLoughlin, L., Spears, B., & Taddeo, C. (2018). The importance of social connection for cybervictims: How connectedness and technology could promote mental health and wellbeing on young children. *International Journal of Emotional Education*, (1), 5. Retrieved on November 4, 2019 from https://search.ebscohost.com/login.aspx?direct=true&AuthType=cookie,ip&db=edsdoj&AN=edsdoj.bfe67b2f840fea266ada6cd93d348&site=eds-live&scope=site

Melhuish, K. & Falloon, G. (2010). Looking to the future: M-learning with the iPad. Computers in New Zealand schools. *Learning, Leading, Technology, 22*(3), 1–16.

Miller, B. T., Krockover, G. H., & Doughty, T. (2013). Using iPads to teach inquiry science to students with a moderate to severe intellectual disability: A pilot study. *Journal of Research in Science Teaching, 50*(8), 887–911.

Miller, T. (2018). Developing numeracy skills using interactive technology in a play-based learning environment. *International Journal of STEM Education, 5*(1), 39. Retrieved on March 12, 2019 from https://www.ncbi.nlm.nih.gov/pmc/articles/PMC6310467/

National Association for the Education of Young Children. (2012). *Technology and interactive media as tools in early childhood programs serving children from birth through age 8*. Joint position statement. Washington, DC: NAEYC. Retrieved on December 22, 2013 from https://www.naeyc.org/files/naeyc/file/positions/PS_technology_WEB2.pdf

Odom, S. L., Thompson, J. L., Hedges, S., Boyd, B. A., Dykstra, J. R., Duda, M. A., . . . Bord, A. (2015). Technology-aided interventions and instruction for adolescents with autism spectrum disorder. *Grantee Submission, 45*(12), 3805–19.

Palmer, S. (2015). *Toxic childhood: How the modern world is damaging our children and what we can do about it*. London: Orion Books.

Park, J. H., Gabbadon, N. G., & Chernin, A. R. (2006). Naturalizing racial differences through comedy: Asian, black, and white views on racial stereotypes in *Rush Hour 2*. *Journal of Communication, 56*, 157–77.

Ramsey, M., Gentzler, A., Morey, J., Oberhauser, A., & Westerman, D. (2013). College students' use of communication technology with parents: Comparisons between two cohorts in 2009 and 2011. *Cyber psychology, Behavior, and Social Networking, 16*, 747–52.

Resnick, M. (2006). Computer as paintbrush: Technology, play, and the creative society. In Singer, D., Golikoff, R., & Hirsh-Pasek, K. (eds.), *Play = learning: How play motivates and enhances children's cognitive and social-emotional growth*. Oxford: Oxford University Press.

Rideout, V., Foehr, U., & Roberts, D. (2010). *Generation M²: Media in the lives of 8 to 18-year-olds*. Menlo Park, CA: The Kaiser Family Foundation.

Rideout, V. J., & Hamel, E. (2006). *The media family: Electronic media in the lives of infants, toddlers, preschoolers and their parents*. Menlo Park, CA: Kaiser Family Foundation.

Rideout, V., Lauricella, A., & Wartella, E. (2011). *Children, media, and race: Media use among White, Black, Hispanic, and Asian American children. Report for the Center on Media and Human Development*. Evanston, IL: School of Communication, Northwestern University.

Richards, R., McGee, R., Williams, S., Welch, D., & Hancox, R. (2010). Adolescent screen time and attachment to parents and peers. *Archives of Pediatrics and Adolescent Medicine, 164*(3), 258–62.

Rorty, R. (1989). *Contingency, irony, and solidarity*. New York, NY: Cambridge University Press.

Royse, P., Joon, L., Undrahbuyan, B., Hopson, M., & Consalvo, M. (2007). Women and games: technologies of the gendered self. *New Media & Society, 9*(4), 555–76.

Shu-Fang, L. (2010). Gender differences and the effect of contextual features on game enjoyment and responses. *Cyberpsychology & Behavior, 13*(5). 533–37.

Small, G., & Vorgan, G. (2008). *iBrain: Surviving the technological alteration of the modern mind*. New York, NY: Harper Collins Publishers.

Trevarthen, C. (1980). The foundations of intersubjectivity: Development of interpersonal and cooperative understanding in infants. In D. R. Olson (Ed.), *The social foundations of language and thought* (p. 316–42). Toronto: W. W. Norton.

van der Meer, L., Kagohara, D., Achmadi, D., Green, V. A., Herrington, C., Sigafoos, J., . . . Rispoli, M. (2011). Teaching functional use of an iPod-based speech-generating device to individuals with developmental disabilities. *Journal of Special Education Technology, 26*(3), 1–11. Retrieved on August 15, 2013 from https://search-ebscohost-com.proxy.lib.miamioh.edu/login.aspx?direct=true&AuthType=cookie,ip&db=eric&AN=EJ1001788&site=eds-live&scope=site

Vygotsky, L. S. (1978). *Mind in society: The development of higher psychological processes*. Cambridge, MA: Harvard University Press.

Vygotsky, L.S. (1981). The development of higher forms of attention in childhood. In J. V. Wertsch (Ed.), *The concept of activity in Soviet psychology* (p. 134–43). Armonk, NY: Sharpe.

Wakefield, J. (2018). *Gaming addiction classified as disorder by WHO*. BBC News. Retrieved on June 29, 2019 from https://www.bbc.com/news/technology-42541404

Warschauer, M., Knobel, M., & Stone, L.A. (2004). Technology and equity in schooling: Deconstructing the digital divide. *Educational Policy, 18*(4), 562–88.

DESIGNING DEVELOPMENTALLY APPROPRIATE TOYS

Barry Kudrowitz

At least two schools in the United States (OTIS and FIT) offer degrees specifically in the field of "toy design." However, professional toy designers can come from a variety of backgrounds including engineering, design, fine arts, and marketing. Perhaps the most common field of study for those pursuing careers in toy design is industrial design or product design. This chapter provides an industrial design—or product design—perspective on designing developmentally appropriate toys. As toys are a product, there are many tools, methods, and techniques discussed here that are also often used in other general product industries. No matter what discipline one comes from when developing a toy concept, there is responsibility and obligation to understand the developmental nature of the users for whom they are designing.

A DESIGN PROCESS FOR DEVELOPING DEVELOPMENTALLY APPROPRIATE TOYS

Design is about creating things for others. It is therefore crucial to understand the end user if one is going to create something of value. With any product, this involves conducting both user research and market research throughout the design process. Just as a designer developing a professional table saw would spend hours understanding the mind-set, abilities, and needs of professional carpenters and woodworkers, a designer developing a toy must have a basic understanding of the mindset, abilities, and needs of their intended user: the child.

It is the designer's role to translate the (obvious and latent) needs and desires of a specific user into solutions and opportunities. Although a popular view of design is about making things "look pretty," design is a much larger *process* for creation and creative problem solving. In the next few sections, the stages of this process are discussed as well as the means in which the child can be involved throughout this process to ensure the end-result is developmentally appropriate.

Human-centered design (HCD) is a creative problem-solving approach made popular by the Stanford D-School and IDEO. This approach is so common it is almost synonymous with general design process as well as the term "design thinking." This process involves a series of steps: research/empathize, gather insights/define a problem, generate ideas, prototype ideas, test ideas/get feedback, iterate. A representation of this process is shown in figure 24.1. To find more information about doing user-centered design, the D-School offers a free online PDF tutorial called the Bootcamp Bootleg: https://dschool.stanford.edu/resources/design-thinking-bootleg.

Design Research

The first stage of this process, the research phase, is where the designer directly interacts with the user (in this case, the child and caregivers) to assess their state of development in addition to things like their interests, current products, and environment. Designers use a variety of tools to do user research (observation, interviews, focus groups, cultural probes, etc.) and many are adapted from the field of anthropology/ethnography. If designers do not interact with their target user prior to ideation and prototyping, they will be designing based upon unvalidated or false assumptions about a user's abilities and desires.

Tom Kelly, founder of the Stanford D-school and IDEO, describes an example of this in his talk, "Field Observations with Fresh Eyes."

> [W]e're on like the first day of observations and we make a small discovery . . . every kid's toothbrush in the history of the world has had the same implicit assumption . . . parents have big hands. Kids have small hands. And so when you want to make the kid's version, make it like the parent's brush only smaller and skinnier. Perfectly logical—until you go out in the field, until you actually watch humans, little tiny humans, brushing their teeth. And what you notice right away, you get a five-year-old boy brushing his teeth, he's not holding his toothbrush in his fingertips the way mom and dad do; he's fisting it. He's holding it like this because he doesn't have the

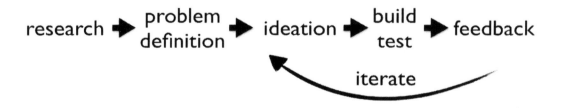

Figure 24.1.   A representation of design process or "design thinking"

dexterity. He doesn't have the fine motor controls that his parents have . . . Kids don't need little skinny toothbrushes. Kids need big fat toothbrushes. Let's make a big, fat, squishy toothbrushes. And you may have noticed, now every toothbrush company in the world makes these. But our client reports that after we made that little tiny discovery out in the field, sitting in a bathroom watching a five year-old boy brush his teeth, they had the bestselling kid's toothbrush in the world for 18 months.

Just as when designing for adults, an interview with a child will not always result in an explicit request for a product concept (e.g., the child is not likely going to say, "I wish toothbrushes had fat squishy handles"). And when designing for younger children and babies, designers must rely simply on observation as in the case with the IDEO toothbrush. The designer must observe how the child behaves, responds, interacts, plays, and then use these observations to inform their design decisions. Research could uncover obvious solutions and ideas, but often the purpose is to question the status quo and find hidden or latent needs that the user doesn't necessarily realize they want or need.

User research (interviews, observations) and market research (such as benchmarking) are always helpful when developing a product for a user group for which you are not a part. However, in the field of toy design, it is even more important because the toy industry, like the fashion industry, is constantly changing. Designers need to stay up to date on current trends and properties in addition to empathizing with a user group that may be several decades younger. Age compression further complicates the research phase of design process as toys, games, brands, products, and activities that may be trending for an age group one year may not be for the same age group the following year. Design process is not as linear as corporate infographics or literature presents it to be. Designers may be doing user research in parallel with the following stages and even after the product gets developed.

Idea Generation

In the movie *Big* (1988), Tom Hanks plays Josh, a 12-year-old who suddenly becomes an adult overnight and manages to find himself at a toy design brainstorming session at FAO Schwarz. In this scene, Josh gets a glimpse of what it looks like when adults attempt to design things for children, relying solely on clinical data from focus groups, prior revenue, market share of comparable products, and double-blind testing. Josh, being a child, questions their proposed new toy concept of a building that turns into a robot: *"So what's so fun about playing with a building?. . . Couldn't it be like a robot that turns into something like a bug or something?"*

Although this example is from fiction, it is representative of the toy industry in that adult designers and engineers sit in a room together and share ideas for toy concepts that they believe children will want. Unless one is regularly studying children, it is difficult to recall what it is like to be a child or remember what would be fun or developmentally appropriate for a specific age group. This is why it is sometimes helpful to have children involved in the idea generation process (like Tom Hanks' character as in *Big*, who was unintentionally involved).

When end-users and other stakeholders are involved in the design process, this is called codesign, cocreation, or participatory design. Typically, in design process, the designer does the research and development and then receives feedback and input from end users, clients, and stakeholders. In a codesign process, the end user or client actively participates in parts of the process, including the idea generation. As children are not necessarily versed in design techniques (such as sketching), the designer takes on more of a facilitator role and helps translate ideas from participants into viable solutions and products. There is additional rational to include children in toy design idea generation phases.

First, one of the tenets of brainstorming (Osborn, 1963) is to have a diverse group of participants in the session, including diversity in age. Brainstorming is about bringing together different viewpoints and perspectives in order to uncover non-obvious connections and develop a variety of different ideas. Involving children (assuming they are old enough to fully participate) brings the end-user's voice to the table.

Second, children are creative. The classic anecdote of the child transforming the cardboard box into a variety of different things has been studied explicitly. A study by Land and Jarman (1999) found that young children are really good at divergent thinking, a cognitive process strongly linked to creativity. This study also found that as children get older their ability to think divergently decreases significantly. Two relevant takeaways from this study are that (1) when designing toys, we should not over-specify affordances or, in other words, open ended toys that can be used in a variety of different ways may help to encourage creativity; and (2) if children are good at divergent thinking, perhaps they should be more involved in idea generation to help question the status quo.

Play Testing

It's difficult to determine the goodness or appropriateness of any idea without testing it. In product design, idea generation is followed by low-fidelity prototyping or sketch modeling. If a designer wants to get reliable feedback from users, a physical representation of the idea is required to share with those intended users. In general design, this is called "user testing," but in the toy/game industry it is referred to as "play testing."

In the process of sharing a prototype with potential users, the designer gains valuable insights into both user-centered qualities like play value and ergonomics as well as production-related qualities such as feasibility and material specifications. This process is crucial for the iterative nature of design. Prototypes are tested with users and those interactions provide the feedback necessary for the designer to make improvements to the concept to better meet the users' needs. In the toy industry, this is the stage in which the designer determines if the intended developmental play matches the observed developmental play.

Research suggests that designers who make these low-fidelity prototypes early in the design process will have better design results than those who reserve prototyping to later stages (Haggman, Honda, & Yang, 2013). These physical models allow for better and earlier feedback from the user. The value of these early-stage prototypes is greater in the toy industry for a number of reasons. First, children may not be able to express their thoughts orally based on a visual representation and would require observation of the play with a prototype to get any useful data. Second, play is manipulative. If a designer wants a reliable representation of how a child would play with a given toy, a physical object is necessary.

Designers also should not assume to know what children want or what children will do with a toy. Brian Sutton-Smith writes, "It is dangerous to pretend we know what a child will do with a toy just from its characteristics alone; children have a way of doing things with toys over and beyond the apparent character of the toy" (1986, 37–38). When playtesting, the designer shouldn't instruct the child on how the toy prototype should work. This would be biasing the research. Without instructions, the designer can observe problems with the design and uncover opportunities for new directions. During this process, designers may take notes, ask questions, and/or take video. They may also present multiple toy models of different concepts to compare ideas.

WHAT MAKES A "GOOD," DEVELOPMENTALLY APPROPRIATE TOY?

Brian Sutton-Smith suggested that "play is a pleasure for its own sake" (2008). Similarly, the primary purpose of a toy, being a medium for play, should simply be pleasure for its own sake. However, play additionally has inherent developmental benefits and therefore toys can also act as a medium for child development. Children acquire physical, social, cognitive, creative, and emotional skills through play. One could argue that a good toy is one that contributes to the development of one or more of these skills. However, the primary function of a toy is to provide pleasure via play. Regardless of how many developmental skills the toy intends to teach, the toy must first be fun and something that for which the child is self-motivated to engage. To determine other qualities that make for a good toy, one could begin with qualities that make for a good product in general. According to Dieter Ram's *10 Principles of Good Design* (2019), good product design:

1. Is innovative
2. Makes a product useful
3. Is aesthetic
4. Makes a product understandable
5. Is unobtrusive
6. Is honest
7. Is long-lasting
8. Is thorough down to the last detail
9. Is environmentally friendly
10. Involves as little design as possible

All of these principles are valuable, but when focusing on toys, some of these items can be clustered into three principles of good toy design.

Good Toy Design is Timeless

"Timeless" meaning that the toy can be used as the child ages in different ways but *also* over generations. This relates to both Rams' (2019) principles of "long-lasting" and "aesthetic." The toy industry is (perhaps unfortunately) more like the fashion industry than the consumer product industry. Properties, themes, colors, trends, and brands are fickle and go out of style with the seasons and with popular media. This "fast-fashion" perspective makes toys less valuable with age and forces industry to drive cost down at the sacrifice of quality. This abundance of short-play-life plastic toys are designed for the landfill. Good general design is timeless.

For example, much of the work of mid-century designers like Arne Jacobsen, Isamu Noguchi, Harry Bertoia, and Charles and Ray Eames look as if they were designed today. Looking specifically at the collection of Charles and Ray Eames toys, including their "House of Cards," "The Toy," and their molded elephant design (which is now mass produced as "The Plastic Elephant"). These were all designed in the 1950s and 1960s, but they are still sold today and could pass as a new concept (Eames Official Site, 2019).

Good Toy Design is Multifunctional Through Simplicity

"Multifunctional" meaning that the toy can be used with a variety of different play patterns, activities, games, or ages (like a cardboard box). Multifunctional is not synonymous with multiple *features* (i.e., a "Swiss Army Knife"–like toy). The toy itself should be simple enough for the child to find alternative functions for it and explore their own creativity (like the Bilibo, which can be used as a chair, a hat, a bucket, a top, etc.) or a game like Spot-it, which has a variety of different game play options that allow it to be played with younger children, adults or both. This relates to the Rams' principles of "as little design as possible" and is understandable.

A toy with many rules and multiple features is also a toy with very specific uses and likely very specific audiences. A simple design likely also requires fewer components, less material, and will have fewer components that can fail. A simple design should also make the product last longer and be less expensive to manufacture. This evokes the minimalist design philosophy "less is more" used by designer Ludwig Mies Van Der Rohe and the more recent "no unitaskers" philosophy of celebrity chef Alton Brown.

Good Toy Design is Robust

"Robust" product design is a concept from Dr. Genichi Taguchi, a quality engineer. It refers to products being resilient and durable to both internal factors (designed with quality material, not likely to break over normal use) and external factors (not likely to deteriorate with environmental conditions unless that is desired), as well as product components having little unintended variation over time in manufacturing (Lochner & Matar, 1990). A robust design could also be designed for ease of repair and disassembly for recycling. This relates to the Rams' principles of "environmentally friendly" and "long-lasting." Even though LEGO blocks are made of plastic, a nonrenewable re-source, they are environmentally friendly because they are unlikely to be thrown away. If someone uses a toy for their lifetime and passes it down for generations, it could be a more environmentally friendly toy than something made of a renewable material (such as bamboo) in which the embodied time/materials/energy to produce it is discarded after minimal use.

LEGO blocks embody all three of these principles. They are (1) *timeless* with their simple minimalist form; (2) *multifunctional* in that they can be used for a variety of play, structures, games, and ages; and (3) *robust* in that they last for lifetimes in both their durability and also in that the manufacturing tolerances and specifications have main-tained the same such that bricks from 1958 can still connect with bricks from today (Mortensen, 2017).

The antithesis of LEGO might be McDonalds Happy Meal Toys, such that they are typically tied to a media property (not timeless), designed for one specific purpose (not multifunctional, and are manufactured to be as inexpensive as possible (not robust), which leads to a significant amount of toy plastic going directly to the landfill after only a short amount of play. McDonalds is under recent scrutiny for this very issue and is exploring redesigning toys for ease of recycling and switching to books instead of toys (Chaudhuri, 2019).

In summary, designing toys is challenging. Designing "good," developmentally appropriate toys is even more challenging. A designer needs to have the empathetic abilities, creative skills, and the traditional hands-on skills associated with the profession. They also need to have a finger on the pulse of the market to understand the current trends, an understanding of current manufacturing processes and safety standards, and the ability to relate to both children and parents. Toys may seem like an "easy" thing to design as they are "just playthings," but they are perhaps one of the most complicated and nuanced of consumer products.

REFERENCES

Big. Dir. Penny Marshall. 20th Century Fox, 1988.

Chaudhuri, S. (July 8, 2019). McDonald's Happy Meal toys caught in backlash over plastic."*The Wall Street Journal*. Retrieved fromhttps://www.wsj.com/articles/mcdonalds-happy-meal-toys-caught-in-backlash-over-plastic-11562583605

Eames Official Site. (July 1, 2019). Retrieved fromhttps://www.eamesoffice.com/catalog-category/toys/

Haggman, A., Honda, T., & Yang, M. (2013). The influence of timing in exploratory prototyping and other activities in design projects. Proceedings of the *ASME 2013 International Design Engineering Technical Conferences and Computers and Information in Engineering Conference*. Portland, Oregon, USA, August 4–7, 2013.

Kelley, T. Field observations with fresh eyes. *Stanford eCorner*. November 12, 2008. Video URL: http://ecorner.stanford.edu/videos/2100/Field-Observations-with-Fresh-Eyes

Land, G., & Beth J. *Break point and beyond: Mastering the future today*. Champaign, IL: Leadership Two Thousand, 1999.

Lochner, R., & Matar, J. (1990). *Designing for quality*. London, UK: Chapman and Hall.

Mortensen, T. (October 17, 2017). "Lego History Timeline." Lego.com. Retrieved fromhttps://www.lego.com/en-us/aboutus/lego-group/the_lego_history

Osborn, A. (1963). *Applied imagination: Principles and procedures of creative problem solving*. New York, NY: Charles Scribners Sons.

Vitsœ. "The power of good design: Dieter Rams's ideology, engrained within Vitsœ." Retrieved from https://www.vitsoe.com/gb/about/good-design, July 1, 2019.

Shapiro, A. (Host). (2015, Dec 23). The "unitasker" kitchen gadgets Alton Brown loves to loathe. *All Things Considered* [Radio broadcast episode]. NPR. Retrieved fromhttps://www.npr.org/sections/thesalt/2015/12/23/460833325/

Sutton-Smith, Brian. (1986). *Toys as culture*. Mattituck, NY: Gardner Press.

Sutton-Smith, Brian. (2008). Play theory. A personal journey and new thoughts. *American Journal of Play*, 1, 80–123.

Vitsœ. "The power of good design: Dieter Rams's ideology, engrained within Vitsœ" Retrieved fromhttps://www.vitsoe.com/gb/about/good-design, July 1, 2019.

25

PROMOTING DEVELOPMENTALLY APPROPRIATE TOYS IN A CHANGING CHILD CULTURAL WORLD

Doris Bergen

As the authors of this handbook have demonstrated, toys have been very important facilitators of children's development throughout the centuries of human existence. Although their specific appearances and designs have changed over that time, their basic qualities have remained similar. Toys have continued to engage and strengthen children's physical, cognitive, language, social, emotional, and creative abilities, as well as to foster children's optimal brain development. They also have been major vehicles for introducing children to the specific values and demands of their own cultures.

For example, toy play has enhanced children's understanding of their cultural roles and development of culturally expected skills. In earliest times, the skills children gained through toy play were related to basic survival (e.g., bow and arrows for "hunting," toy pots for "cooking," dolls for "baby caring") but some early toys also engaged children in expanding their thinking skills and aesthetic interests (e.g., puzzles, musical instruments). In ongoing centuries, up to the present day, toys also have promoted children's learning of culturally required academic skills such as literacy, mathematics, and scientific knowledge. Most recently, toys also have introduced children to the technological innovations of our present society. Most significantly, toys have been an important vehicle through which children can learn about their own feelings, their creative thoughts, and their understanding of their world.

While the specific features of toys will continue to change in the future, it is very likely that versions of the toys that children have always loved will continue to be made and loved by children. There are two aspects of the present cultural environment, however, that could be problematic for children's toy play: (1) not having enough time for extended toy play and (2) having play with real, physically present toys replaced by virtual toy play.

NO TIME FOR TOY PLAY

Today's children, especially in "advanced" societies, are not as likely to have the long periods of time for toy play that children had in the past. In addition to the time they must spend in group-organized programs (e.g., daycare, preschool, kindergarten, elementary school) that have adult-directed toy play (or sometimes no toys at all!), many children participate mainly in adult-structured out-of-school learning experiences, such as adult-directed sports activities, dancing or music classes, science and art camps, and other "learning" adult-organized activities. The attitude of many adults that it is "dangerous" to allow children freely chosen unstructured time in the outdoors is also problematic. Today's children have much less time and very little space to engage in self-designed creative play activities involving the many variety of toys discussed in this handbook.

This loss of child-directed play time is of concern not only to early childhood professionals but also to pediatricians and other professionals who are concerned about children's optimum development (Bergen, 2018). Authors from many disciplines have begun to express concern about the constriction of children's extended free play times (Gray, 2011, 2013), the lack of outdoor play time (Rivkin, 2015) and the loss of play in natural settings that may cause a "nature deficit" (Louv, 2008). Pediatricians who have raised concern about this "play deficit" include Klass (2018) and Ginsburg (2008), who has urged pediatricians to make parents aware of the importance of children's active, child-centered play with "true toys" (e.g., blocks, dolls). He and a colleague (Milteer & Ginsburg, 2012) also have noted that low-income children who experience "play deprivation" may be especially affected by the lack of free play time and especially lack of recess access and creative opportunities in their low income area schools.

In contrast to this recent concern about the loss of child play time, studies of adults' memories of their childhood play conducted over the past 25 years (see Bergen, Liu, & Liu, 1997; Bergen & Williams, 2008; Davis & Bergen, 2014), have found that adults commonly report remembering many examples of their engagement in extensive time periods of active toy play, often in "games-with-rules" play or in elaborate child-directed pretense scenarios. In the types of lightly supervised ("free") play they loved, the children engaged in play with many types of toys involving physical skills (e.g., balls, bicycles), toys supporting extended pretense themes (e.g., dolls, puppets, blocks), and toys that engaged them in interactions with other children (e.g., board games, fort building). They lived in worlds that they designed and ruled, often for many hours at a time, and the adults at that time allowed them the opportunity to control their own imaginative worlds.

According to many influential developmental theorists such as Piaget (1962), Erikson (1977), and Vygotsky (1967), the time that children play in self-chosen pretense, games, and exploration is essential and fosters their development in many important ways. Typically, this play involves many toys that can facilitate their experiences in solving problems, creating meaningful and child-directed "worlds," learn about their emotions and those of others, and engage in creative thought. Therefore, it is presently unclear how, if it continues to occur, the loss of extensive types of child-chosen and controlled playtime will affect future generations of children's physical, social, emotional, cognitive, and moral development.

VIRTUAL TOY PLAY RATHER THAN "REAL TOY" PLAY

A second factor that is very likely to influence toy play is the increasing role of "virtual toy play" in children's lives. Even very young children are presently involved in playing with virtual toys on various devices and, while this type of play may not be harmful, it may still result in lowering the amount of time that "real world toy play" can be experienced by children. If the virtual toy play experiences substitute for physical toy play experiences, young children may lose essential experiences that foster *enactive* cognition (see Bruner, 1964). This type of cognition, which is gained by touching, feeling, mouthing, holding, shaking, and engaging in a range of other physical behaviors with the toys in their environment, always has provided the foundation for children's later understanding of the world. That is, this "real world" enactive cognition has typically provided the basis for later *iconic* (understanding pictures) and *symbolic* (understanding written symbols) cognition, and its diminishment or loss may be problematic for future generations.

Thus, as play changes with ever increasing virtual world experiences, it is important that children's self-chosen play continues to have space and time and that physically present, versatile, and challenging toys continue to be available for their enjoyment and learning.

SUMMARY

Since earliest times, toys have provided an important vehicle for children. They have served as companions, helped them engage with other children, taught them about the "real world," given them opportunities to create their own worlds, supported their cognitive, social, emotional, physical, and creative learning experiences, and introduced them to the cultural values of the civilizations in which they lived. It is likely that toys (in whatever form they will be) will continue to have many similar values in the future.

REFERENCES

Bergen, D. (2018). Commentary: The "play deficit" discovered by physicians! Implications for policy and practice. *Journal of Psychiatry and Psychiatric Disorders*, 2:5; 128–32; doi: 10.26502/jppd.2572-519X0050

Bergen, D., Liu, W., & Liu, G. (1997). Chinese and American students' memories of childhood play: A comparison. *International Journal of Educology*, 1(2), 109–27.

Bergen, D., & Williams, E. (2008, May). *Differing childhood play experiences of three young adult cohorts have implications for physical, social and academic development.* Poster presentation at the Association for Psychological Science, Chicago, IL.

Davis, D., & Bergen, D. (2014). Relationships among play behaviors reported by college students and their responses to moral issues: A pilot study. *Journal of Research in Childhood Education, 28*, 484–98.

Erikson, E. H. (1977). *Toys and reason.* New York, NY: Norton.

Ginsburg, K. R. (2008). The importance of play in promoting healthy child development and maintaining strong parent-child bonds. *Pediatrics 2007, 119*, 182; doi: 10.1542/peds.2006–2697

Gray, P. (2013). The play deficit. *Aeon Magazine.*

Gray, P. (2011). The decline of play and the rise of psychopathology in children and adolescents. *American Journal of Play*, 3(4), 443–63.

Klass, P. (2018). Let kids play, doctor's orders. *New York Times; Section D4*; 8/28/2018

Louv, R. (2008). *Last child in the woods: Saving our children from nature-deficit disorder.* Chapel Hill, NC: Algonquin Books.

Miller, R. M., & Ginsburg, K. R. (2012). The importance of play in promoting healthy child development and maintaining strong parent-child bond: Focus on children in poverty. *Pediatrics, 129*(1), 204–13; www.pediatrics.org/cgi/doi/10.1542/peds.2011-2953; doi:10.1542/peds. 2011–2953

Piaget, J. (1962). *Play, dreams, and imitation in childhood.* New York, NY: Norton.

Rivkin, M. S. (1995). *The great outdoors: Restoring children's right to play outside.* National Association for the Education of Young Children, Washington, DC.

Rivkin, M. S. (2015). Children's outdoor play: An endangered activity. In *Play from birth to twelve*, 341–48. Philadelphia: Routledge.

Vygotsky, L. (1967). Play and the role of mental development in the child. *Soviet Psychology, 5*, 6–18.

ABOUT THE AUTHORS

Jason Abbitt, PhD, is associate professor of educational psychology at Miami University. His scholarly work focuses on aspects of technology in modern society including the integration of technology in teaching and learning environments. Dr. Abbitt also is active in developing innovative distance education programs in higher education.

Christopher Bensch, MA, Winterthur Program in American Material Culture, is curator at The Strong National Museum of Play. He serves as vice president for collections and chief curator, overseeing the museum's curatorial, conservation, library, and archives staff and the over 510,000 items and resources in the museum's collection. Bensch also is the spokesperson for the National Toy Hall of Fame, which is housed at The Strong.

Doris Bergen, PhD, is a Distinguished Professor of Educational Psychology Emerita at Miami University, Oxford, Ohio. Her research interests have focused on play theory and humor development, including effects of technology-enhanced toys on play, adult memories of childhood play, and gifted children's humor. She also is a Miami University distinguished scholar.

Annerieke Bolland, PhD, is a professor in early childhood education at Hogeschool iPabo, a university for education in Amsterdam. Through practice-oriented research, she works on play-based curricula and play guidance in close cooperation with early childhood education teachers. Connecting with children in their play is one of the major themes in her work.

Gail Burnett, MA, is an early childhood music educator, performer and preschool teacher trainer. Her experience includes 20 years working in music education with infants to mid-elementary age children. She received a Teacher's Choice Award, Parent

Choice Awards, and a Grammy ballot for her original children's music. She is listed on the Teaching Artists Registry, Georgia Council for the Arts.

Lynn Cohen, PhD, is professor in the Department of Teaching and Learning at LIU/Post. Prior to joining the faculty, she worked for over 25 years as a preschool, kindergarten, and literacy teacher. Her research interests are related to school readiness, young children's play, technology and engineering, language development, emergent literacy, dual language learners, and contemporary literacies.

Brooke R. Spangler Cropenbaker, PhD, is an associate teaching professor and developmental psychologist at Miami University. She teaches large courses about human development across the lifespan and small seminars on the psychology of play. When she isn't teaching you can find her exhibiting her "explorer" play personality, traveling to faraway places or exploring her own backyard with family.

Darrel R. Davis, PhD, is associate professor in the Department of Educational Psychology at Miami University. His research focuses on issues at the intersection of play, technology, and human development and learning. He is also interested in teaching and learning in the online environment and the use of technology in diverse educational settings.

Myae Han, PhD, is a professor in the Department of Human Development and Family Sciences at the University of Delaware, and a past president of The Association for the Study of Play (TASP). She studies early childhood education, a play-based intervention, and early language and literacy.

Olga S. Jarrett, PhD, is professor emerita of early childhood and elementary education at Georgia State University where she taught a wide variety of courses. She is a past president of The Association of the Study of Play and the American Association for the Child's Right to Play and recipient of four play awards. A lifetime lover of puppets, she joined the international puppetry organization, Union Internationale de la Marionnette (UNIMA) while working on her chapter.

James E. Johnson, PhD, professor of early childhood education, The Pennsylvania State University–University Park is Series Editor of *Play & Culture Studies* and past president of The Association for the Study of Play. He is lead coeditor of *The Handbook of the Study of Play* (2015) with Scott Eberle, Thomas Henricks, and David Kuschner.

Barry Kudrowitz, PhD, is associate professor and Director of Product Design at the University of Minnesota. His research focuses on how creativity is perceived, evaluated, and learned. He has taught Toy Product Design, an interdisciplinary project-based class, at both MIT and the University of Minnesota.

Lena Lee, PhD, is professor of early childhood education, Department of Teacher Education, at Miami University. Her research focuses on how diversity in education is manifested and understood in different sociocultural contexts. A recent project was to examine effective technology uses for low-income preschool children's learning and curriculum.

Eleni Loizou, PhD, is associate professor of early childhood education at the University of Cyprus. Her research interests include play, humor and infancy, taking young children's perspectives, and considering early childhood teachers' training.

Sohyun Meacham PhD, is associate professor of literacy education at the University of Northern Iowa. Her research interests center around young children's language use during play.

Shirley K. Morgenthaler, PhD, is distinguished professor of education at Concordia University Chicago (CUC). At CUC, she is the chief editor of *Lutheran Education Journal*, a 156-year faculty publication. Dr. Morgenthaler works on dissertations with doctoral students in early childhood education.

Kathleen Roskos, PhD, is professor emerita at John Carroll University located in Cleveland, Ohio. Her scholarly work focuses on the relationship between play and early literacy development. Her recent studies examine the design and use of digital books as instructional resources that promote early literacy skills.

Jean-Pierre Rossie, PhD, is associated researcher of the Centre for Philosophical and Humanistic Studies, Faculty of Philosophy, Catholic University of Portugal, Braga. All his books, articles, and PowerPoints are available on https://ucp.academia.edu/JeanPierreRossie

Dorothy Justus Sluss, PhD, is professor emerita at James Madison University. She has been a kindergarten teacher, professor, and consultant. She is the author of numerous journal articles and four books, recipient of several awards for play scholarship and advocacy.

Tracy Settleberry, PhD, is a visiting assistant professor at Miami University. She is a licensed K–12 art educator and currently teaches human development courses at the collegiate level. Her research area is family quality of life for children with autism.

Sandra J. Stone, PhD, is professor emeritus at Northern Arizona University. She has written multiple articles on play, symbolic play, and literacy and play. She is the author of the book *Playing: A Kid's Curriculum* (GoodYear Books).

John A. Sutterby, PhD, is an associate professor at the University of Texas San Antonio. His research interests include children's play and play environments both indoors and out. He is also interested in children's popular culture including dolls and other playthings.

Sonia Tiwari is a PhD student at Penn State University's Learning, Design, and Technology program. She earned her MFA in animation from Academy of Art University, San Francisco, and previously worked as a game designer in Bay Area, and briefly taught toy design at National Institute of Design, India.

Valerie A. Ubbes, PhD, MCHES, is a professor of Health education at Miami University. She also directs the Digital Literacy Partnership (http://dlp.lib.miamioh.edu) and an oral health curriculum that promotes "Reading for a Healthy Smile" for children and their parents. Her research and teaching focuses on health literacy and health communication message design.